CLARENDON LAW SERIES

Edited by
PAUL CRAIG

CLARENDON LAW SERIES

Natural Law and Natural Rights
(2nd edition)
JOHN FINNIS

Philosophy of Private Law
WILLIAM LUCY

Law in Modern Society
DENIS GALLIGAN

Criminal Justice
LUCIA ZEDNER

Contract Theory
STEPHEN A. SMITH

Law of Property (3rd edition)
F. H. LAWSON AND BERNARD RUDDEN

Legal Reasoning and Legal
Theory
NEIL MACCORMICK

Playing by the Rules

A Philosophical Examination of
Rule-Based Decision-Making
FREDERICK SCHAUER

Precedent in English Law
(4th edition)
RUPERT CROSS AND
J. W. HARRIS

Conflicts of Law and Morality
KENT GREENAWALT

An Introduction to Roman Law
BARRY NICHOLAS

Land Law (2nd edition)
ELIZABETH COOK

Administrative Law (5th edition)
PETER CANE

Discrimination Law (2nd edition)
SANDRA FREDMAN

An Introduction to the Law of
Trusts (3rd edition)
SIMON GARDNER

Introduction to Company Law
(2nd edition)
PAUL DAVIES

Equity (2nd edition)
SARAH WORTHINGTON

Atiyah's Introduction to the Law
of Contract (6th edition)
STEPHEN A. SMITH,
P. S. ATIYAH

Unjust Enrichment
(2nd edition)
PETER BIRKS

Public Law
ADAM TOMKINS

Employment Law
(2nd edition)
HUGH COLLINS

The Conflict of Laws
(2nd edition)
ADRIAN BRIGGS

International Law
VAUGHAN LOWE

Intellectual Property
MICHAEL SPENCE

An Introduction to Tort Law
(2nd edition)
TONY WEIR

THE CONCEPT OF LAW

THIRD EDITION

By

H. L. A. HART

With a Postscript edited by
Penelope A. Bulloch and Joseph Raz
And with an Introduction and Notes by
Leslie Green

OXFORD
UNIVERSITY PRESS

Great Clarendon Street, Oxford, OX2 6DP,
United Kingdom

Oxford University Press is a department of the University of Oxford.
It furthers the University's objective of excellence in research, scholarship,
and education by publishing worldwide. Oxford is a registered trade mark of
Oxford University Press in the UK and in certain other countries

© Oxford University Press 1961, 1994, 2012; Introduction © Leslie Green 2012

The moral rights of the authors have been asserted

First Edition published in 1961
Second Edition published in 1994
Third Edition published in 2012

3

Crown copyright material is reproduced under Class Licence
Number C01P0000148 with the permission of OPSI
and the Queen's Printer for Scotland

British Library Cataloguing in Publication Data
Data available

ISBN 978–0–19–964469–8 (Hbk)
ISBN 978–0–19–964470–4 (Pbk)

Printed in Great Britain by
Clays Ltd, St Ives plc

TO J.H.

PREFACE

My aim in this book has been to further the understanding of law, coercion, and morality as different but related social phenomena. Though it is primarily designed for the student of jurisprudence, I hope it may also be of use to those whose chief interests are in moral or political philosophy, or in sociology, rather than in law. The lawyer will regard the book as an essay in analytical jurisprudence, for it is concerned with the clarification of the general framework of legal thought, rather than with the criticism of law or legal policy. More over, at many points, I have raised questions which may well be said to be about the meanings of words. Thus I have considered: how 'being obliged' differs from 'having an obligation'; how the statement that a rule is a valid rule of law differs from a prediction of the behaviour of officials; what is meant by the assertion that a social group observes a rule and how this differs from and resembles the assertion that its members habitually do certain things. Indeed, one of the central themes of the book is that neither law nor any other form of social structure can be understood without an appreciation of certain crucial distinctions between two different kinds of statement, which I have called 'internal' and 'external' and which can both be made whenever social rules are observed.

Notwithstanding its concern with analysis the book may also be regarded as an essay in descriptive sociology; for the suggestion that inquiries into the meanings of words merely throw light on words is false. Many important distinctions, which are not immediately obvious, between types of social situation or relationships may best be brought to light by an examination of the standard uses of the relevant expressions and of the way in which these depend on a social context, itself often left unstated. In this field of study it is particularly true that we may use, as Professor J. L. Austin said, 'a sharpened awareness of words to sharpen our perception of the phenomena'.

I am heavily and obviously indebted to other writers; indeed much of the book is concerned with the deficiencies of a simple model of a legal system, constructed along the lines of Austin's imperative theory. But in the text the reader will find very few references to other writers and very few footnotes. Instead, he will find at the end of the book extensive notes designed to be read after each chapter; here the views expressed in the text are related to those of my predecessors and contemporaries, and suggestions are made as to the way in which the argument may be further pursued in their writings. I have taken this course, partly because the argument of the book is a continuous one; which comparison with other theories would interrupt. But I have also had a pedagogic aim: I hope that this arrangement may discourage the belief that a book on legal theory is primarily a book from which one learns what other books contain. So long as this belief is held by those who write, little progress will be made in the subject; and so long as it is held by those who read, the educational value of the subject must remain very small.

I have been indebted for too long to too many friends to be capable now of identifying all my obligations. But I have a special debt to acknowledge to Mr A. M. Honoré whose detailed criticisms exposed many confusions of thought and infelicities of style. These I have tried to eliminate, but I fear that much is left of which he would disapprove. I owe to conversations with Mr G. A. Paul anything of value in the political philosophy of this book and in its reinterpretation of natural law, and I have to thank him for reading the proofs. I am also most grateful to Dr Rupert Cross and Mr P. F. Strawson, who read the text, for their beneficial advice and criticism.

H. L. A. HART

EDITORS' NOTE
(Written for the Second Edition)

Within a few years of its publication *The Concept Of Law* transformed the way jurisprudence was understood and studied in the English-speaking world and beyond. Its enormous impact led to a multitude of publications discussing the book and its doctrines, and not only in the context of legal theory, but in political and moral philosophy too.

For many years Hart had it in mind to add a chapter to *The Concept of Law.* He did not wish to tinker with the text whose influence has been so great, and in accordance with his wishes it is here published unchanged, except for minor corrections. But he wanted to respond to the many discussions of the book, defending his position against those who misconstrued it, refuting unfounded criticism, and—of equal importance in his eyes conceding the force of justified criticism and suggesting ways of adjusting the book's doctrines to meet those points. That the new chapter, first thought of as a preface, but finally as a postscript, was unfinished at the time of his death was due only in part to his meticulous perfectionism. It was also due to persisting doubts about the wisdom of the project, and a nagging uncertainty whether he could do justice to the vigour and insight of the theses of the book as originally conceived. Nevertheless, and with many interruptions, he persisted with work on the postscript and at the time of his death the first of the two intended sections was nearly complete.

When Jennifer Hart asked us to look at the drafts and decide whether there was anything publishable there our foremost thought was not to let anything be published that Hart would not have been happy with. We were, therefore, delighted to discover that for the most part the first section of the postscript was in such a finished state. We found only hand-written notes intended for the second section, and they were too fragmentary and inchoate to be publishable. In contrast the first section existed in several versions, having been typed, revised, retyped, and rerevised. Even the most recent version was obviously not thought by him to be in a final state. There are numerous alterations in pencil and Biro. Moreover, Hart did not discard earlier versions, but seems to have continued to work on whichever version was to hand. While this made the editorial task more difficult, the changes introduced over the last two years were mostly changes of stylistic nuance, which itself indicated that he was essentially satisfied with the text as it was.

Our task was to compare the alternative versions, and where they did not match establish whether segments of text which appeared in only one of them were missing from the others because he discarded them, or because he never had one version incorporating all the emendations. The published text includes all the emendations which were not discarded by Hart, and which appear in versions of the text that he continued to revise. At times the text itself was incoherent. Often this must have been the result of a misreading of a manuscript by the typist, whose mistakes Hart did not always notice. At other times it was no doubt due to the natural way in which sentences get mangled in the course of composition, to be sorted out at the final drafting, which he did not live to do. In these cases we tried to restore the original text, or to recapture, with minimum intervention, Hart's thought. One special problem was presented by Section 6 (on discretion). We found two versions of its opening paragraph, one in a copy which ended at that point, and another in a copy containing the rest of the section. As the truncated version was in a copy incorporating many of his most recent revisions, and was never discarded by him, and as it is consonant with his general discussion in the postscript, we decided to allow both versions to be published, the one which was not continued appearing in an endnote.

Hart never had the notes, mostly references, typed. He had a hand-written version of the notes, the cues for which were most easily traced in the earliest typed copy of the main text. Later he occasionally added references in marginal comments, but for the most part these were incomplete, sometimes indicating no more than the need to trace the reference. Timothy Endicott has checked all the references, traced all that were incomplete, and added references where Hart quoted Dworkin or closely paraphrased him without indicating a source. Endicott also corrected the text where the quotations were inaccurate. In the course of this work, which involved extensive research and resourcefulness, he has also suggested several corrections to the main text, in line with the editorial guidelines set out above, which we gratefully incorporated.

There is no doubt in our mind that given the opportunity Hart would have further polished and improved the text before publishing it. But we believe that the published postscript contains his considered response to many of Dworkin's arguments.

Penelope A. Bulloch
Joseph Raz
1994

PREFACE TO THE THIRD EDITION

The Concept of Law is based on introductory lectures in jurisprudence that Herbert Hart gave to law students at the University of Oxford. After its first publication in 1961, it quickly became the most influential book in legal philosophy ever written in English. Scholars in law, in philosophy, and in political theory continue to develop, build on, and criticize its arguments. At the same time, it remains a widely used introduction to its subject and is read by students, whether in the original or in one of its many translations, around the globe.

As the fiftieth anniversary of the first publication of the book approached, Oxford University Press approached me about the possibility of preparing a new edition. A posthumous second edition, published in 1994 under the editorship of Penelope Bulloch and Joseph Raz, included a Postscript based on Hart's unpublished replies to Ronald Dworkin. That edition set off a new wave of debate about Hart's theories and about jurisprudence in general. After several more reprints, it was time to correct a few errors in the text and to redesign the book. This opened the door to the possibility of including some new material.

Although *The Concept of Law* needs no apology, after half a century it is no longer true that it needs no introduction. In the one that follows I highlight some main themes, sketch a few criticisms and, most important, try to forestall some misunderstandings of its project. Hart had added notes giving references, elaborating points, and suggesting further readings. These have been left intact. But many of those readings have been superseded and many later books and articles take up his arguments. A fresh set of notes has therefore been added to point students in the direction of some key debates. Finally, although earlier works do give citations to the pagination of the first edition, fewer and fewer copies of that edition are still in circulation. (And fewer and fewer people familiar with its pagination are still in circulation.) I therefore decided to follow the pagination of the second edition.

The Introduction draws on material previously published in my paper 'The Concept of Law Revisited' (1997) 94 *Michigan Law Review* 1687. I am very grateful to Alex Flach of Oxford University Press, who first proposed this project and who gave valuable advice at many points. My colleague John Finnis helped with corrections to Hart's text; Tom Adams assisted with research for the Notes: warm thanks to both of them. And thanks especially to Denise Réaume, who read and commented on the Introduction.

Leslie Green
Balliol College, Oxford
Trinity 2012

CONTENTS

INTRODUCTION, *by Leslie Green*   xv

1. Hart's Message   xv
2. Law as a Social Construction   xvii
3. Law and Power   xxvii
4. Law and Morality   xxxiii
5. Fact, Value, and Method   xliv
6. The Point   lii

I. PERSISTENT QUESTIONS   1

1. Perplexities of Legal Theory   1
2. Three Recurrent Issues   6
3. Definition   13

II. LAWS, COMMANDS, AND ORDERS   18

1. Varieties of Imperatives   18
2. Law as Coercive Orders   20

III. THE VARIETY OF LAWS   26

1. The Content of Laws   27
2. The Range of Application   42
3. Modes of Origin   44

IV. SOVEREIGN AND SUBJECT   50

1. The Habit of Obedience and the Continuity of Law   51
2. The Persistence of Law   61
3. Legal Limitations on Legislative Power   66
4. The Sovereign Behind the Legislature   71

V. LAW AS THE UNION OF PRIMARY AND
SECONDARY RULES   79

I. A Fresh Start   79
2. The Idea of Obligation   82
3. The Elements of Law   91

VI. THE FOUNDATIONS OF A LEGAL SYSTEM 100

1. Rule of Recognition and Legal Validity 100
2. New Questions 110
3. The Pathology of a Legal System 117

VII. FORMALISM AND RULE-SCEPTICISM 124

1. The Open Texture of Law 124
2. Varieties of Rule-Scepticism 136
3. Finality and Infallibility in Judicial Decision 141
4. Uncertainty in the Rule of Recognition 147

VIII. JUSTICE AND MORALITY 155

1. Principles of Justice 157
2. Moral and Legal Obligation 167
3. Moral Ideals and Social Criticism 180

IX. LAWS AND MORALS 185

1. Natural Law and Legal Positivism 185
2. The Minimum Content of Natural Law 193
3. Legal Validity and Moral Value 200

X. INTERNATIONAL LAW 213

1. Sources of Doubt 213
2. Obligations and Sanctions 216
3. Obligation and the Sovereignty of States 220
4. International Law and Morality 227
5. Analogies of Form and Content 232

POSTSCRIPT 238

Introductory 238
1. The Nature of Legal Theory 239
2. The Nature of Legal Positivism 244
3. The Nature of Rules 254
4. Principles and the Rule of Recognition 263
5. Law and Morality 268
6. Judicial Discretion 272

Notes 277
Notes to the Third Edition 309
Index 327

INTRODUCTION

Leslie Green

I. HART'S MESSAGE

Law is a social construction. It is an historically contingent feature of certain societies, one whose emergence is signalled by the rise of a systematic form of social control administered by institutions. In one way law supersedes custom, in another it rests on it, for law is a system of primary rules that direct and appraise conduct together with secondary social rules about how to identify, enforce, and change the primary rules. A set-up like that can be beneficial, but only in some contexts and always at a price, for it poses special risks of injustice and of alienating its subjects from some of the most important norms that govern their lives. The appropriate attitude to take towards law is therefore one of caution rather than celebration. What is more, law sometimes pretends to an objectivity it does not have for, whatever judges may say, they in fact wield serious power to create law. So law and adjudication are political. In a different way, so is legal theory. There can be no 'pure' theory of law: a jurisprudence built only using concepts drawn from the law itself is inadequate to understand law's nature; it needs the help of resources from social theory and philosophic inquiry. Jurisprudence is thus neither the sole preserve, nor even the natural habitat, of lawyers or law professors. It is but one part of a more general political theory. Its value lies not in helping advise clients or decide cases but in understanding our culture and institutions and in underpinning any moral assessment of them. That assessment must be sensitive to the nature of law, and also to the nature of morality, which comprises plural and conflicting values.

These are the most important ideas of H. L. A. Hart's *The Concept of Law*, one of the most influential works in modern legal philosophy. Like some other important books, however, Hart's is known as much by rumour as by reading. To some who know of it, but do not really know it, the precis I just gave may sound unfamiliar. What they have heard makes them wonder: doesn't Hart think law is a closed logical system of rules? Doesn't he think law is a good thing, a social achievement that cures defects in other forms of social order? Doesn't he think laws are mostly clear and to be applied by courts without regard to moral values? Doesn't he think law and morality are conceptually separate and to be kept apart? And doesn't he think jurisprudence is value-free, and that its truths can be established by attending to the true meaning of words like 'law'?

The short answer is 'no', Hart does not think any of those things. These garbled versions of Hart's message have three sources. The first is a difficulty familiar throughout philosophy: the problems he addresses are complex, and the space between truth and falsehood is often a subtle, or easily overlooked, distinction. (For example: to claim that law and morality are separable is not to claim that they are separate.) The second is historical: after half a century, the book's language and examples feel socially, and sometimes philosophically, remote. Not many of us would still refer to customary social orders as 'primitive', or call an account of the nature of something an 'elucidation' of its concept. The third has to do with the audience's expectations. Each book has, as they say, an 'implied reader': Hart's is someone who is philosophically curious about the nature of one of our major political institutions and about its relations to morality and coercive force. That is not always his actual reader. Some turn to jurisprudence looking for practical help—for instance, they want to know how we should interpret constitutions, or what kind of people to choose as judges. They imagine that a book on the theory of law will stand to law as a book on the theory of catering might stand to catering—a general 'how-to' applicable to a range of different occasions.

Hart's book is clear enough to need no summary, but an exploration of some of its themes might help guard against misunderstandings like those. I'm going to examine his views about the law and social rules, coercion, and morality, and then briefly glance at some methodological points. I make no effort to remain neutral: Hart's theory of law is correct in part, mistaken in part, and, here and there, a bit obscure. But what follows is not an assessment. I highlight areas where people tend to go, or to be led, astray, and I make critical comments on a few points; but an appraisal is work for the reader.

2. LAW AS A SOCIAL CONSTRUCTION

Laws and legal systems are not matters of nature but artifice. We might say they are social constructions. Does that mark any contrast worth mentioning? Some think law is a social construction because they think everything is: '*il n'y a pas de hors-texte*', Derrida used to tease. Were that intelligible it would be irrelevant. Imagine someone said 'race is a social construction', only to follow up by clarifying, 'just like truncheons and prisons'. It would be like being told God doesn't exist, only to find out that the interlocutor doesn't believe in the existence of dogs either. When I say law is a social construction, I mean that it is one in the way that some things are *not*. Law is made up of institutional facts like orders and rules, and those are made by people thinking and acting.[1] But law exists in a physical universe that is not socially constructed, and it is created by and for people who are not socially constructed either. Perhaps this is banal. One might, to sound trendy, talk about the 'social construction of etiquette', but there isn't much point, since everyone already knows that manners are conventional.[2] They depend on common practice, they have a history, and they vary from place to place. Isn't it blindingly obvious that law is like that too? Well, consider this famous summary of a Stoic 'natural law' view:

True law is right reason in agreement with Nature; it is of universal application, unchanging and everlasting . . . [T]here will not be different laws at Rome and at Athens, or different laws now and in the future, but one eternal and unchangeable law will be valid for all nations and for all times. . . .[3]

---

[1] See eg. John Searle, *The Construction of Social Reality* (Allen Lane, 1995); and Neil MacCormick, *Institutions of Law: An Essay in Legal Theory* (Oxford University Press, 2007).

[2] Cf. Ian Hacking, *The Social Construction of What?* (Harvard University Press, 1999).

[3] Cicero, *De Re Republica* III. xii. 33, tr. C. W. Keyes (Harvard University Press, Loeb Classical Library, 1943) 211.

This eternal and universal law isn't something anyone made up and, we are told, it isn't something anyone can change. Natural law is not a matter of will but reason. It is hard to find legal theorists who still believe all of this,[4] but there are many who believe some of it. Ronald Dworkin, for example, argues that our law includes not only norms found in treaties, customs, constitutions, statutes, and cases, but also moral principles that provide the best justification for the norms found there.[5] On his account the *things justified* by moral principles are socially constructed, but the justifications themselves are not. It is important to bear in mind that a justification is not an event; it is an argument. Believing, or accepting, or asserting a justification are events. But Dworkin does not say that law consists of the constructed stuff plus things people believed to be, or accepted as, or asserted to be justifications for it. He says it consists of the constructed stuff plus moral principles that *actually are* justifications for it. If you believe that it is sufficient for something to be law that it is, or follows from, the best moral justification for something else that is law then, just as much as Cicero did, you believe there is law that owes its status to the fact that it is a requirement of 'right reason'. Since nothing we do can turn a justification that is sound into one that is not, you are also committed to the existence of law we cannot change. And since whether a moral principle justifies some arrangement does not depend on anyone knowing or believing that it does, there can be law—lots of law—that no one has ever heard of. Depending on the prospects for moral knowledge, there can be law that is not even knowable.

Hart's approach rejects all that. Anything in the law is there because some person or group put it there, either intentionally or accidentally. It all has a history; it all can be changed; it is all either known or knowable. Some of our laws have good justifications, some do not, and justifications do not anyway suffice to make law. To do that, we need actual human intervention:

[4] Perhaps John Finnis comes closest, in his *Natural Law and Natural Rights* (2nd edn., Oxford University Press, 2011).

[5] Ronald Dworkin, *Taking Rights Seriously* (Harvard University Press, 1978), chap. 4; Ronald Dworkin, *Law's Empire* (Harvard University Press, 1986), chaps. 2–3.

orders need to be given, rules to be applied, decisions to be taken, customs to emerge, or justifications to be endorsed or asserted.

Legal philosophers often use an antique term to cover things set by human interventions like that: they say they are 'posited'. Someone who thinks all law is posited is a *legal positivist*, of which social constructivists are one kind. Not all positivists are social constructivists, however. Hans Kelsen was not. He thought that all laws are posited, but he also thought that every legal system contains at least one norm that is not posited but only 'presupposed'.[6] A legal norm, Kelsen said, exists only if it is valid, where 'valid' means its subjects ought to conform to it. He followed Hume and Kant in holding that there can be no 'ought' from an 'is' alone; hence, no social construction, or bunch of them, can ever add up to a norm. If they are to produce norms, fundamental law-making processes in a society must therefore be presupposed to be valid. The original constitution needs to have genuine authority or nothing below it does, so if we are to regard materials created under its ground rules as law, we need to presuppose that the original constitution is binding. Now, a presupposition is no more an event than a justification is. Kelsen did not deny that if we want to know what law requires we need to know what people have actually posited. But he argued that if we want to know the product of their activities *as law*, then we need to add something that is not social or historical. So while Kelsen is a legal positivist he is not a social constructivist. That is why he regards the ways we study socially constructed norms— including sociological, psychological, and historical inquiry—as 'alien elements' in jurisprudence.[7]

Hart rejects Kelsen's view, too.[8] The ultimate basis of law is neither a justification nor a presupposition but a social construction that arises from people thinking and doing certain things. Jurisprudence explains what this construction is and how it is built up from more mundane social facts. Hart goes so far as to

---

[6] Hans Kelsen, *Pure Theory of Law* (Max Knight tr., 2nd edn., University of California Press, 1967) 193–205.

[7] Ibid. 1.

[8] See below, 292–3, and Hart's essays 'Kelsen Visited' and 'Kelsen's Doctrine of the Unity of Law' in H. L. A. Hart, *Essays in Jurisprudence and Philosophy* (Oxford University Press, 1983).

call his account of this 'an essay in descriptive sociology' (vi).[9]
That is probably going too far. It is an essay in analytic legal philosophy, but it is one that draws on concepts that a theoretically
astute sociology of law could profitably use. The most important
of these is the concept of a social rule.

(i) *Law, Rules, and Conventions*

Hart came to think that rules are the most important building
blocks of law after rejecting an earlier positivist account found
in Hobbes, Bentham, and Austin. They thought that law is constructed from commands, threats, and obedience. A sovereign is
a person or group who enjoys the habitual obedience of most
others but does not habitually obey anyone else. Law is a general
command of a sovereign backed by threat of force.

In 1977 Michel Foucault said, 'What we need ... is a
political philosophy that isn't erected around the problem of
sovereignty.... We need to cut off the King's head: in political
theory that still has to be done.'[10] News of regicide must not
have crossed the Channel, for Hart had long finished the job. In
Chapters III and IV he shows that not all laws are commands;
that a legal system need not have any person or group with the
attributes of a sovereign; that law continues after its creators
have perished; and that while threats can oblige people to do
things, they cannot create obligations to do them. At bottom,
what is missing from the sovereignty account is the concept of
a social rule. Once we understand rules we will find that they
are the key to explaining many phenomena in law, including
sovereignty, powers, jurisdiction, validity, authority, courts,
laws, legal systems—and even, argues Hart, one kind of justice.
Law itself is a *union* of social rules: primary rules that guide
behaviour by imposing duties or conferring powers on people,
and secondary rules that provide for the identification, alteration,
and enforcement of the primary rules. Among the secondary
rules, the ultimate *rule of recognition* has special importance.

---

[9] Parenthetical page references are all to this volume.

[10] Michel Foucault, 'Truth and Power' in his *Power/Knowledge: Selected
Interviews and Other Writings, 1972–1977* (Colin Gordon ed., Vintage, 1980) 121.

A customary practice of those whose role it is to apply primary rules, a rule of recognition provides criteria of legal validity by determining which acts create law. So the fundamental constitution of a legal system does not rest on moral justifications or logical presuppositions, but on this customary social rule created by 'a complex...practice of the courts, officials, and private persons' (107). Hart suggests that the rule of recognition in the United Kingdom is something like this, 'Whatever the Queen in Parliament enacts is law'. Parliamentary enactments are law, then, not because of their moral credentials, or because of any logical presupposition, but because an actually practised customary rule recognizes them as such.

So law is constructed of social rules. What about rules themselves? They too are social constructions, and Hart says they are made up of practice. (This is often called the 'practice theory of rules'.) Customary rules have an 'external aspect' in behavioural regularity: people act in a common way. (Depending on the rule, this may involve conforming to what it requires, or applying it to others.) Rules also have an 'internal aspect' involving a complex attitude Hart calls 'acceptance': a willingness to use the regularity as a standard to guide and appraise behaviour, especially to commend conformity and criticize breaches, and to treat such commendation and criticism as appropriate. Acceptance does not require approval; it is not a matter of how people feel about the rule but of their willingness to use it. People can accept rules in Hart's sense because they think they are good rules, or to please others, or out of fear or conformism (56–7, 115, 257). If Milton is to be believed, Satan could even accept a rule on the ground that it is a bad one: 'Evil be thou my good'. All that matters is that people converge on a standard and use it as a guide to conduct and in that way treat it as normative.

The practice theory of rules is controversial. Let us notice a few difficulties, and then turn to Hart's attempt to deflect certain objections. Hart wants a test for the existence of a rule that discriminates between rule-following and accidental or purely habitual patterns in behaviour, and he wants to explain what it is for a customary rule to be obligatory or binding.

However, the practice theory fails to deliver.[11] There are rules that are not social practices (e.g. an individual's rules); there are accepted social practices that are not rules (e.g. the common and accepted practice of surrendering one's wallet to a robber rather than resisting); and citing a rule can be offered *as* a justification for one's behaviour, not merely a sign that one supposes *there is* some justification for it. None of this fits the practice theory. Moreover, it is not clear that we need the concept of a social rule to understand the idea of obligation: one can believe that one has an obligation to purchase carbon offsets against air travel without supposing there is a common practice of doing it.

In the Postscript to this book, Hart tries to meet such criticisms by confining his account. Not all rules, he now admits, are practice rules, but *conventional* rules are and they form the basis of law. A rule is conventional provided 'general conformity of a group to them is part of the reasons which its individual members have for acceptance...' (255). The rule that one must drive on the right is a convention because people wouldn't follow it if most others didn't. The rule that one must not drive when sleepy is not a convention in the relevant sense, because on a road with lots of sleepy drivers you have more, not less, reason to stay awake. Hart holds that the ultimate rule of recognition is a convention: '[S]urely an English judge's reason for treating Parliament's legislation (or an American judge's reason for treating the Constitution) as a source of law having supremacy over other sources includes the fact that his judicial colleagues concur in this as their predecessors have done' (267). Law rests on 'a mere conventional rule of recognition accepted by the judges and lawyers' (267). We should delete the word 'mere' in the second formulation. It is not plausible to think that the only reason officials conform to a rule of recognition (or other fundamental rules) is that others do so. Recognition rules are rarely believed to be wholly arbitrary (even if they are believed to be arbitrary at the margins). In the United Kingdom, for example, the supremacy of parliamentary statutes as a source of

---

[11] See Ronald Dworkin, *Taking Rights Seriously* (rev. edn., Harvard University Press, 1978) 48–58; Joseph Raz, *Practical Reason and Norms* (2nd edn., Oxford University Press, 1999) 49–58.

law may rest, not only on a common practice of treating them as supreme, but also on a belief that this practice is democratic or is central to our culture. In the United States, the supremacy of the Constitution may rest, not only on common practice, but also on a belief that it sets up a just form of government, or that it was ordained by wise people with whom it is important to keep faith. Such beliefs do not have to be correct, and they do not have to be uniformly shared, but some such beliefs are typically present along with reasons based on common practice. What is needed for a rule of recognition to be conventional in Hart's sense is that, whatever other reasons officials have for applying it, they would not do so unless there was also a shared common practice to that effect.

Allowing for this modification, there is another problem to confront.[12] The rule of recognition is an obligation- or duty-imposing rule: it not only identifies the sources of law; it directs judges and others to apply the law so identified. According to the practice theory, a social rule imposes a duty if and only if (a) the rule is believed socially necessary, (b) it is reinforced by serious social pressure, and (c) it can conflict with the norm-subject's immediate self-interest (86–8). Are these conditions met here? The conditions are factual, so in any given case we would need to investigate. It does seem probable that courts and others will think it necessary to have settled tests for law, and that significant deviation from these would be reinforced by serious pressure to conform. (Imagine the reaction if, for example, a US district court simply ignored all rulings of the Supreme Court, or started to apply Sharia as a binding source of law.) But it is harder, in the case of a conventional rule, to see why condition (c) would be satisfied. The more important a conventional standard is believed to be, the less temptation there is to non-conformity, assuming it is known to be conventional. We could all drive on the left, or on the right, but when there is a common practice there isn't much temptation to break ranks and drive on the wrong side.

---

[12] For other doubts about Hart's argument on this point see Leslie Green, 'Positivism and Conventionalism' (1999) 12 *Canadian Journal of Law and Jurisprudence* 35; and Julie Dickson, 'Is the Rule of Recognition Really a Conventional Rule?' (2007) 27 *Oxford Journal of Legal Studies* 373.

A temptation to defect is characteristic of rules of other sorts, especially those that support public goods that are subject to free-riding. But when a rule is conventional, duty and desire pull in the same direction; there isn't 'the standing possibility of conflict between obligation or duty and interest' (87). As I said above, judges may have preferences among recognition rules, preferences that reflect views about legitimacy and so forth. But if the predominant attitude of each were a desire to run with the crowd, then the familiar sense of normative push and pull we find with obligations would be unusual. On this point, Hart came nearer the truth the first time round: breaking ranks can be tempting, even for judges, but it is also an occasion for criticism and serious pressure to conform. Alas, that also holds where there is no rule at all, but only a reason of general application. Debate about the precise characterization of social rules therefore continues, and there are other options that could fit within a broadly Hartian account of law.[13] But neither the simple practice theory, nor Hart's conventionalist revision of it, will work on its own.

(ii) *The Reach of Rules*

An independent source of doubt about a rule-based theory of law has to do with its scope. Supposing social rules prove necessary to understand legal phenomena, are they sufficient? They are not, for several reasons.

The first is stressed by Hart himself. Not all systems of primary and secondary rules are legal systems. The National Hockey League has a system of rules: primary rules that direct the conduct of players, officials, and the Commissioner, together with secondary rules of recognition, change, and adjudication that operate on the official rules. Yet the hockey rules are not a legal system. (Of course, they are a lot *like* a legal system; no one denies that.) What is missing? Hockey rules

---

[13] For example: Joseph Raz, *Practical Reason and Norms*; Frederick F. Schauer, *Playing by the Rules: A Philosophical Examination of Rule-based Decision-making in Law and in Life* (Oxford University Press, 1993); Andrei Marmor, *Social Conventions: From Language to Law* (Princeton University Press, 2009); Scott J. Shapiro, *Legality* (Harvard University Press, 2011).

are special-purpose: they regulate one game, whereas law can regulate much of life. And the legal system regulates hockey, including the hockey rules, but the hockey rules do not regulate the law. Hart further argues that, not only *can* law regulate comprehensively, a system of rules is not a legal system unless it actually *does* regulate a wide range of things including property, agreements, and the use of force (193–200). Hart calls this the 'minimum content' of a legal system, and he thinks that since regulating that content promotes human survival, and since human survival is (he assumes) morally good, all legal systems are oriented to some sort of good. Hence, there is no question of having a 'formal' test for legal systems. That is one of the reasons why, as I said at the outset, it is mistaken to think that Hart's theory represents legal systems as being like some kind of formal system in logic or mathematics. And this point packs an even bigger punch. Because nothing is a law that does not belong to some legal system, there can be no purely formal test for law either. Laws are rules that play a role in a particular *kind* of normative system, one distinguished in part by its content.

A second point leads to a clarification. Some writers think Hart's account is incorrect or incomplete because not everything in a legal system is a rule. It is said that we find other kinds of norms as well, for example, 'standards' or 'principles'.[14] As we have seen above (xviii), if these are supposed to pick out moral justifications for laws then, on Hart's account, they are not part of the law unless they are somehow officially adopted or endorsed. But 'standards' and 'principles' are also in common use to pick out general legal norms that are flexible or defeasible. Understood in this way, they fit easily with Hart's theory. To know the bearing of the law on some issue one needs to know the net effect of many different rules that intersect and may conflict, and there may be more than one permissible way to resolve that conflict. That is one source of

---

[14] A distinction between rules and standards is drawn in Henry M. Hart and Albert Sacks, *The Legal Process: Basic Problems in the Making and Application of Law* (W. N. Eskridge, Jr. and P. P. Frickey eds., Foundation Press, 1994) 139–41. A distinction between rules and principles is drawn in Ronald Dworkin, *Taking Rights Seriously* 22–8.

defeasibility. Another flows from the fact that, as Hart explains in Chapter VII, every rule is somewhat vague and open-textured. There are cases to which it clearly applies and clearly does not apply, but there are also cases to which it arguably applies, and a lot of work, especially in appellate courts, involves arguable but legally uncertain cases. Although legal indeterminacy in one sense occurs at the margins of a rule, it is not a marginal phenomenon. It is a feature of every legal system and of every rule in that system, with the consequence that 'a large and important field is left open for the discretion of courts and other officials' (136). Courts have a special task in making authoritative applications of law, but they also have another task they share with legislatures, that of creating new law. Knowing when and how to use this law-creating power is mostly not about applying rules of any kind; it calls for practical judgement. The role of courts in resolving indeterminacy means that it would be misleading to develop a general theory of law by looking only, or mainly, at the work of appellate courts, or indeed any courts. Owing to a 'selection effect' one would be over-emphasizing legal uncertainty. Many who find the very idea of a rule too cut-and-dried to capture the fluid and controversial character of law fall into this trap. They don't notice the fairly settled rules that constitute courts themselves, or the ordinary legal rules that people use to determine what to do without going near courts at all. Drivers know that 'Stop' on a road sign means 'Stop the car', not 'Stop blinking'. No one needs a judicial ruling on the point, and this is a typical case of law in action.

A third point reminds us that not everything in a system of legal rules is a rule of any kind. Section 6 of the UK Human Rights Act 1998 says, 'In this section "public authority" includes—(a) a court or tribunal, and (b) any person certain of whose functions are functions of a public nature. . . .' Is that a rule? It is a definition; but perhaps a definition is a rule for using words? If so, it is a rule that is not a norm, since it does not require or empower or permit any action. The legal role of definitions is explained by showing how they work *along with* rules that are norms, including the norm in Section 1 of that Act: 'It is unlawful for a public authority to act in a way which is incompatible with a Convention right,' and the remedies for unlawful action provided elsewhere. This does tell people to do things (though implicitly: you need to know what 'unlawful' means in a context like this). And this is also how we should approach materials in law that are norms but are not rules. For example, a judicial decision often ends with a particular order: a directive telling someone or other to do something, or pay something, or suffer something. A one-off order is not a rule; it is an individual norm. It is practically impossible to govern by using individual norms alone; but it is logically impossible to govern without them. For courts to be able authoritatively to determine people's legal positions they need to issue rulings that bind particular people.

Although rules are necessary to understand laws and legal systems, they are therefore not sufficient. We also need to know what the rules are about and what they are expected to do; we need to know about other materials that fit together with rules, and we need to know about legal decision making that is not rule-governed. Hart spends more time on some of these topics than on others, but all of them can be accommodated within the theory. Contrary to a common misunderstanding, Hart never says that law is *simply* a matter of rules, or that rules explain *all* legal phenomena. Indeed, he cautions against that error: 'though the combination of primary and secondary rules merits, because it explains many aspects of law, the central place assigned to it, this cannot by itself illuminate every problem.... [It] is at the centre of the legal system; but it is not the whole....' (99). There are many other things of interest, and jurisprudence needs to take account of them.

3. LAW AND POWER

So we have this: law is a construction of social rules, which are themselves constructed from practice. That may sound like a rather complacent view of an institution that is, in the end, an instrument of social control. What about conflict, coercion, and power?

(i) *The Division of Labour in Law*

Hart argues against Austin's top-down, pyramidal view of law as orders of a sovereign backed by threats. It is widely acknowledged that that view was crude, but some may feel that it was salutary and that Hart, while making legal positivism more subtle, loses some of its punch. Law is not just about consensus and agreement, it is also about conflict and disagreement.[15] Now, if this is the familiar claim that a lot of activity in appellate courts is highly politicized and consists not of applying settled law but settling arguable cases, there is no reason to dissent. We have just seen how that fits Hart's theory. He does, however, require a degree of consensus at other points if things are to get off the ground: at least the rule of recognition needs to rest on agreement about which activities make law. But whose agreement? Here is Dworkin's rendition of Hart's theory:

The true grounds of law lie in the acceptance by the community as a whole of a fundamental master rule (he calls this a 'rule of recognition').... For Austin the proposition that the speed limit in California is 55 is true just because the legislators who enacted that rule happen to be in control there; for Hart it is true because the people of California have accepted, and continue to accept, the scheme of authority in the state and national constitutions.[16]

What is wrong with that as an account of the 'grounds' of law is obvious enough. Many people in California have no idea what the 'scheme of authority in the state and national constitutions' amounts to; some are not even aware that there *is* a state constitution. There is also something wrong with it as an interpretation of Hart's theory. In a pre-legal society, social norms can exist only with broad support. 'In the simpler structure [before the emergence of law], since there are no officials, the rules must be widely accepted as setting critical standards for the behaviour of the group. If, there, the internal point of view is not widely disseminated there could not logically be any rules (117).' Customary rules require general buy-in. However,

... where there is a union of primary and secondary rules ... the acceptance of rules as common standards for the group may be split off from the relatively passive matter of the ordinary individual acquiescing

---

[15] On other aspects of this theme see Jeremy Waldron, *Law and Disagreement* (Oxford University Press, 1999).

[16] Ronald Dworkin, *Law's Empire* 34.

in the rules by obeying them for his part alone. In an extreme case the internal point of view with its characteristic normative use of language ('This is a valid rule') might be confined to the official world. In this more complex system, only officials might accept and use the system's criteria of validity. The society in which this was so might be deplorably sheeplike; the sheep might end in the slaughterhouse. But there is little reason for thinking that it could not exist or for denying it the title of a legal system (117).

I have quoted this passage at length because the point it makes is critical to understanding the nature of law and also the political significance of the fact that law has that nature. Custom and social morality, Hart notes, are immune to deliberate change; they evolve only gradually. For a small and stable community, they are fairly good ways of running things—throughout much of private life that is how we normally run things—but large and complex societies also need deliberate mechanisms of social control that enable customs and other norms to be publicly ascertained and to be changeable forthwith, by the say-so of the rulers, by majority vote, or whatever. This is made possible by institutionalization: the emergence of specialized organs with power to identify, alter, and enforce the rules. The resulting division of normative labour is a mixed blessing, bringing both gains and costs: 'The gains are those of adaptability to change, certainty, and efficiency ... the cost is the risk that the centrally organized power may well be used for the oppression of numbers with whose support it can dispense, in a way that the simpler regime of primary rules could not' (202). So law is *not* universally good or good without qualification. Its institutional character makes certain gains possible, but it also makes certain costs possible, costs that a society without law is unlikely to bear. Even short of the limiting case Hart discusses above, a typical society under law depends less on a broad social consensus than it does on a narrow official consensus.[17] What the existence of law requires

---

[17] This skates over the question of precisely which officials matter, and of how the role of 'official' should be characterized. Generally speaking, Hart means to include at least judges and legislators, and 'official' takes a socio-political rather than legal definition.

of the population in general is little more than acquiescence with respect to the mandatory norms of the system.

There is, then, nothing cosy or communal about the consensus on which law rests. It does not presuppose an agreement on values; it does not exclude significant dissent in the operation of law. And this shows why the romantic belief that every legal system necessarily expresses the values of its community is incorrect. Even a just and valuable legal system can end up arcane, technical, and remote from the lives of those it governs. Owing to the division of normative labour, law runs a standing risk of becoming, in a word, legalistic. Every legal theorist acknowledges that law is morally fallible. Hart's special contribution here is in showing that some of the ways law can fail are intimately connected to its nature as a social institution.

(ii) *Coercion and Power*

The idea that law is essentially a coercive apparatus resonates with the layperson's view and has been popular in jurisprudence. Hart thinks it mistaken. Every legal system contains some norms that are not coercively enforced, and it is conceivable that a legal system might be composed entirely of such norms (199–200). What would be the point of sanction-free law? The same as the point of law with sanctions: to direct people how to behave. Sanctions are the law's Plan B. Plan A is that its subjects should conform to it without further supervision. Where a need for direction exists without a need for reinforcing motivation it is not so uncommon to find laws without sanctions. The United States Code, for example, contains norms telling people how to show respect for the flag. ('The flag should never be used as a receptacle for receiving, holding, carrying, or delivering anything.'[18]) Yet it provides no penalties for breach of these norms. Were human nature other than what it is, all legal norms could be like that.

Even with human nature being what it is, many legal norms are not reinforced by sanctions. One important class is power-conferring norms, legal rules that create the capacity

---

[18] 4 U.S.C. § 8 (h).

to change legal norms and statuses, for example the rules that empower people to legislate, incorporate, contract, or marry. Where the powers in question are voluntary (as these examples generally are), people are free to exercise them or not at their option. Someone who does not follow the law's recipe for legislating, incorporating, contracting or marrying fails to do so, and the resulting 'marriage', for example, would be null and void. But no one is punished for failing. Or should we say that nullity is itself a kind of punishment and that these are, after all, coercive laws? Hart explains why we should not: we do not have two distinct things here, an order to do something and a sanction for disobedience. There is no order at all, and the 'sanction' is nothing other than the power-conferring rule itself. Kelsen proposed a work-around to save the coercion theory. He said power-conferring rules are really only fragments of laws, so it isn't surprising that the sanction isn't found in them: they are tucked away elsewhere in the legal system. There are sanction-bearing rules requiring one to support one's spouse; what the power-conferring rules of marriage do is tell us whether someone has a spouse and, if so, who it is. One way or another, it is all eventually linked back to coercion. Hart's reply to this move is revealing. He does not say that Kelsen's reconstruction is impossible or illogical. He says that it is unmotivated and at variance with a methodological constraint on jurisprudence:

The principal functions of the law as a means of social control are not to be seen in private litigation or prosecutions, which represent vital but still ancillary provisions for the failures of the system. It is to be seen in the diverse ways in which the law is used to control, to guide, and to plan life out of court (40).

There is no essentialist, 'metaphysical', answer to the question of how to divide up the legal material into individual laws; the best approach is one that lets us understand law as it is for those who actually use it, most of whom live outside courtrooms. Power-conferring rules are thought of, spoken of, and used in social life differently from rules that impose duties, and they are valued for different reasons. 'What other tests for difference in character could there be?' (41). This epitomizes Hart's method. To Holmes's 'bad man', law is all about costs to be avoided; to the lawyer it is all about possible and actual court cases (and legal costs to be earned). Theories of law have been spun out of these cyclopic viewpoints. They treat what is real but marginal as if it were central. Whole dimensions of legal importance are left out of their flat and reductive pictures.

All that is correct as far as it goes. However, if we want to attend to *all* the 'principal functions of the law as a means of social control' we must go further than Hart does here. It is indeed a mistake to try to reduce power-conferring rules to duty-imposing rules, or to represent nullity as a kind of sanction. But it is not a mistake to notice the ways that power-conferring rules are bound up with social power. Why care about coercion in the first place? One answer is connected to responsibility: people who are forced by threat to do things are generally not held responsible for having done them; their will is overborne. Many legal penalties are not that severe, however (short of persistent refusal to pay them). Nonetheless, they still affect people's incentives, and that is true of power-conferring rules as well. Coercion is the hard edge of law's power; the incentivizing and expressive character of legal norms belongs to its soft edge.

Think again of the rules that confer the power to marry. They do so subject to conditions. These used to include (and in some places still include) restrictions on the race or sex of the people one can marry. Marriages between people of different races, or between people of the same sex, were legal nullities. Now, it would be wrong, for the reasons Hart gives, to see this as a kind of coercion, forcing people into heterosexual or homoracial relationships. No one need marry at all. So these laws were not like criminal punishments for homosexual conduct, or like the fugitive slave laws. Still, it was no accident or unintended by-product of the relevant power-conferring rules (or the combination of power-conferring rules and interpretation rules) that rendered these marriages void. That was their purpose. Without resorting to anything as crude as orders and sanctions these laws attempted to shape both individuals' lives and the common culture. They did so with some success. We need to bear this in mind when we think about the functions of rules that Hart benignly refers to as providing 'facilities'. Not all laws are coercive, but non-coercive laws do something that coercive laws also do: they express and channel social power. They can do it through their content and through more general features. Voluntary powers, for example, parcel out legal control to those who are capable of exercising their will; individual powers parcel it out to individuals. That may not force anyone to do anything, but it does shape the social world in ways that are not only predictable, but often intended by those who create and apply such laws.

4. LAW AND MORALITY

A central problem in this book involves the pluriform relations between law and morality—both customary, or 'social' morality and ideal, or 'critical', morality. Hart is famous for insisting on some kind of disjunction between law and morality—people who know nothing else about his theory know that he holds, as he put it in his landmark Holmes Lecture, that 'there is no necessary connection between law and morals'.[19] We have already seen above, in 3 (i), why law need not reflect the moral values actually endorsed by the population it governs. But what about the moral values that *should* govern them? Does Hart mean to say that there is no necessary connection here either? In *The Concept of Law*, he sometimes formulates the thought differently. At one point he describes the core positivist thesis as holding that, 'it is in no sense a necessary truth that laws reproduce or satisfy certain demands of morality' (185–6). That seems narrower: it is possible that there are necessary relations between law and morality that do not require that all laws 'reproduce or satisfy' sound moral standards.

Hart's first, broader, formulation found little favour, not even among those who share his view that law is a social construction.[20] Surely it is not just a contingent matter that law and morality

---

[19] H. L. A. Hart, 'Positivism and the Separation of Law and Morals' (1958) 71 *Harvard Law Review* 593, at 601 n. 25.

[20] See John Gardner, 'Legal Positivism: 5½ Myths', chap. 2 of his *Law as a Leap of Faith* (Oxford University Press, 2012); and Leslie Green, 'Positivism and the Inseparability of Law and Morals' (2008) 83 *New York University Law Review* 1035.

both regulate human conduct? A system of norms that had nothing to say about how we should live would not be legal norms, and they would not be moral norms either. That suggests one necessary connection between law and morals; there are others. In fact, Hart's mature theory actually endorses two more interesting necessary connections between law and morality, one via the purpose of law and the other via a putative connection between law and justice. It also allows for a contingent connection between law and morality that many other positivists are reluctant to credit. These three claims are as important to Hart's theory as either version of the disjunction thesis. But only the first of them is clearly correct.

(i) *Law's Purpose*

Law is not just a system of rules; it is a system that serves various purposes. Thomas Aquinas thought law also has an *overall* purpose for it is, he claimed, 'an ordinance of reason made for the common good'.[21] Modern suggestions along these lines include the idea that law is made for guiding conduct, or for coordinating activity for the common good, or for doing justice, or for licensing coercion.[22] These claims should be understood, not as suggestions about possible ideals for law, but about *constitutive aims* of law. The basic idea is that a system of social control that did not have these aims would not be a legal system, just as an institution that did not aim at the pursuit of knowledge would not be a university. Having constitutive aims does not establish any connection with morality. That depends on what the aims are. No appliance is a dishwasher unless it is for washing dishes, and its capacity to wash dishes is one of the main criteria for judging whether a dishwasher is good. Washing dishes is not normally a morally significant activity, however, so a good dishwasher is not a morally good dishwasher. The above suggestions for a constitutive aim of

---

[21] *Summa Theologica* II-I, q. 90 a. 4.

[22] Guiding conduct: Lon L. Fuller, *The Morality of Law* (rev. edn., Yale University Press, 1969); coordinating activity: John Finnis, *Natural Law And Natural Rights* (Oxford University Press, 1980); doing justice: Michael Moore, 'Law as a Functional Kind,' in R. P. George ed., *Natural Law Theory: Contemporary Essays* (Oxford University Press, 1992) 221; licensing coercion: Ronald Dworkin, *Law's Empire* 93.

law vary from the morally charged to the morally neutral. Doing justice is morally good; guiding conduct is morally neutral; and licensing coercion is morally ambiguous.[23]

The connection to morality also depends on how far the constitutive aim succeeds. Hart's argument in Chapter IX assumes that human survival is morally good, and that a normative system that did not aim at it would not be a legal system. It also holds that, for a legal system to exist, it must actually deliver the goods, if not to everyone all of the time, then to some people much of the time. Generally speaking, however, a thing with a constitutive aim gets quite a lot of latitude before we disqualify it as a member of the relevant kind. A dishwasher that is defective or broken is still a dishwasher, provided that, if modified or repaired, it would have some capacity to wash dishes. The same holds for legal systems. Unified sets of laws that are very defective at doing what laws are supposed to do can nonetheless count as a legal system. This follows from the fact that to *aim* at something does not require *succeeding* at it.

In his last reflections on this problem, Hart seems no longer to think that law need even aim at survival. He joins Max Weber and Hans Kelsen, who deny that law has an interesting constitutive aim of any kind. (Kelsen said 'law is a means, a specific social means, not an end'.[24]) Hart writes, 'I think it quite vain to seek any more specific purpose which law as such serves beyond providing guides to human conduct and standards of criticism of such conduct' (249). No mention of survival here. But perhaps Hart is not withdrawing his earlier claim that law has the purpose of promoting survival, or other purposes. Perhaps he is denying that law can be *identified* by any such purposes—there is no purpose that is both universal among and unique to legal systems. Law may have the aim of promoting survival; it may have the aim of guiding and appraising conduct. Neither will

---

[23] Does licensing coercion mean 'providing a justification for such coercion as is going on'; or 'ensuring that no coercion goes on that is not justified' or 'coercing people when it would be justified to do so'?

[24] Hans Kelsen, *General Theory of Law and State* (A. Wedberg tr., Harvard University Press, 1949) 20.

distinguish law from things like custom, religion, and morality; on the contrary, they are points of overlap. Law and morality attend to similar tasks; they do so for related reasons; and they use some similar techniques.

(ii) *Law and Justice*

In Chapter VIII, Hart defends a surprising connection between law and morality. The argument associates rule-following with justice, through the idea that, in both, like cases are to be treated alike. By the practice theory, general rules cannot exist unless they are conformed to or applied with some constancy. But constancy, Hart says, is *itself* a kind of justice: '[T]hough the most odious laws may be justly applied, we have, in the bare notion of applying a general rule of law, the germ at least of justice' (206, cf. 160). It follows, then, that every existing legal system does some justice. Not, to be sure, 'substantive' justice. Steady application of an odious law in no way compensates for or mitigates its odiousness. But it nonetheless produces justice in the *application* of law, or as some say 'formal' justice.[25] This requires that a law be applied to all and only those who are alike in the ways that the law itself regards—rightly or wrongly—as relevant to their treatment under that law. And the requirement covers every law, even those that are 'hideously oppressive', or deny to 'rightless slaves' the minimum benefits of any functioning legal system.[26]

I've quoted Hart's words about how bad law can be ('odious', 'hideously oppressive', etc.) to make clear that his 'germ of justice' thesis is a bold one. Constancy in application can seem sensible if one is thinking of laws that are only mildly unjust; say, laws that are over- or under-inclusive with respect to their justifying aims. (A norm prohibiting anyone under 17 from driving allows too few of some, and too many of others, to drive.) Perfection is not to be had, however, and there are plenty of reasons for steadfastly applying laws that fall short

---

[25] David Lyons criticizes it under that label in 'On Formal Justice' (1973) 58 *Cornell Law Review* 833. Matthew Kramer defends it under the better label of 'constancy': Matthew Kramer, 'Justice as Constancy' (1997) 16 *Law and Philosophy* 561.

[26] H. L. A. Hart, 'Positivism and the Separation of Law and Morals' 593, at 626.

in modest ways. But that will not establish Hart's case. He says that it applies also to odious laws and that even when we allow substantive justice—or equity, or mercy, or sanity—to win out, we do so in the recognition that we have lost something valuable along the way: we have been unjust in at least one respect.

There is something odd in this idea of 'formal' justice. After all, not everything that has *the form of* justice is *a* form of justice, any more than everything that has the form of a camel is a camel. Worse, norms of justice and norms of injustice need not differ in their forms.[27] The norm 'men and women are to be paid equally for work of equal value' is a norm of justice. The norm 'men and women are to be paid unequally for work of equal value' is a norm of *injustice*. They have the same form. What about the norm, 'Apply every rule to all and only those covered by it'? That has the same form as 'Be friends with all and only those people you have already decided to befriend'. Is the second a norm of justice? It seems clear that we can't tell whether a norm is a norm of justice, or injustice, or neither, on grounds of its form alone.

Imagine the case of a judge working in a legal system where adultery is to be punished by stoning a convicted woman to death. Is there any reason to apply this law to everyone covered by it? Perhaps in special cases: his life may be in jeopardy if he doesn't; to refuse may cause riots and the killing of even more women; he may apply it on one occasion in order to secure his credibility long enough to more effectively attack it on another occasion. But is there a reason to be steadfast in the application of such a law on *all* occasions? Here we need more than the principle *nulla poena sine lege*. That tells us *not* to punish people who *have not* broken a law. The condition is met in our hypothetical case. But that principle does not tell us to punish everyone who *has* broken a law. Would refusing to do so be an injustice? If so, to whom? It beggars belief to suppose that other convicted women who are to be stoned to death, or the families of women who already were, are entitled to demand that every other convicted woman be treated just as odiously.

---

[27] Following John Gardner, 'The Virtue of Justice and the Character of Law', chap. 10 of his *Law as a Leap of Faith*.

Hart may be confusing 'formal' justice with two sound, but unrelated, ideas. One is that there can be justice and injustice not only in outcomes but also in *procedures*. It is a requirement of natural justice, for instance, that both sides to a legal dispute be heard. A procedure that does not provide for that is unjust. But an unjust rule may *itself* prescribe a violation of natural justice: if the law permits the rich to have twice as much time to present their case as the poor, strict application of that law will set back natural justice, not advance it. The other idea in this neighbourhood is that we should be *impartial* in our application of rules, and that those who judge should not act out of 'prejudice, interest or caprice' (161). That is also correct, but there need be no such motivation on the part of one who refuses to apply an unjust law according to its terms. In fact, the odious law may itself be prejudicial or capricious, and selective non-application of it may be done with the best of motivation.

Can we rescue anything from Hart's 'germ of justice' thesis? Perhaps this: once we are attuned to rule-application, we are perforce thinking about how rules ought to be applied *in particular cases*—we are thinking about how people fare or should fare under them. This focuses attention on distributive questions, not just on aggregative questions. It requires us to ask not merely whether enough punishment is being meted out these days, but whether the right people are being punished in the right way for the right offences. To think about how benefits and burdens should be distributed among people is to think about questions of justice. An attentive concern with whether A was treated as A deserves, or whether any difference in treatment between A and B can be justified, is a concern for justice. When we have institutions, such as courts, that have the power to consider and settle such questions we have institutions that are able to do justice. (And, of course, injustice.) Perhaps in a large and complex society, justice cannot be done without institutions like that.

(iii) *Legal Validity and Moral Principles*

The third point of contact between law and morality is different. Hart allows that while moral principles are not necessarily a source of law, they *could* be, provided they were so authorized by things that *are* a source of law. One way of putting this is to say that Hart thinks that, while the rule of recognition is necessarily a social construction, the criteria it deploys need not be. He does not think that moral principles are law because they are valuable principles or because they justify existing law. But they can become law if, one way or another, they are put into law.

Here Hart takes a stand on one of two ways of interpreting the constructivist thesis, in favour of what is often called 'inclusive' legal positivism, according to which the sources of law may include principles of ideal morality, and against 'exclusive' legal positivism, according to which they cannot.[28] His route to this conclusion is hard to retrace, partly because, when he wrote the main text, these alternatives were not yet distinguished. But his conclusion in the Postscript is that legal validity need not be purely a matter of a norm's 'pedigree', that is, features 'concerned only with the manner in which laws are adopted or created by legal institutions and not with their content...' (247).[29] Instead, legal validity could turn on moral propriety.

We cannot evaluate the inclusive positivist thesis here.[30] But it is worth trying to clear away one confusion Hart brings to the debate. The question whether the criteria in the rule of recognition can include moral principles is not the same as the question whether these criteria are matters of pedigree. There are two possible contrasts with 'pedigree'. There is a contrast with *substance*, and a different contrast with *morality*. Confusion reigns owing to the common habit of using 'substantive' to mean 'justified', or 'moral' (as we saw in the notion of 'substantive justice', above, 4 (ii)). In the main text, Hart introduces these issues in criticizing Austin's view that every legal system comprises a

---

[28] Hart calls his position 'soft' positivism, but 'inclusive' positivism is more perspicuous since it holds that law *includes* anything to which law refers.

[29] The metaphor is first used by Ronald Dworkin, *Taking Rights Seriously* 17.

[30] The theory is defended by W. J. Waluchow, *Inclusive Legal Positivism* (Oxford University Press, 1994), and by Jules Coleman, *The Practice of Principle: In Defence of a Pragmatist Approach to Legal Theory* (Oxford University Press, 2001). It is criticized by Joseph Raz, *Ethics in the Public Domain: Essays in the Morality of Law and Politics* (Oxford University Press, 1994), chaps. 9, 10; and Scott Shapiro, 'On Hart's Way Out' (1998) 4 *Legal Theory* 469.

power that is legally unlimited. An Austinian could, perhaps, allow that a sovereign legislator could be limited as to the 'manner and form' in which it legislates—for example, it may be subject to special requirements of notice and debate, or to supermajority decision making—but there are also constraints in many written constitutions that cannot be characterized in that way. These 'exclud[e] altogether certain matters from the scope of its legislative competence, thus imposing limitations of substance' (68). They impose disabilities that 'are legal and not merely moral or conventional' (69).[31] Hart offers as an example the Sixteenth Amendment to the United States Constitution, which requires, in part, that 'No Capitation, or other direct, Tax shall be laid, unless in proportion to the Census or Enumeration herein before directed to be taken'. That is certainly not a manner-and-form requirement, so it is in one sense substantive. But Hart also says that 'in some systems of law, as in the United States, the ultimate criteria of validity might explicitly incorporate besides pedigree, principles of justice or substantive moral values, and these may form the content of legal constitutional constraints' (247). This is a rather different notion of 'substantive'. Compare the following fragments of a possible recognition rule:

(S1) Congress shall make no law establishing a religion.
(S2) Congress shall make no law that is unfair.
(P1) Congress shall make no law secretly.
(P2) Congress shall make no law unfairly.

Rules (S1) and (S2) set substantive criteria of validity; (P1) and (P2) set procedural criteria. But we can also pair them another way: (S2) and (P2) set moral criteria for validity, whereas (S1) and (P1) set factual criteria. (This is not to say that they set fully determinate criteria, but that we can tell whether a law establishes religion or was made in secret without coming to any view about the propriety of doing either.) But now we ask: does (P2) also state a test of *pedigree*? It does in the sense that to apply it we examine the manner in which the law was adopted rather

---

[31] Here Hart is using 'moral or conventional' to cover both what Austin called non-legal limitations of 'positive morality' on legal power, as well as what Dicey called constitutional 'conventions'.

than the content of law that ended up being adopted. It does not in the sense that we cannot know *whether* (P2) is satisfied without deciding about the moral propriety of how it was made. The pedigree metaphor is thus likely to mislead, and we should dispense with it in favour of a distinction between matters of social fact and matters requiring moral judgement.

Matters are further complicated by three other things. The first is homonymy. That there are moral-sounding *terms* in constitutions, or elsewhere, does not even suggest that there may be moral tests for law. Some such terms have, or have come to have, a special meaning in legal contexts, a meaning controlled by customary morality and by judicial decisions and traditions of legal interpretation.[32] A constitution that says 'Every individual is equal before the law' may or may not be reaching out to a moral ideal of equality. We would have to see what courts and others actually do with it. And even when a provision begins its constitutional life stating a moral ideal, judicial decisions can encrust it with factual paradigms of inequality, and multi-prong doctrinal tests for inequality, and so on. These are ordinary source-based tests for the validity of law. They can be so remote from the original, abstract moral ideal that it is unclear whether it is even still in play.

The second complication is supervenience. It is plausible to think that, for example, if something is 'unfair' there are facts *in virtue of which* it is unfair, and that one arrangement cannot be unfair and another fair without there also being some difference in these facts. Suppose a constitution bans statutes that are discriminatory, where discrimination is understood to be morally wrong. If it is wrong in virtue of ordinary social facts— for example, facts about the intention with which a decision was taken, or facts about the relative impact of that decision on various people—these facts may, on any view, be part of a test for law. Exclusive positivism does not require that the ultimate tests for law include no facts that could be mentioned in a case for thinking something fair or unfair. That would be unintelligible. It requires only that it is possible to ascertain the relevant

---

[32] As always, 'controlled' does not mean 'completely controlled'.

facts without coming to a view about their impact on such moral properties.

The third complication is uncertainty. Hart considers a case in which the legislature requires an industry to charge only a 'fair rate' for its services (131–2). Although there will be some extreme cases of unfairness that are so obvious as to have been clearly contemplated by the legislation (e.g. 'a rate so high that it would hold the public up to ransom for a vital service' (131)), there will be many other cases which it would be both impossible and unwise to try to specify in advance:

In these cases it is clear that the rule-making authority must exercise a discretion, and there is no possibility of treating the question raised by the various cases as if there were one uniquely correct answer to be found, as distinct from an answer which is a reasonable compromise between many conflicting interests (131–2).

At least to the extent that 'fairness' is uncertain, then, reference to this term in a statute requires courts to exercise discretion. A legislator mandating a 'fair rate' would know this, and should be understood as conferring on courts a discretionary power—not a power to do whatever they like, but a power to determine what is unfair and for their determination to bind. In the Postscript the picture seems different. Here, constitutional provisions such as those referring to 'due process', 'equality', etc. are offered as examples of moral principles being incorporated into the law. Whether they confer discretion is now said to depend, not on the extent of their uncertainty, but on whether any moral judgements that would be needed to resolve disputes about them have, or do not have, 'objective standing' (253–4). If moral judgements are objective, then uncertainty-resolving decisions merely apply pre-existing law that refers to moral standards; if moral judgements are not objective, these 'can only constitute directions to courts to *make* law in accordance with morality' (254). Hart wants jurisprudence to avoid commitments to controversial meta-ethical theories, so he leaves the question open.

If this intimates that moral language in constitutions functions differently from moral language in statutes it seems unmotivated. A written constitution is, after all, just a special kind of statute. Why think that in a statute a reference to 'fairness' confers discretionary power at least when it is uncertain what fairness requires, but in a constitution a reference to, say, 'fundamental justice' confers discretionary power only if it is uncertain what that requires *and* moral resolution of that uncertainty would not be 'objective'? Isn't it sufficient that resolution is required, never mind the status of the principles to be deployed in achieving that resolution? Maybe discretion seems more worrying in the case of constitutional fundamentals than in the case of a mere statute; but that does not show that it is absent. Moreover, discretion is not an all-or-nothing affair. Fact-based criteria may have partial control over discretionary decisions, not only, in Kelsen's metaphor, by providing a 'frame' within which they have to fit, but also as non-conclusive reasons for decisions of one sort or another.[33]

The closest Hart comes to an argument for his position is the following. He considers a hypothetical constitution that makes broad moral propriety a test for law. Nothing is to count as law if it is in any way wrong, unjust, unfair, etc. He says there would be nothing illogical about this. '[T]he objection to this extraordinary arrangement would not be "logic" but the gross indeterminacy of such criteria of legal validity. Constitutions do not invite trouble by taking this form.'[34] If 'logic' includes conceptual argument, however, there may be such an objection. Joseph Raz argues that this would not merely be inviting trouble, it would be incompatible with law having the sort of authority it claims.[35] All law claims legitimate authority, and it can coherently do so only if it is the kind of thing that *could* have authority. Law's claim may be hollow—it may be insincere, unjust or unwise—but it must be intelligible. The role of practical authorities, including legal systems, is to help people conform to what they have reason to do.[36] Authorities can do that only if they base their directives on those reasons, and only if trying to follow their directives makes it more likely that the subjects will

---

[33] Hans Kelsen, *Pure Theory of Law* 350–1.

[34] H. L. A. Hart, *Essays in Jurisprudence and Philosophy* 361.

[35] Joseph Raz, *The Morality of Freedom* (Oxford University Press, 1986), chap. 2; *Ethics in the Public Domain*, chap. 10; and *Between Authority and Interpretation: On the Theory of Law and Practical Reason* (Oxford University Press, 2009), chap. 5.

[36] This means what they have 'objective' reason to do, not merely what would be in their *selfish* interest to do, or what they *think* they have reason to do.

comply with the underlying reasons that apply to them. That is in turn possible only if the directives can be identified in a way independent of appeal to those very reasons. So law cannot help anyone know what he ought to do if in order to know what the law requires he must first *figure out* what he ought to do. A statute cannot secure fairer outcomes just by telling people to deal fairly with each other; a constitution cannot produce a more equal society just by declaring everyone to be equals. To provide authoritative direction they need to tell people what these things in fact require. So argues Raz. This is one of the most-discussed arguments in analytical jurisprudence. There are many steps in it and several of them are controversial. But it is an argument of the sort Hart declares unavailable, and it would have to be tested before we could sign up to Hart's view.[37]

Inclusive legal positivism seems to suggest that morality could properly find a role in legal argument only if it were invited to do so. Hart issues an invitation via the ultimate criteria of validity.[38] But is an invitation really needed?[39] No one thinks that judges can rely on principles of logical inference or simple arithmetic only if the law specially invites these principles in. No one thinks the rules of English grammar need a place in the rule of recognition in English law. Perhaps no invitation is needed after all, and moral principles, like these other standards, are already at home in court. If that is so, Hart may be proposing a solution to a problem that does not exist.

5. FACT, VALUE, AND METHOD

The aim of this book, Hart tells us in the Preface, is 'to further the understanding of law, coercion, and morality as different but related social phenomena'. He predicts that lawyers will see it as an exercise in 'analytical jurisprudence', since it is 'concerned

---

[37] Moreover, in a later article Hart himself adopts some of its key ideas. See H. L. A. Hart, 'Commands and Authoritative Legal Reasons' in his *Essays On Bentham* (Oxford University Press, 1982).

[38] Tony Honoré thinks the invitation comes through the moral claims that law makes. See his 'The Necessary Connection between Law and Morality' (2002) 22 *Oxford Journal of Legal Studies* 489.

[39] See Joseph Raz, *Between Authority and Interpretation*, chap. 7.

with the clarification of the general framework of legal thought rather than with the criticism of law or legal policy'. He also says we can think of it as 'an essay in descriptive sociology' (vi). What are we to make of these remarks?

(i) *Jurisprudence and Sociology*

It is a funny sort of sociology that presents no fieldwork, no statistical modelling, and even few legal cases. On later reflection, Hart says he shouldn't have suggested that the book is a *kind* of sociology, but rather that it is somehow preparatory to sociology.[40] These five words cause more grief than they warrant. Their point is merely to emphasize that Hart's method, *like* descriptive sociological methods, holds itself responsible to the facts without taking any moral or political stand about them. Time and again he appeals to his reader to use an informed person's knowledge of the legal world to test the claims of legal philosophy. Are there really such things as legal rules? Look and see (136). Does every legal system have an illimitable sovereign? Look and see. If there is a conflict between an *a priori* theory and ordinary knowledge of the law, go with the latter. It may need revision, it will probably need disciplining, but it is the place to start. The empirical basis of the book is no more sophisticated than that; but, like descriptive sociology, it has an empirical basis. It does not begin with definitions or axioms and purport to derive necessary truths about law. It does not begin with moral claims about how law should be and infer conclusions about how law really is.

Descriptive sociology goes beyond ordinary knowledge in the quantity and quality of its observations. It often tries to assemble them into generalizations or, more ambitiously, predictions. Hart does neither. He works with basic things we already know. He offers a theory about the nature of law that is, he claims, consistent with them in a way that other influential theories are not. His theory is not a set of generalizations caught when trawling oceans of socio-legal data, and it does not try to predict anything at all. How then can it add value to what we already know? By deepening our understanding of it. It shows

---

[40] David Sugarman, 'Hart Interviewed: H. L. A. Hart in Conversation with David Sugarman' (2005) 32 *Journal of Law and Society* 267, 291.

us surprising relations among ordinary facts, unnoticed presuppositions of those facts, and, especially, the wider significance of certain facts. Of course there is no sharp break between explanation and understanding. Rich works in the sociology of law, and in the philosophy of law, do some of each. Understanding is not a rival to explanatory and predictive inquiry into law. Nor is it a licensing scheme that purports to regulate how anyone should study or what they should study. It is its own thing.

This suggests that analytic jurisprudence and legal sociology can largely run in parallel. Could any case be made for Hart's suggestion that the first might sometimes be preparatory to the second? Kelsen said '[S]ociological jurisprudence presupposes the juristic concept of law, the concept of law defined by normative jurisprudence.'[41] His basic idea was that, insofar as sociology seeks to study and make generalizations about legal institutions and practices, it will have to start *with them*. If you are interested in the social consequences of power-conferring rules, you had better be able to tell which ones those are. That will take some 'normative jurisprudence'. Or another example: sociologists are trying to develop empirical measures of the rule of law. To know whether these are valid measures of their target, we need to know what the rule of law is. As far as I can tell, none of the leading indices tries to estimate the extent to which laws in a given jurisdiction are not retrospective, or vague, or in conflict with each other—all central requirements of the rule of law.[42] Some of them do, however, estimate the security of private property or freedom of contract in various jurisdictions, and they give higher rule-of-law marks to places that have more of it. This betrays an obvious political bias; it also signals conceptual confusion. There is controversy about the concept of the rule of law, but anyone who thinks it means 'the prerequisites for capitalism' has a very poor grasp of the idea. It may be replied that at least these empirical measures are reliable, correlate with variables

---

[41] Hans Kelsen, *General Theory of Law and State* 178. 'Normative' here means 'having to do with norms', *not* 'morally appraisive'.

[42] For a review some attempts at an index, and the problems in constructing one, see Tom Ginsburg, 'Pitfalls of Measuring the Rule of Law' (2011) 3 *Hague Journal on the Rule of Law* 269.

of interest, and are continuous with other knowledge we have of law and society.[43] Even so, when the sociology of law drifts so far from the core of what the pertinent concepts pick out, it has changed the subject. Some subjects may need changing—progress in the natural sciences sometimes came about by tearing up an ontology and starting again. But if progress in social science requires tearing up our familiar legal ontology of rules, duties, powers, courts etc., or familiar legal values like the rule of law, it will become a sociology of something other than law. That gives jurisprudence some priority.

If we are going to hang on to 'the juristic concept of law' and related concepts, how do we achieve the deeper understanding that Hart promises? Where do we start? Hart often tries to elicit our ordinary knowledge by asking how we would judge or classify certain things, and sometimes he does *that* by asking what we would *say* about them. Does that make his jurisprudence a branch of semantics? Hart was influenced by, and saw himself as an advocate of, the 'linguistic turn' in philosophy.[44] His particular path was influenced by the ordinary language philosophy developed at Oxford by his colleagues J. L. Austin and Gilbert Ryle.[45] For all that, what is most striking, given its vintage and provenance, is how *little* linguistic analysis there is in *The Concept of Law*. We are reminded that language has various functions, that sentences have contexts, and that some theories can be understood as giving criteria for use of concepts. A few points are reinforced with linguistic distinctions. (Hart claims there is a difference between being 'obliged' to do something and being 'obligated' to do it, between doing something 'as a rule' and 'having a rule'.) That's about it. There is none of the linguistic philosophers' hostility to theory building;

---

[43] For a spirited defence of a social-scientific approach to jurisprudence see Brian Leiter, *Naturalizing Jurisprudence: Essays on American Legal Realism and Naturalism in Legal Philosophy* (Oxford University Press, 2007).

[44] See Richard Rorty ed., *The Linguistic Turn: Recent Essays in Philosophical Method* (University of Chicago Press, 1967).

[45] And also the later Wittgenstein, especially as received through his pupil, Friedrich Waismann. For an illuminating account of Hart's personal and intellectual relationships with the Oxford philosophers of his day see Nicola Lacey, *A Life of H. L. A. Hart: The Nightmare and the Noble Dream* (Oxford University Press, 2004).

no suggestion that legal system is a 'family-resemblance' concept or anything like it. Hart even works out necessary and sufficient conditions for something to be a legal system! He does not approach this problem, or any central problem in jurisprudence, by appeal to the meaning of words. Time and again Hart warns us of the futility of a linguistic approach. To try to answer the question 'What is law?' by 'remind[ing] the questioner of the existing conventions governing the use of the words "law" and "legal system" is,' he says, 'useless' (5). To try to choose between a broader and a narrower concept of law we need more than semantics; 'we cannot grapple adequately with this issue if we see it as one concerning the proprieties of linguistic usage' (209). If one were writing a book on the methodology of jurisprudence, rather than a book on jurisprudence, one would need to square these warnings with the friendliness to other aspects of linguistic philosophy that is also on display here. But Hart is not writing a book on the methodology of anything.

It cannot be denied that linguistic philosophy colours the rhetoric of the book including, of course, its title. But a good historian of ideas needs to look beyond style to substance. There is a difference between what a philosopher thought he was doing, what he said he was doing, and what he was actually doing. (David Hume said politics could be reduced to a science. Not a single experiment or proof was reported in either the *Treatise* or the *Enquiry*.) Current rhetorical styles in philosophy are as different from Hart's as his own was from that of Bentham. How far these mark real differences of technique is hard to say.

(ii) *Clarification and Criticism*

This book advocates a kind of legal theory Hart calls 'general and descriptive' (239–40). He means that it is a theory of law *as such*, not a theory of English law, or common law, or capitalist law—and it 'is morally neutral and has no justificatory aims: it does not seek to justify or commend on moral or other grounds the forms and structures which appear in my general account of law, though', he adds optimistically, 'a clear understanding of these is, I think, an important preliminary to any useful moral criticism of law' (240).

Even if the book lacks justificatory aims, it does not follow that it is morally neutral. Perhaps moral bias creeps in unintentionally. Some people think it does on the basis that any description must be more than a list of facts about the thing described. Observations are theory-laden; descriptions built from observations are value-laden; so descriptive legal philosophy is impossible. But that is too quick. A statement of fact may be appraised as true or false. A description is not normally thought of as being true or false, but as being helpful or unhelpful, illuminating or unilluminating, etc. There are an infinite number of possible descriptions of any object or state of affairs, because there are infinitely many facts about each. An actual description of something is not a list of *all* the facts about it; it is a selection and arrangement of facts that are for some reason taken to be important, salient, relevant, interesting, etc. Every description presupposes, or is made from the point of view of, certain values. This does not, however, entail that the person offering the description endorses those values, or that they are moral values. A description of a case-management system as 'inefficient' is not value-neutral. It selects for attention certain features of the system. The reason for selection, however, need not be that the speaker himself thinks efficiency is valuable, let alone most valuable, or of moral value. He may focus on that because he thinks that his audience thinks it salient, or that most people think it, or that judges using that case-management system think it. The possibilities are many.

It may be helpful to explore one point at which critics think they detect moral seepage into Hart's descriptive project. He famously introduces his main argument through a fictional history of social development (91–9). We begin with a 'primitive' society in which social order is achieved by consensus on what is to be done. With social change these arrangements are liable to uncertainty, they are static, and they become inefficient. The emergence of law with its secondary rules cures these 'defects', and thus in a 'developed', 'complex' society things are better in as much as we gain certainty, dynamism, and efficiency through the use of rules of recognition, change, and adjudication. And here the critics pounce:[46] how can Hart say law cures 'defects'

---

[46] Among many pouncers, see Stephen Guest, 'Two Strands in Hart's Concept of Law' in Stephen Guest ed., *Positivism Today* (Dartmouth, 1996) 29.

while claiming to be neutral on the merits of law? How can he call pre-legal societies 'primitive' and not implicitly condemn them?

In this context 'primitive' clearly means simple; it does not mean foolish or barbaric. And the reason simple societies do not have law is not that they aren't sufficiently civilized to have invented it: it is that they do not *need* it. There is nothing in human nature or society that requires law; many have got along well without it (91). As we can see from the international realm, highly systematized rule systems are 'not a necessity, but a luxury' (235). Simple forms of social order actually work well, for example, when the societies in which they operate are small, stable, and socially and ideologically united (91). However, 'In any other conditions such a simple form of social control must prove defective and will require supplementation in different ways' (92). Notice, first, that the defect in question is not a *moral* vice, it is a functional deficit in the mechanisms of social control. Whether that is a matter for moral regret depends on whether or not these mechanisms are oriented to good or to evil. More efficient social control can be a bad thing. Second, the defect is not so much in the simple society as in the mis-match between modes of governance and social complexity. The defect lies in trying to rule a large society of strangers as if it were a small society of friends—the mistake of some modern communitarian political theories, for example. There is no suggestion here that if we could choose between a simple society without law and a complex society with it we should prefer the latter.

This argument cannot, then, be accused of abandoning the sort of neutrality Hart is after. Obviously, Hart focuses on the emergence of secondary rules because he thinks that is a salient and important fact about law. But *not* because he thinks it desirable: in fact, as we saw above, he thinks it is morally risky. Ironically, a bias more often lies with those who read into his argument some kind of modernist triumphalism. They suppose that, if a society lacks a legal system, then it lacks one of the achievements of modernity. Since it would be parochial and demeaning to think 'primitive' societies uncivilized, by *modus tollens*, they must have legal systems. Any jurisprudence that fails to acknowledge these *as* legal systems is therefore biased in favour of modern or Western law. The form of that argument is startling. It begins from the premise that all societies ought to have law and draws the inference that all societies actually have it. The inference is obviously invalid. It also rests on a premise Hart rejects. Not sharing an enthusiasm for law, he does not feel compelled to find it all over the place.

Similar considerations apply to Hart's claim, in Chapter X, that international law is not a system but a *set* of rules, and in that way a bit like a simple social order. International lawyers are scandalized: Hart gives international law 'low marks'; he treats it as an 'outcast' rather than the special thing it is.[47] They are so worried about the status of their subject that they scarcely notice that the main burden of this chapter is to *defend* international law from the misguided suggestion that, since it lacks a central sovereign or compulsory jurisdiction, it cannot be law. Hart does doubt that international law is very systematized; he finds nothing in the field like an overall rule of recognition. But this does not exclude the possibility that other secondary rules exist, including rules that tell us, for example, when an entity is a state or what it takes to adopt a treaty. It is striking that when writing about the international order itself (rather than writing about jurisprudential theories of it) international lawyers readily acknowledge that many of its central rules have patchy effectiveness, that tests for some important norms are seriously unsettled, that adjudicative institutions are fragmented into special-purpose tribunals, and that many areas of international law remain aspirational. But the systematization of law is anyway a matter of degree, and it may be correct to think that international law is more systematic now than it was in 1961.[48] That it is already on a par with what we find in domestic legal systems is not plausible. In pointing this out Hart is not condemning international law, or celebrating Westphalian statism. He is trying to understand

---

[47] Ian Brownlie, 'The Reality and Efficacy of International Law' (1981) 52 *British Yearbook of International Law* 1, 7–8.

[48] For a review of some of the issues see the editors' introduction to Samantha Besson and John Tasioulas eds., *The Philosophy of International Law* (Oxford University Press, 2010) 1–13, and sources therein cited.

the ways international law is like domestic law, and the ways it is not.

None of this is to deny that *The Concept of Law* is a book framed by views about political morality. There is not much here of Hart's version of Millian liberalism, or his democratic socialism. There are, however, clear traces of another of his moral views, namely, value pluralism. Like his friend Isaiah Berlin,[49] Hart thinks that what is good is irreducibly plural, and the world is such that genuine goods are often in conflict. Even a justified gain in one may come at the expense of another. Hart therefore stands against both reductive monism of the sort we see in utilitarianism or welfare economics, according to which there is really only one thing worth pursuing, and also against a non-reductive position that allows for various values, but insists that (properly interpreted) they can never conflict.[50] Hart tells us that 'laws and the administration of laws may have or lack excellences of different kinds' (157) and he says that even justice is only one of those excellences. His value pluralism is on prominent display also in his remarks on legal reasoning. 'Judicial decision, especially on matters of high constitutional import, often involves a choice between moral values, and not merely the application of some single outstanding moral principle' (204). This will have profound implications for judicial reasoning: 'because a plurality of such principles is always possible it cannot be *demonstrated* that a [judicial] decision is uniquely correct...' (205).

6. THE POINT

Suppose a general jurisprudence along Hart's lines could be successfully developed. Why bother? Grappling with the ideas in this book has become the price of admission to a vast literature in contemporary legal philosophy. It contains helpful treatments of earlier works in philosophy. But the idea that we should read a book of jurisprudence mainly to find out about *other* books

---

[49] Isaiah Berlin, *Four Essays on Liberty* (Oxford University Press, 1969), and also his 'On Value Pluralism' (1998) *New York Review of Books*, vol. XLV No. 8.

[50] For the most sustained defence of this position see Ronald Dworkin, *Justice for Hedgehogs* (Harvard University Press, 2011).

of jurisprudence has no sharper critic than Hart himself. There aren't many scholarly notes in *The Concept of Law*, and they are relegated to the back of the book with the suggestion that we read them later, if at all:

I hope that this arrangement may discourage the belief that a book on legal theory is primarily a book from which one learns what other books contain. So long as this belief is held by those who write, little progress will be made in the subject; and so long as it is held by those who read, the educational value of the subject must remain very small (vii).

Clearing obstacles to progress is of value, however, only if progress in that field is itself of value. No doubt analytic legal philosophy of Hart's sort has non-specific value: it prizes and promotes close reading, clear thinking, and careful argument. All handy skills, and of educational value, too. But there are many ways to learn them, and no reason to think the study of jurisprudence is the quickest or easiest route.

A fully adequate apology for general jurisprudence is that law is an important social institution, and that a deeper understanding of such institutions is of value in itself. We want to understand the nature of law for the same reasons we want to understand the nature of the market or the family. That will not prove that we should train our attention on law rather than on the market or family; it will not even prove that we should pursue deeper understanding of law rather than prediction of law-related behaviour or reform of laws and legal institutions. But none of these alternatives undermines the distinctive value of jurisprudence.

Some people read books of jurisprudence hoping for guidance about life and law. Some write books of jurisprudence hoping to offer it. (Including some who write for the reason Machiavelli did, to catch the ear of a prince.) If those are your ambitions general jurisprudence may disappoint you. Its influence as a kind of high-brow *amicus curiae* brief has not been notable. To be sure, it is possible that a court case could raise or rely on jurisprudential theses. There are decisions in which judges express views on the relation between the validity and efficacy of law, on the difference between penalties and taxes, even on the difference between law and custom. But when they do address such questions courts try to answer them within local doctrinal constraints that legal philosophy is not bound to respect. We have good theoretical grounds for distinguishing customary social orders from legal systems; yet a given legal system may hold that aboriginal custom is a legal system in its own right. Would that refute Hart's theory? Not in the least. That the Fisheries Act regulates whaling does nothing to shake our confidence in the view that whales are not fish. (Neither does it show there is anything wrong with the Fisheries Act.)

Historically, *The Concept of Law* stands at the cusp of the revival of political philosophy in the English-speaking world. Soon after it was first published, attention turned fairly dramatically to problems of value. The big books of the next generation focused on ideas like justice, liberty, and equality, while attention to legal institutions and structures diminished.[51] Hart's book casts sideways glances at evaluative issues—as we saw, it has something to say about justice—but it is overwhelmingly a book about institutions and structures. Because of that, and because of its steady determination to remain descriptive in orientation, it sometimes attracts the favourite slurs of the advocate: its theory is declared 'sterile' or 'boring'. It is hard to know what to make of that. The slurs betray intellectual narrowness, but also a lack of self-awareness. It is a lawyer's conceit that law is *unquestionably* interesting and that other things are made interesting by showing their relevance to a possible lawsuit (an idea not far removed from the thought that a *really* interesting question is one a client might pay you to answer).

Ronald Dworkin writes that jurisprudence matters because 'It matters how judges decide cases'.[52] Much earlier he had written, 'What, in general, is a good reason for a decision by a court of law? This is *the* question of jurisprudence ... '.[53] Hart is not only a value pluralist; he is an intellectual pluralist as well. He does not take part in the race to the bottom line. The first chapter of this

<hr />

[51] For the suggestion that the subject ended up going too far in the direction of applied moral philosophy, see Jeremy Waldron, '*Political* Political Theory: An Oxford Inaugural Lecture', http://ssrn.com/abstract=2060344.

[52] Ronald Dworkin, *Law's Empire* 1.

[53] Ronald Dworkin, 'Does Law Have a Function? A Comment on the Two-Level Theory of Decision' (1965) 74 *Yale Law Journal* 640.

book is entitled 'Persistent Questions', in the plural. They are: How is law related to coercive threats? What does the obligatory force of law amount to, and how is it related to moral obligation? What are social rules and in what way is law about rules? But none of these is *the* question of jurisprudence; they are all just *questions* of jurisprudence.

Are they, in the end, interesting questions? Of course they are; but the simple truth is that people are interested in different things. Reflecting on his own life, David Hume wrote, 'My studious disposition, my sobriety, and my industry, gave my family a notion that the law was a proper profession for me; but I found an insurmountable aversion to everything but the pursuit of philosophy and general learning...'.[54] Hume found the law impossibly boring; he is not alone. No doubt others have the opposite aversions. But whatever one's intellectual proclivities one should be able to see—Hume certainly did—that being 'interesting' is not a property of the object in question, but of a relation between it and a person. Hart's jurisprudence may have a limited bearing on lawsuits, but it should hold interest for anyone who sees the intrinsic importance of its problems, as well as for those who have larger political concerns. In court it is more important to know what *the law* is than it is to know what *law* is. But outside court where, as Hart reminds us, most law-in-action takes place, questions about the nature of law come into their own. What might we hope for from law as a means of governance; what are its benefits and its risks? Why value the rule of law? Should we obey the law; if so, how far? And, of course, why even have law at all? Anyone drawn to ask such questions, or who finds he can no longer avoid them, will need the help of general jurisprudence to find answers. That Hart made such a good start on it is, for us, extremely lucky.

---

[54] David Hume, 'My Own Life' in his *Essays, Moral, Political and Literary*, E. F. Miller, ed. (Liberty Press, 1987).

I

PERSISTENT QUESTIONS

I. PERPLEXITIES OF LEGAL THEORY

Few questions concerning human society have been asked with such persistence and answered by serious thinkers in so many diverse, strange, and even paradoxical ways as the question 'What is law?' Even if we confine our attention to the legal theory of the last 150 years and neglect classical and medieval speculation about the 'nature' of law, we shall find a situation not paralleled in any other subject systematically studied as a separate academic discipline. No vast literature is dedicated to answering the questions 'What is chemistry?' or 'What is medicine?', as it is to the question 'What is law?' A few lines on the opening page of an elementary textbook is all that the student of these sciences is asked to consider; and the answers he is given are of a very different kind from those tendered to the student of law. No one has thought it illuminating or important to insist that medicine is 'what doctors do about illnesses', or 'a prediction of what doctors will do', or to declare that what is ordinarily recognized as a characteristic, central part of chemistry, say the study of acids, is not really part of chemistry at all. Yet, in the case of law, things which at first sight look as strange as these have often been said, and not only said but urged with eloquence and passion, as if they were revelations of truths about law, long obscured by gross misrepresentations of its essential nature.

'What officials do about disputes is ... the law itself';[1] 'The prophecies of what the courts will do ... are what I mean by the law';[2] Statutes are 'sources of Law ... not parts of the Law itself';[3] 'Constitutional law is positive morality merely';[4] 'One shall not steal; if somebody steals he shall be punished.

---

[1] Llewellyn, *The Bramble Bush* (2nd edn., 1951), p. 9.
[2] O. W. Holmes, 'The Path of the Law' in *Collected Papers* (1920), p. 173.
[3] J. C. Gray, *The Nature and Sources of the Law* (1902), s. 276.
[4] Austin, *The Province of Jurisprudence Determined* (1832), Lecture VI (1954 edn., p. 259).

... If at all existent, the first norm is contained in the second norm which is the only genuine norm. ... Law is the primary norm which stipulates the sanction'.[1]

These are only a few of many assertions and denials concerning the nature of law which at first sight, at least, seem strange and paradoxical. Some of them seem to conflict with the most firmly rooted beliefs and to be easily refutable; so that we are tempted to reply, 'Surely statutes *are* law, at least one kind of law even if there are others': 'Surely law cannot just mean what officials do or courts will do, since it takes a law to make an official or a court'.

Yet these seemingly paradoxical utterances were not made by visionaries or philosophers professionally concerned to doubt the plainest deliverances of common sense. They are the outcome of prolonged reflection on law made by men who were primarily lawyers, concerned professionally either to teach or practise law, and in some cases to administer it as judges. Moreover, what they said about law actually did in their time and place increase our understanding of it. For, understood in their context, such statements are *both* illuminating and puzzling: they are more like great exaggerations of some truths about law unduly neglected, than cool definitions. They throw a light which makes us see much in law that lay hidden; but the light is so bright that it blinds us to the remainder and so leaves us still without a clear view of the whole.

To this unending theoretical debate in books we find a strange contrast in the ability of most men to cite, with ease and confidence, examples of law if they are asked to do so. Few Englishmen are unaware that there is a law forbidding murder, or requiring the payment of income tax, or specifying what must be done to make a valid will. Virtually everyone except the child or foreigner coming across the English word 'law' for the first time could easily multiply such examples, and most people could do more. They could describe, at least in outline, how to find out whether something is the law in England; they know that there are experts to consult and courts with a final authoritative voice on all such questions.

[1] Kelsen, *General Theory of Law and State* (1949), p. 61.

Much more than this is quite generally known. Most educated people have the idea that the laws in England form some sort of system, and that in France or the United States or Soviet Russia and, indeed, in almost every part of the world which is thought of as a separate 'country' there are legal systems which are broadly similar in structure in spite of important differences. Indeed an education would have seriously failed if it left people in ignorance of these facts, and we would hardly think it a mark of great sophistication if those who knew this could also say what are the important points of similarity between different legal systems. Any educated man might be expected to be able to identify these salient features in some such skeleton way as follows. They comprise (i) rules forbidding or enjoining certain types of behaviour under penalty; (ii) rules requiring people to compensate those whom they injure in certain ways; (iii) rules specifying what must be done to make wills, contracts or other arrangements which confer rights and create obligations; (iv) courts to determine what the rules are and when they have been broken, and to fix the punishment or compensation to be paid; (v) a legislature to make new rules and abolish old ones.

If all this is common knowledge, how is it that the question 'What is law?' has persisted and so many various and extraordinary answers have been given to it? Is it because, besides the clear standard cases constituted by the legal systems of modern states, which no one in his senses doubts are legal systems, there exist also doubtful cases, and about their 'legal quality' not only ordinary educated men but even lawyers hesitate? Primitive law and international law are the foremost of such doubtful cases, and it is notorious that many find that there are reasons, though usually not conclusive ones, for denying the propriety of the now conventional use of the word 'law' in these cases. The existence of these questionable or challengeable cases has indeed given rise to a prolonged and somewhat sterile controversy, but surely they cannot account for the perplexities about the general nature of law expressed by the persistent question 'What is law?' That these cannot be the root of the difficulty seems plain for two reasons.

First, it is quite obvious why hesitation is felt in these cases. International law lacks a legislature, states cannot be brought before international courts without their prior consent, and there is no centrally organized effective system of sanctions. Certain types of primitive law, including those out of which some contemporary legal systems may have gradually evolved, similarly lack these features, and it is perfectly clear to everyone that it is their deviation in these respects from the standard case which makes their classification appear questionable. There is no mystery about this.

Secondly, it is not a peculiarity of complex terms like 'law' and 'legal system' that we are forced to recognize both clear standard cases and challengeable borderline cases. It is now a familiar fact (though once too little stressed) that this distinction must be made in the case of almost every general term which we use in classifying features of human life and of the world in which we live. Sometimes the difference between the clear, standard case or paradigm for the use of an expression and the questionable cases is only a matter of degree. A man with a shining smooth pate is clearly bald; another with a luxuriant mop clearly is not; but the question whether a third man, with a fringe of hair here and there, is bald might be indefinitely disputed, if it were thought worth while or any practical issue turned on it.

Sometimes the deviation from the standard case is not a mere matter of degree but arises when the standard case is in fact a complex of normally concomitant but distinct elements, some one or more of which may be lacking in the cases open to challenge. Is a flying boat a 'vessel'? Is it still 'chess' if the game is played without a queen? Such questions may be instructive because they force us to reflect on, and make explicit, our conception of the composition of the standard case; but it is plain that what may be called the borderline aspect of things is too common to account for the long debate about law. Moreover, only a relatively small and unimportant part of the most famous and controversial theories of law is concerned with the propriety of using the expressions 'primitive law' or 'international law' to describe the cases to which they are conventionally applied.

When we reflect on the quite general ability of people to recognize and cite examples of laws and on how much is generally known about the standard case of a legal system, it might seem that we could easily put an end to the persistent question, 'What is law?', simply by issuing a series of reminders of what is already familiar. Why should we not just repeat the skeleton account of the salient features of a municipal legal system which, perhaps optimistically, we put (on page 3) into the mouth of an educated man? We can then simply say, 'Such is the standard case of what is meant by "law" and "legal system"; remember that besides these standard cases you will also find arrangements in social life which, while sharing some of these salient features, also lack others of them. These are disputed cases where there can be no conclusive argument for or against their classification as law.'

Such a way with the question would be agreeably short. But it would have nothing else to recommend it. For, in the first place, it is clear that those who are most perplexed by the question 'What is law?' have not forgotten and need no reminder of the familiar facts which this skeleton answer offers them. The deep perplexity which has kept alive the question, is not ignorance or forgetfulness or inability to recognize the phenomena to which the word 'law' commonly refers. Moreover, if we consider the terms of our skeleton account of a legal system, it is plain that it does little more than assert that in the standard, normal case laws of various sorts go together. This is so because both a court and a legislature, which appear in this short account as typical elements of a standard legal system, are themselves creatures of law. Only when there are certain types of laws giving men jurisdiction to try cases and authority to make laws do they constitute a court or a legislature.

This short way with the question, which does little more than remind the questioner of the existing conventions governing the use of the words 'law' and 'legal system', is therefore useless. Plainly the best course is to defer giving any answer to the query 'What is law?' until we have found out what it is about law that has in fact puzzled those who have asked or attempted to answer it, even though their familiarity with the law and their ability to recognize examples are beyond question. What more do they want to know and why do they want to know it? To *this* question something like a general answer can be given. For there are certain recurrent main themes which have formed a constant focus of argument and counter-argument about the nature of law, and provoked exaggerated and paradoxical assertions about law such as those we have already cited. Speculation about the nature of law has a long and complicated history; yet in retrospect it is apparent that it has centred almost continuously upon a few principal issues. These were not gratuitously chosen or invented for the pleasure of academic discussion; they concern aspects of law which seem naturally, at all times, to give rise to misunderstanding, so that confusion and a consequent need for greater clarity about them may coexist even in the minds of thoughtful men with a firm mastery and knowledge of the law.

2. THREE RECURRENT ISSUES

We shall distinguish here three such principal recurrent issues, and show later why they come together in the form of a request for a *definition* of law or an answer to the question 'What is law?', or in more obscurely framed questions such as 'What is the nature (or the essence) of law?'

Two of these issues arise in the following way. The most prominent general feature of law at all times and places is that its existence means that certain kinds of human conduct are no longer optional, but in *some* sense obligatory. Yet this apparently simple characteristic of law is not in fact a simple one; for within the sphere of non-optional obligatory conduct we can distinguish different forms. The first, simplest sense in which conduct is no longer optional, is when one man is forced to do what another tells him, not because he is physically compelled in the sense that his body is pushed or pulled about, but because the other threatens him with unpleasant consequences if he refuses. The gunman orders his victim to hand over his purse and threatens to shoot if he refuses; if the victim complies we refer to the way in which he was forced to do so by saying that he was *obliged* to do so. To some it has seemed clear that in this situation where one person gives another an order backed by threats, and, in this sense of 'oblige', obliges him to comply, we have the essence of law, or at least 'the key to the science of jurisprudence'.[1] This is

---

[1] Austin, op. cit., Lecture I, p. 13. He adds 'and morals'.

the starting-point of Austin's analysis by which so much English jurisprudence has been influenced.

There is of course no doubt that a legal system often presents this aspect among others. A penal statute declaring certain conduct to be an offence and specifying the punishment to which the offender is liable, may appear to be the gunman situation writ large; and the only difference to be the relatively minor one, that in the case of statutes, the orders are addressed generally to a group which customarily obeys such orders. But attractive as this reduction of the complex phenomena of law to this simple element may seem, it has been found, when examined closely, to be a distortion and a source of confusion even in the case of a penal statute where an analysis in these simple terms seems most plausible. How then do law and legal obligation differ from, and how are they related to, orders backed by threats? This at all times has been one cardinal issue latent in the question 'What is law?'.

A second such issue arises from a second way in which conduct may be not optional but obligatory. Moral rules impose obligations and withdraw certain areas of conduct from the free option of the individual to do as he likes. Just as a legal system obviously contains elements closely connected with the simple cases of orders backed by threats, so equally obviously it contains elements closely connected with certain aspects of morality. In both cases alike there is a difficulty in identifying precisely the relationship and a temptation to see in the obviously close connection an identity. Not only do law and morals share a vocabulary so that there are both legal and moral obligations, duties, and rights; but all municipal legal systems reproduce the substance of certain fundamental moral requirements. Killing and the wanton use of violence are only the most obvious examples of the coincidence between the prohibitions of law and morals. Further, there is one idea, that of justice, which seems to unite both fields: it is both a virtue specially appropriate to law and the most legal of the virtues. We think and talk of 'justice *according to* law' and yet also of the justice or injustice *of* the laws.

These facts suggest the view that law is best understood as a 'branch' of morality or justice and that its congruence with the principles of morality or justice rather than its incorporation of orders and threats is of its 'essence'. This is the doctrine characteristic not only of scholastic theories of natural law but of some contemporary legal theory which is critical of the legal 'positivism' inherited from Austin. Yet here again theories that make this close assimilation of law to morality seem, in the end, often to confuse one kind of obligatory conduct with another, and to leave insufficient room for differences in kind between legal and moral rules and for divergences in their requirements. These are at least as important as the similarity and convergence which we may also find. So the assertion that 'an unjust law is not a law'[1] has the same ring of exaggeration and paradox, if not falsity, as 'statutes are not laws' or 'constitutional law is not law'. It is characteristic of the oscillation between extremes which makes up the history of legal theory, that those who have seen in the close assimilation of law and morals nothing more than a mistaken inference from the fact that law and morals share a common vocabulary of rights and duties, should have protested against it in terms equally exaggerated and paradoxical. 'The prophecies of what the courts will do in fact, and nothing more pretentious, are what I mean by the law.'[2]

The third main issue perennially prompting the question 'What is law?' is a more general one. At first sight it might seem that the statement that a legal system consists, in general at any rate, of *rules* could hardly be doubted or found difficult to understand. Both those who have found the key to the understanding of law in the notion of orders backed by threats, and those who have found it in its relation to morality or justice, alike speak of law as containing, if not consisting largely of, rules. Yet dissatisfaction, confusion, and uncertainty concerning this seemingly unproblematic notion underlies much of the perplexity about the nature of law. What *are* rules? What does it mean to say that a rule *exists*? Do courts really apply rules or merely pretend to do so? Once the notion is queried, as it has been especially in the jurisprudence of this century, major divergencies in opinion appear. These we shall merely outline here.

---

[1] 'Nam mihi lex esse non videtur quae justa non fuerit': St. Augustine I, *De Libero Arbitrio*; Aquinas, *Summa Theologica*, I–II, Qu. 95 Art. 2; Qu. 96 Art. 4.

[2] Holmes, loc. cit.

It is of course true that there are rules of many different types, not only in the obvious sense that besides legal rules there are rules of etiquette and of language, rules of games and clubs, but in the less obvious sense that even within any one of these spheres, what are called rules may originate in different ways and may have very different relationships to the conduct with which they are concerned. Thus even within the law some rules are made by legislation; others are not made by any such deliberate act. More important, some rules are mandatory in the sense that they require people to behave in certain ways, e.g. abstain from violence or pay taxes, whether they wish to or not; other rules such as those prescribing the procedures, formalities, and conditions for the making of marriages, wills, or contracts indicate what people should do to give effect to the wishes they have. The same contrast between these two types of rule is also to be seen between those rules of a game which veto certain types of conduct under penalty (foul play or abuse of the referee) and those which specify what must be done to score or to win. But even if we neglect for the moment this complexity and consider only the first sort of rule (which is typical of the criminal law) we shall find, even among contemporary writers, the widest divergence of view as to the meaning of the assertion that a rule of this simple mandatory type exists. Some indeed find the notion utterly mysterious.

The account which we are at first perhaps naturally tempted to give of the apparently simple idea of a mandatory rule has soon to be abandoned. It is that to say that a rule exists means only that a group of people, or most of them, behave 'as a rule' i.e. *generally*, in a specified similar way in certain kinds of circumstances. So to say that in England there is a rule that a man must not wear a hat in church or that one must stand up when 'God Save the Queen' is played means, on this account of the matter, only that most people generally do these things. Plainly this is not enough, even though it conveys part of what is meant. Mere convergence in behaviour between members of a social group may exist (all may regularly drink tea at breakfast or go weekly to the cinema) and yet there may be no rule *requiring* it. The difference between the two social situations of mere convergent behaviour and the existence of a social rule shows itself often linguistically. In describing the latter we may, though we need not, make use of certain words which would be misleading if we meant only to assert the former. These are the words 'must', 'should', and 'ought to', which in spite of differences share certain common functions in indicating the presence of a rule requiring certain conduct. There is in England no rule, nor is it true, that everyone must or ought to or should go to the cinema each week: it is only true that there is regular resort to the cinema each week. But there *is* a rule that a man must bare his head in church.

What then is the crucial difference between merely convergent habitual behaviour in a social group and the existence of a rule of which the words 'must', 'should', and 'ought to' are often a sign? Here indeed legal theorists have been divided, especially in our own day when several things have forced this issue to the front. In the case of legal rules it is very often held that the crucial difference (the element of 'must' or 'ought') consists in the fact that deviations from certain types of behaviour will probably meet with hostile reaction, and in the case of legal rules be punished by officials. In the case of what may be called mere group habits, like that of going weekly to the cinema, deviations are not met with punishment or even reproof; but wherever there are rules requiring certain conduct, even non-legal rules like that requiring men to bare their heads in church, something of this sort is likely to result from deviation. In the case of legal rules this predictable consequence is definite and officially organized, whereas in the non-legal case, though a similar hostile reaction to deviation is probable, this is not organized or definite in character.

It is obvious that predictability of punishment is one important aspect of legal rules; but it is not possible to accept this as an exhaustive account of what is meant by the statement that a social rule exists or of the element of 'must' or 'ought' involved in rules. To such a predictive account there are many objections, but one in particular, which characterizes a whole school of legal theory in Scandinavia, deserves careful consideration. It is that if we look closely at the activity of the judge or official who punishes deviations from legal rules (or those private persons who reprove or criticize deviations from non-legal rules), we see that rules are involved in this activity in a way which this predictive account leaves quite unexplained. For the judge, in punishing, takes the rule as his *guide* and the breach of the rule as his *reason* and *justification* for punishing the offender. He does not look upon the rule as a statement that he and others are likely to punish deviations, though a spectator might look upon the rule in just this way. The predictive aspect of the rule (though real enough) is irrelevant to his purposes, whereas its status as a guide and justification is essential. The same is true of informal reproofs administered for the breach of non-legal rules. These too are not merely predictable reactions to deviations, but something which existence of the rule guides and is held to justify. So we say that we reprove or punish a man *because* he has broken the rule: and not merely that it was probable that we would reprove or punish him.

Yet among critics who have pressed these objections to the predictive account some confess that there is something obscure here; something which resists analysis in clear, hard, factual terms. What *can* there be in a rule apart from regular and hence predictable punishment or reproof of those who deviate from the usual patterns of conduct, which distinguishes it from a mere group habit? Can there really be something over and above these clear ascertainable facts, some extra element, which guides the judge and justifies or gives him a reason for punishing? The difficulty of saying what exactly this extra element is has led these critics of the predictive theory to insist at this point that all talk of rules, and the corresponding use of words like 'must', 'ought', and 'should', is fraught with a confusion which perhaps enhances their importance in men's eyes but has no rational basis. We merely *think*, so such critics claim, that there is something in the rule which binds us to do certain things and guides or justifies us in doing them, but this is an illusion even if it is a useful one. All that there is, over and above the clear ascertainable facts of group behaviour and predictable reaction to deviation, are our own powerful 'feelings' of compulsion to behave in accordance with the rule and to act against those who do not. We do not recognize these feelings for what they are but imagine that there is something external, some invisible part of the fabric of the universe guiding and controlling us in these activities. We are here in the realm of fiction, with which it is said the law has always been connected. It is only because we adopt this fiction that we can talk solemnly of the government 'of laws not men'. This type of criticism, whatever the merits of its positive contentions, at least calls for further elucidation of the distinction between social rules and mere convergent habits of behaviour. This distinction is crucial for the understanding of law, and much of the early chapters of this book is concerned with it.

Scepticism about the character of legal rules has not, however, always taken the extreme form of condemning the very notion of a binding rule as confused or fictitious. Instead, the most prevalent form of scepticism in England and the United States invites us to reconsider the view that a legal system *wholly*, or even *primarily*, consists of rules. No doubt the courts so frame their judgments as to give the impression that their decisions are the necessary consequence of predetermined rules whose meaning is fixed and clear. In very simple cases this may be so; but in the vast majority of cases that trouble the courts, neither statutes nor precedents in which the rules are allegedly contained allow of only one result. In most important cases there is always a choice. The judge has to choose between alternative meanings to be given to the words of a statute or between rival interpretations of what a precedent 'amounts to'. It is only the tradition that judges 'find' and do not 'make' law that conceals this, and presents their decisions as if they were deductions smoothly made from clear pre-existing rules without intrusion of the judge's choice. Legal rules may have a central core of undisputed meaning, and in some cases it may be difficult to imagine a dispute as to the meaning of a rule breaking out. The provision of s. 9 of the Wills Act, 1837, that there must be two witnesses to a will may not seem likely to raise problems of interpretation. Yet all rules have a penumbra of uncertainty where the judge must choose between alternatives. Even the meaning of the innocent-seeming provision of the Wills Act that the testator must *sign* the will may prove doubtful in certain circumstances. What if the testator used a pseudonym? Or if his hand was guided by another? Or if he wrote his initials only? Or if he put his full, correct, name unaided, but at the top of the first page instead of at the bottom of the last? Would all these cases be 'signing' within the meaning of the legal rule?

If so much uncertainty may break out in humble spheres of private law, how much more shall we find in the magniloquent phrases of a constitution such as the Fifth and Fourteenth Amendments to the Constitution of the United States, providing that no person shall be 'deprived of life liberty or property without due process of law'? Of this one writer[1] has said that the true meaning of this phrase is really quite clear. It means 'no *w* shall be *x* or *y* without *z* where *w*, *x*, *y*, and *z* can assume any values within a wide range'. To cap the tale sceptics remind us that not only are the rules uncertain, but the court's interpretation of them may be not only authoritative but final. In view of all this, is not the conception of law as essentially a matter of rules a gross exaggeration if not a mistake? Such thoughts lead to the paradoxical denial which we have already cited: 'Statutes are sources of law, not part of the law itself.'[2]

3. DEFINITION

Here then are the three recurrent issues: How does law differ from and how is it related to orders backed by threats? How does legal obligation differ from, and how is it related to, moral obligation? What are rules and to what extent is law an affair of rules? To dispel doubt and perplexity on these three issues has been the chief aim of most speculation about the 'nature' of law. It is possible now to see why this speculation has usually been conceived as a search for the definition of law, and also why at least the familiar forms of definition have done so little to resolve the persistent difficulties and doubts. Definition, as the word suggests, is primarily a matter of drawing lines or distinguishing between one kind of thing and another, which language marks off by a separate word. The need for such a drawing of lines is often felt by those who are perfectly at home with the day-to-day use of the word in question, but cannot state or explain the distinctions

---

[1] J. D. March, 'Sociological Jurisprudence Revisited', 8 *Stanford Law Review* (1956), p. 518.   [2] Gray, loc. cit.

which, they sense, divide one kind of thing from another. All of us are sometimes in this predicament: it is fundamentally that of the man who says, 'I can recognize an elephant when I see one but I cannot define it.' The same predicament was expressed by some famous words of St Augustine[1] about the notion of time. 'What then is time? If no one asks me I know: if I wish to explain it to one that asks I know not.' It is in this way that even skilled lawyers have felt that, though they know the law, there is much about law and its relations to other things that they cannot explain and do not fully understand. Like a man who can get from one point to another in a familiar town but cannot explain or show others how to do it, those who press for a definition need a map exhibiting clearly the relationships dimly felt to exist between the law they know and other things.

Sometimes in such cases a definition of a word can supply such a map: at one and the same time it may make explicit the latent principle which guides our use of a word, and may exhibit relationships between the type of phenomena to which we apply the word and other phenomena. It is sometimes said that definition is 'merely verbal' or 'just about words'; but this may be most misleading where the expression defined is one in current use. Even the definition of a triangle as a 'three-sided rectilinear figure', or the definition of an elephant as a 'quadruped distinguished from others by its possession of a thick skin, tusks, and trunk', instructs us in a humble way both as to the standard use of these words and about the things to which the words apply. A definition of this familiar type does two things at once. It simultaneously provides a code or formula translating the word into other well-understood terms and locates for us the kind of thing to which the word is used to refer, by indicating the features which it shares in common with a wider family of things and those which mark it off from others of that same family. In searching for and finding such definitions we 'are looking not merely at words...but also at the realities we use words to talk about. We are using a sharpened awareness of words to sharpen our perception of the phenomena.'[2]

---

[1] *Confessiones*, xiv. 17.
[2] J. L. Austin, 'A Plea for Excuses', *Proceedings of the Aristotelian Society*, vol. 57 (1956–7), p. 8.

This form of definition (*per genus et differentiam*) which we see in the simple case of the triangle or elephant is the simplest and to some the most satisfying, because it gives us a form of words which can always be substituted for the word defined. But it is not always available nor, when it is available, always illuminating. Its success depends on conditions which are often not satisfied. Chief among these is that there should be a wider family of things or *genus*, about the character of which we are clear, and within which the definition locates what it defines; for plainly a definition which tells us that something is a member of a family cannot help us if we have only vague or confused ideas as to the character of the family. It is this requirement that in the case of law renders this form of definition useless, for here there is no familiar well-understood general category of which law is a member. The most obvious candidate for use in this way in a definition of law is the general family of *rules of behaviour*; yet the concept of a rule as we have seen is as perplexing as that of law itself, so that definitions of law that start by identifying laws as a species of rule usually advance our understanding of law no further. For this, something more fundamental is required than a form of definition which is successfully used to locate some special, subordinate, kind within some familiar, well-understood, general kind of thing.

There are, however, further formidable obstacles to the profitable use of this simple form of definition in the case of law. The supposition that a general expression can be defined in this way rests on the tacit assumption that all the instances of what is to be defined as triangles and elephants have common characteristics which are signified by the expression defined. Of course, even at a relatively elementary stage, the existence of borderline cases is forced upon our attention, and this shows that the assumption that the several instances of a general term must have the same characteristics may be dogmatic. Very often the ordinary, or even the technical, usage of a term is quite 'open' in that it does not *forbid* the extension of the term to cases where only some of the normally concomitant characteristics are present. This, as we have already observed, is true of international law and of certain forms of primitive law, so that it is always possible to argue with plausibility for and against such an extension. What is more important is that, apart from such borderline cases, the several instances of a general term are often linked together in quite different ways from that postulated by the simple form of definition. They may be linked by analogy as when we speak of the 'foot' of a man and also of the 'foot' of a mountain. They may be linked by *different* relationships to a central element. Such a unifying principle is seen in the application of the word 'healthy' not only to a man but to his complexion and to his morning exercise; the second being a *sign* and the third a *cause* of the first central characteristic. Or again—and here perhaps we have a principle similar to that which unifies the different types of rules which make up a legal system—the several instances may be different constituents of some complex activity. The use of the adjectival expression 'railway' not only of a train but also of the lines, of a station, of a porter, and of a limited company, is governed by this type of unifying principle.

There are of course many other kinds of definition besides the very simple traditional form which we have discussed, but it seems clear, when we recall the character of the three main issues which we have identified as underlying the recurrent question 'What is law?', that nothing concise enough to be recognized as a definition could provide a satisfactory answer to it. The underlying issues are too different from each other and too fundamental to be capable of this sort of resolution. This the history of attempts to provide concise definitions has shown. Yet the instinct which has often brought these three questions together under a single question or request for definition has not been misguided; for, as we shall show in the course of this book, it is possible to isolate and characterize a central set of elements which form a common part of the answer to all three. What these elements are and why they deserve the important place assigned to them in this book will best emerge, if we first consider, in detail, the deficiencies of the theory which has dominated so much English jurisprudence since Austin expounded it. This is the claim that the key to the understanding of law is to be found in the simple notion of an order backed by threats, which Austin himself termed a 'command'. The investigation of the deficiencies of this theory occupies the next three chapters. In criticizing it first and deferring to the later chapters of this book consideration of its main rival, we have consciously disregarded the historical order in which modern legal theory has developed; for the rival claim that law is best understood through its 'necessary' connection with morality is an older doctrine which Austin, like Bentham before him, took as a principal object of attack. Our excuse, if one is needed, for this unhistorical treatment, is that the errors of the simple imperative theory are a better pointer to the truth than those of its more complex rivals.

At various points in this book the reader will find discussions of the borderline cases where legal theorists have felt doubts about the application of the expression 'law' or 'legal system', but the suggested resolution of these doubts, which he will also find here, is only a secondary concern of the book. For its purpose is not to provide a definition of law, in the sense of a rule by reference to which the correctness of the use of the word can be tested; it is to advance legal theory by providing an improved analysis of the distinctive structure of a municipal legal system and a better understanding of the resemblances and differences between law, coercion, and morality, as types of social phenomena. The set of elements identified in the course of the critical discussion of the next three chapters and described in detail in Chapters V and VI serve this purpose in ways which are demonstrated in the rest of the book. It is for this reason that they are treated as the central elements in the concept of law and of prime importance in its elucidation.

II

LAWS, COMMANDS, AND ORDERS

1. VARIETIES OF IMPERATIVES

The clearest and the most thorough attempt to analyse the concept of law in terms of the apparently simple elements of commands and habits, was that made by Austin in the *Province of Jurisprudence Determined*. In this and the next two chapters we shall state and criticize a position which is, in substance, the same as Austin's doctrine but probably diverges from it at certain points. For our principal concern is not with Austin but with the credentials of a certain type of theory which has perennial attractions whatever its defects may be. So we have not hesitated where Austin's meaning is doubtful or where his views seem inconsistent to ignore this and to state a clear and consistent position. Moreover, where Austin merely gives hints as to ways in which criticisms might be met, we have developed these (in part along the lines followed by later theorists such as Kelsen) in order to secure that the doctrine we shall consider and criticize is stated in its strongest form.

In many different situations in social life one person may express a wish that another person should do or abstain from doing something. When this wish is expressed not merely as a piece of interesting information or deliberate self-revelation but with the intention that the person addressed should conform to the wish expressed, it is customary in English and many other languages, though not necessary, to use a special linguistic form called the *imperative mood*, 'Go home!' 'Come here!' 'Stop!' 'Do not kill him!' The social situations in which we thus address others in imperative form are extremely diverse; yet they include some recurrent main types, the importance of which is marked by certain familiar classifications. 'Pass the salt, please', is usually a mere *request*, since normally it is addressed by the speaker to one who is able to render him a service, and there is no suggestion either of any great urgency or any hint of what may follow on failure to comply. 'Do not kill me', would normally be uttered as a *plea* where the speaker is at the mercy of the person addressed or in a predicament from which the latter has the power to release him. 'Don't move', on the other hand, may be a *warning* if the speaker knows of some impending danger to the person addressed (a snake in the grass) which his keeping still may avert.

The varieties of social situation in which use is characteristically, though not invariably, made of imperative forms of language are not only numerous but shade into each other; and terms like 'plea', 'request', or 'warning', serve only to make a few rough discriminations. The most important of these situations is one to which the word 'imperative' seems specially appropriate. It is that illustrated by the case of the gunman who says to the bank clerk, 'Hand over the money or I will shoot.' Its distinctive feature which leads us to speak of the gunman *ordering* not merely *asking*, still less *pleading with* the clerk to hand over the money, is that, to secure compliance with his expressed wishes, the speaker threatens to do something which a normal man would regard as harmful or unpleasant, and renders keeping the money a substantially less eligible course of conduct for the clerk. If the gunman succeeds, we would describe him as having *coerced* the clerk, and the clerk as in that sense being in the gunman's power. Many nice linguistic questions may arise over such cases: we might properly say that the gunman *ordered* the clerk to hand over the money and the clerk obeyed, but it would be somewhat misleading to say that the gunman *gave an order* to the clerk to hand it over, since this rather military-sounding phrase suggests some right or authority to give orders not present in our case. It would, however, be quite natural to say that the gunman gave an order to his henchman to guard the door.

We need not here concern ourselves with these subtleties. Although a suggestion of authority and deference to authority may often attach to the words 'order' and 'obedience', we shall use the expressions 'orders backed by threats' and 'coercive orders' to refer to orders which, like the gunman's, are supported only by threats, and we shall use the words 'obedience' and 'obey' to include compliance with such orders. It is, however, important to notice, if only because of the great influence on jurists of Austin's definition of the notion of a command, that the simple situation, where threats of harm and nothing else is used to force obedience, is *not* the situation where we naturally speak of 'commands'. This word, which is not very common outside military contexts, carries with it very strong implications that there is a relatively stable hierarchical organization of men, such as an army or a body of disciples in which the commander occupies a position of pre-eminence. Typically it is the general (not the sergeant) who is the commander and gives commands, though other forms of special pre-eminence are spoken of in these terms, as when Christ in the New Testament is said to command his disciples. More important—for this is a crucial distinction between different forms of 'imperative'— is the point that it need not be the case, where a command is given, that there should be a latent threat of harm in the event of disobedience. To command is characteristically to exercise authority over men, not power to inflict harm, and though it may be combined with threats of harm a command is primarily an appeal not to fear but to respect for authority.

It is obvious that the idea of a command with its very strong connection with authority is much closer to that of law than our gunman's order backed by threats, though the latter is an instance of what Austin, ignoring the distinctions noticed in the last paragraph, misleadingly calls a command. A command is, however, too close to law for our purpose; for the element of authority involved in law has always been one of the obstacles in the path of any easy explanation of what law is. We cannot therefore profitably use, in the elucidation of law, the notion of a command which also involves it. Indeed it is a virtue of Austin's analysis, whatever its defects, that the elements of the gunman situation are, unlike the element of authority, not themselves obscure or in need of much explanation; and hence we shall follow Austin in an attempt to build up from it the idea of law. We shall not, however, hope, as Austin did, for success, but rather to learn from our failure.

2. LAW AS COERCIVE ORDERS

Even in a complex large society, like that of a modern state, there are occasions when an official, face to face with an individual, orders him to do something. A policeman orders a particular motorist to stop or a particular beggar to move on. But these simple situations are not, and could not be, the standard way in which law functions, if only because no society could support the number of officials necessary to secure that every member of the society was officially and separately informed of every act which he was required to do. Instead such particularized forms of control are either exceptional or are ancillary accompaniments or reinforcements of general forms of directions which do not name, and are not addressed to, particular individuals, and do not indicate a particular act to be done. Hence the *standard* form even of a criminal statute (which of all the varieties of law has the closest resemblance to an order backed by threats) is general in two ways; it indicates a general type of conduct and applies to a general class of persons who are expected to see that it applies to them and to comply with it. Official individuated face-to-face directions here have a secondary place: if the primary general directions are not obeyed by a particular individual, officials may draw his attention to them and demand compliance, as a tax inspector does, or the disobedience may be officially identified and recorded and the threatened punishment imposed by a court.

Legal control is therefore primarily, though not exclusively, control by directions which are in this double sense *general*. This is the first feature which we must add to the simple model of the gunman if it is to reproduce for us the characteristics of law. The range of persons affected and the manner in which the range is indicated may vary with different legal systems and even different laws. In a modern state it is normally understood that, in the absence of special indications widening or narrowing the class, its general laws extend to all persons within its territorial boundaries. In canon law there is a similar understanding that normally all the members of the church are within the range of its law except when a narrower class is indicated. In all cases the range of application of a law is a question of interpretation of the particular law aided by such general understandings. It is here worth noticing that though jurists, Austin among them, sometimes speak of laws being *addressed*[1] to classes of persons this is misleading in

---

[1] 'Addressed to the community at large', Austin, above, p. 1 n. 4 at p. 22.

suggesting a parallel to the face-to-face situation which really does not exist and is not intended by those who use this expression. Ordering people to do things is a form of communication and does entail actually 'addressing' them, i.e. attracting their attention or taking steps to attract it, but making laws for people does not. Thus the gunman by one and the same utterance, 'Hand over those notes', expresses his wish that the clerk should do something and actually *addresses* the clerk, i.e. he does what is normally sufficient to bring this expression to the clerk's attention. If he did not do the latter but merely said the same words in an empty room, he would not have addressed the clerk at all and would not have *ordered* him to do anything: we might describe the situation as one where the gunman merely said the words, 'Hand over those notes'. In this respect making laws differs from ordering people to do things, and we must allow for this difference in using this simple idea as a model for law. It may indeed be desirable that laws should as soon as may be after they are made, be brought to the attention of those to whom they apply. The legislator's purpose in making laws would be defeated unless this were generally done, and legal systems often provide, by special rules concerning promulgation, that this shall be done. But laws may be complete as laws before this is done, and even if it is not done at all. In the absence of special rules to the contrary, laws are validly made even if those affected are left to find out for themselves what laws have been made and who are affected thereby. What is usually intended by those who speak of laws being 'addressed' to certain persons, is that these are the persons to whom the particular law applies, i.e. whom it requires to behave in certain ways. If we use the word 'addressed' here we may both fail to notice an important difference between the making of a law and giving a face-to-face order, and we may confuse the two distinct questions: 'To whom does the law apply?' and 'To whom has it been published?'

Besides the introduction of the feature of generality a more fundamental change must be made in the gunman situation if we are to have a plausible model of the situation where there is law. It is true there is a sense in which the gunman has an ascendancy or superiority over the bank clerk; it lies in his temporary ability to make a threat, which might well be sufficient to make the bank clerk do the particular thing he is told to do. There is no other form of relationship of superiority and inferiority between the two men except this short-lived coercive one. But for the gunman's purposes this may be enough; for the simple face-to-face order 'Hand over those notes or I'll shoot' dies with the occasion. The gunman does not issue to the bank clerk (though he may to his gang of followers) *standing orders* to be followed time after time by classes of persons. Yet laws pre-eminently have this 'standing' or persistent characteristic. Hence if we are to use the notion of orders backed by threats as explaining what laws are, we must endeavour to reproduce this enduring character which laws have.

We must therefore suppose that there is a general belief on the part of those to whom the general orders apply that disobedience is likely to be followed by the execution of the threat not only on the first promulgation of the order, but continuously until the order is withdrawn or cancelled. This continuing belief in the consequences of disobedience may be said to keep the original orders alive or 'standing', though as we shall see later there is difficulty in analysing the persistent quality of laws in these simple terms. Of course the concurrence of many factors which could not be reproduced in the gunman situation may, in fact, be required if such a general belief in the continuing likelihood of the execution of the threat is to exist: it may be that the power to carry out threats attached to such standing orders affecting large numbers of persons could only in fact exist, and would only be thought to exist, if it was known that some considerable number of the population were prepared both themselves to obey voluntarily, i.e. independently of fear of the threat, and to co-operate in the execution of the threats on those who disobeyed.

Whatever the basis of this general belief in the likelihood of the execution of the threats, we must distinguish from it a further necessary feature which we must add to the gunman situation if it is to approximate to the settled situation in which there is law. We must suppose that, whatever the motive, most of the orders are more often obeyed than disobeyed by most of those affected. We shall call this here, following Austin, 'a general habit of obedience' and note, with him, that like many other aspects of law it is an essentially vague or imprecise notion. The question how many people must obey how many such general orders, and for how long, if there is to be law, no more admits of definite answers than the question how few hairs must a man have to be bald. Yet in this fact of general obedience lies a crucial distinction between laws and the original simple case of the gunman's order. Mere temporary ascendancy of one person over another is naturally thought of as the polar opposite of law, with its relatively enduring and settled character, and, indeed, in most legal systems to exercise such short-term coercive power as the gunman has would constitute a criminal offence. It remains indeed to be seen whether this simple, though admittedly vague, notion of general habitual obedience to general orders backed by threats is really enough to reproduce the settled character and continuity which legal systems possess.

The concept of general orders backed by threats given by one generally obeyed, which we have constructed by successive additions to the simple situation of the gunman case, plainly approximates closer to a penal statute enacted by the legislature of a modern state than to any other variety of law. For there are types of law which seem prima facie very unlike such penal statutes, and we shall have later to consider the claim that these other varieties of law also, in spite of appearances to the contrary, are really just complicated or disguised versions of this same form. But if we are to reproduce the features of even a penal statute in our constructed model of general orders generally obeyed, something more must be said about the person who gives the orders. The legal system of a modern state is characterized by a certain kind of *supremacy* within its territory and *independence* of other systems which we have not yet reproduced in our simple model. These two notions are not as simple as they may appear, but what, on a common-sense view (which may not prove adequate) is essential to them, may be expressed as follows. English law, French law, and the law of any modern country regulates the conduct of populations inhabiting territories with fairly well-defined geographical limits. Within the territory of each country there may be many different persons or bodies of persons giving general orders backed by threats and receiving habitual obedience. But we should distinguish some of these persons or bodies (e.g. the LCC or a minister exercising what we term powers of delegated legislation) as *subordinate* lawmakers in contrast to the Queen in Parliament who is supreme. We can express this relationship in the simple terminology of habits by saying that whereas the Queen in Parliament in making laws obeys no one habitually, the subordinate lawmakers keep within limits statutorily prescribed and so may be said in making law to be agents of the Queen in Parliament. If they did not do so we should not have one system of law in England but a plurality of systems; whereas in fact just because the Queen in Parliament is supreme in relation to all within the territory in this sense and the other bodies are not, we have in England a single system in which we can distinguish a hierarchy of supreme and subordinate elements.

The same negative characterization of the Queen in Parliament, as *not* habitually obeying the orders of others, roughly defines the notion of *independence* which we use in speaking of the separate legal systems of different countries. The supreme legislature of the Soviet Union is not in the habit of obeying the Queen in Parliament, and whatever the latter enacted about Soviet affairs (though it would constitute part of the law of England) would not form part of the law of the USSR. It would do so only if the Queen in Parliament were habitually obeyed by the legislature of the USSR.

On this simple account of the matter, which we shall later have to examine critically, there must, wherever there is a legal system, be some persons or body of persons issuing general orders backed by threats which are generally obeyed, and it must be generally believed that these threats are likely to be implemented in the event of disobedience. This person or body must be internally supreme and externally independent. If, following Austin, we call such a supreme and independent person or body of persons the sovereign, the laws of any country will be the general orders backed by threats which are issued either by the sovereign or subordinates in obedience to the sovereign.

THE VARIETY OF LAWS

If we compare the varieties of different kinds of law to be found in a modern system such as English Law with the simple model of coercive orders constructed in the last chapter, a crowd of objections leap to mind. Surely not all laws order people to do or not to do things. Is it not misleading so to classify laws which confer powers on private individuals to make wills, contracts, or marriages, and laws which give powers to officials, e.g. to a judge to try cases, to a minister to make rules, or a county council to make by-laws? Surely not all laws are enacted nor are they all the expression of someone's desire like the general orders of our model. This seems untrue of custom which has a genuine though modest place in most legal systems. Surely laws, even when they are statutes deliberately made, need not be orders given only to *others*. Do not statutes often bind the legislators themselves? Finally, must enacted laws to be laws really express any legislator's actual desires, intentions, or wishes? Would an enactment duly passed not be law if (as must be the case with many a section of an English Finance Act) those who voted for it did not know what it meant?

These are some of the most important of many possible objections. Plainly some modification of the original simple model will be necessary to deal with them and, when they have all been accommodated, we may find that the notion of general orders backed by threats has been transformed out of recognition.

The objections we have mentioned fall into three main groups. Some of them concern the *content* of laws, others their *mode of origin*, and others again their *range of application*. All legal systems, at any rate, *seem* to contain laws which in respect of one or more of these three matters diverge from the model of general orders which we have set up. In the rest of this chapter we shall consider separately these three types of objection. We shall leave to the next chapter a more fundamental criticism that apart from these objections on the score of content, mode of origin, and range of application, the whole conception of a supreme and independent sovereign habitually obeyed, on which the model rests, is misleading, since there is little in any actual legal system which corresponds to it.

1. THE CONTENT OF LAWS

The criminal law is something which we either obey or disobey and what its rules require is spoken of as a 'duty'. If we disobey we are said to 'break' the law and what we have done is legally 'wrong', a 'breach of duty', or an 'offence'. The social function which a criminal statute performs is that of setting up and defining certain kinds of conduct as something to be avoided or done by those to whom it applies, irrespective of their wishes. The punishment or 'sanction' which is attached by the law to breaches or violations of the criminal law is (whatever other purpose punishment may serve) intended to provide one motive for abstaining from these activities. In all these respects there is at least a strong analogy between the criminal law and its sanctions and the general orders backed by threats of our model. There is some analogy (notwithstanding many important differences) between such general orders and the law of torts, the primary aim of which is to provide individuals with compensation for harm suffered as the result of the conduct of others. Here too the rules which determine what types of conduct constitute actionable wrongs are spoken of as imposing on persons, irrespective of their wishes, 'duties' (or more rarely 'obligations') to abstain from such conduct. This conduct is itself termed a 'breach of duty' and the compensation or other legal remedies a 'sanction'. But there are important classes of law where this analogy with orders backed by threats altogether fails, since they perform a quite different social function. Legal rules defining the ways in which valid contracts or wills or marriages are made do not require persons to act in certain ways whether they wish to or not. Such laws do not impose duties or obligations. Instead, they provide individuals with *facilities* for realizing their wishes, by conferring legal powers upon them to create, by certain specified procedures and subject to certain conditions, structures of rights and duties within the coercive framework of the law.

The power thus conferred on individuals to mould their legal relations with others by contracts, wills, marriages, &c., is one of the great contributions of law to social life; and it is a feature of law obscured by representing all law as a matter of orders backed by threats. The radical difference in function between laws that confer such powers and the criminal statute is reflected in much of our normal ways of speaking about this class of laws. We may or may not 'comply' in making our will with the provision of s. 9 of the Wills Act, 1837, as to the number of witnesses. If we do not comply the document we have made will not be a 'valid' will creating rights and duties; it will be a 'nullity' without legal 'force' or 'effect'. But, though it is a nullity our failure to comply with the statutory provision is not a 'breach' or a 'violation' of any obligation or duty nor an 'offence' and it would be confusing to think of it in such terms.

If we look into the various legal rules that confer legal powers on private individuals we find that these themselves fall into distinguishable kinds. Thus behind the power to make wills or contracts are rules relating to *capacity* or minimum personal qualification (such as being adult or sane) which those exercising the power must possess. Other rules detail the manner and form in which the power is to be exercised, and settle whether wills or contracts may be made orally or in writing, and if in writing the form of execution and attestation. Other rules delimit the variety, or maximum or minimum duration, of the structure of rights and duties which individuals may create by such acts-in-the-law. Examples of such rules are those of public policy in relation to contract, or the rules against accumulations in wills or settlements.

We shall consider later the attempts made by jurists to assimilate those laws which provide facilities or powers and say, 'If you wish to do this, this is the way to do it' to the criminal laws which, like orders backed by threats, say, 'Do this whether you wish to or not.' Here, however, we shall consider a further class of laws which also confer legal powers but, in contrast to those just discussed, the powers are of a public or official rather than a private nature. Examples of

these are to be found in all the three departments, judicial, legislative, and administrative, into which government is customarily
though vaguely divided.

Consider first those laws which lie behind the operation of a
law court. In the case of a court some rules specify the subject-
matter and content of the judge's jurisdiction or, as we say, give
him 'power to try' certain types of case. Other rules specify
the manner of appointment, the qualifications for, and tenure
of judicial office. Others again will lay down canons of correct
judicial behaviour and determine the procedure to be followed
in the court. Examples of such rules, forming something like a
judicial code, are to be found in the County Courts Act, 1959, the
Court of Criminal Appeal Act, 1907, or Title 28 of the United
States Code. It is salutary to observe the variety of provisions
made in these statutes for the constitution and normal operation
of a law court. Few of these seem at first sight to be orders given
to the judge to do or abstain from doing anything; for though of
course there is no reason why the law should not also by special
rules prohibit a judge under penalty from exceeding his jurisdiction or trying a case in which he has a financial interest, these
rules imposing such legal duties would be additional to those
conferring judicial powers on him and defining his jurisdiction.
For the concern of rules conferring such powers is not to deter
judges from improprieties but to define the conditions and limits
under which the court's decisions shall be valid.

It is instructive to examine in a little detail a typical provision
specifying the extent of a court's jurisdiction. We may take as a
very simple example the section of the County Courts Act, 1959,
as amended, which confers jurisdiction on the county courts to
try actions for the recovery of land. Its language which is very
remote from that of 'orders', is as follows:

A county court shall have jurisdiction to hear and determine any
action for the recovery of land where the net annual value for rating of
the land in question does not exceed one hundred pounds.[1]

If a county court judge exceeds his jurisdiction by trying
a case for the recovery of land with an annual value greater

---

[1] Section 48 (I).

than £100 and makes an order concerning such land, neither he nor the parties to the action commit an *offence*. Yet the position is not quite like that which arises when a private person does something which is a 'nullity' for lack of compliance with some condition essential for the valid exercise of some legal power. If a would-be testator omits to sign or obtain two witnesses to his will, what he writes has no legal status or effect. A court's order is not, however, treated in this way even if it is plainly one outside the jurisdiction of the court to make. It is obviously in the interests of public order that a court's decision should have legal authority until a superior court certifies its invalidity, even if it is one which the court should not legally have given. Hence, until it is set aside on appeal as an order given in excess of jurisdiction, it stands as a legally effective order between the parties which will be enforced. But it has a legal defect: it *is liable* to be set aside or 'quashed' on appeal because of the lack of jurisdiction. It is to be noted that there is an important difference between what is ordinarily spoken of in England as a 'reversal' by a superior court of an inferior court's order and the 'quashing' of an order for lack of jurisdiction. If an order is reversed, it is because what the lower court has said either about the law applicable to the case or the facts, is considered wrong. But an order of the lower court which is quashed for lack of jurisdiction may be impeccable in both these respects. It is not *what* the judge in the lower court has said or ordered that is wrong, but *his* saying or ordering of it. He has purported to do something which he is not legally empowered to do though other courts may be so empowered. But for the complication that, in the interests of public order a decision given in excess of jurisdiction stands till quashed by a superior court, conformity or failure to conform to rules of jurisdiction is like conformity and failure to conform to rules defining the conditions for the valid exercise of legal powers by private individuals. The relationship between the conforming action and the rule is ill-conveyed by the words 'obey' and 'disobey', which are more apposite in the case of the criminal law where the rules are analogous to orders.

A statute conferring legislative power on a subordinate legislative authority similarly exemplifies a type of legal rule that cannot, except at the cost of distortion, be assimilated to a general order. Here too, as in the exercise of private powers, conformity with the conditions specified by the rules conferring the legislative powers is a step which is like a 'move' in a game such as chess; it has consequences definable in terms of the rules, which the system enables persons to achieve. Legislation is an exercise of legal powers 'operative' or effective in creating legal rights and duties. Failure to conform to the conditions of the enabling rule makes what is done ineffective and so a nullity for this purpose.

The rules which lie behind the exercise of legislative powers are themselves even more various than those which lie behind the jurisdiction of a court, for provision must be made by them for many different aspects of legislation. Thus some rules specify the subject-matter over which the legislative power may be exercised; others the qualifications or identity of the members of the legislative body; others the manner and form of legislation and the procedure to be followed by the legislature. These are only a few of the relevant matters; a glance at any enactment such as the Municipal Corporations Act, 1882, conferring and defining the powers of an inferior legislature or rule-making body will reveal many more. The consequence of failure to conform to such rules may not always be the same, but there will always be some rules, failure to conform to which renders a purported exercise of legislative power a nullity or, like the decision of an inferior court, liable to be declared invalid. Sometimes a certificate that the required procedures have been followed may by law be made conclusive as to matters of internal procedure, and sometimes persons not qualified under the rules, who participate in legislative proceedings, may be liable to a penalty under special criminal rules making this an offence. But, though partly hidden by these complications, there is a radical difference between rules conferring and defining the manner of exercise of legislative powers and the rules of criminal law, which at least resemble orders backed by threats.

In some cases it would be grotesque to assimilate these two broad types of rule. If a measure before a legislative body obtains the required majority of votes and is thus duly passed, the voters in favour of the measure have not 'obeyed' the law requiring a majority decision nor have those who voted against it either obeyed or disobeyed it: the same is of course true if the measure fails to obtain the required majority and so no law is passed. The radical difference in function between such rules as these prevents the use here of the terminology appropriate to conduct in its relation to rules of the criminal law.

A full detailed taxonomy of the varieties of law comprised in a modern legal system, free from the prejudice that all *must* be reducible to a single simple type, still remains to be accomplished. In distinguishing certain laws under the very rough head of laws that confer powers from those that impose duties and are analogous to orders backed by threats, we have made only a beginning. But perhaps enough has been done to show that some of the distinctive features of a legal system lie in the provision it makes, by rules of this type, for the exercise of private and public legal powers. If such rules of this distinctive kind did not exist we should lack some of the most familiar concepts of social life, since these logically presuppose the existence of such rules. Just as there could be no crimes or offences and so no murders or thefts if there were no criminal laws of the mandatory kind which do resemble orders backed by threats, so there could be no buying, selling, gifts, wills, or marriages if there were no power-conferring rules; for these latter things, like the orders of courts and the enactments of law-making bodies, just consist in the valid exercise of legal powers.

Nevertheless the itch for uniformity in jurisprudence is strong: and since it is by no means disreputable, we must consider two alternative arguments in favour of it which have been sponsored by great jurists. These arguments are designed to show that the distinction between varieties of law which we have stressed is superficial, if not unreal, and that 'ultimately' the notion of orders backed by threats is adequate for the analysis of rules conferring powers as well as for the rules of criminal law. As with most theories which have persisted long in jurisprudence there is an element of truth in these arguments. There certainly are points of resemblance between the legal rules of the two sorts which we have distinguished. In both cases actions may be criticized or assessed by reference to the rules as legally the 'right' or 'wrong' thing to do. Both the power-conferring rules concerning the making of a will and the rule of criminal law prohibiting assault under penalty constitute *standards* by which particular actions may be thus critically appraised. So much is perhaps implied in speaking of them both as rules. Further it is important to realize that rules of the power-conferring sort, though different from rules which impose duties and so have some analogy to orders backed by threats, are always related to such rules; for the powers which they confer are powers to make general rules of the latter sort or to impose duties on particular persons who would otherwise not be subject to them. This is most obviously the case when the power conferred is what would ordinarily be termed a power to legislate. But, as we shall see, it is also true in the case of other legal powers. It might be said, at the cost of some inaccuracy, that whereas rules like those of the criminal law impose duties, power-conferring rules are recipes for creating duties.

Nullity as a sanction

The first argument, designed to show the fundamental identity of the two sorts of rule and to exhibit both as coercive orders, fastens on the 'nullity' which ensues when some essential condition for the exercise of the power is not fulfilled. This, it is urged, is like the punishment attached to the criminal law, a threatened evil or sanction exacted by law for breach of the rule; though it is conceded that in certain cases this sanction may only amount to a slight inconvenience. It is in this light that we are invited to view the case of one who seeks to enforce by law, as contractually binding, a promise made to him, and finds, to his chagrin, that, since it is not under seal and he gave no consideration for the promise, the written promise is legally a nullity. Similarly we are to think of the rule providing that a will without two witnesses will be inoperative, as moving testators to compliance with s. 9 of the Wills Act, just as we are moved to obedience to the criminal law by the thought of imprisonment.

No one could deny that there are, in some cases, these associations between nullity and such psychological factors as disappointment of the hope that a transaction will be valid. None the less the extension of the idea of a sanction to include nullity is a source (and a sign) of confusion. Some minor objections to it are well known. Thus, in many cases, nullity may not be an 'evil' to the person who has failed to satisfy some condition required for legal validity. A judge may have no material interest in and may be indifferent to the validity of his order; a party who finds that the contract on which he is sued is not binding on him, because he was under age or did not sign the memorandum in writing required for certain contracts, might not recognize here a 'threatened evil' or 'sanction'. But apart from these trivialities, which might be accommodated with some ingenuity, nullity cannot, for more important reasons, be assimilated to a punishment attached to a rule as an inducement to abstain from the activities which the rule forbids. In the case of a rule of criminal law we can identify and distinguish two things: a certain type of conduct which the rule prohibits, and a sanction intended to discourage it. But how could we consider in this light such desirable social activities as men making each other promises which do not satisfy legal requirements as to form? This is not like the conduct discouraged by the criminal law, something which the legal rules stipulating legal forms for contracts are designed to suppress. The rules merely withhold legal recognition from them. Even more absurd is it to regard as a sanction the fact that a legislative measure, if it does not obtain the required majority, fails to attain the status of a law. To assimilate this fact to the sanctions of the criminal law would be like thinking of the scoring rules of a game as designed to eliminate all moves except the kicking of goals or the making of runs. This, if successful, would be the end of all games; yet only if we think of power-conferring rules as designed to make people behave in certain ways and as adding 'nullity' as a motive for obedience, can we assimilate such rules to orders backed by threats.

The confusion inherent in thinking of nullity as similar to the threatened evil or sanctions of the criminal law may be brought out in another form. In the case of the rules of the criminal law, it is logically possible and might be desirable that there should be such rules even though no punishment or other evil were threatened. It may of course be argued that in that case they would not be *legal* rules; none the less, we can distinguish clearly the rule prohibiting certain behaviour from the provision for penalties to be exacted if the rule is broken, and suppose the first to exist without the latter. We can, in a sense, subtract the sanction and still leave an intelligible standard of behaviour which it was designed to maintain. But we cannot logically make such a distinction between the rule requiring compliance with certain conditions, e.g. attestation for a valid will, and the so-called sanction of 'nullity'. In this case, if failure to comply with this essential condition did not entail nullity, the rule itself could not be intelligibly said to exist without sanctions even as a non-legal rule. The provision for nullity is *part* of this type of rule itself in a way which punishment attached to a rule imposing duties is not. If failure to get the ball between the posts did not mean the 'nullity' of not scoring, the scoring rules could not be said to exist.

The argument which we have here criticized is an attempt to show the fundamental identity of power-conferring rules with coercive orders by *widening* the meaning of a sanction or threatened evil, so as to include the nullity of a legal trans-action when it is vitiated by non-compliance with such rules. The second argument which we shall consider takes a differ-ent, indeed an opposite, line. Instead of attempting to show that these rules are a species of coercive orders, it denies them the status of 'law'. To exclude them it *narrows* the meaning of the word 'law'. The general form of this argument, which appears in a more or less extreme form in different jurists, is to assert that what are loosely or in popular modes of expression referred to as complete rules of law, are really incomplete fragments of coercive rules which are the only 'genuine' rules of law.

Power-conferring rules as fragments of laws

In its extreme form this argument would deny that even the rules of the criminal law, in the words in which they are often stated, are genuine laws. It is in this form that the argument is adopted by Kelsen: 'Law is the primary norm which stipu-lates the sanction'.[1] There is no law prohibiting murder: there

---

[1] *General Theory of Law and State*, p. 63. See above, p. 2.

is only a law directing officials to apply certain sanctions in certain circumstances to those who do murder. On this view, what is ordinarily thought of as the content of law, designed to guide the conduct of ordinary citizens, is merely the antecedent or 'if-clause' in a rule which is directed not to them but to officials, and orders them to apply certain sanctions if certain conditions are satisfied. All genuine laws, on this view, are conditional orders to officials to apply sanctions. They are all of the form, 'If anything of a kind X is done or omitted or happens, then apply sanction of a kind Y.'

By greater and greater elaboration of the antecedent or if-clauses, legal rules of every type, including the rules conferring and defining the manner of exercise of private or public powers, can be restated in this conditional form. Thus, the provisions of the Wills Act requiring two witnesses would appear as a common part of many different directions to courts to apply sanctions to an executor who, in breach of the provisions of the will, refuses to pay the legacies: 'if and only if there is a will duly witnessed containing these provisions and if ... then sanctions must be applied to him.' Similarly, a rule specifying the extent of a court's jurisdiction would appear as a common part of the conditions to be satisfied before it applies any sanctions. So too, the rules conferring legislative powers and defining the manner and form of legislation (including the provisions of a constitution concerning the supreme legislature) can also be restated and exhibited as specifying certain common conditions on the fulfilment of which (among others) the courts are to apply the sanctions mentioned in the statutes. Thus, the theory bids us disentangle the substance from the obscuring forms; then we shall see that constitutional forms such as 'what the Queen in Parliament enacts is law', or the provisions of the American constitution as to the law-making power of Congress, merely specify the general conditions under which courts are to apply sanctions. These forms are essentially 'if-clauses', not complete rules: '*If* the Queen in Parliament has so enacted ...' or '*if* Congress within the limits specified in the Constitution has so enacted ...' are forms of conditions common to a vast number of directions to courts to apply sanctions or punish certain types of conduct.

This is a formidable and interesting theory, purporting to disclose the true, uniform nature of law latent beneath a variety of common forms and expressions which obscure it. Before we consider its defects it is to be observed that, in this extreme form, the theory involves a shift from the original conception of law as consisting of orders backed by threats of sanctions which are to be exacted when the orders are disobeyed. Instead, the central conception now is that of orders to officials to apply sanctions. On this view it is not necessary that a sanction be prescribed for the *breach* of every law; it is only necessary that every 'genuine' law shall direct the application of some sanction. So it may well be the case that an official who disregards such directions will not be punishable; and of course this is in fact often the case in many legal systems.

This general theory may, as we have said, take one of two forms, one less extreme than the other. In the less extreme form the original conception of law (which many find intuitively more acceptable) as orders backed by threats directed to ordinary citizens, among others, is preserved at least for those rules that, on a common-sense view, refer primarily to the conduct of ordinary citizens, and not merely to officials. The rules of the criminal law, on this more moderate view, are laws as they stand, and need no recasting as fragments of other complete rules; for they are already orders backed by threats. Recasting is, however, needed in other cases. Rules which confer legal powers on private individuals are, for this as for the more extreme theory, mere fragments of the real complete laws—the orders backed by threats. These last are to be discovered by asking: what persons does the law order to do things, subject to a penalty if they do not comply? When this is known the provisions of such rules as those of the Wills Act, 1837, in relation to witnesses, and other rules conferring on individuals powers and defining the conditions for valid exercise of them, may be recast as specifying some of the conditions under which ultimately such a legal duty arises. They will then appear as part of the antecedent or 'if-clause' of conditional orders backed by threats or rules imposing duties. 'If and only if a will has been signed by the testator and witnessed by two witnesses in the specified manner and if ... then the executor (or other legal representative) shall give effect to the provisions of the will.' Rules relating to the formation of contract will similarly appear as mere fragments of rules ordering persons, if certain things are the case or have been said or done (if the party is of full age, has covenanted under seal or been promised consideration) to do the things which by the contract are to be done.

A recasting of rules conferring legislative powers (including the provisions of a constitution as to the supreme legislature), so as to represent them as fragments of the 'real' rules, may be carried through along the lines similar to those explained on page 36 in the case of the more extreme version of this theory. The only difference is that on the more moderate view the power-conferring rules are represented by the antecedents or if-clauses of rules ordering ordinary citizens, under threat of sanctions, to do things and not merely (as in the more extreme theory) as the if-clauses of directions to officials to apply sanctions.

Both versions of this theory attempt to reduce apparently distinct varieties of legal rule to a single form alleged to convey the quintessence of law. Both, in different ways, make the sanction a centrally important element, and both will fail if it is shown that law without sanctions is perfectly conceivable. This general objection must be, however, left till later. The specific criticism of both forms of the theory which we shall develop here is that they purchase the pleasing uniformity of pattern to which they reduce all laws at too high a price: that of distorting the different social functions which different types of legal rule perform. This is true of both forms of the theory, but is most evident in the recasting of the criminal law demanded by the theory in its more extreme form.

Distortion as the price of uniformity

The distortion effected by this recasting is worth considering for it illuminates many different aspects of law. There are many techniques by which society may be controlled, but the characteristic technique of the criminal law is to designate by rules certain types of behaviour as standards for the guidance either of the members of society as a whole or of special classes within it: they are expected without the aid or intervention of officials to understand the rules and to see that the rules apply to them and to conform to them. Only when the law is broken, and this primary function of the law fails, are officials concerned to identify the fact of breach and impose the threatened sanctions. What is distinctive of this technique, as compared with individuated face-to-face orders which an official, like a policeman on traffic duty, might give to a motorist, is that the members of society are left to discover the rules and conform their behaviour to them; in this sense they 'apply' the rules themselves to themselves, though they are provided with a motive for conformity in the sanction added to the rule. Plainly we shall conceal the characteristic way in which such rules function if we concentrate on, or make primary, the rules requiring the courts to impose the sanctions in the event of disobedience; for these latter rules make provision for the breakdown or failure of the primary purpose of the system. They may indeed be indispensable but they are ancillary.

The idea that the substantive rules of the criminal law have as their function (and, in a broad sense, their meaning) the guidance not merely of officials operating a system of penalties, but of ordinary citizens in the activities of non-official life, cannot be eliminated without jettisoning cardinal distinctions and obscuring the specific character of law as a means of social control. A punishment for a crime, such as a fine, is not the same as a tax on a course of conduct, though both involve directions to officials to inflict the same money loss. What differentiates these ideas is that the first involves, as the second does not, an offence or breach of duty in the form of a violation of a rule set up to guide the conduct of ordinary citizens. It is true that this generally clear distinction may in certain circumstances be blurred. Taxes may be imposed not for revenue purposes but to discourage the activities taxed, though the law gives no express indications that these are to be abandoned as it does when it 'makes them criminal'. Conversely the fines payable for some criminal offence may, because of the depreciation of money, become so small that they are cheerfully paid. They are then perhaps felt to be 'mere taxes', and 'offences' are frequent, precisely because in these circumstances the sense is lost that the rule is, like the bulk of the criminal law, meant to be taken seriously as a standard of behaviour.

It is sometimes urged in favour of theories like the one under consideration that, by recasting the law in a form of a direction to apply sanctions, an advance in clarity is made, since this form makes plain all that the 'bad man' wants to know about the law. This may be true but it seems an inadequate defence for the theory. Why should not law be equally if not more concerned with the 'puzzled man' or 'ignorant man' who is willing to do what is required, if only he can be told what it is? Or with the 'man who wishes to arrange his affairs' if only he can be told how to do it? It is of course very important, if we are to understand the law, to see how the courts administer it when they come to apply its sanctions. But this should not lead us to think that all there is to understand is what happens in courts. The principal functions of the law as a means of social control are not to be seen in private litigation or prosecutions, which represent vital but still ancillary provisions for the failures of the system. It is to be seen in the diverse ways in which the law is used to control, to guide, and to plan life out of court.

We may compare the inversion of ancillary and principal, which this extreme form of the theory makes, to the following suggestion for recasting the rules of a game. A theorist, considering the rules of cricket or baseball, might claim that he had discovered a uniformity hidden by the terminology of the rules and by the conventional claim that some were primarily addressed to players, some primarily to officials (umpire and scorer), some to both. 'All rules', the theorist might claim, 'are *really* rules directing officials to do certain things under certain conditions.' The rules that certain motions after hitting the ball constitute a 'run', or that being caught makes a man 'out', are really just complex directions to officials; in the one case to the scorer to write down 'a run' in the scoring-book and in the other to the umpire to order the man 'off the field'. The natural protest is that the uniformity imposed on the rules by this transformation of them conceals the ways in which the rules operate, and the manner in which the players use them in guiding purposive activities, and so obscures their function in the co-operative, though competitive, social enterprise which is the game.

The less extreme form of the theory would leave the criminal law and all other laws which impose duties untouched, since these already conform to the simple model of coercive orders. But it would reduce all rules conferring and defining the manner of exercise of legal powers to this single form. It is open here to the same criticism as the extreme form of the theory. If we look at all law simply from the point of view of the persons on whom its duties are imposed, and reduce all other aspects of it to the status of more or less elaborate conditions in which duties fall on them, we treat as something merely subordinate, elements which are at least as characteristic of law and as valuable to society as duty. Rules conferring private powers must, if they are to be understood, be looked at from the point of view of those who exercise them. They appear then as an additional element introduced by the law into social life over and above that of coercive control. This is so because possession of these legal powers makes of the private citizen, who, if there were no such rules, would be a mere duty-bearer, a private legislator. He is made competent to determine the course of the law within the sphere of his contracts, trusts, wills, and other structures of rights and duties which he is enabled to build. Why should rules which are used in this special way, and confer this huge and distinctive amenity, not be recognized as distinct from rules which impose duties, the incidence of which is indeed in part determined by the exercise of such powers? Such power-conferring rules are thought of, spoken of, and used in social life differently from rules which impose duties, and they are valued for different reasons. What other tests for difference in character could there be?

The reduction of rules conferring and defining legislative and judicial powers to statements of the conditions under which duties arise has, in the public sphere, a similar obscuring vice. Those who exercise these powers to make authoritative enactments and orders use these rules in a form of purposive activity utterly different from performance of duty or submission to coercive control. To represent such rules as mere aspects or fragments of the rules of duty is, even more than in the private sphere, to obscure the distinctive characteristics of law and of the activities possible within its framework. For the introduction into society of rules enabling legislators to change and add to the rules of duty, and judges to determine when the rules of duty have been broken, is a step forward as important to society as the invention of the wheel. Not only was it an important step; but it is one which, as we shall argue in Chapter V, may fairly be considered as the step from the pre-legal into the legal world.

2. THE RANGE OF APPLICATION

Plainly a penal statute, of all the varieties of law, approximates most closely to the simple model of coercive orders. Yet even these laws have certain characteristics, examined in this section, to which the model is apt to blind us, and we shall not understand them till we shake off its influence. The order backed by threats is essentially the expression of a wish that *others* should do or abstain from doing certain things. It is, of course, possible that legislation might take this exclusively other-regarding form. An absolute monarch wielding legislative power may, in certain systems, always be considered exempt from the scope of the laws he makes; and even in a democratic system laws may be made which do not apply to those who made them, but only to special classes indicated in the law. But the range of application of a law is always a question of its interpretation. It may or may not be found on interpretation to exclude those who made it, and, of course, many a law is now made which imposes legal obligations on the makers of the law. Legislation, as distinct from just ordering *others* to do things under threats, may perfectly well have such a self-binding force. There is nothing *essentially* other-regarding about it. This is a legal phenomenon which is puzzling only so long as we think, under the influence of the model, of the laws as always laid down by a man or men above the law for others subjected to it.

This vertical or 'top-to-bottom' image of law-making, so attractive in its simplicity, is something which can only be reconciled with the realities by the device of distinguishing between the legislator in his official capacity as one person and in his private capacity as another. Acting in the first capacity he then makes law which imposes obligations on other persons, including himself in his 'private capacity'. There is nothing objectionable in these forms of expression, but the notion of different capacities, as we shall see in Chapter IV, is intelligible only in terms of power-conferring rules of law which cannot be reduced to coercive orders. Meanwhile it is to be observed that this complicated device is really quite unnecessary; we can explain the self-binding quality of legislative enactment without it. For we have to hand, both in daily life and in the law, something which will enable us to understand it far better. This is the operation of a *promise* which in many ways is a far better model than that of coercive orders for understanding many, though not all, features of law.

To promise is to say something which creates an obligation for the promisor: in order that words should have this kind of effect, rules must exist providing that if words are used by appropriate persons on appropriate occasions (i.e. by sane persons understanding their position and free from various sorts of pressure) those who use these words shall be bound to do the things designated by them. So, when we promise, we make use of specified procedures to change our own moral situation by imposing obligations on ourselves and conferring rights on others; in lawyers' parlance we exercise 'a power' conferred by rules to do this. It would be indeed possible, but not helpful, to distinguish two persons 'within' the promisor: one acting in the capacity of creator of obligations and the other in the capacity of person bound: and to think of one as ordering the other to do something.

Equally we can dispense with this device for understanding the self-binding force of legislation. For the making of a law, like the making of a promise, presupposes the existence of certain rules which govern the process: words said or written by the persons qualified by these rules, and following the procedure specified by them, create obligations for all within the ambit designated explicitly or implicitly by the words. These may include those who take part in the legislative process.

Of course, though there is this analogy which explains the self-binding character of legislation, there are many differences between the making of promises and the making of laws. The rules governing the latter are very much more complex and the bilateral character of a promise is not present. There is usually no person in the special position of the promisee *to whom* the promise is made and who has a special, if not the only, claim to its performance. In these respects certain other forms of self-imposition of obligation known to English law, such as that whereby a person declares himself trustee of property for other persons, offer a closer analogy to the self-binding aspect of legislation. Yet, in general, making of law by enactment is something we shall understand best by considering such private ways of creating particular legal obligations.

What is most needed as a corrective to the model of coercive orders or rules, is a fresh conception of legislation as the introduction or modification of general standards of behaviour to be followed by the society generally. The legislator is not necessarily like the giver of orders to another: someone by definition outside the reach of what he does. Like the giver of a promise he exercises powers conferred by rules: very often he may, as the promisor *must*, fall within their ambit.

3. MODES OF ORIGIN

So far we have confined our discussion of the varieties of law to statutes which, in spite of the differences we have emphasized, have one salient point of analogy with coercive orders. The enactment of a law, like the giving of an order, *is* a deliberate datable act. Those who take part in legislation consciously operate a procedure for making law, just as the man who gives an order consciously uses a form of words to secure recognition of, and compliance with, his intentions. Accordingly, theories which use the model of coercive orders in the analysis of law make the claim that all law can be seen, if we strip away the disguises, to have this point of resemblance to legislation and to owe its status as law to a deliberate law-creating act. The type of law which most obviously conflicts with this claim is custom; but the discussion whether custom is 'really' law has often been confused by the failure to disentangle two distinct issues. The first is whether 'custom as such' is law or not. The meaning and good sense of the denial that custom, as such, is law lie in the simple truth that, in any society, there are many customs which form no part of its law. Failure to take off a hat to a lady is not a breach of any rule of law; it has no legal status save that of being permitted by law. This shows that custom is law only if it is one of a class of customs which is 'recognized' as law by a particular legal system. The second issue concerns the meaning of 'legal recognition'. What is it for a custom to be legally recognized? Does it, as the model of coercive orders requires, consist in the fact that someone, perhaps 'the sovereign' or his agent, has ordered the custom to be obeyed, so that its status as law is due to something which, in this respect, resembles the act of legislation?

Custom is not in the modern world a very important 'source' of law. It is usually a subordinate one, in the sense that the legislature may by statute deprive a customary rule of legal status; and in many systems the tests which courts apply, in determining whether a custom is fit for legal recognition, incorporate such fluid notions as that of 'reasonableness' which provide at least some foundation for the view that in accepting or rejecting a custom courts are exercising a virtually uncontrolled discretion. Even so, to attribute the legal status of a custom to the fact that a court or the legislature or the sovereign has so 'ordered' is to adopt a theory which can only be carried through if a meaning is given to 'order' so extended as to rob the theory of its point.

In order to present this doctrine of legal recognition we must recall the part played by the sovereign in the conception of law as coercive orders. According to this theory, law is the order of either the sovereign or of his subordinate whom he may choose to give orders on his behalf. In the first case law is made by the order of the sovereign in the most literal sense of 'order'. In the second case the order given by the subordinate will only rank as law if it is, in its own turn, given in pursuance of some order issued by the sovereign. The subordinate must have some authority delegated by the sovereign to issue orders on his behalf. Sometimes this may be conferred by an express direction to a minister to 'make orders' on a certain subject-matter. If the theory stopped here, plainly it could not account for the facts; so it is extended and claims that sometimes the sovereign may express his will in less direct fashion. His orders may be 'tacit'; he may, without giving an express order, signify his intentions that his subjects should do certain things, by not interfering when his subordinates both give orders to his subjects and punish them for disobedience.

A military example may make the idea of a 'tacit order' as clear as it is possible to make it. A sergeant who himself regularly obeys his superiors, orders his men to do certain fatigues and punishes them when they disobey. The general, learning of this, allows things to go on, though if he had ordered the sergeant to stop the fatigues he would have been obeyed. In these circumstances the general may be considered tacitly to have expressed his will that the men should do the fatigues. His non-interference, when he could have interfered, is a silent substitute for the words he might have used in ordering the fatigues.

It is in this light that we are asked to view customary rules which have the status of law in a legal system. Till the courts apply them in particular cases such rules are *mere* customs, in no sense law. When the courts use them, and make orders in accordance with them which are enforced, then for the first time these rules receive legal recognition. The sovereign who might have interfered has tacitly ordered his subjects to obey the judges' orders 'fashioned' on pre-existing custom.

This account of the legal status of custom is open to two different criticisms. The first is that it is not *necessarily* the case that until they are used in litigation customary rules have no status as law. The assertion that this is necessarily the case is either merely dogmatic or fails to distinguish what is necessary from what may be the case in certain systems. Why, if statutes made in certain defined ways are law before they are applied by the courts in particular cases, should not customs of certain defined kinds also be so? Why should it not be true that, just as the courts recognize as binding the general principle that what the legislature enacts is law, they also recognize as binding another general principle: that customs of certain defined sorts are law? What absurdity is there in the contention that, when particular cases arise, courts apply custom, as they apply statute, as something which is already law and because it is law? It is, of course, *possible* that a legal system should provide that no customary rule should have the status of law until the courts, in their uncontrolled discretion, declared that it should. But this would be just *one* possibility, which cannot exclude the possibility of systems in which the courts have no such discretion. How can it establish the general contention that a customary rule *cannot* have the status of law till applied in court?

The answers made to these objections sometimes reduce to no more than the reassertion of the dogma that nothing can be law unless and until it has been *ordered* by someone to be so. The suggested parallel between the relationships of courts to statute and to custom is then rejected on the ground that, before it is applied by a court, a statute has already been 'ordered' but a custom has not. Less dogmatic arguments are inadequate because they make too much of the particular arrangements of particular systems. The fact that in English law a custom may be rejected by the courts if it fails to pass the test of 'reasonableness' is sometimes said to show that it is not law till applied by the courts. This again could at the most only prove something about custom in English law. Even this cannot be established, unless it is true, as some claim, that it is meaningless to distinguish a system in which courts are only bound to apply certain customary rules if they are reasonable from a system in which they have an uncontrolled discretion.

The second criticism of the theory that custom, when it is law, owes its legal status to the sovereign's tacit order is more fundamental. Even if it is conceded that it is not law till enforced by the court in the particular case, is it possible to treat the failure of the sovereign to interfere as a tacit expression of the wish that the rules should be obeyed? Even in the very simple military example on page 46 it is not a necessary inference from the fact that the general did not interfere with the sergeant's orders that he wished them to be obeyed. He may merely have wished to placate a valued subordinate and hoped that the men would find some way of evading the fatigues. No doubt we might in some cases draw the inference that he wished the fatigues to be done, but if we did this, a material part of our evidence would be the fact that the general knew that the orders had been given, had time to consider them, and decided to do nothing. The main objection to the use of the idea of tacit expressions of the sovereign's will to explain the legal status of custom is that, in any modern state, it is rarely possible to ascribe such knowledge, consideration and decision not to interfere to the 'sovereign', whether we identify the sovereign with the supreme legislature or the electorate. It is, of course, true that in most legal systems custom is a source of law subordinate to statute. This means that the legislature *could* take away their legal status; but failure to do this may not be a sign of the legislator's wishes. Only very rarely is the attention of a legislature, and still more rarely that of the electorate, turned to the customary rules applied by courts. Their non-interference can therefore not be compared to the general's non-interference with his sergeant; even if, in his case, we are prepared to infer from it a wish that his subordinate's orders be obeyed.

In what then does the legal recognition of custom consist? To what does a customary rule owe its legal status, if it is not to the order of the court which applied it to a particular case or to the tacit order of the supreme law-making power? How can it, like statute, be law before the court applies it? These questions can only be fully answered when we have scrutinized in detail, as we shall in the next chapter, the doctrine that, where there is law, there must be some sovereign person or persons whose general orders, explicit or tacit, alone are law. Meanwhile we may summarize the conclusions of this chapter as follows:

The theory of law as coercive orders meets at the outset with the objection that there are varieties of law found in all systems which, in three principal respects, do not fit this description. First, even a penal statute, which comes nearest to it, has often a range of application different from that of orders given to others; for such a law may impose duties on those who make it as well as on others. Secondly, other statutes are unlike orders in that they do not require persons to do things, but may confer powers on them; they do not impose duties but offer facilities for the free creation of legal rights and duties within the coercive framework of the law. Thirdly, though the enactment of a statute is in some ways analogous to the giving of an order, some rules of law originate in custom and do not owe their legal status to any such conscious law-creating act.

To defend the theory against these objections a variety of expedients have been adopted. The originally simple idea of a threat of evil or 'sanction' has been stretched to include the nullity of a legal transaction; the notion of a legal rule has been narrowed so as to exclude rules which confer powers, as being mere fragments of law; within the single natural person of the legislator whose enactments are self-binding two persons have been discovered; the notion of an order has been extended from a verbal to a 'tacit' expression of will, consisting in non-interference with orders given by subordinates. Notwithstanding the ingenuity of these devices, the model of orders backed by threats obscures more of law than it reveals; the effort to reduce to this single simple form the variety of laws ends by imposing upon them a spurious uniformity. Indeed, to look for uniformity here may be a mistake, for, as we shall argue in Chapter V, a distinguishing, if not the distinguishing, characteristic of law lies in its fusion of different types of rule.

IV

SOVEREIGN AND SUBJECT

In criticizing the simple model of law as coercive orders we have so far raised no questions concerning the 'sovereign' person or persons whose general orders constitute, according to this conception, the law of any society. Indeed in discussing the adequacy of the idea of an order backed by threats as an account of the different varieties of law, we provisionally assumed that in any society where there is law, there actually is a sovereign, characterized affirmatively and negatively by reference to the habit of obedience: a person or body of persons whose orders the great majority of the society habitually obey and who does not habitually obey any other person or persons.

We must now consider in some detail this general theory concerning the foundations of all legal systems; for in spite of its extreme simplicity the doctrine of sovereignty is nothing less than this. The doctrine asserts that in every human society, where there is law, there is ultimately to be found latent beneath the variety of political forms, in a democracy as much as in an absolute monarchy, this simple relationship between subjects rendering habitual obedience and a sovereign who renders habitual obedience to no one. This vertical structure composed of sovereign and subjects is, according to the theory, as essential a part of a society which possesses law, as a backbone is of a man. Where it is present, we may speak of the society, together with its sovereign, as a single independent state, and we may speak of *its* law: where it is not present, we can apply none of these expressions, for the relation of sovereign and subject forms, according to this theory, part of their very meaning.

Two points in this doctrine are of special importance and we shall emphasize them here in general terms in order to indicate the lines of criticism pursued in detail in the rest of the chapter. The first concerns the idea of a *habit* of obedience, which is all that is required on the part of those to whom the sovereign's laws apply. Here we shall inquire whether such a habit is sufficient to account for two salient features of most legal systems: the *continuity* of the authority to make law possessed by a succession of different legislators, and the *persistence* of laws long after their maker and those who rendered him habitual obedience have perished. Our second point concerns the position occupied by the sovereign above the law: he creates law for others and so imposes legal duties or 'limitations' upon them whereas he is said himself to be legally unlimited and illimitable. Here we shall inquire whether this legally illimitable status of the supreme lawgiver is necessary for the existence of law, and whether either the presence or the absence of legal limits on legislative power can be understood in the simple terms of habit and obedience into which this theory analyses these notions.

I. THE HABIT OF OBEDIENCE AND THE CONTINUITY OF LAW

The idea of obedience, like many other apparently simple ideas used without scrutiny, is not free from complexities. We shall disregard the complexity already noticed[1] that the word 'obedience' often suggests deference to authority and not merely compliance with orders backed by threats. Even so, it is not easy to state, even in the case of a single order given face to face by one man to another, precisely what connection there must be between the giving of the order and the performance of the specified act in order that the latter should constitute obedience. What, for example, is the relevance of the fact, when it is a fact, that the person ordered would certainly have done the very same thing without any order? These difficulties are particularly acute in the case of laws, some of which prohibit people from doing things which many of them would never think of doing. Till these difficulties are settled the whole idea of a 'general habit of obedience' to the laws of a country must remain somewhat obscure. We may, however, for our present purposes imagine a very simple case to which the words 'habit' and 'obedience' would perhaps be conceded to have a fairly obvious application.

[1] See p. 19 above.

We shall suppose that there is a population living in a territory in which an absolute monarch (Rex) reigns for a very long time: he controls his people by general orders backed by threats requiring them to do various things which they would not otherwise do, and to abstain from doing things which they would otherwise do; though there was trouble in the early years of the reign, things have long since settled down and, in general, the people can be relied on to obey him. Since what Rex requires is often onerous, and the temptation to disobey and risk the punishment is considerable, it is hardly to be supposed that the obedience, though generally rendered, is a 'habit' or 'habitual' in the full sense or most usual sense of that word. Men can indeed quite literally acquire the habit of complying with certain laws: driving on the left-hand side of the road is perhaps a paradigm, for Englishmen, of such an acquired habit. But where the law runs counter to strong inclinations as, for example, do laws requiring the payment of taxes, our eventual compliance with them, even though regular, has not the unreflective, effortless, engrained character of a habit. None the less, though the obedience accorded to Rex will often lack this element of habit, it will have other important ones. To say of a person that he has habit, e.g. of reading a newspaper at breakfast, entails that he has for some considerable time past done this and that he is likely to repeat this behaviour. If so, it will be true of most people in our imagined community, at any time after the initial period of trouble, that they have generally obeyed the orders of Rex and are likely to continue to do so.

It is to be noted that, on this account of the social situation under Rex, the habit of obedience is a personal relationship between each subject and Rex: each regularly does what Rex orders him, among others, to do. If we speak of the *population* as 'having such a habit', this, like the assertion that people habitually frequent the tavern on Saturday nights, will mean only that the habits of most of the people are convergent: they each habitually obey Rex, just as they might each habitually go to the tavern on Saturday night.

It is to be observed that in this very simple situation all that is required from the community to constitute Rex the sovereign are the personal acts of obedience on the part of the population. Each of them need, for his part, only obey; and, so long as obedience is regularly forthcoming, no one in the community need have or express any views as to whether his own or others' obedience to Rex is in any sense right, proper, or legitimately demanded. Plainly, the society we have described, in order to give as literal application as possible to the notion of a habit of obedience, is a very simple one. It is probably far too simple ever to have existed anywhere, and it is certainly not a primitive one; for primitive society knows little of absolute rulers like Rex, and its members are not usually concerned merely to obey but have pronounced views as to the rightness of obedience on the part of all concerned. None the less the community under Rex has certainly some of the important marks of a society governed by law, at least during the lifetime of Rex. It has even a certain unity, so that it may be called 'a state'. This unity is constituted by the fact that its members obey the same person, even though they may have no views as to the rightness of doing so.

Let us now suppose that, after a successful reign, Rex dies leaving a son Rex II who then starts to issue general orders. The mere fact that there was a general habit of obedience to Rex I in his lifetime does not by itself even render probable that Rex II will be habitually obeyed. Hence if we have nothing more to go on than the fact of obedience to Rex I and the likelihood that *he* would continue to be obeyed, we shall not be able to say of Rex II's first order, as we could have said of Rex I's last order, that it was given by one who was sovereign and was therefore law. There is as yet no established habit of obedience to Rex II. We shall have to wait and see whether such obedience will be accorded to Rex II, as it was to his father, before we can say, in accordance with the theory, that he is now sovereign and his orders are law. There is nothing to make him sovereign from the start. Only after we know that his orders have been obeyed for some time shall we be able to say that a habit of obedience has been established. Then, but not till then, we shall be able to say of any further order that it is already law as soon as it is issued and before it is obeyed. Till this stage is reached there will be an interregnum in which no law can be made.

Such a state of affairs is of course possible and has occasionally been realized in troubled times: but the dangers of discontinuity are obvious and not usually courted. Instead, it is characteristic of a legal system, even in an absolute monarchy, to secure the uninterrupted continuity of law-making power by rules which bridge the transition from one lawgiver to another: these regulate the succession *in advance*, naming or specifying in general terms the qualifications of and mode of determining the lawgiver. In a modern democracy the qualifications are highly complex and relate to the composition of a legislature with a frequently changing membership, but the essence of the rules required for continuity can be seen in the simpler forms appropriate to our imaginary monarchy. If the rule provides for the succession of the eldest son, then Rex II has a *title* to succeed his father. He will have the *right* to make law on his father's death, and when his first orders are issued we may have good reason for saying that they are already law, before any relationship of habitual obedience between him personally and his subjects has had time to establish itself. Indeed such a relationship may never be established. Yet his word may be law; for Rex II may himself die immediately after issuing his first orders; he will not have lived to receive obedience, yet he may have had the *right* to make law and his orders may be law.

In explaining the continuity of law-making power through a changing succession of individual legislators, it is natural to use the expressions 'rule of succession', 'title', 'right to succeed', and 'right to make law'. It is plain, however, that with these expressions we have introduced a new set of elements, of which no account can be given in terms of habits of obedience to general orders, out of which, following the prescription of the theory of sovereignty, we constructed the simple legal world of Rex I. For in that world there were no rules, and so no rights or titles, and hence *a fortiori* no right or title to succeed: there were just the facts that orders were given by Rex I, and his orders were habitually obeyed. To constitute Rex sovereign during his lifetime and to make his orders law, no more was needed; but this is not enough to account for his successor's *rights*. In fact, the idea of habitual obedience fails, in two different though related ways, to account for the continuity to be observed in every normal legal system, when one legislator succeeds another. First, mere habits of obedience to orders given by one legislator cannot confer on the new legislator any *right* to succeed the old and give orders in his place. Secondly, habitual obedience to the old lawgiver cannot by itself render probable, or found any presumption, that the new legislator's orders will be obeyed. If there is to be this right and this presumption at the moment of succession there must, during the reign of the earlier legislator, have been somewhere in the society a general social practice more complex than any that can be described in terms of habit of obedience: there must have been the acceptance of the rule under which the new legislator is entitled to succeed.

What is this more complex practice? What is the acceptance of a rule? Here we must resume the inquiry already outlined in Chapter I. To answer it we must, for the moment, turn aside from the special case of legal rules. How does a habit differ from a rule? What is the difference between saying of a group that they have the habit, e.g. of going to the cinema on Saturday nights, and saying that it is the rule with them that the male head is to be bared on entering a church? We have already mentioned in Chapter I some of the elements which must be brought into the analysis of this type of rule, and here we must pursue the analysis further.

There is certainly one point of similarity between social rules and habits: in both cases the behaviour in question (e.g. baring the head in church) must be general though not necessarily invariable; this means that it is repeated when occasion arises by most of the group: so much is, as we have said, implied in the phrase, 'They do it *as a rule*.' But though there is this similarity there are three salient differences.

First, for the group to have a *habit* it is enough that their behaviour in fact converges. Deviation from the regular course need not be a matter for any form of criticism. But such general convergence or even identity of behaviour is not enough to constitute the existence of a rule requiring that behaviour: where there is such a rule deviations are generally regarded as lapses or faults open to criticism, and threatened deviations meet with pressure for conformity, though the forms of criticism and pressure differ with different types of rule.

Secondly, where there are such rules, not only is such criticism in fact made but deviation from the standard is generally accepted as a *good reason* for making it. Criticism for deviation is regarded as legitimate or justified in this sense, as are demands for compliance with the standard when deviation is threatened. Moreover, except by a minority of hardened offenders, such criticism and demands are generally regarded as legitimate, or made with good reason, both by those who make them and those to whom they are made. How many of the group must in these various ways treat the regular mode of behaviour as a standard of criticism, and how often and for how long they must do so to warrant the statement that the group has a rule, are not definite matters; they need not worry us more than the question as to the number of hairs a man may have and still be bald. We need only remember that the statement that a group has a certain rule is compatible with the existence of a minority who not only break the rule but refuse to look upon it as a standard either for themselves or others.

The third feature distinguishing social rules from habits is implicit in what has already been said, but it is one so important and so frequently disregarded or misrepresented in jurisprudence that we shall elaborate it here. It is a feature which throughout this book we shall call the *internal aspect* of rules. When a habit is general in a social group, this generality is merely a fact about the observable behaviour of most of the group. In order that there should be such a habit no members of the group need in any way think of the general behaviour, or even know that the behaviour in question is general; still less need they strive to teach or intend to maintain it. It is enough that each for his part behaves in the way that others also in fact do. By contrast, if a social rule is to exist some at least must look upon the behaviour in question as a general standard to be followed by the group as a whole. A social rule has an 'internal' aspect, in addition to the external aspect which it shares with a social habit and which consists in the regular uniform behaviour which an observer could record.

This internal aspect of rules may be simply illustrated from the rules of any game. Chess players do not merely have similar habits of moving the Queen in the same way which an external observer, who knew nothing about their attitude to the moves which they make, could record. In addition, they have a reflective critical attitude to this pattern of behaviour: they regard it as a standard for all who play the game. Each not only moves the Queen in a certain way himself but 'has views' about the propriety of all moving the Queen in that way. These views are manifested in the criticism of others and demands for conformity made upon others when deviation is actual or threatened, and in the acknowledgement of the legitimacy of such criticism and demands when received from others. For the expression of such criticisms, demands, and acknowledgements a wide range of 'normative' language is used. 'I (You) ought not to have moved the Queen like that', 'I (You) must do that', 'That is right', 'That is wrong'.

The internal aspect of rules is often misrepresented as a mere matter of 'feelings' in contrast to externally observable physical behaviour. No doubt, where rules are generally accepted by a social group and generally supported by social criticism and pressure for conformity, individuals may often have psychological experiences analogous to those of restriction or compulsion. When they say they 'feel bound' to behave in certain ways they may indeed refer to these experiences. But such feelings are neither necessary nor sufficient for the existence of 'binding' rules. There is no contradiction in saying that people accept certain rules but experience no such feelings of compulsion. What is necessary is that there should be a critical reflective attitude to certain patterns of behaviour as a common standard, and that this should display itself in criticism (including self-criticism), demands for conformity, and in acknowledgements that such criticism and demands are justified, all of which find their characteristic expression in the normative terminology of 'ought', 'must', and 'should', 'right' and 'wrong'.

These are the crucial features which distinguish social rules from mere group habits, and with them in mind we may return to the law. We may suppose that our social group has not only rules which, like that concerning baring the head in church, makes a specific kind of behaviour standard, but a rule which provides for the identification of standards of behaviour in a less direct fashion, by reference to the words, spoken or written, of a given person. In its simplest form this rule will be to the effect that whatever actions Rex specifies (perhaps in certain formal ways) are to be done. This transforms the situation which we first depicted in terms of mere habits of obedience to Rex; for where such a rule is accepted Rex will not only in fact specify what is to be done but will have the *right* to do this; and not only will there be general obedience to his orders, but it will be generally accepted that it is *right* to obey him. Rex will in fact be a legislator with the *authority* to legislate, i.e. to introduce new standards of behaviour into the life of the group, and there is no reason, since we are now concerned with standards, not 'orders', why he should not be bound by his own legislation.

The social practices which underlie such legislative authority will be, in all essentials, the same as those which underlie the simple direct rules of conduct, like that concerning baring the head in church, which we may now distinguish as mere customary rules, and they will differ in the same way from general habits. Rex's *word* will now be a standard of behaviour so that deviations from the behaviour he designates will be open to criticism; his word will now generally be referred to and accepted as justifying criticism and demands for compliance.

In order to see how such rules explain the continuity of legislative authority, we need only notice that in some cases, even before a new legislator has begun to legislate, it may be clear that there is a firmly established rule giving him, as one of a *class* or line of persons, the right to do this in his turn. Thus we may find it generally accepted by the group, during the lifetime of Rex I, that the person whose word is to be obeyed is not limited to the individual Rex I but is that person who, for the time being, is qualified in a certain way, e.g. as the eldest living descendant in the direct line of a certain ancestor: Rex I is merely the particular person so qualified at a particular time. Such a rule, unlike the habit of obeying Rex I, looks forward, since it refers to future possible lawgivers as well as the present actual lawgiver.

The acceptance, and so the existence, of such a rule will be manifested during Rex I's lifetime in part by obedience to him, but also by acknowledgements that obedience is something to which he has a right by virtue of his qualification under the general rule. Just because the scope of a rule accepted at a given time by a group may look forward in general terms to successors in the office of legislator in this way, its acceptance affords us grounds *both* for the statement of law that the successor has a right to legislate, even before he starts to do so, and for the statement of fact that he is likely to receive the same obedience as his predecessor does.

Of course, acceptance of a rule by a society at one moment does not *guarantee* its continued existence. There may be a revolution: the society may cease to accept the rule. This may happen either during the lifetime of one legislator, Rex I, or at the point of transition to a new one, Rex II, and, if it does happen, Rex I will lose or Rex II will not acquire, the right to legislate. It is true that the position may be obscure: there may be intermediate confused stages, when it is not clear whether we are faced with a mere insurrection or temporary interruption of the old rule, or a full-scale effective abandonment of it. But in principle the matter is clear. The statement that a new legislator has a right to legislate presupposes the existence, in the social group, of the rule under which he has this right. If it is clear that the rule which now qualifies him was accepted during the lifetime of his predecessor, whom it also qualified, it is to be assumed, in the absence of evidence to the contrary, that it has not been abandoned and still exists. A similar continuity is to be observed in a game when the scorer, in the absence of evidence that the rules of the game have been changed since the last innings, credits the new batsman with the runs which he makes, assessed in the usual way.

Consideration of the simple legal worlds of Rex I and Rex II is perhaps enough to show that the continuity of legislative authority which characterizes most legal systems depends on that form of social practice which constitutes the acceptance of a rule, and differs, in the ways we have indicated, from the simpler facts of mere habitual obedience. We may summarize the argument as follows. Even if we concede that a person, such as Rex, whose general orders are habitually obeyed, may be called a legislator and his orders laws, habits of obedience to each of a succession of such legislators are not enough to account for the *right* of a successor to succeed and for the consequent continuity in legislative power. First, because habits are not 'normative'; they cannot confer rights or authority on anyone. Secondly, because habits of obedience to one individual cannot, though accepted rules can, refer to a class or line of future successive legislators as well as to the current legislator, or render obedience to them likely. So the fact that there is habitual obedience to one legislator neither affords grounds for the statement that his successor has the right to make law, nor for the factual statement that he is likely to be obeyed.

At this point, however, an important point must be noticed which we shall develop fully in a later chapter. It constitutes one of the strong points of Austin's theory. In order to reveal the essential differences between accepted rules and habits we have taken a very simple form of society. Before we leave this aspect of sovereignty we must inquire how far our account of the acceptance of a rule conferring authority to legislate could be transferred to a modern state. In referring to our simple society we spoke as if most ordinary people not only obeyed the law but understood and accepted the rule qualifying a succession of lawgivers to legislate. In a simple society this might be the case; but in a modern state it would be absurd to think of the mass of the population, however law-abiding, as having any clear realization of the rules specifying the qualifications of a continually changing body of persons entitled to legislate. To speak of the populace 'accepting' these rules, in the same way as the members of some small tribe might accept the rule giving authority to its successive chiefs, would involve putting into the heads of ordinary citizens an understanding of constitutional matters which they might not have. We would only require such an understanding of the officials or experts of the system; the courts, which are charged with the responsibility of determining what the law is, and the lawyers whom the ordinary citizen consults when he wants to know what it is.

These differences between a simple tribal society and a modern state deserve attention. In what sense, then, are we to think of the continuity of the legislative authority of the Queen in Parliament, preserved throughout the changes of successive legislators, as resting on some fundamental rule or rules generally accepted? Plainly, general acceptance is here a complex phenomenon, in a sense divided between official and ordinary citizens, who contribute to it and so to the *existence* of a legal system in different ways. The officials of the system may be said to acknowledge explicitly such fundamental rules conferring legislative authority: the legislators do this when they make laws in accordance with the rules which empower them to do so: the courts when they identify, as laws to be applied by them, the laws made by those thus qualified, and the experts when they guide the ordinary citizens by reference to the laws so made. The ordinary citizen manifests his acceptance largely by acquiescence in the results of these official operations. He keeps the law which is made and identified in this way, and also makes claims and exercises powers conferred by it. But he may know little of its origin or its makers: some may know nothing more about the laws than that they are 'the law'. It forbids things ordinary citizens want to do, and they know that they may be arrested by a policeman and sentenced to prison by a judge if they disobey. It is the strength of the doctrine which insists that habitual obedience to orders backed by threats is the foundation of a legal system that it forces us to think in realistic terms of this relatively passive aspect of the complex phenomenon which we call the existence of a legal system. The weakness of the doctrine is that it obscures or distorts the other relatively active aspect, which is seen primarily, though not exclusively, in the law-making, law-identifying, and law-applying operations of the officials or experts of the system. Both aspects must be kept in view if we are to see this complex social phenomenon for what it actually is.

2. THE PERSISTENCE OF LAW

In 1944 a woman was prosecuted in England and convicted for telling fortunes in violation of the Witchcraft Act, 1735.[1] This is only a picturesque example of a very familiar legal phenomenon: a statute enacted centuries ago may still be law today. Yet familiar though it is, the persistence of laws in this way is something which cannot be made intelligible in terms of the simple scheme which conceives of laws as orders given

---

[1] *R. v. Duncan* [1944] 1 KB 713.

by a person habitually obeyed. We have in fact here the converse of the problem of the continuity of law-making authority which we have just considered. There the question was how, on the basis of the simple scheme of habits of obedience, it could be said that the first law made by a successor to the office of legislator is *already* law before he personally had received habitual obedience. Here the question is: how can law made by an earlier legislator, long dead, *still* be law for a society that cannot be said habitually to obey him? As in the first case, no difficulty arises for the simple scheme if we confine our view to the lifetime of the legislator. Indeed, it seems to explain admirably why the Witchcraft Act was law in England but would not have been law in France, even if its terms extended to French citizens telling fortunes in France, though of course it could have been applied to those Frenchmen who had the misfortune to be brought before English courts. The simple explanation would be that in England there was a habit of obedience to those who enacted this law whereas in France there was not. Hence it was law for England but not for France.

We cannot, however, narrow our view of laws to the lifetime of their makers, for the feature which we have to explain is just their obdurate capacity to survive their makers and those who habitually obeyed them. Why is the Witchcraft Act law still for us, if it was not law for the contemporary French? Surely, by no stretch of language can we, the English of the twentieth century, now be said habitually to obey George II and his Parliament. In this respect, the English now and the French then are alike: neither habitually obey or obeyed the maker of this law. The Witchcraft Act might be the sole Act surviving from this reign and yet it would still be law in England now. The answer to this problem of 'Why law still?' is in principle the same as the answer to our first problem of 'Why law already?' and it involves the substitution, for the too simple notion of habits of obedience to a sovereign person, of the notion of currently accepted fundamental rules specifying a class or line of persons whose word is to constitute a standard of behaviour for the society, i.e. who have the *right* to legislate. Such a rule, though it must exist now, may in a sense be timeless in its reference: it may not only look forward and refer to the legislative operation of a future legislator but it may also look back and refer to the operations of a past one.

Presented in the simple terms of the Rex dynasty the position is this. Each of a line of legislators, Rex I, II, and III, may be qualified under the same general rule that confers the right to legislate on the eldest living descendant in the direct line. When the individual ruler dies his legislative work lives on; for it rests upon the foundation of a general rule which successive generations of the society continue to respect regarding each legislator whenever he lived. In the simple case Rex I, II, and III, are each entitled, under the same general rule, to introduce standards of behaviour by legislation. In most legal systems matters are not quite so simple, for the presently accepted rule under which past legislation is recognized as law may differ from the rule relating to contemporary legislation. But, given the present acceptance of the underlying rule, the persistence of laws is no more mysterious than the fact that the decision of the umpire, in the first round of a tournament between teams whose membership has changed, should have the same relevance to the final result as those of the umpire who took his place in the third round. None the less, if not mysterious, the notion of an accepted rule conferring authority on the orders of past and future, as well as present, legislators, is certainly more complex and sophisticated than the idea of habits of obedience to a present legislator. Is it possible to dispense with this complexity, and by some ingenious extension of the simple conception of orders backed by threats show that the persistence of laws rests, after all, on the simpler facts of habitual obedience to the present sovereign?

One ingenious attempt to do this has been made: Hobbes, echoed here by Bentham and Austin, said that 'the legislator is he, not by whose authority the laws were first made, but by whose authority they now continue to be laws'.[1] It is not immediately clear, if we dispense with the notion of a rule in favour of the simpler idea of habit, what the 'authority' as distinct from the 'power' of a legislator can be. But the general

[1] *Leviathan*, chap. xxvi.

argument expressed by this quotation is clear. It is that, though as a matter of history the source or origin of a law such as the Witchcraft Act was the legislative operation of a past sovereign, its present status as law in twentieth-century England is due to its recognition as law by the present sovereign. This recognition does not take the form of an *explicit* order, as in the case of statutes made by the now living legislators, but of a *tacit* expression of the sovereign's will. This consists in the fact that, though he could, he does not interfere with the enforcement by his agents (the courts and possibly the executive) of the statute made long ago.

This is, of course, the same theory of tacit orders already considered, which was invoked to explain the legal status of certain customary rules, which appeared not to have been ordered by any one at any time. The criticisms which we made of this theory in Chapter III apply even more obviously when it is used to explain the continued recognition of past legislation as law. For though, owing to the wide discretion accorded to the courts to reject unreasonable customary rules, there may be some plausibility in the view that until the courts actually apply a customary rule in a given case, it has no status as law, there is very little plausibility in the view that a statute made by a past 'sovereign' is not law until it is actually applied by the courts in the particular case, and enforced with the acquiescence of the present sovereign. If this theory is right it follows that the courts do not enforce it because it is already law: yet this would be an absurd inference to draw from the fact that the present legislator could repeal the past enactments but has not exercised this power. For Victorian statutes and those passed by the Queen in Parliament today surely have precisely the same legal status in present-day England. Both are law even before cases to which they are applied arise in the courts and, when such cases do arise, the courts apply both Victorian and modern statutes because they are already law. In neither case are these law only after they are applied by the courts; and in both cases alike their status as law is due to the fact that they were enacted by persons whose enactments are now authoritative under presently accepted rules, irrespective of the fact that these persons are alive or dead.

The incoherence of the theory that past statutes owe their present status as law to the acquiescence of the present legislature in their application by the courts, may be seen most clearly in its incapacity to explain why the courts of the present day should distinguish between a Victorian statute which has not been repealed as still law, and one which was repealed under Edward VII as no longer law. Plainly, in drawing such distinctions the courts (and with them any lawyer or ordinary citizen who understands the system) use as a criterion a fundamental rule or rules of what is to count as law which embraces past as well as present legislative operations: they do not rest their discrimination between the two statutes on knowledge that the present sovereign has tacitly commanded (i.e. allowed to be enforced) one but not the other.

Again, it seems that the only virtue in the theory we have rejected is that of a blurred version of a realistic reminder. In this case it is the reminder that unless the officials of the system and above all the courts accept the rule that certain legislative operations, *past or present*, are authoritative, something essential to their status as law will be lacking. But realism of this humdrum sort must not be inflated into the theory sometimes known as Legal Realism, the main features of which are discussed in detail later,[1] and which, in some versions, holds *no* statute to be law until it is actually applied by a court. There is a difference, crucial for the understanding of law, between the truth that if a statute is to be law, the courts must accept the rule that certain legislative operations make law, and the misleading theory that nothing is law till it is applied in a particular case by a court. Some versions of the theory of Legal Realism of course go far beyond the false explanation of the persistence of laws which we have criticized; for they go the full length of denying that the status of law can belong to any statute whether made by a past or *present* sovereign, before the courts have actually applied it. Yet an explanation of the persistence of laws which stops short of the full Realist theory and acknowledges that statutes of the present sovereign, as distinguished from past sovereigns, are law before they are applied by the courts has the worst of both worlds and is surely quite absurd. This halfway position is untenable because there is nothing to distinguish the legal status of a statute of the present sovereign and an unrepealed statute of an earlier one. Either both (as ordinary lawyers would acknowledge) or neither, as the full Realist theory claims, are law before they are applied by the courts of the present day to a particular case.

3. LEGAL LIMITATIONS ON LEGISLATIVE POWER

In the doctrine of sovereignty the general habit of obedience of the subject has, as its complement, the absence of any such habit in the sovereign. He makes law for his subjects and makes it from a position outside any law. There are, and can be, no legal limits on his law-creating power. It is important to understand that the legally unlimited power of the sovereign is his by definition: the theory simply asserts that there could only be legal limits on legislative power if the legislator were under the orders of another legislator whom he habitually obeyed; and in that case he would no longer be sovereign. If he is sovereign he does not obey any other legislator and hence there can be no legal limits on his legislative power. The importance of the theory does not of course lie in these definitions and their simple necessary consequences which tell us nothing about the facts. It lies in the claim that in every society where there is law there is a sovereign with these attributes. We may have to look behind legal or political forms, which suggest that all legal powers are limited and that no person or persons occupy the position outside the law ascribed to the sovereign. But if we are resolute in our search we shall find the reality which, as the theory claims, exists behind the forms.

We must not misinterpret the theory as making either a weaker or a stronger claim than it in fact makes. The theory does not merely state that there are *some* societies where a sovereign subject to no legal limits is to be found, but that everywhere the existence of law implies the existence of such a sovereign. On the other hand the theory does not insist that there are no limits on the sovereign's power but only that there are no *legal* limits on it. So the sovereign may in fact defer, in exercising legislative power, to popular opinion either from fear of the consequences of flouting it, or because he thinks himself morally bound to respect it. Very many different factors may influence him in this, and, if a fear of popular revolt or moral conviction leads him not to legislate in ways which he otherwise would, he may indeed think and speak of these factors as 'limits' on his power. But they are not legal limits. He is under no legal duty to abstain from such legislation, and the law courts, in considering whether they have before them a law of the sovereign, would not listen to the argument that its divergence from the requirements of popular opinion or morality prevented it from ranking as law, unless there was an order of the sovereign that they should.

The attractions of this theory as a general account of law are manifest. It seems to give us in satisfying simple form an answer to two major questions. When we have found the sovereign who receives habitual obedience but yields it to no one, we can do two things. First, we can identify in his general orders the law of a given society and distinguish it from many other rules, principles, or standards, moral or merely customary, by which the lives of its members are also governed. Secondly, within the area of law we can determine whether we are confronted with an independent legal system or merely a subordinate part of some wider system.

It is usually claimed that the Queen in Parliament, considered as a single continuing legislative entity, fills the requirements of this theory and the sovereignty of Parliament consists in the fact that it does so. Whatever the accuracy of this belief (some aspects of which we later consider in Chapter VI), we can certainly reproduce quite coherently in the imaginary simple world of Rex I what the theory demands. It is instructive to do this before considering the more complex case of a modern state, since the full implications of the theory are best brought out in this way. To accommodate the criticisms made in Section 1 of the notion of habits of obedience we can conceive of the situation in terms of rules rather than habits. On this footing we shall imagine a society in which there is a rule generally accepted by courts, officials, and citizens that, whenever Rex orders anything to be done, his word constitutes a standard of behaviour for the group. It may well be that, in order to distinguish among these orders those expressions of 'private' wishes, which Rex does not wish to have 'official' status, from those which he does, ancillary rules will also be adopted specifying a special style which the monarch is to use when he legislates 'in the character of a monarch' but not when he gives private orders to his wife or mistress. Such rules concerning the manner and form of legislation must be taken seriously if they are to serve their purpose, and they may at times inconvenience Rex. None the less, though we may well rank them as legal rules, we need not count them as 'limits' on his legislative power, since if he does follow the required form there is no subject on which he cannot legislate so as to give effect to his wishes. The 'area' if not the 'form' of his legislative power is unlimited by law.

The objection to the theory as a general theory of law is that the existence of a sovereign such as Rex in this imagined society, who is subject to no legal limitations, is not a necessary condition or presupposition of the existence of law. To establish this we need not invoke disputable or challengeable types of law. Our argument therefore is not drawn from systems of customary law or international law, to which some wish to deny the title of law just because they lack a legislature. Appeal to these cases is quite unnecessary; for the conception of the legally unlimited sovereign misrepresents the character of law in many modern states where no one would question that there is law. Here there are legislatures but sometimes the supreme legislative power within the system is far from unlimited. A written constitution may restrict the competence of the legislature not merely by specifying the form and manner of legislation (which we may allow not to be limitations) but by excluding altogether certain matters from the scope of its legislative competence, thus imposing limitations of substance.

Again, before examining the complex case of a modern state, it is useful to see what, in the simple world where Rex is the supreme legislator, 'legal limitations on his legislative power' would actually mean, and why it is a perfectly coherent notion.

In the simple society of Rex it may be the accepted rule (whether embodied in a written constitution or not) that no law of Rex shall be valid if it excludes native inhabitants from the territory or provides for their imprisonment without trial, and that any enactment contrary to these provisions shall be void and so treated by all. In such a case Rex's powers to legislate would be subject to limitations which surely would be legal, even if we are disinclined to call such a fundamental constitutional rule 'a law'. Unlike disregard of popular opinion or popular moral convictions to which he might often defer even against his inclinations, disregard of these specific restrictions would render his legislation void. The courts would therefore be concerned with these in a way in which they would not be concerned with the other merely moral or *de facto* limits on the legislator's exercise of his power. Yet, in spite of these legal limitations, surely Rex's enactments within their scope are laws, and there is an independent legal system in his society.

It is important to dwell a little longer on this imaginary simple case in order to see precisely what legal limits of this type are. We might often express the position of Rex by saying that he '*cannot*' pass laws providing for imprisonment without trial; it is illuminating to contrast this sense of 'cannot' with that which signifies that a person is under some legal duty or obligation not to do something. 'Cannot' is used in this latter sense when we say, 'You cannot ride a bicycle on the pavement.' A constitution which effectively restricts the legislative powers of the supreme legislature in the system does not do so by imposing (or at any rate need not impose) duties on the legislature not to attempt to legislate in certain ways; instead it provides that any such purported legislation shall be void. It imposes not legal duties but legal disabilities. 'Limits' here implies not the presence of *duty* but the absence of legal power.

Such restrictions on the legislative power of Rex may well be called constitutional: but they are not mere conventions or moral matters with which courts are unconcerned. They are parts of the rule conferring authority to legislate and they vitally concern the courts, since they use such a rule as a criterion of the validity of purported legislative enactments coming before them. Yet though such restrictions are legal and not merely moral or conventional, their presence or absence cannot be expressed in terms of the presence or absence of a habit of obedience on the part of Rex to other persons. Rex may well be subject to such restrictions and never seek to evade them; yet there may be no one whom he habitually obeys. He merely fulfils the conditions for making valid law. Or he may try to evade the restrictions by issuing orders inconsistent with them; yet if he does this he will not have disobeyed any one; he will not have broken any superior legislators' law or violated a legal duty. He will surely have failed to make (though he does not break) a valid law. Conversely, if in the constitutional rule qualifying Rex to legislate there are no legal restrictions on Rex's authority to legislate, the fact that he habitually obeys the orders of Tyrannus, the king of the neighbouring territory, will neither deprive Rex's enactments of their status as law nor show that they are subordinate parts of a single system in which Tyrannus has supreme authority.

The foregoing very obvious considerations establish a number of points much obscured by the simple doctrine of sovereignty yet vital for the understanding of the foundation of a legal system. These we may summarize as follows: First, legal limitations on legislative authority consist not of duties imposed on the legislator to obey some superior legislator but of disabilities contained in rules which qualify him to legislate.

Secondly, in order to establish that a purported enactment is law we do not have to trace it back to the enactment, express or tacit, of a legislator who is 'sovereign' or 'unlimited' either in the sense that his authority to legislate is legally unrestricted or in the sense that he is a person who obeys no one else habitually. Instead we have to show that it was made by a legislator who was qualified to legislate under an existing rule and that either no restrictions are contained in the rule or there are none affecting this particular enactment.

Thirdly, in order to show that we have before us an independent legal system we do not have to show that its supreme legislator is legally unrestricted or obeys no other person habitually. We have to show merely that the rules which qualify the legislator do not confer superior authority on those who have also authority over other territory. Conversely, the fact that he is not subject to such foreign authority does not mean that he has unrestricted authority within his own territory.

Fourthly, we must distinguish between a legally unlimited

legislative authority and one which, though limited, is supreme in the system. Rex may well have been the highest legislating authority known to the law of the land, in the sense that all other legislation may be repealed by his, even though his own is restricted by a constitution.

Fifthly, and last, whereas the presence or absence of rules limiting the legislator's competence to legislate is crucial, the legislator's habits of obedience are at the most of some indirect evidential importance. The only relevance of the fact, if it be the fact, that the legislator is not in a habit of obedience to other persons is that sometimes it may afford some, though far from conclusive, evidence that his authority to legislate is not subordinate, by constitutional or legal rule, to that of others. Similarly, the only relevance of the fact that the legislator does habitually obey someone else is that this is some evidence that under the rules his authority to legislate is subordinate to that of others.

4. THE SOVEREIGN BEHIND THE LEGISLATURE

There are in the modern world many legal systems in which the body, normally considered to be the supreme legislature within the system, is subject to legal limitations on the exercise of its legislative powers; yet, as both lawyer and legal theorist would agree, the enactments of such a legislature within the scope of its limited powers are plainly law. In these cases, if we are to maintain the theory that wherever there is law there is a sovereign incapable of legal limitation, we must search for such a sovereign behind the legally limited legislature. Whether he is there to be found is the question which we must now consider.

We may neglect for the moment the provisions, which every legal system must make in one form or another, though not necessarily by a written constitution, as to the qualification of the legislators and 'the manner and form' of legislation. These may be considered as specifications of the identity of the legislative body and of what it must do to legislate rather than legal limitations on the scope of its legislative power; though, in fact, as the experience of South Africa has shown,[1] it is

---

[1] See *Harris* v. *Dönges* [1952] 1 TLR 1245.

difficult to give general criteria which satisfactorily distinguish mere provisions as to 'manner and form' of legislation or definitions of the legislative body from 'substantial' limitations.

Plain examples of substantive limitations are, however, to be found in federal constitutions such as those of the United States or Australia, where the division of powers between the central government and the member states, and also certain individual rights, cannot be changed by the ordinary processes of legislation. In these cases an enactment, either of the state or federal legislature, purporting to alter or inconsistent with the federal division of powers or with the individual rights protected in this way, is liable to be treated as *ultra vires*, and declared legally invalid by the courts to the extent that it conflicts with the constitutional provisions. The most famous of such legal limitations on legislative powers is the Fifth Amendment to the Constitution of the United States. This provides, among other things, that no person shall be deprived 'of life liberty or property without due process of law'; and statutes of Congress have been declared invalid by the courts when found to conflict with these or with other restrictions placed by the constitution on their legislative powers.

There are, of course, many different devices for protecting the provisions of a constitution from the operations of the legislature. In some cases, such as that of Switzerland, some provisions as to the rights of the member states of a federation and the rights of individuals, though mandatory in form, are treated as 'merely political' or hortatory. In such cases the courts are not accorded jurisdiction to 'review' the enactment of the federal legislature and to declare it invalid even though it may be in plain conflict with the provisions of the constitution as to the proper scope of the legislature's operations.[1] Certain provisions of the United States Constitution have been held to raise 'political questions', and where a case falls within this category the courts will not consider whether a statute violates the constitution.

Where legal limitations on the normal operations of the supreme legislature are imposed by a constitution, these themselves may or may not be immune from certain forms of

---

[1] See Art. 113 of the Constitution of Switzerland.

legal change. This depends on the nature of the provision made by the constitution for its amendment. Most constitutions contain a wide amending power to be exercised either by a body distinct from the ordinary legislature, or by the members of the ordinary legislature using a special procedure. The provision of Article V of the Constitution of the United States for amendments ratified by the legislatures of three-fourths of the States or by conventions in three-fourths thereof is an example of the first type of amending power; and the provision for amendment in the South Africa Act of 1909 s. 152 is an example of the second. But not all constitutions contain an amending power, and sometimes even where there is such an amending power certain provisions of the constitution which impose limits on the legislature are kept outside its scope; here the amending power is itself limited. This may be observed (though some limitations are no longer of practical importance) even in the Constitution of the United States. For Article V provides that 'no amendment made prior to the Year 1808 shall in any Manner affect the first and fourth Clauses in the Ninth Section of the first Article and that no State without its consent shall be deprived of its equal suffrage in the Senate'.

Where the legislature is subject to limitations which can, as in South Africa, be removed by the members of the legislature operating a special procedure, it is arguable that it may be identified with the sovereign incapable of legal limitation which the theory requires. The difficult cases for the theory are those where the restrictions on the legislature can, as in the United States, only be removed by the exercise of an amending power entrusted to a special body, or where the restrictions are altogether outside the scope of any amending power.

In considering the claim of the theory to account consistently for these cases we must recall, since it is often overlooked, that Austin himself in elaborating the theory did *not* identify the sovereign with the legislature even in England. This was his view although the Queen in Parliament is, according to the normally accepted doctrine, free from legal limitations on its legislative power, and so is often cited as a paradigm of what is meant by 'a sovereign legislature' in contrast with Congress or other legislatures limited by a 'rigid' constitution. None the less, Austin's view was that in any democracy it is not the elected representatives who constitute or form part of the sovereign body but the electors. Hence in England 'speaking accurately the members of the commons house are merely trustees for the body by which they are elected and appointed: and consequently the sovereignty always resides in the Kings Peers and the electoral body of the commons'.[1] Similarly, he held that in the United States sovereignty of each of the states and 'also of the larger state arising from the Federal Union resided in the states' governments as forming one aggregate body, meaning by a state's government not its ordinary legislature but the body of citizens which appoints its ordinary legislature'.[2]

Viewed in this perspective, the difference between a legal system in which the ordinary legislature is free from legal limitations, and one where the legislature is subject to them, appears merely as a difference between the manner in which the sovereign electorate chooses to exercise its sovereign powers. In England, on this theory, the only direct exercise made by the electorate of their share in the sovereignty consists in their election of representatives to sit in Parliament and the delegation to them of their sovereign power. This delegation is, in a sense, absolute since, though a trust is reposed in them not to abuse the powers thus delegated to them, this trust in such cases is a matter only for moral sanctions and the courts are not concerned with it, as they are with legal limitations on legislative power. By contrast, in the United States, as in every democracy where the ordinary legislature is legally limited, the electoral body has not confined its exercise of sovereign power to the election of delegates, but has subjected them to legal restrictions. Here the electorate may be considered an 'extraordinary and ulterior legislature' superior to the ordinary legislature which is legally 'bound' to observe the constitutional restrictions and, in cases of conflict, the courts will declare the Acts of the ordinary legislature invalid. Here then, in the electorate, is the sovereign free from all legal limitations which the theory requires.

[1] Austin, *Province of Jurisprudence Determined*, Lecture VI, pp. 230–1.
[2] Ibid., p. 251.

It is plain that in these further reaches of the theory the initial, simple conception of the sovereign has undergone a certain sophistication, if not a radical transformation. The description of the sovereign as 'the person or persons to whom the bulk of the society are in the habit of obedience' had, as we showed in Section 1 of this chapter, an almost literal application to the simplest form of society, in which Rex was an absolute monarch and no provision was made for the succession to him as legislator. Where such a provision was made, the consequent continuity of legislative authority, which is such a salient feature of a modern legal system, could not be expressed in the simple terms of habits of obedience, but required for its expression the notion of an accepted rule under which the successor had the right to legislate before actually doing so and receiving obedience. But the present identification of the sovereign with the electorate of a democratic state has no plausibility whatsoever, unless we give to the key words 'habit of obedience' and 'person or persons' a meaning which is quite different from that which they had when applied to the simple case; and it is a meaning which can only be made clear if the notion of an accepted rule is surreptitiously introduced. The simple scheme of habits of obedience and orders cannot suffice for this.

That this is so may be shown in many different ways. It emerges most clearly if we consider a democracy in which the electorate excludes only infants and mental defectives and so itself constitutes 'the bulk' of the population, or if we imagine a simple social group of sane adults where all have the right to vote. If we attempt to treat the electorate in such cases as the sovereign and apply to it the simple definitions of the original theory, we shall find ourselves saying that here the 'bulk' of the society habitually obey themselves. Thus the original clear image of a society divided into two segments: the sovereign free from legal limitation who gives orders, and the subjects who habitually obey, has given place to the blurred image of a society in which the majority obey orders given by the majority or by all. Surely we have here neither 'orders' in the original sense (expression of intention that *others* shall behave in certain ways) or 'obedience'.

To meet this criticism, a distinction may be made between the members of the society in their private capacity as individuals and the same persons in their official capacity as electors or legislators. Such a distinction is perfectly intelligible; indeed many legal and political phenomena are most naturally presented in such terms; but it cannot rescue the theory of sovereignty even if we are prepared to take the further step of saying that the individuals in their official capacity constitute *another person* who is habitually obeyed. For if we ask what is meant by saying of a group of persons that in electing a representative or in issuing an order, they have acted not 'as individuals' but 'in their official capacity', the answer can only be given in terms of their qualifications under certain rules and their compliance with other rules, which define what is to be done by them to make a valid election or a law. It is only by reference to such rules that we can identify something as an election or a law made by this body of persons. Such things are to be attributed to the body 'making' them not by the same simple natural test which we use in attributing an individual's spoken or written orders to him.

What then is it for such rules to exist? Since they are rules defining what the members of the society must do to function as an electorate (and so for the purposes of the theory as a sovereign) they cannot themselves have the status of orders issued by the sovereign, for nothing can count as orders issued by the sovereign unless the rules already exist and have been followed.

Can we then say that these rules are just parts of the description of the population's *habits* of obedience? In a simple case where the sovereign is a single person whom the bulk of the society obey if, and only if, he gives his orders in a certain form, e.g. in writing signed and witnessed, we might say (subject to the objections made in Section 1 to the use here of the notion of habit) that the rule that he must legislate in this fashion is just part of the description of the society's habit of obedience: they habitually obey him *when* he gives orders in this way. But, where the sovereign person is not identifiable independently of the rules, we cannot represent the rules in this way as merely the terms or conditions under which the society habitually obeys the sovereign. The rules are *constitutive* of the sovereign, not merely things which we should have to mention in a description of the habits of obedience to the sovereign. So we cannot say that in the present case the rules specifying the procedure of the electorate represent the conditions under which the society, as so many individuals, obeys itself as an electorate; for 'itself as an electorate' is not a reference to a person identifiable apart from the rules. It is a condensed reference to the fact that the electors have complied with rules in electing their representatives. At the most we might say (subject to the objections in Section 1) that the rules set forth the conditions under which the *elected persons* are habitually obeyed: but this would take us back to a form of the theory in which the legislature, not the electorate, is sovereign, and all the difficulties, arising from the fact that such a legislature might be subject to legal limitations on its legislative powers, would remain unsolved.

These arguments against the theory, like those of the earlier section of this chapter, are fundamental in the sense that they amount to the contention that the theory is not merely mistaken in detail, but that the simple idea of orders, habits, and obedience, cannot be adequate for the analysis of law. What is required instead is the notion of a rule conferring powers, which may be limited or unlimited, on persons qualified in certain ways to legislate by complying with a certain procedure.

Apart from what may be termed the general conceptual inadequacy of the theory, there are many ancillary objections to this attempt to accommodate within it the fact that what would ordinarily be regarded as the supreme legislature may be legally limited. If in such cases the sovereign is to be identified with the electorate, we may well ask, even where the electorate has an unlimited amending power by which the restrictions on the ordinary legislature could all be removed, if it is true that these restrictions are legal because the electorate has given orders which the ordinary legislature habitually obeys. We might waive our objection that legal limitations on legislative power are misrepresented as orders and so as *duties* imposed on it. Can we, even so, suppose that these restrictions are duties which the electorate has even *tacitly* ordered the legislature to fulfil? All the objections taken in earlier chapters to the idea of tacit orders apply with even greater force to its use here. Failure to exercise an amending power as complex in its manner of exercise as that in the United States constitution, may be a poor sign of the wishes of the electorate, though often a reliable sign of its ignorance and indifference. We are a long way indeed from the general who may, perhaps plausibly, be considered tacitly to have ordered his men to do what he knows the sergeant tells them to do.

Again, what are we to say, in the terms of the theory, if there are some restrictions on the legislature which are altogether outside the scope of the amending power entrusted to the electorate? This is not merely conceivable but actually is the position in some cases. Here the electorate is subject to legal limitations, and though it may be called an extraordinary legislature it is not free from legal limitation and so is not sovereign. Are we to say here that the society as a whole is sovereign and these legal limitations have been tacitly ordered by *it*, since it has failed to revolt against them? That this would make the distinction between revolution and legislation untenable is perhaps a sufficient reason for rejecting it.

Finally, the theory treating the electorate as sovereign only provides at the best for a limited legislature in a democracy where an electorate exists. Yet there is no absurdity in the notion of an hereditary monarch like Rex enjoying limited legislative powers which are both limited and supreme within the system.

V

LAW AS THE UNION OF PRIMARY AND SECONDARY RULES

I. A FRESH START

In the last three chapters we have seen that, at various crucial points, the simple model of law as the sovereign's coercive orders failed to reproduce some of the salient features of a legal system. To demonstrate this, we did not find it necessary to invoke (as earlier critics have done) international law or primitive law which some may regard as disputable or borderline examples of law; instead we pointed to certain familiar features of municipal law in a modern state, and showed that these were either distorted or altogether unrepresented in this over-simple theory.

The main ways in which the theory failed are instructive enough to merit a second summary. First, it became clear that though of all the varieties of law, a criminal statute, forbidding or enjoining certain actions under penalty, most resembles orders backed by threats given by one person to others, such a statute none the less differs from such orders in the important respect that it commonly applies to those who enact it and not merely to others. Secondly, there are other varieties of law, notably those conferring legal powers to adjudicate or legislate (public powers) or to create or vary legal relations (private powers) which cannot, without absurdity, be construed as orders backed by threats. Thirdly, there are legal rules which differ from orders in their mode of origin, because they are not brought into being by anything analogous to explicit prescription. Finally, the analysis of law in terms of the sovereign, habitually obeyed and necessarily exempt from all legal limitation, failed to account for the continuity of legislative authority characteristic of a modern legal system, and the sovereign person or persons could not be identified with either the electorate or the legislature of a modern state.

It will be recalled that in thus criticizing the conception of law as the sovereign's coercive orders we considered also a number of ancillary devices which were brought in at the cost of corrupting the primitive simplicity of the theory to rescue it from its difficulties. But these too failed. One device, the notion of a *tacit* order, seemed to have no application to the complex actualities of a modern legal system, but only to very much simpler situations like that of a general who deliberately refrains from interfering with orders given by his subordinates. Other devices, such as that of treating power-conferring rules as mere fragments of rules imposing duties, or treating all rules as directed only to officials, distort the ways in which these are spoken of, thought of, and actually used in social life. This had no better claim to our assent than the theory that all the rules of a game are 'really' directions to the umpire and the scorer. The device, designed to reconcile the self-binding character of legislation with the theory that a statute is an order given to *others*, was to distinguish the legislators acting in their official capacity, as *one* person ordering *others* who include themselves in their private capacities. This device, impeccable in itself, involved supplementing the theory with something it does not contain: this is the notion of a rule defining what must be done to legislate; for it is only in conforming with such a rule that legislators have an official capacity and a separate personality to be contrasted with themselves as private individuals.

The last three chapters are therefore the record of a failure and there is plainly need for a fresh start. Yet the failure is an instructive one, worth the detailed consideration we have given it, because at each point where the theory failed to fit the facts it was possible to see at least in outline why it was bound to fail and what is required for a better account. The root cause of failure is that the elements out of which the theory was constructed, viz. the ideas of orders, obedience, habits, and threats, do not include, and cannot by their combination yield, the idea of a rule, without which we cannot hope to elucidate even the most elementary forms of law. It is true that the idea of a rule is by no means a simple one: we have already seen in Chapter III the need, if we are to do justice to the complexity of a legal system, to discriminate between two different though related types. Under rules of the one type, which may well be considered the basic or primary type, human beings are required to do or abstain from certain actions, whether they wish to or not. Rules of the other type are in a sense parasitic upon or secondary to the first; for they provide that human beings may by doing or saying certain things introduce new rules of the primary type, extinguish or modify old ones, or in various ways determine their incidence or control their operations. Rules of the first type impose duties; rules of the second type confer powers, public or private. Rules of the first type concern actions involving physical movement or changes; rules of the second type provide for operations which lead not merely to physical movement or change, but to the creation or variation of duties or obligations.

We have already given some preliminary analysis of what is involved in the assertion that rules of these two types exist among a given social group, and in this chapter we shall not only carry this analysis a little farther but we shall make the general claim that in the combination of these two types of rule there lies what Austin wrongly claimed to have found in the notion of coercive orders, namely, 'the key to the science of jurisprudence'. We shall not indeed claim that wherever the word 'law' is 'properly' used this combination of primary and secondary rules is to be found; for it is clear that the diverse range of cases of which the word 'law' is used are not linked by any such simple uniformity, but by less direct relations—often of analogy of either form or content—to a central case. What we shall attempt to show, in this and the succeeding chapters, is that most of the features of law which have proved most perplexing and have both provoked and eluded the search for definition can best be rendered clear, if these two types of rule and the interplay between them are understood. We accord this union of elements a central place because of their explanatory power in elucidating the concepts that constitute the framework of legal thought. The justification for the use of the word 'law' for a range of apparently heterogeneous cases is a secondary matter which can be undertaken when the central elements have been grasped.

2. THE IDEA OF OBLIGATION

It will be recalled that the theory of law as coercive orders, notwithstanding its errors, started from the perfectly correct appreciation of the fact that where there is law, there human conduct is made in some sense non-optional or obligatory. In choosing this starting-point the theory was well inspired, and in building up a new account of law in terms of the interplay of primary and secondary rules we too shall start from the same idea. It is, however, here, at this crucial first step, that we have perhaps most to learn from the theory's errors.

Let us recall the gunman situation. A orders B to hand over his money and threatens to shoot him if he does not comply. According to the theory of coercive orders this situation illustrates the notion of obligation or duty in general. Legal obligation is to be found in this situation writ large; A must be the sovereign habitually obeyed and the orders must be general, prescribing courses of conduct not single actions. The plausibility of the claim that the gunman situation displays the meaning of obligation lies in the fact that it is certainly one in which we would say that B, if he obeyed, was 'obliged' to hand over his money. It is, however, equally certain that we should misdescribe the situation if we said, on these facts, that B 'had an obligation' or a 'duty' to hand over the money. So from the start it is clear that we need something else for an understanding of the idea of obligation. There is a difference, yet to be explained, between the assertion that someone *was obliged* to do something and the assertion that he *had an obligation* to do it. The first is often a statement about the beliefs and motives with which an action is done: B was obliged to hand over his money may simply mean, as it does in the gunman case, that he believed that some harm or other unpleasant consequences would befall him if he did not hand it over and he handed it over to avoid those consequences. In such cases the prospect of what would happen to the agent if he disobeyed has rendered something he would otherwise have preferred to have done (keep the money) less eligible.

Two further elements slightly complicate the elucidation of the notion of being obliged to do something. It seems clear that we should not think of B as obliged to hand over the money if the threatened harm was, according to common judgments, trivial in comparison with the disadvantage or serious consequences, either for B or for others, of complying with the orders, as it would be, for example, if A merely threatened to pinch B. Nor perhaps should we say that B was obliged, if there were no reasonable grounds for thinking that A could or would probably implement his threat of relatively serious harm. Yet, though such references to common judgments of comparative harm and reasonable estimates of likelihood, are implicit in this notion, the statement that a person was obliged to obey someone is, in the main, a psychological one referring to the beliefs and motives with which an action was done. But the statement that someone *had an obligation* to do something is of a very different type and there are many signs of this difference. Thus not only is it the case that the facts about B's action and his beliefs and motives in the gunman case, though sufficient to warrant the statement that B was obliged to hand over his purse, are *not sufficient* to warrant the statement that he had an obligation to do this; it is also the case that facts of this sort, i.e. facts about beliefs and motives, are *not necessary* for the truth of a statement that a person had an obligation to do something. Thus the statement that a person had an obligation, e.g. to tell the truth or report for military service, remains true even if he believed (reasonably or unreasonably) that he would never be found out and had nothing to fear from disobedience. Moreover, whereas the statement that he had this obligation is quite independent of the question whether or not he in fact reported for service, the statement that someone was obliged to do something, normally carries the implication that he actually did it.

Some theorists, Austin among them, seeing perhaps the general irrelevance of the person's beliefs, fears, and motives to the question whether he had an obligation to do something, have defined this notion not in terms of these subjective facts, but in terms of the *chance* or *likelihood* that the person having the obligation will suffer a punishment or 'evil' at the hands of others in the event of disobedience. This, in effect, treats statements of obligation not as psychological statements but as predictions or assessments of chances of incurring punishment or 'evil'. To many later theorists this has appeared as a revelation, bringing down to earth an elusive notion and restating it in the same clear, hard, empirical terms as are used in science. It has, indeed, been accepted sometimes as the only alternative to metaphysical conceptions of obligation or duty as invisible objects mysteriously existing 'above' or 'behind' the world of ordinary, observable facts. But there are many reasons for rejecting this interpretation of statements of obligation as predictions, and it is not, in fact, the only alternative to obscure metaphysics.

The fundamental objection is that the predictive interpretation obscures the fact that, where rules exist, deviations from them are not merely grounds for a prediction that hostile reactions will follow or that a court will apply sanctions to those who break them, but are also a reason or justification for such reaction and for applying the sanctions. We have already drawn attention in Chapter IV to this neglect of the internal aspect of rules and we shall elaborate it later in this chapter.

There is, however, a second, simpler, objection to the predictive interpretation of obligation. If it were true that the statement that a person had an obligation meant that *he* was likely to suffer in the event of disobedience, it would be a contradiction to say that he had an obligation, e.g. to report for military service but that, owing to the fact that he had escaped from the jurisdiction, or had successfully bribed the police or the court, there was not the slightest chance of his being caught or made to suffer. In fact, there is no contradiction in saying this, and such statements are often made and understood.

It is, of course, true that in a normal legal system, where sanctions are exacted for a high proportion of offences, an offender usually runs a risk of punishment; so, usually the statement that a person has an obligation and the statement that he is likely to suffer for disobedience will both be true together. Indeed, the connection between these two statements is somewhat stronger than this: at least in a municipal system it may well be true that, unless *in general* sanctions were likely to be exacted from offenders, there would be little or no point in making particular statements about a person's obligations. In this sense, such statements may be said to presuppose belief in the continued normal operation of the system of sanctions much as the statement 'he is out' in cricket presupposes, though it does not assert, that players, umpire, and scorer will probably take the usual steps. None the less, it is crucial for the understanding of the idea of obligation to see that in individual cases the statement that a person has an obligation under some rule and the prediction that he is likely to suffer for disobedience may diverge.

It is clear that obligation is not to be found in the gunman situation, though the simpler notion of being obliged to do something may well be defined in the elements present there. To understand the general idea of obligation as a necessary preliminary to understanding it in its legal form, we must turn to a different social situation which, unlike the gunman situation, includes the existence of social rules; for this situation contributes to the meaning of the statement that a person has an obligation in two ways. First, the existence of such rules, making certain types of behaviour a standard, is the normal, though unstated, background or proper context for such a statement; and, secondly, the distinctive function of such statement is to apply such a general rule to a particular person by calling attention to the fact that his case falls under it. We have already seen in Chapter IV that there is involved in the existence of any social rules a combination of regular conduct with a distinctive attitude to that conduct as a standard. We have also seen the main ways in which these differ from mere social habits, and how the varied normative vocabulary ('ought', 'must', 'should') is used to draw attention to the standard and to deviations from it, and to formulate the demands, criticisms, or acknowledgements which may be based on it. Of this class of normative words the words 'obligation' and 'duty' form an important sub-class, carrying with them certain implications not usually present in the others. Hence, though a grasp of the elements generally differentiating social rules from mere habits is certainly indispensable for understanding the notion of obligation or duty, it is not sufficient by itself.

The statement that someone has or is under an obligation does indeed imply the existence of a rule; yet it is not always the case that where rules exist the standard of behaviour required by them is conceived of in terms of obligation. 'He ought to have' and 'He had an obligation to' are not always interchangeable expressions, even though they are alike in carrying an implicit reference to existing standards of conduct or are used in drawing conclusions in particular cases from a general rule. Rules of etiquette or correct speech are certainly rules: they are more than convergent habits or regularities of behaviour; they are taught and efforts are made to maintain them; they are used in criticizing our own and other people's behaviour in the characteristic normative vocabulary. 'You ought to take your hat off', 'It is wrong to say "you was"'. But to use in connection with rules of this kind the words 'obligation' or 'duty' would be misleading and not merely stylistically odd. It would misdescribe a social situation; for though the line separating rules of obligation from others is at points a vague one, yet the main rationale of the distinction is fairly clear.

Rules are conceived and spoken of as imposing obligations when the general demand for conformity is insistent and the social pressure brought to bear upon those who deviate or threaten to deviate is great. Such rules may be wholly customary in origin: there may be no centrally organized system of punishments for breach of the rules; the social pressure may take only the form of a general diffused hostile or critical reaction which may stop short of physical sanctions. It may be limited to verbal manifestations of disapproval or of appeals to the individuals' respect for the rule violated; it may depend heavily on the operation of feelings of shame, remorse, and guilt. When the pressure is of this last-mentioned kind we may be inclined to classify the rules as part of the morality of the social group and the obligation under the rules as moral obligation. Conversely, when physical sanctions are prominent or usual among the forms of pressure, even though these are neither closely defined nor administered by officials but are left to the community at large, we shall be inclined to classify the rules as a primitive or rudimentary form of law. We may, of course, find both these types of serious social pressure behind what is, in an obvious sense, the same rule of conduct; sometimes this may occur with no indication that one of them is peculiarly appropriate as primary and the other secondary, and then the question whether we are confronted with a rule of morality or rudimentary law may not be susceptible of an answer. But for the moment the possibility of drawing the line between law and morals need not detain us. What is important is that the insistence on importance or *seriousness* of social pressure behind the rules is the primary factor determining whether they are thought of as giving rise to obligations.

Two other characteristics of obligation go naturally together with this primary one. The rules supported by this serious pressure are thought important because they are believed to be necessary to the maintenance of social life or some highly prized feature of it. Characteristically, rules so obviously essential as those which restrict the free use of violence are thought of in terms of obligation. So too rules which require honesty or truth or require the keeping of promises, or specify what is to be done by one who performs a distinctive role or function in the social group are thought of in terms of either 'obligation' or perhaps more often 'duty'. Secondly, it is generally recognized that the conduct required by these rules may, while benefiting others, conflict with what the person who owes the duty may wish to do. Hence obligations and duties are thought of as characteristically involving sacrifice or renunciation, and the standing possibility of conflict between obligation or duty and interest is, in all societies, among the truisms of both the lawyer and the moralist.

The figure of a *bond* binding the person obligated, which is buried in the word 'obligation', and the similar notion of a debt latent in the word 'duty' are explicable in terms of these three factors, which distinguish rules of obligation or duty from other rules. In this figure, which haunts much legal thought, the social pressure appears as a chain binding those who have obligations so that they are not free to do what they want. The other end of the chain is sometimes held by the group or their official representatives, who insist on performance or exact the penalty: sometimes it is entrusted by the group to a private individual who may choose whether or not to insist on performance or its equivalent in value to him. The first situation typifies the duties or obligations of criminal law and the second those of civil law where we think of private individuals having rights correlative to the obligations.

Natural and perhaps illuminating though these figures or metaphors are, we must not allow them to trap us into a misleading conception of obligation as essentially consisting in some feeling of pressure or compulsion experienced by those who have obligations. The fact that rules of obligation are generally supported by serious social pressure does not entail that to have an obligation under the rules is to experience feelings of compulsion or pressure. Hence there is no contradiction in saying of some hardened swindler, and it may often be true, that he had an obligation to pay the rent but felt no pressure to pay when he made off without doing so. To *feel* obliged and to have an obligation are different though frequently concomitant things. To identify them would be one way of misinterpreting, in terms of psychological feelings, the important internal aspect of rules to which we drew attention in Chapter III.

Indeed, the internal aspect of rules is something to which we must again refer before we can dispose finally of the claims of the predictive theory. For an advocate of that theory may well ask why, if social pressure is so important a feature of rules of obligation, we are yet so concerned to stress the inadequacies of the predictive theory; for it gives this very feature a central place by defining obligation in terms of the likelihood that threatened punishment or hostile reaction will follow deviation from certain lines of conduct. The difference may seem slight between the analysis of a statement of obligation as a prediction, or assessment of the chances, of hostile reaction to deviation, and our own contention that though this statement presupposes a background in which deviations from rules are generally met by hostile reactions, yet its characteristic use is not to predict this but to say that a person's case falls under such a rule. In fact, however, this difference is not a slight one. Indeed, until its importance is grasped, we cannot properly understand the whole distinctive style of human thought, speech, and action which is involved in the existence of rules and which constitutes the normative structure of society.

The following contrast again in terms of the 'internal' and

'external' aspect of rules may serve to mark what gives this distinction its great importance for the understanding not only of law but of the structure of any society.｜When a social group has certain rules of conduct, this fact affords an opportunity for many closely related yet different kinds of assertion; for it is possible to be concerned with the rules, either merely as an observer who does not himself accept them, or as a member of the group which accepts and uses them as guides to conduct. We may call these respectively the 'external' and the 'internal points of view'.｜Statements made from the external point of view may themselves be of different kinds. For the observer may, without accepting the rules himself, assert that the group accepts the rules, and thus may from outside refer to the way in which *they* are concerned with them from the internal point of view. But whatever the rules are, whether they are those of games, like chess or cricket, or moral or legal rules, we can if we choose occupy the position of an observer who does not even refer in this way to the internal point of view of the group. Such an observer is content merely to record the regularities of observable behaviour in which conformity with the rules partly consists and those further regularities, in the form of the hostile reaction, reproofs, or punishments, with which deviations from the rules are met. After a time the external observer may, on the basis of the regularities observed, correlate deviation with hostile reaction, and be able to predict with a fair measure of success, and to assess the chances that a deviation from the group's normal behaviour will meet with hostile reaction or punishment. Such knowledge may not only reveal much about the group, but might enable him to live among them without unpleasant consequences which would attend one who attempted to do so without such knowledge.

If, however, the observer really keeps austerely to this extreme external point of view and does not give any account of the manner in which members of the group who accept the rules view their own regular behaviour, his description of their life cannot be in terms of rules at all, and so not in the terms of the rule-dependent notions of obligation or duty. Instead, it will be in terms of observable regularities of conduct, predictions, probabilities, and signs. For such an observer, deviations by a member of the group from normal conduct will be a sign that hostile reaction is likely to follow, and nothing more. His view will be like the view of one who, having observed the working of a traffic signal in a busy street for some time, limits himself to saying that when the light turns red there is a high probability that the traffic will stop. He treats the light merely as a natural *sign that* people will behave in certain ways, as clouds are a *sign that* rain will come. In so doing he will miss out a whole dimension of the social life of those whom he is watching, since for them the red light is not merely a sign that others will stop: they look upon it as a *signal for* them to stop, and so a reason for stopping in conformity to rules which make stopping when the light is red a standard of behaviour and an obligation. To mention this is to bring into the account the way in which the group regards its own behaviour. It is to refer to the internal aspect of rules seen from their internal point of view.

The external point of view may very nearly reproduce the way in which the rules function in the lives of certain members of the group, namely those who reject its rules and are only concerned with them when and because they judge that unpleasant consequences are likely to follow violation. Their point of view will need for its expression, 'I was obliged to do it', 'I am likely to suffer for it if ...', 'You will probably suffer for it if ...', 'They will do that to you if ...'. But they will not need forms of expression like 'I had an obligation' or 'You have an obligation' for these are required only by those who see their own and other persons' conduct from the internal point of view. What the external point of view, which limits itself to the observable regularities of behaviour, cannot reproduce is the way in which the rules function as rules in the lives of those who normally are the majority of society. These are the officials, lawyers, or private persons who use them, in one situation after another, as guides to the conduct of social life, as the basis for claims, demands, admissions, criticism, or punishment, viz., in all the familiar transactions of life according to rules. For them the violation of a rule is not merely a basis for the prediction that a hostile reaction will follow but a *reason* for hostility.

At any given moment the life of any society which lives by

rules, legal or not, is likely to consist in a tension between those who, on the one hand, accept and voluntarily co-operate in maintaining the rules, and so see their own and other persons' behaviour in terms of the rules, and those who, on the other hand, reject the rules and attend to them only from the external point of view as a sign of possible punishment. One of the difficulties facing any legal theory anxious to do justice to the complexity of the facts is to remember the presence of both these points of view and not to define one of them out of existence. Perhaps all our criticisms of the predictive theory of obligation may be best summarized as the accusation that this is what it does to the internal aspect of obligatory rules.

3. THE ELEMENTS OF LAW

It is, of course, possible to imagine a society without a legislature, courts, or officials of any kind. Indeed, there are many studies of primitive communities which not only claim that this possibility is realized but depict in detail the life of a society where the only means of social control is that general attitude of the group towards its own standard modes of behaviour in terms of which we have characterized rules of obligation. A social structure of this kind is often referred to as one of 'custom'; but we shall not use this term, because it often implies that the customary rules are very old and supported with less social pressure than other rules. To avoid these implications we shall refer to such a social structure as one of primary rules of obligation. If a society is to live by such primary rules alone, there are certain conditions which, granted a few of the most obvious truisms about human nature and the world we live in, must clearly be satisfied. The first of these conditions is that the rules must contain in some form restrictions on the free use of violence, theft, and deception to which human beings are tempted but which they must, in general, repress, if they are to coexist in close proximity to each other. Such rules are in fact always found in the primitive societies of which we have knowledge, together with a variety of others imposing on individuals various positive duties to perform services or make contributions to the common life. Secondly, though such a society may exhibit the tension, already described, between those who accept the rules and those who reject the rules except where fear of social pressure induces them to conform, it is plain that the latter cannot be more than a minority, if so loosely organized a society of persons, approximately equal in physical strength, is to endure: for otherwise those who reject the rules would have too little social pressure to fear. This too is confirmed by what we know of primitive communities where, though there are dissidents and malefactors, the majority live by the rules seen from the internal point of view.

More important for our present purpose is the following consideration. It is plain that only a small community closely knit by ties of kinship, common sentiment, and belief, and placed in a stable environment, could live successfully by such a regime of unofficial rules. In any other conditions such a simple form of social control must prove defective and will require supplementation in different ways. In the first place, the rules by which the group lives will not form a system, but will simply be a set of separate standards, without any identifying or common mark, except of course that they are the rules which a particular group of human beings accepts. They will in this respect resemble our own rules of etiquette. Hence if doubts arise as to what the rules are or as to the precise scope of some given rule, there will be no procedure for settling this doubt, either by reference to an authoritative text or to an official whose declarations on this point are authoritative. For, plainly, such a procedure and the acknowledgement of either authoritative text or persons involve the existence of rules of a type different from the rules of obligation or duty which *ex hypothesi* are all that the group has. This defect in the simple social structure of primary rules we may call its *uncertainty*.

A second defect is the *static* character of the rules. The only mode of change in the rules known to such a society will be the slow process of growth, whereby courses of conduct once thought optional become first habitual or usual, and then obligatory, and the converse process of decay, when deviations, once severely dealt with, are first tolerated and then pass unnoticed. There will be no means, in such a society, of deliberately adapting the rules to changing circumstances, either by eliminating old rules or introducing new ones: for, again, the possibility of doing this presupposes the existence of rules of a different type from the primary rules of obligation by which alone the society lives. In an extreme case the rules may be static in a more drastic sense. This, though never perhaps fully realized in any actual community, is worth considering because the remedy for it is something very characteristic of law. In this extreme case, not only would there be no way of deliberately changing the general rules, but the obligations which arise under the rules in particular cases could not be varied or modified by the deliberate choice of any individual. Each individual would simply have fixed obligations or duties to do or abstain from doing certain things. It might indeed very often be the case that others would benefit from the performance of these obligations; yet if there are only primary rules of obligation they would have no power to release those bound from performance or to transfer to others the benefits which would accrue from performance. For such operations of release or transfer create changes in the initial positions of individuals under the primary rules of obliga-tion, and for these operations to be possible there must be rules of a sort different from the primary rules.

The third defect of this simple form of social life is the *inefficiency* of the diffuse social pressure by which the rules are maintained. Disputes as to whether an admitted rule has or has not been violated will always occur and will, in any but the smallest societies, continue interminably, if there is no agency specially empowered to ascertain finally, and authoritatively, the fact of violation. Lack of such final and authoritative determinations is to be distinguished from another weakness associated with it. This is the fact that punishments for viola-tions of the rules, and other forms of social pressure involv-ing physical effort or the use of force, are not administered by a special agency but are left to the individuals affected or to the group at large. It is obvious that the waste of time involved in the group's unorganized efforts to catch and punish offenders, and the smouldering vendettas which may result from self-help in the absence of an official monopoly of 'sanctions', may be serious. The history of law does, however, strongly suggest that the lack of official agencies to determine authoritatively the fact of violation of the rules is a much more serious defect; for many societies have remedies for this defect long before the other.

The remedy for each of these three main defects in this simplest form of social structure consists in supplementing the *primary* rules of obligation with *secondary* rules which are rules of a different kind. The introduction of the remedy for each defect might, in itself, be considered a step from the pre-legal into the legal world; since each remedy brings with it many elements that permeate law: certainly all three remedies together are enough to convert the regime of primary rules into what is indisputably a legal system. We shall consider in turn each of these remedies and show why law may most illuminatingly be characterized as a union of primary rules of obligation with such secondary rules. Before we do this, however, the following general points should be noted. Though the remedies consist in the introduction of rules which are certainly different from each other, as well as from the primary rules of obligation which they supplement, they have important features in common and are connected in various ways. Thus they may all be said to be on a different level from the primary rules, for they are all *about* such rules; in the sense that while primary rules are concerned with the actions that individuals must or must not do, these secondary rules are all concerned with the primary rules themselves. They specify the ways in which the primary rules may be conclusively ascertained, introduced, eliminated, varied, and the fact of their violation conclusively determined.

The simplest form of remedy for the *uncertainty* of the regime of primary rules is the introduction of what we shall call a 'rule of recognition'. This will specify some feature or features possession of which by a suggested rule is taken as a conclusive affirmative indication that it is a rule of the group to be supported by the social pressure it exerts. The existence of such a rule of recognition may take any of a huge variety of forms, simple or complex. It may, as in the early law of many societies, be no more than that an authoritative list or text of the rules is to be found in a written document or carved on some public monument. No doubt as a matter of history this step from the pre-legal to the legal may be accomplished in distinguishable stages, of which the first is the mere reduction to writing of hitherto unwritten rules. This is not itself the crucial step, though it is a very important one: (what is crucial is the acknowledgement of reference to the writing or inscription as *authoritative*, i.e. as the *proper* way of disposing of doubts as to the existence of the rule. Where there is such an acknowledgement there is a very simple form of secondary rule: a rule for conclusive identification of the primary rules of obligation.)

In a developed legal system the rules of recognition are of course more complex (instead of identifying rules exclusively by reference to a text or list they do so by reference to some general characteristic possessed by the primary rules. This may be the fact of their having been enacted by a specific body, or their long customary practice, or their relation to judicial decisions.) Moreover, where more than one of such general characteristics are treated as identifying criteria, provision may be made for their possible conflict by their arrangement in an order of superiority, as by the common subordination of custom or precedent to statute, the latter being a 'superior source' of law. Such complexity may make the rules of recognition in a modern legal system seem very different from the simple acceptance of an authoritative text: yet even in this simplest form, such a rule brings with it many elements distinctive of law. By providing an authoritative mark it introduces, although in embryonic form, the idea of a legal system: for the rules are now not just a discrete unconnected set but are, in a simple way, unified. (Further, in the simple operation of identifying a given rule as possessing the required feature of being an item on an authoritative list of rules we have the germ of the idea of legal validity.)

The remedy for the *static* quality of the regime of primary rules consists in the introduction of what we shall call 'rules of change'. The simplest form of such a rule is that which empowers an individual or body of persons to introduce new primary rules for the conduct of the life of the group, or of some class within it, and to eliminate old rules. As we have already argued in Chapter IV it is in terms of such a rule, and not in terms of orders backed by threats, that the ideas of legislative enactment and repeal are to be understood. Such rules of change may be very simple or very complex: the powers conferred may be unrestricted or limited in various ways: and the rules may, besides specifying the persons who are to legislate, define in more or less rigid terms the procedure to be followed in legislation. Plainly, there will be a very close connection between the rules of change and the rules of recognition: for where the former exist the latter will necessarily incorporate a reference to legislation as an identifying feature of the rules, though it need not refer to all the details of procedure involved in legislation. Usually some official certificate or official copy will, under the rules of recognition, be taken as a sufficient proof of due enactment. Of course if there is a social structure so simple that the only 'source of law' is legislation, the rule of recognition will simply specify enactment as the unique identifying mark or criterion of validity of the rules. This will be the case for example in the imaginary kingdom of Rex I depicted in Chapter IV: there the rule of recognition would simply be that whatever Rex I enacts is law.

We have already described in some detail the rules which confer on individuals power to vary their initial positions under the primary rules. Without such private power-conferring rules society would lack some of the chief amenities which law confers upon it. For the operations which these rules make possible are the making of wills, contracts, transfers of property, and many other voluntarily created structures of rights and duties which typify life under law, though of course an elementary form of power-conferring rule also underlies the moral institution of a promise. The kinship of these rules with the rules of change involved in the notion of legislation is clear, and as recent theory such as Kelsen's has shown, many of the features which puzzle us in the institutions of contract or property are clarified by thinking of the operations of making a contract or transferring property as the exercise of limited legislative powers by individuals.

The third supplement to the simple regime of primary rules, intended to remedy the *inefficiency* of its diffused social pressure, consists of secondary rules empowering individuals to make authoritative determinations of the question whether, on a particular occasion, a primary rule has been broken.

The minimal form of adjudication consists in such determinations, and we shall call the secondary rules which confer the power to make them 'rules of adjudication'. Besides identifying the individuals who are to adjudicate, such rules will also define the procedure to be followed. Like the other secondary rules these are on a different level from the primary rules: though they may be reinforced by further rules imposing duties on judges to adjudicate, they do not impose duties but confer judicial powers and a special status on judicial declarations about the breach of obligations. Again these rules, like the other secondary rules, define a group of important legal concepts: in this case the concepts of judge or court, jurisdiction and judgment. Besides these resemblances to the other secondary rules, rules of adjudication have intimate connections with them. Indeed, a system which has rules of adjudication is necessarily also committed to a rule of recognition of an elementary and imperfect sort. This is so because, if courts are empowered to make authoritative determinations of the fact that a rule has been broken, these cannot avoid being taken as authoritative determinations of what the rules are. So the rule which confers jurisdiction will also be a rule of recognition, identifying the primary rules through the judgments of the courts and these judgments will become a 'source' of law. It is true that this form of rule of recognition, inseparable from the minimum form of jurisdiction, will be very imperfect. Unlike an authoritative text or a statute book, judgments may not be couched in general terms and their use as authoritative guides to the rules depends on a somewhat shaky inference from particular decisions, and the reliability of this must fluctuate both with the skill of the interpreter and the consistency of the judges.

It need hardly be said that in few legal systems are judicial powers confined to authoritative determinations of the fact of violation of the primary rules. Most systems have, after some delay, seen the advantages of further centralization of social pressure; and have partially prohibited the use of physical punishments or violent self help by private individuals. Instead they have supplemented the primary rules of obligation by further secondary rules, specifying or at least limiting the penalties for violation, and have conferred upon judges, where they have ascertained the fact of violation, the exclusive power to direct the application of penalties by other officials. These secondary rules provide the centralized official 'sanctions' of the system.

If we stand back and consider the structure which has resulted from the combination of primary rules of obligation with the secondary rules of recognition, change and adjudication, it is plain that we have here not only the heart of a legal system, but a most powerful tool for the analysis of much that has puzzled both the jurist and the political theorist.

Not only are the specifically legal concepts with which the lawyer is professionally concerned, such as those of obligation and rights, validity and source of law, legislation and jurisdiction, and sanction, best elucidated in terms of this combination of elements. The concepts (which bestride both law and political theory) of the state, of authority, and of an official require a similar analysis if the obscurity which still lingers about them is to be dissipated. The reason why an analysis in these terms of primary and secondary rules has this explanatory power is not far to seek. Most of the obscurities and distortions surrounding legal and political concepts arise from the fact that these essentially involve reference to what we have called the internal point of view: the view of those who do not merely record and predict behaviour conforming to rules, but *use* the rules as standards for the appraisal of their own and others' behaviour. This requires more detailed attention in the analysis of legal and political concepts than it has usually received. Under the simple regime of primary rules the internal point of view is manifested in its simplest form, in the use of those rules as the basis of criticism, and as the justification of demands for conformity, social pressure, and punishment. Reference to this most elementary manifestation of the internal point of view is required for the analysis of the basic concepts of obligation and duty. With the addition to the system of secondary rules, the range of what is said and done from the internal point of view is much extended and diversified. With this extension comes a whole set of new concepts and they demand a reference to the internal point of view for their analysis. These include the notions of legislation, jurisdiction, validity, and, generally, of legal powers, private and public. There is a constant pull towards an analysis of these in the terms of ordinary or 'scientific', fact-stating or predictive discourse. But this can only reproduce their external aspect: to do justice to their distinctive, internal aspect we need to see the different ways in which the law-making operations of the legislator, the adjudication of a court, the exercise of private or official powers, and other 'acts-in-the-law' are related to secondary rules.

In the next chapter we shall show how the ideas of the validity of law and sources of law, and the truths latent among the errors of the doctrines of sovereignty may be rephrased and clarified in terms of rules of recognition. But we shall conclude this chapter with a warning: though the combination of primary and secondary rules merits, because it explains many aspects of law, the central place assigned to it, this cannot by itself illuminate every problem. The union of primary and secondary rules is at the centre of a legal system; but it is not the whole, and as we move away from the centre we shall have to accommodate, in ways indicated in later chapters, elements of a different character.

THE FOUNDATIONS OF A
LEGAL SYSTEM

I. RULE OF RECOGNITION AND LEGAL VALIDITY

According to the theory criticized in Chapter IV the foundations
of a legal system consist of the situation in which the majority of
a social group habitually obey the orders backed by threats of the
sovereign person or persons, who themselves habitually obey no
one. This social situation is, for this theory, both a necessary and
a sufficient condition of the existence of law. We have already
exhibited in some detail the incapacity of this theory to account
for some of the salient features of a modern municipal legal system:
yet none the less, as its hold over the minds of many thinkers suggests, it does contain, though in a blurred and misleading form,
certain truths about certain important aspects of law. These truths
can, however, only be clearly presented, and their importance
rightly assessed, in terms of the more complex social situation
where a secondary rule of recognition is accepted and used for the
identification of primary rules of obligation. It is this situation
which deserves, if anything does, to be called the foundations of
a legal system. In this chapter we shall discuss various elements
of this situation which have received only partial or misleading
expression in the theory of sovereignty and elsewhere.

Wherever such a rule of recognition is accepted, both private
persons and officials are provided with authoritative criteria for
identifying primary rules of obligation. The criteria so provided
may, as we have seen, take any one or more of a variety of forms:
these include reference to an authoritative text; to legislative enactment; to customary practice; to general declarations of specified
persons, or to past judicial decisions in particular cases. In a very
simple system like the world of Rex I depicted in Chapter IV,
where only what he enacts is law and no legal limitations upon his
legislative power are imposed by customary rule or constitutional

document, the sole criterion for identifying the law will be a simple reference to the fact of enactment by Rex I. The existence of this simple form of rule of recognition will be manifest in the general practice, on the part of officials or private persons, of identifying the rules by this criterion. In a modern legal system where there are a variety of 'sources' of law, the rule of recognition is correspondingly more complex: the criteria for identifying the law are multiple and commonly include a written constitution, enactment by a legislature, and judicial precedents. In most cases, provision is made for possible conflict by ranking these criteria in an order of relative subordination and primacy. It is in this way that in our system 'common law' is subordinate to 'statute'.

It is important to distinguish this relative *subordination* of one criterion to another from *derivation*, since some spurious support for the view that all law is essentially or 'really' (even if only 'tacitly') the product of legislation, has been gained from confusion of these two ideas. In our own system, custom and precedent are subordinate to legislation since customary and common law rules may be deprived of their status as law by statute. Yet they owe their status of law, precarious as this may be, not to a 'tacit' exercise of legislative power but to the\acceptance of a rule of recognition which accords them this independent though subordinate place.\Again, as in the simple case, the existence of such a complex rule of recognition with this hierarchical ordering of distinct criteria is manifested in the general practice of identifying the rules by such criteria.

In the day-to-day life of a legal system its rule of recognition is very seldom expressly formulated as a rule; though occasionally, courts in England may announce in general terms the relative place of one criterion of law in relation to another, as when they assert the supremacy of Acts of Parliament over other sources or suggested sources of law. For the most part the rule of recognition is not stated, but its existence is *shown* in the way in which particular rules are identified, either by courts or other officials or private persons or their advisers. There is, of course, a difference in the use made by courts of the criteria provided by the rule and the use of them by others: for when courts reach a particular conclusion on the footing that a particular rule has been correctly identified as law, what they say has a special authoritative status conferred on it by other rules. In this respect, as in many others, the rule of recognition of a legal system is like the scoring rule of a game. In the course of the game the general rule defining the activities which constitute scoring (runs, goals, &c.) is seldom formulated; instead it is *used* by officials and players in identifying the particular phases which count towards winning. Here too, the declarations of officials (umpire or scorer) have a special authoritative status attributed to them by other rules. Further, in both cases there is the possibility of a conflict between these authoritative applications of the rule and the general understanding of what the rule plainly requires according to its terms. This, as we shall see later, is a complication which must be catered for in any account of what it is for a system of rules of this sort to exist.

The use of unstated rules of recognition, by courts and others, in identifying particular rules of the system is characteristic of the internal point of view. Those who use them in this way thereby manifest their own acceptance of them as guiding rules and with this attitude there goes a characteristic vocabulary different from the natural expressions of the external point of view. Perhaps the simplest of these is the expression, 'It is the law that . . .', which we may find on the lips not only of judges, but of ordinary men living under a legal system, when they identify a given rule of the system. This, like the expression 'Out' or 'Goal', is the language of one assessing a situation by reference to rules which he in common with others acknowledges as appropriate for this purpose. This attitude of shared acceptance of rules is to be contrasted with that of an observer who records *ab extra* the fact that a social group accepts such rules but does not himself accept them. The natural expression of this external point of view is not 'It is the law that . . .' but 'In England they recognize as law . . . whatever the Queen in Parliament enacts. . . .' The first of these forms of expression we shall call an *internal statement* because it manifests the internal point of view and is naturally used by one who, accepting the rule of recognition and without stating the fact that it is accepted, applies the rule in recognizing some particular rule of the system as valid. The second form of expression we shall call an *external statement* because it is the natural language of an external observer of the system who, without himself accepting its rule of recognition, states the fact that others accept it.

If this use of an accepted rule of recognition in making internal statements is understood and carefully distinguished from an external statement of fact that the rule is accepted, many obscurities concerning the notion of legal 'validity' disappear. For the word 'valid' is most frequently, though not always, used, in just such internal statements, applying to a particular rule of a legal system, an unstated but accepted rule of recognition. To say that a given rule is valid is to recognize it as passing all the tests provided by the rule of recognition and so as a rule of the system. We can indeed simply say that the statement that a particular rule is valid means that it satisfies all the criteria provided by the rule of recognition. This is incorrect only to the extent that it might obscure the internal character of such statements; for, like the cricketers' 'Out', these statements of validity normally apply to a particular case a rule of recognition accepted by the speaker and others, rather than expressly state that the rule is satisfied.

Some of the puzzles connected with the idea of legal validity are said to concern the relation between the validity and the 'efficacy' of law. If by 'efficacy' is meant that the fact that a rule of law which requires certain behaviour is obeyed more often than not, it is plain that there is no necessary connection between the validity of any particular rule and *its* efficacy, unless the rule of recognition of the system includes among its criteria, as some do, the provision (sometimes referred to as a rule of obsolescence) that no rule is to count as a rule of the system if it has long ceased to be efficacious.

From the inefficacy of a particular rule, which may or may not count against its validity, we must distinguish a general disregard of the rules of the system. This may be so complete in character and so protracted that we should say, in the case of a new system, that it had never established itself as the legal system of a given group, or, in the case of a once-established system, that it had ceased to be the legal system of the group. In either case, the normal context or background for making any internal statement in terms of the rules of the system is absent. In such cases it would be generally *pointless* either to assess the rights and duties of particular persons by reference to the primary rules of a system or to assess the validity of any of its rules by reference to its rules of recognition. To insist on applying a system of rules which had either never actually been effective or had been discarded would, except in special circumstances mentioned below, be as futile as to assess the progress of a game by reference to a scoring rule which had never been accepted or had been discarded.

One who makes an internal statement concerning the validity of a particular rule of a system may be said to *presuppose* the truth of the external statement of fact that the system is generally efficacious. For the normal use of internal statements is in such a context of general efficacy. It would however be wrong to say that statements of validity 'mean' that the system is generally efficacious. For though it is normally pointless or idle to talk of the validity of a rule of a system which has never established itself or has been discarded, none the less it is not meaningless nor is it always pointless. One vivid way of teaching Roman Law is to speak *as if* the system were efficacious still and to discuss the validity of particular rules and solve problems in their terms; and one way of nursing hopes for the restoration of an old social order destroyed by revolution, and rejecting the new, is to cling to the criteria of legal validity of the old regime. This is implicitly done by the White Russian who still claims property under some rule of descent which was a valid rule of Tsarist Russia.

A grasp of the normal contextual connection between the internal statement that a given rule of a system is valid and the external statement of fact that the system is generally efficacious, will help us see in its proper perspective the common theory that to assert the validity of a rule is to predict that it will be enforced by courts or some other official action taken. In many ways this theory is similar to the predictive analysis of obligation which we considered and rejected in the last chapter. In both cases alike the motive for advancing this predictive theory is the conviction that only thus can metaphysical interpretations be avoided: that either a statement that a rule is valid must ascribe some mysterious property which cannot be detected by empirical means or it must be a prediction of future behaviour of officials. In both cases also the plausibility of the theory is due to the same important fact: that the truth of the external statement of fact, which an observer might record, that the system is generally efficacious and likely to continue so, is normally presupposed by anyone who accepts the rules and makes an internal statement of obligation or validity. The two are certainly very closely associated. Finally, in both cases alike the mistake of the theory is the same: it consists in neglecting the special character of the internal statement and treating it as an external statement about official action.

This mistake becomes immediately apparent when we consider how the judge's own statement that a particular rule is valid functions in judicial decision; for, though here too, in making such a statement, the judge presupposes but does not state the general efficacy of the system, he plainly is not concerned to predict his own or others' official action. His statement that a rule is valid is an internal statement recognizing that the rule satisfies the tests for identifying what is to count as law in his court, and constitutes not a prophecy of but part of the *reason* for his decision. There is indeed a more plausible case for saying that a statement that a rule is valid is a prediction when such a statement is made by a private person; for in the case of conflict between unofficial statements of validity or invalidity and that of a court in deciding a case, there is often good sense in saying that the former must then be withdrawn. Yet even here, as we shall see when we come in Chapter VII to investigate the significance of such conflicts between official declarations and the plain requirements of the rules, it may be dogmatic to assume that it is withdrawn as a statement now shown to be *wrong*, because it has falsely *predicted* what a court would say. For there are more reasons for withdrawing statements than the fact that they are wrong, and also more ways of being wrong than this allows.

The rule of recognition providing the criteria by which the validity of other rules of the system is assessed is in an important sense, which we shall try to clarify, an *ultimate* rule: and where, as is usual, there are several criteria ranked in order of relative subordination and primacy one of them is *supreme*.

These ideas of the ultimacy of the rule of recognition and the supremacy of one of its criteria merit some attention. It is important to disentangle them from the theory, which we have rejected, that somewhere in every legal system, even though it lurks behind legal forms, there must be a sovereign legislative power which is legally unlimited.

Of these two ideas, supreme criterion and ultimate rule, the first is the easiest to define. We may say that a criterion of legal validity or source of law is supreme if rules identified by reference to it are still recognized as rules of the system, even if they conflict with rules identified by reference to the other criteria, whereas rules identified by reference to the latter are not so recognized if they conflict with the rules identified by reference to the supreme criterion. A similar explanation in comparative terms can be given of the notions of 'superior' and 'subordinate' criteria which we have already used. It is plain that the notions of a superior and a supreme criterion merely refer to a *relative* place on a scale and do not import any notion of legally *unlimited* legislative power. Yet 'supreme' and 'unlimited' are easy to confuse—at least in legal theory. One reason for this is that in the simpler forms of legal system the ideas of ultimate rule of recognition, supreme criterion, and legally unlimited legislature seem to converge. For where there is a legislature subject to no constitutional limitations and competent by its enactment to deprive all other rules of law emanating from other sources of their status as law, it is part of the rule of recognition in such a system that enactment by that legislature is the supreme criterion of validity. This is, according to constitutional theory, the position in the United Kingdom. But even systems like that of the United States in which there is no such legally unlimited legislature may perfectly well contain an ultimate rule of recognition which provides a set of criteria of validity, one of which is supreme. This will be so, where the legislative competence of the ordinary legislature is limited by a constitution which contains no amending power, or places some clauses outside the scope of that power. Here there is no legally unlimited legislature, even in the widest interpretation of 'legislature'; but the system of course contains an ultimate rule of recognition and, in the clauses of its constitution, a supreme criterion of validity.

The sense in which the rule of recognition is the *ultimate* rule of a system is best understood if we pursue a very familiar chain of legal reasoning. If the question is raised whether some suggested rule is legally valid, we must, in order to answer the question, use a criterion of validity provided by some other rule. Is this purported by-law of the Oxfordshire County Council valid? Yes: because it was made in exercise of the powers conferred, and in accordance with the procedure specified, by a statutory order made by the Minister of Health. At this first stage the statutory order provides the criteria in terms of which the validity of the by-law is assessed. There may be no practical need to go farther; but there is a standing possibility of doing so. We may query the validity of the statutory order and assess its validity in terms of the statute empowering the minister to make such orders. Finally, when the validity of the statute has been queried and assessed by reference to the rule that what the Queen in Parliament enacts is law, we are brought to a stop in inquiries concerning validity: for we have reached a rule which, like the intermediate statutory order and statute, provides criteria for the assessment of the validity of other rules; but it is also unlike them in that there is no rule providing criteria for the assessment of its own legal validity.

There are, indeed, many questions which we can raise about this ultimate rule. We can ask whether it is the practice of courts, legislatures, officials, or private citizens in England actually to use this rule as an ultimate rule of recognition. Or has our process of legal reasoning been an idle game with the criteria of validity of a system now discarded? We can ask whether it is a satisfactory form of legal system which has such a rule at its root. Does it produce more good than evil? Are there prudential reasons for supporting it? Is there a moral obligation to do so? These are plainly very important questions; but, equally plainly, when we ask them about the rule of recognition, we are no longer attempting to answer the same kind of question about it as those which we answered about other rules with its aid. When we move from saying that a particular enactment is valid, because it satisfies the rule that what the Queen in Parliament enacts is law, to saying that in England this last rule is used by courts, officials, and private persons as the ultimate rule of recognition, we have moved from an internal statement of law asserting the validity of a rule of the system to an external statement of fact which an observer of the system might make even if he did not accept it. So too when we move from the statement that a particular enactment is valid, to the statement that the rule of recognition of the system is an excellent one and the system based on it is one worthy of support, we have moved from a statement of legal validity to a statement of value.

Some writers, who have emphasized the legal ultimacy of the rule of recognition, have expressed this by saying that, whereas the legal validity of other rules of the system can be demonstrated by reference to it, its own validity cannot be demonstrated but is 'assumed' or 'postulated' or is a 'hypothesis'. This may, however, be seriously misleading. Statements of legal validity made about particular rules in the day-to-day life of a legal system whether by judges, lawyers, or ordinary citizens do indeed carry with them certain presuppositions. They are internal statements of law expressing the point of view of those who accept the rule of recognition of the system and, as such, leave unstated much that could be stated in external statements of fact about the system. What is thus left unstated forms the normal background or context of statements of legal validity and is thus said to be 'presupposed' by them. But it is important to see precisely what these presupposed matters are, and not to obscure their character. They consist of two things. First, a person who seriously asserts the validity of some given rule of law, say a particular statute, himself makes use of a rule of recognition which he accepts as appropriate for identifying the law. Secondly, it is the case that this rule of recognition, in terms of which he assesses the validity of a particular statute, is not only accepted by him but is the rule of recognition actually accepted and employed in the general operation of the system. If the truth of this presupposition were doubted, it could be established by reference to actual practice: to the way in which courts identify what is to count as law, and to the general acceptance of or acquiescence in these identifications.

Neither of these two presuppositions are well described as 'assumptions' of a 'validity' which cannot be demonstrated. We only need the word 'validity', and commonly only use it, to answer questions which arise *within* a system of rules where the status of a rule as a member of the system depends on its satisfying certain criteria provided by the rule of recognition. No such question can arise as to the validity of the very rule of recognition which provides the criteria; it can neither be valid nor invalid but is simply accepted as appropriate for use in this way. To express this simple fact by saying darkly that its validity is 'assumed but cannot be demonstrated', is like saying that we assume, but can never demonstrate, that the standard metre bar in Paris which is the ultimate test of the correctness of all measurement in metres, is itself correct.

A more serious objection is that talk of the 'assumption' that the ultimate rule of recognition is valid conceals the essentially factual character of the second presupposition which lies behind the lawyers' statements of validity. No doubt the practice of judges, officials, and others, in which the actual existence of a rule of recognition consists, is a complex matter. As we shall see later, there are certainly situations in which questions as to the precise content and scope of this kind of rule, and even as to its existence, may not admit of a clear or determinate answer. None the less it is important to distinguish 'assuming the validity' from 'presupposing the existence' of such a rule; if only because failure to do this obscures what is meant by the assertion that such a rule *exists*.

In the simple system of primary rules of obligation sketched in the last chapter, the assertion that a given rule existed could only be an external statement of fact such as an observer who did not accept the rules might make and verify by ascertaining whether or not, as a matter of fact, a given mode of behaviour was generally accepted as a standard and was accompanied by those features which, as we have seen, distinguish a social rule from mere convergent habits. It is in this way also that we should now interpret and verify the assertion that in England a rule—though not a legal one—exists that we must bare the head on entering a church. If such rules as these are found to exist in the actual practice of a social group, there is no separate question of their validity to be discussed, though of course their value or desirability is open to question. Once their existence has been established as a fact we should only confuse matters by affirming or denying that they were valid or by saying that 'we assumed' but could not show their validity. Where, on the other hand, as in a mature legal system, we have a system of rules which includes a rule of recognition so that the status of a rule as a member of the system now depends on whether it satisfies certain criteria provided by the rule of recognition, this brings with it a new application of the word 'exist'. The statement that a rule exists may now no longer be what it was in the simple case of customary rules—an external statement of the *fact* that a certain mode of behaviour was generally accepted as a standard in practice. It may now be an internal statement applying an accepted but unstated rule of recognition and meaning (roughly) no more than 'valid given the system's criteria of validity'. In this respect, however, as in others a rule of recognition is unlike other rules of the system. The assertion that it exists can only be an external statement of fact. For whereas a subordinate rule of a system may be valid and in that sense 'exist' even if it is generally disregarded, the rule of recognition exists only as a complex, but normally concordant, practice of the courts, officials, and private persons in identifying the law by reference to certain criteria. Its existence is a matter of fact.

2. NEW QUESTIONS

Once we abandon the view that the foundations of a legal system consist in a habit of obedience to a legally unlimited sovereign and substitute for this the conception of an ultimate rule of recognition which provides a system of rules with its criteria of validity, a range of fascinating and important questions confronts us. They are relatively new questions; for they were veiled so long as jurisprudence and political theory were committed to the older ways of thought. They are also difficult questions, requiring for a full answer, on the one hand a grasp of some fundamental issues of constitutional law and on the other an appreciation of the characteristic manner in which legal forms may silently shift and change. We shall therefore investigate these questions only so far as they bear upon the wisdom or unwisdom of insisting, as we have done, that a central place should be assigned to the union of primary and secondary rules in the elucidation of the concept of law.

The first difficulty is that of classification; for the rule which, in the last resort, is used to identify the law escapes the conventional categories used for describing a legal system, though these are often taken to be exhaustive. Thus, English constitutional writers since Dicey have usually repeated the statement that the constitutional arrangements of the United Kingdom consist partly of laws strictly so called (statutes, orders in council, and rules embodied in precedents) and partly of conventions which are mere usages, understandings, or customs. The latter include important rules such as that the Queen may not refuse her consent to a bill duly passed by Peers and Commons; there is, however, no legal duty on the Queen to give her consent and such rules are called conventions because the courts do not recognize them as imposing a legal duty. Plainly the rule that what the Queen in Parliament enacts is law does not fall into either of these categories. It is not a convention, since the courts are most intimately concerned with it and they use it in identifying the law; and it is not a rule on the same level as the 'laws strictly so called' which it is used to identify. Even if it were enacted by statute, this would not reduce it to the level of a statute; for the legal status of such an enactment necessarily would depend on the fact that the rule existed antecedently to and independently of the enactment. Moreover, as we have shown in the last section, its existence, unlike that of a statute, must consist in an actual practice.

This aspect of things extracts from some a cry of despair: how can we show that the fundamental provisions of a constitution which are surely law are really law? Others reply with the insistence that at the base of legal systems there is something which is 'not law', which is 'pre-legal', 'meta-legal', or is just 'political fact'. This uneasiness is a sure sign that the categories used for the description of this most important feature in any system of law are too crude. The case for calling the rule of recognition 'law' is that the rule providing criteria for the identification of other rules of the system may well be thought a defining feature of a legal system, and so itself worth calling 'law'; the case for calling it 'fact' is that to assert that such a rule exists is indeed to make an external statement of an actual fact concerning the manner in which *define*

the rules of an 'efficacious' system are identified. Both these aspects claim attention but we cannot do justice to them both by choosing one of the labels 'law' or 'fact'. Instead, we need to remember that the ultimate rule of recognition may be regarded from two points of view: one is expressed in the external statement of fact that the rule exists in the actual practice of the system; the other is expressed in the internal statements of validity made by those who use it in identifying the law.

A second set of questions arises out of the hidden complexity and vagueness of the assertion that a legal system *exists* in a given country or among a given social group. When we make this assertion we in fact refer in compressed, portmanteau form to a number of heterogeneous social facts, usually concomitant. The standard terminology of legal and political thought, developed in the shadow of a misleading theory, is apt to oversimplify and obscure the facts. Yet when we take off the spectacles constituted by this terminology and look at the facts, it becomes apparent that a legal system, like a human being, may at one stage be unborn, at a second not yet wholly independent of its mother, then enjoy a healthy independent existence, later decay and finally die. These halfway stages between birth and normal, independent existence and, again, between that and death, put out of joint our familiar ways of describing legal phenomena. They are worth our study because, baffling as they are, they throw into relief the full complexity of what we take for granted when, in the normal case, we make the confident and true assertion that in a given country a legal system exists.

One way of realizing this complexity is to see just where the simple, Austinian formula of a general habit of obedience to orders fails to reproduce or distorts the complex facts which constitute the minimum conditions which a society must satisfy if it is to have a legal system. We may allow that this formula does designate one necessary condition: namely, that where the laws impose obligations or duties these should be generally obeyed or at any rate not generally disobeyed. But, though essential, this only caters for what we may term the 'end product' of the legal system, where it makes its impact on the private citizen; whereas its day-to-day existence consists also in the official creation, the official identification, and the official use and application of law. The relationship with law involved here can be called 'obedience' only if that word is extended so far beyond its normal use as to cease to characterize informatively these operations. In no ordinary sense of 'obey' are legislators obeying rules when, in enacting laws, they conform to the rules conferring their legislative powers, except of course when the rules conferring such powers are reinforced by rules imposing a duty to follow them. Nor, in failing to conform with these rules do they 'disobey' a law, though they may fail to make one. Nor does the word 'obey' describe well what judges do when they apply the system's rule of recognition and recognize a statute as valid law and use it in the determination of disputes. We can of course, if we wish, preserve the simple terminology of 'obedience' in face of the facts by many devices. One is to express, e.g. the use made by judges of general criteria of validity in recognizing a statute, as a case of obedience to orders given by the 'Founders of the Constitution', or (where there are no 'Founders') as obedience to a 'depsychologized command' i.e. a command without a commander. But this last should perhaps have no more serious claims on our attention than the notion of a nephew without an uncle. Alternatively we can push out of sight the whole official side to law and forgo the description of the use of rules made in legislation and adjudication, and instead, think of the whole official world as one person (the 'sovereign') issuing orders, through various agents or mouthpieces, which are habitually obeyed by the citizen. But this is either no more than a convenient shorthand for complex facts which still await description, or a disastrously confusing piece of mythology.

It is natural to react from the failure of attempts to give an account of what it is for a legal system to exist, in the agreeably simple terms of the habitual obedience which is indeed characteristic of (though it does not always exhaustively describe) the relationship of the ordinary citizen to law, by making the opposite error. This consists in taking what is characteristic (though again not exhaustive) of the official activities, especially the judicial attitude or relationship to law, and treating this as an adequate account of what must exist in a social group which has a legal system. This amounts to replacing the simple conception that the bulk of society habitually obey the law with the conception that they must generally share, accept, or regard as binding the ultimate rule of recognition specifying the criteria in terms of which the validity of laws are ultimately assessed. Of course we can imagine, as we have done in Chapter III, a simple society where knowledge and understanding of the sources of law are widely diffused. There the 'constitution' was so simple that no fiction would be involved in attributing knowledge and acceptance of it to the ordinary citizen as well as to the officials and lawyers. In the simple world of Rex I we might well say that there was more than mere habitual obedience by the bulk of the population to his word. There it might well be the case that both they and the officials of the system 'accepted', in the same explicit, conscious way, a rule of recognition specifying Rex's word as the criterion of valid law for the whole society, though subjects and officials would have different roles to play and different relationships to the rules of law identified by this criterion. To insist that this state of affairs, imaginable in a simple society, always or usually exists in a complex modern state would be to insist on a fiction. Here surely the reality of the situation is that a great proportion of ordinary citizens—perhaps a majority—have no general conception of the legal structure or of its criteria of validity. The law which he obeys is something which he knows of only as 'the law'. He may obey it for a variety of different reasons and among them may often, though not always, be the knowledge that it will be best for him to do so. He will be aware of the general likely consequences of disobedience: that there are officials who may arrest him and others who will try him and send him to prison for breaking the law. So long as the laws which are valid by the system's tests of validity are obeyed by the bulk of the population this surely is all the evidence we need in order to establish that a given legal system exists.

But just because a legal system is a complex union of primary and secondary rules, this evidence is not all that is needed to describe the relationships to law involved in the existence of a legal system. It must be supplemented by a description of the relevant relationship of the officials of the system to the secondary rules which concern them as officials. Here what is crucial is that there should be a unified or shared official acceptance of the rule of recognition containing the system's criteria of validity. But it is just here that the simple notion of general obedience, which was adequate to characterize the indispensable minimum in the case of ordinary citizens, is inadequate. The point is not, or not merely, the 'linguistic' one that 'obedience' is not naturally used to refer to the way in which these secondary rules are respected as rules by courts and other officials. We could find, if necessary, some wider expression like 'follow', 'comply', or 'conform to' which would characterize both what ordinary citizens do in relation to law when they report for military service and what judges do when they identify a particular statute as law in their courts, on the footing that what the Queen in Parliament enacts is law. But these blanket terms would merely mask vital differences which must be grasped if the minimum conditions involved in the existence of the complex social phenomenon which we call a legal system are to be understood.

What makes 'obedience' misleading as a description of what legislators do in conforming to the rules conferring their powers, and of what courts do in applying an accepted ultimate rule of recognition, is that obeying a rule (or an order) *need* involve no thought on the part of the person obeying that what he does is the right thing both for himself and for others to do: he need have no view of what he does as a fulfilment of a standard of behaviour for others of the social group. He need not think of his conforming behaviour as 'right', 'correct', or 'obligatory'. His attitude, in other words, need not have any of that critical character which is involved whenever social rules are accepted and types of conduct are treated as general standards. He need not, though he may, share the internal point of view accepting the rules as standards for all to whom they apply. Instead, he may think of the rule only as something demanding action from *him* under threat of penalty; he may obey it out of fear of the consequences, or from inertia, without thinking of himself or others as having an obligation to do so and without being disposed to criticize either himself or others for deviations. But this merely personal concern with the rules, which is all the ordinary citizen *may* have in obeying them, cannot characterize the attitude of the courts to the rules with which they operate as courts. This is most patently the case with the ultimate rule of recognition in terms of which the validity of other rules is assessed. This, if it is to exist at all, must be regarded from the internal point of view as a public, common standard of correct judicial decision, and not as something which each judge merely obeys for his part only. Individual courts of the system though they may, on occasion, deviate from these rules must, in general, be critically concerned with such deviations as lapses from standards, which are essentially common or public. This is not merely a matter of the efficiency or health of the legal system, but is logically a necessary condition of our ability to speak of the existence of a single legal system. If only some judges acted 'for their part only' on the footing that what the Queen in Parliament enacts is law, and made no criticisms of those who did not respect this rule of recognition, the characteristic unity and continuity of a legal system would have disappeared. For this depends on the acceptance, at this crucial point, of common standards of legal validity. In the interval between these vagaries of judicial behaviour and the chaos which would ultimately ensue when the ordinary man was faced with contrary judicial orders, we would be at a loss to describe the situation. We would be in the presence of a *lusus naturae* worth thinking about only because it sharpens our awareness of what is often too obvious to be noticed.

There are therefore two minimum conditions necessary and sufficient for the existence of a legal system. On the one hand, those rules of behaviour which are valid according to the system's ultimate criteria of validity must be generally obeyed, and, on the other hand, its rules of recognition specifying the criteria of legal validity and its rules of change and adjudication must be effectively accepted as common public standards of official behaviour by its officials. The first condition is the only one which private citizens *need* satisfy: they may obey each 'for his part only' and from any motive whatever; though in a healthy society they will in fact often accept these rules as common standards of behaviour and acknowledge an obligation to obey them, or even trace this obligation to a more general obligation to respect the constitution. The second condition must also be satisfied by the officials of the system. They must regard these as common standards of official behaviour and appraise critically their own and each other's deviations as lapses. Of course it is also true that besides these there will be many primary rules which apply to officials in their merely personal capacity which they need only obey.

The assertion that a legal system exists is therefore a Janus-faced statement looking both towards obedience by ordinary citizens and to the acceptance by officials of secondary rules as critical common standards of official behaviour. We need not be surprised at this duality. It is merely the reflection of the composite character of a legal system as compared with a simpler decentralized pre-legal form of social structure which consists only of primary rules. In the simpler structure, since there are no officials, the rules must be widely accepted as setting critical standards for the behaviour of the group. If, there, the internal point of view is not widely disseminated there could not logically be any rules. But where there is a union of primary and secondary rules, which is, as we have argued, the most fruitful way of regarding a legal system, the acceptance of the rules as common standards for the group may be split off from the relatively passive matter of the ordinary individual acquiescing in the rules by obeying them for his part alone. In an extreme case the internal point of view with its characteristic normative use of legal language ('This is a valid rule') might be confined to the official world. In this more complex system, only officials might accept and use the system's criteria of legal validity. The society in which this was so might be deplorably sheeplike; the sheep might end in the slaughter-house. But there is little reason for thinking that it could not exist or for denying it the title of a legal system.

3. THE PATHOLOGY OF A LEGAL SYSTEM

Evidence for the existence of a legal system must therefore be drawn from two different sectors of social life. The normal, unproblematic case where we can say confidently that a legal system exists, is just one where it is clear that the two sectors are congruent in their respective typical concerns with the law. Crudely put, the facts are, that the rules recognized as valid at the official level are generally obeyed. Sometimes, however, the official sector may be detached from the private sector, in the sense that there is no longer general obedience to the rules which are valid according to the criteria of validity in use in the courts. The variety of ways in which this may happen belongs to the pathology of legal systems; for they represent a breakdown in the complex congruent practice which is referred to when we make the external statement of fact that a legal system exists. There is here a partial failure of what is presupposed whenever, from within the particular system, we make internal statements of law. Such a breakdown may be the product of different disturbing factors. 'Revolution', where rival claims to govern are made from within the group, is only one case, and though this will always involve the breach of some of the laws of the existing system, it may entail only the legally unauthorized substitution of a new set of individuals as officials, and not a new constitution or legal system. Enemy occupation, where a rival claim to govern without authority under the existing system comes from without, is another case; and the simple breakdown of ordered legal control in the face of anarchy or banditry without political pretensions to govern is yet another.

In each of these cases there may be half-way stages during which the courts function, either on the territory or in exile, and still use the criteria of legal validity of the old once firmly established system; but these orders are ineffective in the territory. The stage at which it is right to say in such cases that the legal system has finally ceased to exist is a thing not susceptible of any exact determination. Plainly, if there is some considerable chance of a restoration or if the disturbance of the established system is an incident in a general war of which the issue is still uncertain, no unqualified assertion that it has ceased to exist would be warranted. This is so just because the statement that a legal system exists is of a sufficiently broad and general type to allow for interruptions; it is not verified or falsified by what happens in short spaces of time.

Of course difficult questions may arise after such interruptions have been succeeded by the resumption of normal relations between the courts and the population. A government returns from exile on the expulsion of occupying forces or the defeat of a rebel government; then questions arise as to what was or was not 'law' in the territory during the period of interruption. Here what is most important is to understand that this question may *not* be one of fact. If it were one of fact it would have to be settled by asking whether the interruption was so protracted and complete that the situation must be described as one in which the original system had ceased to exist and a new one was set up similar to the old, on the return from exile. Instead the question may be raised as one of international law, or it may, somewhat paradoxically, arise as a question of law within the very system of law existing since the restoration. In the latter case it might well be that the restored system included a retrospective law declaring the system to have been (or, more candidly, to be 'deemed' to have been) continuously the law of the territory. This might be done even if the interruption were so long as to make such a declaration seem quite at variance with the conclusion that might have been reached had the question been treated as a question of fact. In such a case there is no reason why the declaration should not stand as a rule of the restored system, determining the law which its courts must apply to incidents and transactions occurring during the period of interruption.

There is only a paradox here if we think of a legal system's statements of law, concerning what are to be deemed to be phases of its own past, present, or future existence, as rivals to the factual statement about its existence, made from an external point of view. Except for the apparent puzzle of self-reference the legal status of a provision in an existing system concerning the period during which it is to be considered to have existed, is no different from a law of one system declaring that a certain system is still in existence in another country, though the latter is not likely to have many practical consequences. We are, in fact, quite clear that the legal system in existence in the territory of the Soviet Union is not in fact that of the Tsarist regime. But if a statute of the British Parliament declared that the law of Tsarist Russia was still the law of Russian territory this would indeed have meaning and legal effect as part of English law referring to the USSR, but it would leave unaffected the truth of the statement of fact contained in our last sentence. The force and meaning of the statute would be merely to determine the law to be applied in English courts, and so in England, to cases with a Russian element.

The converse of the situation just described is to be seen in the fascinating moments of transition during which a new legal system emerges from the womb of an old one—sometimes only after a Caesarian operation. The recent history of the Commonwealth is an admirable field of study of this aspect of the embryology of legal systems. The schematic, simplified outline of this development is as follows. At the beginning of a period we may have a colony with a local legislature, judiciary, and executive. This constitutional structure has been set up by a statute of the United Kingdom Parliament, which retains full legal competence to legislate for the colony; this includes power to amend or repeal both the local laws and any of its own statutes, including those referring to the constitution of the colony. At this stage the legal system of the colony is plainly a subordinate part of a wider system characterized by the ultimate rule of recognition that what the Queen in Parliament enacts is law for (*inter alia*) the colony. At the end of the period of development we find that the ultimate rule of recognition has shifted, for the legal competence of the Westminster Parliament to legislate for the former colony is no longer recognized in its courts. It is still true that much of the constitutional structure of the former colony is to be found in the original statute of the Westminster Parliament: but this is now only an historical fact, for it no longer owes its contemporary legal status in the territory to the authority of the Westminster Parliament. The legal system in the former colony has now a 'local root' in that the rule of recognition specifying the ultimate criteria of legal validity no longer refers to enactments of a legislature of another territory. The new rule rests simply on the fact that it is accepted and used as such a rule in the judicial and other official operations of a local system whose rules are generally obeyed. Hence, though the composition, mode of enactment, and structure of the local legislature may still be that prescribed in the original constitution, its enactments are valid now not because they are the exercise of powers granted by a valid statute of the Westminster Parliament. They are valid because, under the rule of recognition locally accepted, enactment by the local legislature is an ultimate criterion of validity.

This development may be achieved in many different ways. The parent legislature may, after a period in which it never in fact exercises its formal legislative authority over the colony except with its consent, finally retire from the scene by renouncing legislative power over the former colony. Here it is to be noted that there are theoretical doubts as to whether the courts in the United Kingdom would recognize the legal competence of the Westminster Parliament thus irrevocably to cut down its powers. The break away may, on the other hand, be achieved only by violence. But in either case we have at the end of this development two independent legal systems. This is a factual statement and not the less factual because it is one concerning the existence of legal systems. The main evidence for it is that in the former colony the ultimate rule of recognition now accepted and used no longer includes among the criteria of validity, any reference to the operations of legislatures of other territories.

Again, however, and here Commonwealth history provides intriguing examples, it is possible that though in fact the legal system of the colony is now independent of its parent, the parent system may not recognize this fact. It may still be part of English law that the Westminster Parliament has retained, or can legally regain, power to legislate for the colony; and the domestic English courts may, if any cases involving a conflict between a Westminster statute and one of the local legislature come before them, give effect to this view of the matter. In this case propositions of English law seem to conflict with fact. The law of the colony is *not* recognized in English courts as being what it is in fact: an independent legal system with its own local, ultimate rule of recognition. As a matter of fact there will be two legal systems, where English law will insist that there is only one But, just because one assertion is a statement of fact and the other a proposition of (English) law, the two do not logically conflict. To make the position clear we can, if we like, say that the statement of fact is true and the proposition of English law is 'correct in English law'.

Similar distinctions between the factual assertion (or denial) that two independent legal systems exist, and propositions of law about the existence of a legal system, need to be borne in mind in considering the relationship between public international law and municipal law. Some very strange theories owe their only plausibility to a neglect of this distinction.

To complete this crude survey of the pathology and embryology of legal systems we should notice other forms of partial failure of the normal conditions, the congruence of which is asserted by the unqualified assertion that a legal system exists. The unity among officials, the existence of which is normally presupposed when internal statements of law are made within the system, may partly break down. It may be that, over certain constitutional issues and only over those, there is a division within the official world ultimately leading to a division among the judiciary. The beginning of such a split over the ultimate criteria to be used in identifying the law was seen in the constitutional troubles in South Africa in 1954, which came before the courts in *Harris* v. *Dönges*.[1] Here the legislature acted on a different view of its legal competence and powers from that taken by the courts, and enacted measures which the courts declared invalid. The response to this was the creation by the legislature of a special appellate 'court' to hear appeals from judgments of the ordinary courts which invalidated the enactments of the legislature. This court, in due course, heard such appeals and reversed the judgments of the ordinary courts; in turn, the ordinary courts declared the legislation creating the special courts invalid and their judgments a legal nullity. Had this process not been stopped (because the Government found it unwise to pursue this means of getting its way), we should have had an endless oscillation between two views of the competence of the legislature and so of the criteria of valid law. The normal conditions of official, and especially of judicial, harmony, under which alone it is possible to identify the system's rule of recognition, would have been suspended. Yet the great mass of legal operations not touching on this constitutional issue would go on as before. Till the population became divided and 'law and order'

---

[1] [1952] I TLR 1245.

broke down it would be misleading to say that the original legal system had ceased to exist: for the expression 'the same legal system' is too broad and elastic to permit unified official consensus on *all* the original criteria of legal validity to be a necessary condition of the legal system remaining 'the same'. All we could do would be to describe the situation as we have done and note it as a substandard, abnormal case containing within it the threat that the legal system will dissolve.

This last case brings us to the borders of a wider topic which we discuss in the next chapter both in relation to the high constitutional matter of a legal system's ultimate criteria of validity and its 'ordinary' law. All rules involve recognizing or classifying particular cases as instances of general terms, and in the case of everything which we are prepared to call a rule it is possible to distinguish clear central cases, where it certainly applies and others where there are reasons for both asserting and denying that it applies. Nothing can eliminate this duality of a core of certainty and a penumbra of doubt when we are engaged in bringing particular situations under general rules. This imparts to all rules a fringe of vagueness or 'open texture', and this may affect the rule of recognition specifying the ultimate criteria used in the identification of the law as much as a particular statute. This aspect of law is often held to show that any elucidation of the concept of law in terms of rules must be misleading. To insist on it in the face of the realities of the situation is often stigmatized as 'conceptualism' or 'formalism', and it is to the estimation of this charge that we shall now turn.

VII

FORMALISM AND RULE-SCEPTICISM

I. THE OPEN TEXTURE OF LAW

In any large group general rules, standards, and principles must be the main instrument of social control, and not particular directions given to each individual separately. If it were not possible to communicate general standards of conduct, which multitudes of individuals could understand, without further direction, as requiring from them certain conduct when occasion arose, nothing that we now recognize as law could exist. Hence the law must predominantly, but by no means exclusively, refer to *classes* of person, and to *classes* of acts, things, and circumstances; and its successful operation over vast areas of social life depends on a widely diffused capacity to recognize particular acts, things, and circumstances as instances of the general classifications which the law makes.

Two principal devices, at first sight very different from each other, have been used for the communication of such general standards of conduct in advance of the successive occasions on which they are to be applied. One of them makes a maximal and the other a minimal use of general classifying words. The first is typified by what we call legislation and the second by precedent. We can see the distinguishing features of these in the following simple non-legal cases. One father before going to church says to his son, 'Every man and boy must take off his hat on entering a church.' Another baring his head as he enters the church says, 'Look: this is the right way to behave on such occasions.'

The communication or teaching of standards of conduct by example may take different forms, far more sophisticated than our simple case. Our case would more closely resemble the legal use of precedent, if instead of the child being told on the particular occasion to regard what his father did on entering the church as an example of the right thing to do, the father assumed that the child would regard him as an authority on proper behaviour, and would watch him in order to learn the way to behave. To approach further the legal use of precedent, we must suppose that the father is conceived by himself and others to subscribe to traditional standards of behaviour and not to be introducing new ones.

Communication by example in all its forms, though accompanied by some general verbal directions such as 'Do as I do', may leave open ranges of possibilities, and hence of doubt, as to what is intended even as to matters which the person seeking to communicate has himself clearly envisaged. How much of the performance must be imitated? Does it matter if the left hand is used, instead of the right, to remove the hat? That it is done slowly or smartly? That the hat is put under the seat? That it is not replaced on the head inside the church? These are all variants of general questions which the child might ask himself: 'In what ways must my conduct resemble his to be right?' 'What precisely is it about his conduct that is to be my guide?' In understanding the example, the child attends to some of its aspects rather than others. In so doing he is guided by common sense and knowledge of the general kind of things and purposes which adults think important, and by his appreciation of the general character of the occasion (going to church) and the kind of behaviour appropriate to it.

In contrast with the indeterminacies of examples, the communication of general standards by explicit general forms of language ('Every man must take off his hat on entering a church') seems clear, dependable, and certain. The features to be taken as general guides to conduct are here identified in words; they are verbally extricated, not left embedded with others in a concrete example. In order to know what to do on other occasions the child has no longer to guess what is intended, or what will be approved; he is not left to speculate as to the way in which his conduct must resemble the example if it is to be right. Instead, he has a verbal description which he can use to pick out what he must do in future and when he must do it. He has only to recognize instances of clear verbal terms, to 'subsume' particular facts under general classificatory heads and draw a simple syllogistic conclusion.

He is not faced with the alternative of choosing at his peril or seeking further authoritative guidance. He has a rule which he can apply by himself to himself.

Much of the jurisprudence of this century has consisted of the progressive realization (and sometimes the exaggeration) of the important fact that the distinction between the uncertainties of communication by authoritative example (precedent), and the certainties of communication by authoritative general language (legislation) is far less firm than this naïve contrast suggests. Even when verbally formulated general rules are used, uncertainties as to the form of behaviour required by them may break out in particular concrete cases. Particular fact-situations do not await us already marked off from each other, and labelled as instances of the general rule, the application of which is in question; nor can the rule itself step forward to claim its own instances. In all fields of experience, not only that of rules, there is a limit, inherent in the nature of language, to the guidance which general language can provide. There will indeed be plain cases constantly recurring in similar contexts to which general expressions are clearly applicable ('If anything is a vehicle a motor-car is one') but there will also be cases where it is not clear whether they apply or not. ('Does "vehicle" used here include bicycles, airplanes, roller skates?') The latter are fact-situations, continually thrown up by nature or human invention, which possess only some of the features of the plain cases but others which they lack. Canons of 'interpretation' cannot eliminate, though they can diminish, these uncertainties; for these canons are themselves general rules for the use of language, and make use of general terms which themselves require interpretation. They cannot, any more than other rules, provide for their own interpretation. The plain case, where the general terms seem to need no interpretation and where the recognition of instances seems unproblematic or 'automatic', are only the familiar ones, constantly recurring in similar contexts, where there is general agreement in judgments as to the applicability of the classifying terms.

General terms would be useless to us as a medium of communication unless there were such familiar, generally unchallenged cases. But the variants on the familiar also call for classification under the general terms which at any given moment constitute part of our linguistic resources. Here something in the nature of a crisis in communication is precipitated: there are reasons both for and against our use of a general term, and no firm convention or general agreement dictates its use, or, on the other hand, its rejection by the person concerned to classify. If in such cases doubts are to be resolved, something in the nature of a choice between open alternatives must be made by whoever is to resolve them.

At this point, the authoritative general language in which a rule is expressed may guide only in an uncertain way much as an authoritative example does. The sense that the language of the rule will enable us simply to pick out easily recognizable instances, at this point gives way; subsumption and the drawing of a syllogistic conclusion no longer characterize the nerve of the reasoning involved in determining what is the right thing to do. Instead, the language of the rule seems now only to mark out an authoritative example, namely that constituted by the plain case. This may be used in much the same way as a precedent, though the language of the rule will limit the features demanding attention both more permanently and more closely than precedent does. Faced with the question whether the rule prohibiting the use of vehicles in the park is applicable to some combination of circumstances in which it appears indeterminate, all that the person called upon to answer can do is to consider (as does one who makes use of a precedent) whether the present case resembles the plain case 'sufficiently' in 'relevant' respects. The discretion thus left to him by language may be very wide; so that if he applies the rule, the conclusion, even though it may not be arbitrary or irrational, is in effect a choice. He chooses to add to a line of cases a new case because of resemblances which can reasonably be defended as both legally relevant and sufficiently close. In the case of legal rules, the criteria of relevance and close-ness of resemblance depend on many complex factors running through the legal system and on the aims or purpose which may be attributed to the rule. To characterize these would be to characterize whatever is specific in or peculiar to legal reasoning.

Whichever device, precedent or legislation, is chosen for

the communication of standards of behaviour, these, however smoothly they work over the great mass of ordinary cases, will, at some point where their application is in question, prove indeterminate; they will have what has been termed an *open texture*. So far we have presented this, in the case of legislation, as a general feature of human language; uncertainty at the borderline is the price to be paid for the use of general classifying terms in any form of communication concerning matters of fact. Natural languages like English are when so used irreducibly open-textured. It is, however, important to appreciate why, apart from this dependence on language as it actually is, with its characteristics of open texture, we should not cherish, even as an ideal, the conception of a rule so detailed that the question whether it applied or not to a particular case was always settled in advance, and never involved, at the point of actual application, a fresh choice between open alternatives. Put shortly, the reason is that the necessity for such choice is thrust upon us because we are men, not gods. It is a feature of the human predicament (and so of the legislative one) that we labour under two connected handicaps whenever we seek to regulate, unambiguously and in advance, some sphere of conduct by means of general standards to be used without further official direction on particular occasions. The first handicap is our relative ignorance of fact: the second is our relative indeterminacy of aim. If the world in which we live were characterized only by a finite number of features, and these together with all the modes in which they could combine were known to us, then provision could be made in advance for every possibility. We could make rules, the application of which to particular cases never called for a further choice. Everything could be known, and for everything, since it could be known, something could be done and specified in advance by rule. This would be a world fit for 'mechanical' jurisprudence.

Plainly this world is not our world; human legislators can have no such knowledge of all the possible combinations of circumstances which the future may bring. This inability to anticipate brings with it a relative indeterminacy of aim. When we are bold enough to frame some general rule of conduct (e.g. a rule that no vehicle may be taken into the park), the language used in this context fixes necessary conditions which anything must satisfy if it is to be within its scope, and certain clear examples of what is certainly within its scope may be present to our minds. They are the paradigm, clear cases (the motor-car, the bus, the motor-cycle); and our aim in legislating is so far determinate because we have made a certain choice. We have initially settled the question that peace and quiet in the park is to be maintained at the cost, at any rate, of the exclusion of these things. On the other hand, until we have put the general aim of peace in the park into conjunction with those cases which we did not, or perhaps could not, initially envisage (perhaps a toy motor-car electrically propelled) our aim is, in this direction, indeterminate. We have not settled, because we have not anticipated, the question which will be raised by the unenvisaged case when it occurs: whether some degree of peace in the park is to be sacrificed to, or defended against, those children whose pleasure or interest it is to use these things. When the unenvisaged case does arise, we confront the issues at stake and can then settle the question by choosing between the competing interests in the way which best satisfies us. In doing so we shall have rendered more determinate our initial aim, and shall incidentally have settled a question as to the meaning, for the purposes of this rule, of a general word.

Different legal systems, or the same system at different times, may either ignore or acknowledge more or less explicitly such a need for the further exercise of choice in the application of general rules to particular cases. The vice known to legal theory as formalism or conceptualism consists in an attitude to verbally formulated rules which both seeks to disguise and to minimize the need for such choice, once the general rule has been laid down. One way of doing this is to freeze the meaning of the rule so that its general terms must have the same meaning in every case where its application is in question. To secure this we may fasten on certain features present in the plain case and insist that these are both necessary and sufficient to bring anything which has them within the scope of the rule, whatever other features it may have or lack, and whatever may be the social consequences of applying the rule in this way. To do this is to secure a measure of certainty or predictability at the cost of blindly prejudging what is to be done in a range of future cases, about whose composition we are ignorant. We shall thus indeed succeed in settling in advance, but also in the dark, issues which can only reasonably be settled when they arise and are identified. We shall be forced by this technique to include in the scope of a rule cases which we would wish to exclude in order to give effect to reasonable social aims, and which the open-textured terms of our language would have allowed us to exclude, had we left them less rigidly defined. The rigidity of our classifications will thus war with our aims in having or maintaining the rule.

The consummation of this process is the jurists' 'heaven of concepts'; this is reached when a general term is given the same meaning not only in every application of a single rule, but whenever it appears in any rule in the legal system. No effort is then ever required or made to interpret the term in the light of the different issues at stake in its various recurrences.

In fact all systems, in different ways, compromise between two social needs: the need for certain rules which can, over great areas of conduct, safely be applied by private individuals to themselves without fresh official guidance or weighing up of social issues, and the need to leave open, for later settlement by an informed, official choice, issues which can only be properly appreciated and settled when they arise in a concrete case. In some legal systems at some periods it may be that too much is sacrificed to certainty, and that judicial interpretation of statutes or of precedent is too formal and so fails to respond to the similarities and differences between cases which are visible only when they are considered in the light of social aims. In other systems or at other periods it may seem that too much is treated by courts as perennially open or revisable in precedents, and too little respect paid to such limits as legislative language, despite its open texture, does after all provide. Legal theory has in this matter a curious history; for it is apt either to ignore or to exaggerate the indeterminacies of legal rules. To escape this oscillation between extremes we need to remind ourselves that human inability to anticipate the future, which is at the root of this indeterminacy, varies in degree in different fields of conduct, and that legal systems cater for this inability by a corresponding variety of techniques.

Sometimes the sphere to be legally controlled is recognized from the start as one in which the features of individual cases will vary so much in socially important but unpredictable respects, that uniform rules to be applied from case to case without further official direction cannot usefully be framed by the legislature in advance. Accordingly, to regulate such a sphere the legislature sets up very general standards and then delegates to an administrative, rule-making body acquainted with the varying types of case, the task of fashioning rules adapted to their special needs. Thus the legislature may require an industry to maintain certain standards: to charge only a *fair rate* or to provide *safe systems* of work. Instead of leaving the different enterprises to apply these vague standards to themselves, at the risk of being found to have violated them *ex post facto*, it may be found best to defer the use of sanctions for violations until the administrative body has by regulation specified what, for a given industry, is to count as a 'fair rate' or a 'safe system'. This rule-making power may be exercisable only after something like a judicial inquiry into the facts about the particular industry, and a hearing of arguments pro and con a given form of regulation.

Of course even with very general standards there will be plain indisputable examples of what does, or does not, satisfy them. Some extreme cases of what is, or is not, a 'fair rate' or a 'safe system' will always be identifiable *ab initio*. Thus at one end of the infinitely varied range of cases there will be a rate so high that it would hold the public up to ransom for a vital service, while yielding the entrepreneurs vast profits; at the other end there will be a rate so low that it fails to provide an incentive for running the enterprise. Both these in different ways would defeat any possible aim we could have in regulating rates. But these are only the extremes of a range of different factors and are not likely to be met in practice; between them fall the difficult real cases requiring attention. The anticipatable combinations of relevant factors are few, and this entails a relative indeterminacy in our initial aim of a fair rate or a safe system, and a need for further official choice. In these cases it is clear that the rule-making authority must exercise a discretion, and there is no possibility of treating the question raised by the various cases as if there were one uniquely correct answer to be found, as distinct from an answer which is a reasonable compromise between many conflicting interests.

A second similar technique is used where the sphere to be controlled is such that it is impossible to identify a class of specific actions to be uniformly done or forborne and to make them the subject of a simple rule, yet the range of circumstances, though very varied, covers familiar features of common experience. Here common judgments of what is 'reasonable' can be used by the law. This technique leaves to individuals, subject to correction by a court, the task of weighing up and striking a reasonable balance between the social claims which arise in various unanticipatable forms. In this case they are required to conform to a variable standard *before* it has been officially defined, and they may learn from a court only *ex post facto* when they have violated it, what, in terms of specific actions or forbearances, is the standard required of them. Where the decisions of the court on such matters are regarded as precedents, their specification of the variable standard is very like the exercise of delegated rule-making power by an administrative body, though there are also obvious differences.

The most famous example of this technique in Anglo-American law is the use of the standard of due care in cases of negligence. Civil, and less frequently criminal, sanctions may be applied to those who fail to take reasonable care to avoid inflicting physical injuries on others. But what is reasonable or due care in a concrete situation? We can, of course, cite typical examples of due care: doing such things as stopping, looking, and listening where traffic is to be expected. But we are all well aware that the situations where care is demanded are hugely various and that many other actions are now required besides, or in place of, 'stop, look, and listen'; indeed these may not be enough and might be quite useless if looking would not help to avert the danger. What we are striving for in the application of standards of reasonable care is to ensure (1) that precautions will be taken which will avert substantial harm, yet (2) that the precautions are such that the burden of proper precautions does not involve too great a sacrifice of other respectable interests. Nothing much is sacrificed by stopping, looking, and listening unless of course a man bleeding to death is being driven to the hospital. But owing to the immense variety of possible cases where care is called for, we cannot *ab initio* foresee what combinations of circumstances will arise nor foresee what interests will have to be sacrificed or to what extent, if precaution against harm is to be taken. Hence it is that we are unable to consider, before particular cases arise, precisely what sacrifice or compromise of interests or values we wish to make in order to reduce the risk of harm. Again, our aim of securing people against harm is indeterminate till we put it in conjunction with, or test it against, possibilities which only experience will bring before us; when it does, then we have to face a decision which will, when made, render our aim *pro tanto* determinate.

Consideration of these two techniques throws into relief the characteristics of those wide areas of conduct which are successfully controlled *ab initio* by rule, requiring specific actions, with only a fringe of open texture, instead of a variable standard. They are characterized by the fact that certain distinguishable actions, events, or states of affairs are of such practical importance to us, as things either to avert or bring about, that very few concomitant circumstances incline us to regard them differently. The crudest example of this is the killing of a human being. We are in a position to make a rule against killing instead of laying down a variable standard ('due respect for human life'), although the circumstances in which human beings kill others are very various: this is so because very few factors appear to us to outweigh or make us revise our estimate of the importance of protecting life. Almost always killing, as it were, *dominates* the other factors by which it is accompanied, so when we rule it out in advance as 'killing', we are not blindly prejudging issues which require to be weighed against each other. Of course there are exceptions, factors which override this usually dominant one. There is killing in self-defence and other forms of justifiable homicide. But these are few and identifiable in relatively simple terms; they are admitted as exceptions to a general rule.

It is important to notice that the dominant status of some easily identifiable action, event, or state of affairs may be, in a sense, conventional or artificial, and not due to its 'natural' or 'intrinsic' importance to us as human beings. It does not matter which side of the road is prescribed by the rule of the road, nor (within limits) what formalities are prescribed for the execution of a conveyance; but it does matter very much that there should be an easily identifiable and uniform procedure, and so a clear right and wrong on these matters. When this has been introduced by law the importance of adhering to it is, with few exceptions, paramount; for relatively few attendant circumstances could outweigh it and those that do may be easily identifiable as exceptions and reduced to rule. The English law of real property very clearly illustrates this aspect of rules.

The communication of general rules by authoritative examples brings with it, as we have seen, indeterminacies of a more complex kind. The acknowledgement of precedent as a criterion of legal validity means different things in different systems, and in the same system at different times. Descriptions of the English 'theory' of precedent are, on certain points, still highly contentious: indeed even the key terms used in the theory, 'ratio decidendi', 'material facts', 'interpretation', have their own penumbra of uncertainty. We shall not offer any fresh general description, but merely attempt to characterize briefly, as we have in the case of statute, the area of open texture and the creative judicial activity within it.

Any honest description of the use of precedent in English law must allow a place for the following pairs of contrasting facts. *First*, there is no single method of determining the rule for which a given authoritative precedent is an authority. Notwithstanding this, in the vast majority of decided cases there is very little doubt. The head-note is usually correct enough. *Secondly*, there is no authoritative or uniquely correct formulation of any rule to be extracted from cases. On the other hand, there is often very general agreement, when the bearing of a precedent on a later case is in issue, that a given formulation is adequate. *Thirdly*, whatever authoritative status a rule extracted from precedent may have, it is compatible with the exercise by courts that are bound by it of the following two types of creative or legislative activity. On the one hand, courts deciding a later case may reach an opposite decision to that in a precedent by narrowing the rule extracted from the precedent, and admitting some exception to it not before considered, or, if considered, left open. This process of 'distinguishing' the earlier case involves finding some legally relevant difference between it and the present case, and the class of such differences can never be exhaustively determined. On the other hand, in following an earlier precedent the courts may discard a restriction found in the rule as formulated from the earlier case, on the ground that it is not required by any rule established by statute or earlier precedent. To do this is to widen the rule. Notwithstanding these two forms of legislative activity, left open by the binding force of precedent, the result of the English system of precedent has been to produce, by its use, a body of rules of which a vast number, of both major and minor importance, are as determinate as any statutory rule. They can now only be altered by statute, as the courts themselves often declare in cases where the 'merits' seem to run counter to the requirements of the established precedents.

The open texture of law means that there are, indeed, areas of conduct where much must be left to be developed by courts or officials striking a balance, in the light of circumstances, between competing interests which vary in weight from case to case. None the less, the life of the law consists to a very large extent in the guidance both of officials and private individuals by determinate rules which, unlike the applications of variable standards, do *not* require from them a fresh judgment from case to case. This salient fact of social life remains true, even though uncertainties may break out as to the applicability of any rule (whether written or communicated by precedent) to a concrete case. Here at the margin of rules and in the fields left open by the theory of precedents, the courts perform a rule-producing function which administrative bodies perform centrally in the elaboration of variable standards. In a system where *stare decisis* is firmly acknowledged, this function of the courts is very like the exercise of delegated rule-making powers by an administrative body. In England this fact is often obscured by forms: for the courts often disclaim any such creative function and insist that the proper task of statutory interpretation and the use of precedent is, respectively, to search for the 'intention of the legislature' and the law that already exists.

2. VARIETIES OF RULE-SCEPTICISM

We have discussed at some length the open texture of law because it is important to see this feature in a just perspective. Failure to do justice to it will always provoke exaggerations which will obscure other features of law. In every legal system a large and important field is left open for the exercise of discretion by courts and other officials in rendering initially vague standards determinate, in resolving the uncertainties of statutes, or in developing and qualifying rules only broadly communicated by authoritative precedents. None the less these activities, important and insufficiently studied though they are, must not disguise the fact that both the framework within which they take place and their chief end-product is one of general rules. These are rules the application of which individuals can see for themselves in case after case, without further recourse to official direction or discretion.

It may seem strange that the contention that rules have a central place in the structure of a legal system could ever be seriously doubted. Yet 'rule-scepticism', or the claim that talk of rules is a myth, cloaking the truth that law consists simply of the decisions of courts and the prediction of them, can make a powerful appeal to a lawyer's candour. Stated in an unqualified general form, so as to embrace both secondary and primary rules, it is indeed quite incoherent; for the assertion that there are decisions of courts cannot consistently be combined with the denial that there are any rules at all. This is so because, as we have seen, the existence of a court entails the existence of secondary rules conferring jurisdiction on a changing succession of individuals and so making their decisions authoritative. In a community of people who understood the notions of a decision and a prediction of a decision, but not the notion of a rule, the idea of an *authoritative* decision would be lacking and with it the idea of a court. There would be nothing to distinguish the decision of a private person from that of a court. We might try to eke out, with the notion

of 'habitual obedience', the deficiencies of predictability of decision as a foundation for the authoritative jurisdiction required in
a court. But if we do this we shall find that the notion of a habit
suffers, for this purpose, from all the inadequacies which came
to light when in Chapter IV we considered it as a substitute for a
rule conferring legislative powers.

In some more moderate versions of the theory it may be
conceded that if there are to be courts there must be legal
rules which constitute them, and these themselves cannot
therefore be simply predictions of the decisions of courts.
Little headway can, however, in fact be made with this con-
cession alone. For it is an assertion characteristic of this type
of theory that statutes are not law until applied by courts but
only sources of law, and this is inconsistent with the assertion
that the only rules that exist are those required to constitute
courts. There must also be secondary rules conferring legislative powers on changing successions of individuals. For the
theory does not deny that there are statutes; indeed it cites
them as mere 'sources' of law, and only denies that statutes are
law until applied by courts.

These objections though important and, against an incautious
form of the theory, well taken, do not apply to it in all forms. It
may well be that rule-scepticism was never intended as a denial of
the existence of secondary rules conferring judicial or legislative
power, and was never committed to the claim that these could
be shown to be nothing more than decisions or predictions of
decisions. Certainly, the examples on which this type of theory
has most often relied are drawn from rules imposing duties or
conferring rights or powers on private individuals. Yet, even
if we suppose the denial that there are rules and the assertion
that what are called rules are merely predictions of the decisions
of courts to be limited in this way, there is one sense, at least,
in which it is obviously false. For it cannot be doubted that at
any rate in relation to some spheres of conduct in a modern state
individuals do exhibit the whole range of conduct and attitudes
which we have called the internal point of view. Laws function
in their lives not merely as habits or the basis for predicting
the decisions of courts or the actions of other officials, but as
accepted legal standards of behaviour. That is, they not only do

with tolerable regularity what the law requires of them, but they look upon it as a legal standard of conduct, refer to it in criticizing others, or in justifying demands, and in admitting criticism and demands made by others. In using legal rules in this normative way they no doubt assume that the courts and other officials will continue to decide and behave in certain regular and hence predictable ways, in accordance with the rules of the system; but it is surely an observable fact of social life that individuals do not confine themselves to the external point of view, recording and predicting the decisions of courts or the probable incidence of sanctions. Instead they continuously express in normative terms their shared acceptance of the law as a guide to conduct. We have considered at length in Chapter III the claim that nothing more is meant by normative terms such as 'obligation' than a prediction of official behaviour. If, as we have argued, that claim is false, legal rules function as such in social life: they are *used* as rules not as descriptions of habits or predictions. No doubt they are rules with an open texture and at the points where the texture is open, individuals can only predict how courts will decide and adjust their behaviour accordingly.

Rule-scepticism has a serious claim on our attention, but only as a theory of the function of rules in judicial decision. In this form, while conceding all the objections to which we have drawn attention, it amounts to the contention that, so far as the courts are concerned, there is nothing to circumscribe the area of open texture: so that it is false, if not senseless, to regard judges as themselves subject to rules or 'bound' to decide cases as they do. They may act with sufficient predictable regularity and uniformity to enable others, over long periods, to live by courts' decisions as rules. Judges may even experience feelings of compulsion when they decide as they do, and these feelings may be predictable too; but beyond this there is nothing which can be characterized as a rule which they observe. There is nothing which courts treat as standards of correct judicial behaviour, and so nothing in that behaviour which manifests the internal point of view characteristic of the acceptance of rules.

The theory in this form draws support from a variety of considerations of very different weight. The rule-sceptic is sometimes a disappointed absolutist; he has found that rules are not all they would be in a formalist's heaven, or in a world where men were like gods and could anticipate all possible combinations of fact, so that open texture was not a necessary feature of rules. The sceptic's conception of what it is for a rule to exist, may thus be an unattainable ideal, and when he discovers that it is not attained by what are called rules, he expresses his disappointment by the denial that there are, or can be, any rules. Thus the fact that the rules, which judges claim bind them in deciding a case, have an open texture, or have exceptions not exhaustively specifiable in advance, and the fact that deviation from the rules will not draw down on the judge a physical sanction are often used to establish the sceptic's case. These facts are stressed to show that 'rules are important so far as they help you to predict what judges will do. That is all their importance except as pretty playthings.'[1]

To argue in this way is to ignore what rules actually are in any sphere of real life. It suggests that we are faced with the dilemma: 'Either rules are what they would be in the formalist's heaven and they bind as fetters bind; or there are no rules, only predictable decisions or patterns of behaviour.' Yet surely this is a false dilemma. We promise to visit a friend the next day. When the day comes it turns out that keeping the promise would involve neglecting someone dangerously ill. The fact that this is accepted as an adequate reason for not keeping the promise surely does not mean that there is no rule requiring promises to be kept, only a certain regularity in keeping them. It does not follow from the fact that such rules have exceptions incapable of exhaustive statement, that in every situation we are left to our discretion and are never bound to keep a promise. A rule that ends with the word 'unless...' is still a rule.

Sometimes the existence of rules binding on courts is denied, because the question whether a person, in acting in a certain way, thereby manifested his acceptance of a rule requiring him so to act, is confused with psychological questions as to the processes of thought through which the person

---

[1] Llewellyn, *The Bramble Bush* (2nd edn.), p. 9.

went before or in acting. Very often when a person accepts a rule as binding and as something he and others are not free to change, he may see what it requires in a given situation quite intuitively, and do that without first thinking of the rule and what it requires. When we move a piece in chess in accordance with the rules, or stop at a traffic light when it is red, our rule-complying behaviour is often a direct response to the situation, unmediated by calculation in terms of the rules. The evidence that such actions are genuine applications of the rule is their setting in certain circumstances. Some of these precede the particular action and others follow it: and some of them are stateable only in general and hypothetical terms. The most important of these factors which show that in acting we have applied a rule is that *if* our behaviour is challenged we are disposed to justify it by reference to the rule: and the genuineness of our acceptance of the rule may be manifested not only in our past and subsequent general acknowledgements of it and conformity to it, but in our criticism of our own and others' deviation from it. On such or similar evidence we may indeed conclude that if, before our 'unthinking' compliance with the rule, we had been asked to say what the right thing to do was and why, we would, if honest, have cited the rule in reply. It is this setting of our behaviour among such circumstances, and not its accompaniment by explicit thought of the rule, that is necessary to distinguish an action which is genuinely an observance of a rule from one that merely happens to coincide with it. It is thus that we would distinguish, as a compliance with an accepted rule, the adult chess-player's move from the action of the baby who merely pushed the piece into the right place.

This is not to say that pretence or 'window dressing' is not possible and sometimes successful. Tests for whether a person has merely pretended *ex post facto* that he acted on a rule are, like all empirical tests, inherently fallible but they are not inveterately so. It is possible that, in a given society, judges might always first reach their decisions intuitively or 'by hunches', and then merely choose from a catalogue of legal rules one which, they pretended, resembled the case in hand; they might then claim that this was the rule which they regarded as requiring their decision, although nothing else in their actions or words suggested that they regarded it as a rule binding on them. Some judicial decisions may be like this, but it is surely evident that for the most part decisions, like the chess-player's moves, are reached either by genuine effort to conform to rules consciously taken as guiding standards of decision or, if intuitively reached, are justified by rules which the judge was antecedently disposed to observe and whose relevance to the case in hand would generally be acknowledged.

The last but most interesting form of rule-scepticism does not rest either on the open character of legal rules or on the intuitive character of many decisions; but on the fact that the decision of a court has a unique position as something authoritative, and in the case of supreme tribunals, final. This form of the theory, to which we shall devote the next section, is implicit in Bishop Hoadly's famous phrase echoed so often by Gray in *The Nature and Sources of Law*, 'Nay whoever hath an absolute authority to interpret any written or spoken laws it is he who is the lawgiver to all intents and purposes and not the person who first wrote or spake them.'

3. FINALITY AND INFALLIBILITY IN JUDICIAL DECISION

A supreme tribunal has the last word in saying what the law is and, when it has said it, the statement that the court was 'wrong' has no consequences within the system: no one's rights or duties are thereby altered. The decision may, of course, be deprived of legal effect by legislation, but the very fact that resort to this is necessary demonstrates the empty character, so far as the law is concerned, of the statement that the court's decision was wrong. Consideration of these facts makes it seem pedantic to distinguish, in the case of a supreme tribunal's decisions, between their finality and infallibility. This leads to another form of the denial that courts in deciding are ever bound by rules: 'The law (or the constitution) is what the courts say it is.'

The most interesting and instructive feature of this form of the theory is its exploitation of the ambiguity of such statements as 'the law (or the constitution) is what the courts say it is', and the account which the theory must, to be consistent, give of the relation of non-official statements of law to the official statements of a court. To understand this ambiguity, we shall turn aside to consider its analogue in the case of a game. Many competitive games are played without an official scorer: notwithstanding their competing interests, the players succeed tolerably well in applying the scoring rule to particular cases; they usually agree in their judgments, and unresolved disputes may be few. Before the institution of an official scorer, a statement of the score made by a player represents, if he is honest, an effort to assess the progress of the game by reference to the particular scoring rule accepted in that game. Such statements of the score are internal statements applying the scoring rule, which though they presuppose that the players will, in general, abide by the rules and will object to their violation, are not statements or predictions of these facts.

Like the changes from a regime of custom to a mature system of law, the addition to the game of secondary rules providing for the institution of a scorer whose rulings are final, brings into the system a new kind of internal statement; for unlike the players' statements as to the score, the scorer's determinations are given, by secondary rules, a status which renders them unchallengeable. In *this* sense it is true that for the purposes of the game 'the score is what the scorer says it is'. But it is important to see that the scoring *rule* remains what it was before and it is the scorer's duty to apply it as best he can. 'The score is what the scorer says it is' would be false if it meant that there was no rule for scoring save what the scorer in his discretion chose to apply. There might indeed be a game with such a rule, and some amusement might be found in playing it if the scorer's discretion were exercised with some regularity; but it would be a different game. We may call such a game the game of 'scorer's discretion'.

It is plain that the advantages of quick and final settlement of disputes, which a scorer brings, are purchased at a price. The institution of a scorer may face the players with a predicament: the wish that the game should be regulated, as before, by the scoring rule and the wish for final authoritative decisions as to its application, where it is doubtful, may turn out to be conflicting aims. The scorer may make honest mistakes, be drunk or may wantonly violate his duty to apply the scoring rule to the best of his ability. He may for any of these reasons record a 'run' when the batsman has never moved. Provision may be made for correcting his rulings by appeal to a higher authority: but this must end somewhere in a final, authoritative judgment, which will be made by fallible human beings and so will carry with it the same risk of honest mistake, abuse, or violation. It is impossible to provide by rule for the correction of the breach of every rule.

The risk inherent in setting up an authority to make final authoritative applications of rules may materialize in any sphere. Those that might materialize in the humble sphere of a game are worth consideration, since they show, in a particularly clear fashion, that some of the inferences drawn by the rule-sceptic ignore certain distinctions which are necessary for the understanding of this form of authority wherever it is used. When an official scorer is established and his determinations of the score are made final, statements as to the score made by the players or other non-officials have no status within the game; they are irrelevant to its result. If they happen to coincide with the scorer's statement, well and good; if they conflict, they must be neglected in computing the result. But these very obvious facts would be distorted if the players' statements were classified as predictions of the scorer's rulings, and it would be absurd to explain the neglect of these statements, when they conflicted with the scorer's rulings, by saying that they were predictions of those rulings which had turned out to be false. The player, in making his own statements as to the score after the introduction of an official scorer, is doing what he did before: namely, assessing the progress of the game, as best he can, by reference to the scoring rule. This, too, is what the scorer himself, so long as he fulfils the duties of his position, is also doing. The difference between them is not that one is predicting what the other will say, but that the players' statements are unofficial applications of the scoring rule and hence have no significance in computing the result; whereas the scorer's statements are authoritative and final. It is important to observe that if the game played were 'scorer's discretion' then the relationship between unofficial and official statements would necessarily be different: the players' statements not only *would* be a prediction of the scorer's rulings but *could* be nothing else. For in that case 'the score is what the scorer says it is' would itself be the scoring *rule*; there would be no possibility of the players' statements being merely unofficial versions of what the scorer does officially. Then the scorer's rulings would be both final and infallible—or rather the question whether they were fallible or infallible would be meaningless; for there would be nothing for him to get 'right' or 'wrong'. But in an ordinary game 'the score is what the scorer says it is' is not the scoring rule: it is a rule providing for the authority and finality of his application of the scoring rule in particular cases.

The second lesson to be learnt from this example of authoritative decision touches more fundamental matters. We are able to distinguish a normal game from the game of 'scorer's discretion' simply because the scoring rule, though it has, like other rules, its area of open texture where the scorer has to exercise a choice, yet has a core of settled meaning. It is this which the scorer is not free to depart from, and which, so far as it goes, constitutes the standard of correct and incorrect scoring, both for the player, in making his unofficial statements as to the score, and for the scorer in his official rulings. It is this that makes it true to say that the scorer's rulings are, though final, not infallible. The same is true in law.

Up to a certain point, the fact that some rulings given by a scorer are plainly wrong is not inconsistent with the game continuing: they count as much as rulings which are obviously correct; but there is a limit to the extent to which tolerance of incorrect decisions is compatible with the continued existence of the same game, and this has an important legal analogue. The fact that isolated or exceptional official aberrations are tolerated does not mean that the game of cricket or baseball is no longer being played. On the other hand, if these aberrations are frequent, or if the scorer repudiates the scoring rule, there must come a point when either the players no longer accept the scorer's aberrant rulings or, if they do, the game has changed. It is no longer cricket or baseball but 'scorer's discretion'; for it is a defining feature of these other games that, in general, their results should be assessed in the way demanded by the plain meaning of the rule, whatever

latitude its open texture may leave to the scorer. In some imaginable condition we should say that in truth the game being
played was 'scorer's discretion' but the fact that in all games
the scorer's rulings are final does not mean that that is what all
games are.

These distinctions should be borne in mind when we are
appraising the form of rule-scepticism that rests on the unique
status of a court's decision as a final, authoritative statement
of what the law is in a particular case. The open texture of
law leaves to courts a law-creating power far wider and more
important than that left to scorers, whose decisions are not used
as law-making precedents. Whatever courts decide, both on
matters lying within that part of the rule which seems plain to
all, and those lying on its debatable border, stands till altered by
legislation; and over the interpretation of that, courts will again
have the same last authoritative voice. None the less there still
remains a distinction between a constitution which, after setting
up a system of courts, provides that the law shall be whatever
the supreme court thinks fit, and the actual Constitution of
the United States—or for that matter the constitution of any
modern State. 'The constitution (or the law) is whatever the
judges say it is', if interpreted as denying this distinction, is
false. At any given moment judges, even those of a supreme
court, are parts of a system the rules of which are determinate
enough at the centre to supply standards of correct judicial
decision. These are regarded by the courts as something which
they are not free to disregard in the exercise of the authority
to make those decisions which cannot be challenged within
the system. Any individual judge coming to his office, like
any scorer coming to his, finds a rule, such as the rule that the
enactments of the Queen in Parliament are law, established as
a tradition and accepted as the standard for the conduct of that
office. This circumscribes, while allowing, the creative activity
of its occupants. Such standards could not indeed continue to
exist unless most of the judges of the time adhered to them, for
their existence at any given time consists simply in the acceptance and use of them as standards of correct adjudication. But
this does not make the judge who uses them the author of these
standards, or in Hoadly's language the 'lawgiver' competent to

decide as he pleases. The adherence of the judge is required to maintain the standards, but the judge does not make them.

It is, of course, possible that behind the shield of the rules which make judicial decisions final and authoritative, judges might combine in rejecting the existing rules and cease to regard even the clearest Acts of Parliament as imposing any limits on their decisions. If the majority of their rulings were of this character and were accepted this would amount to a transformation of the system parallel to the conversion of a game from cricket to 'scorer's discretion'. But the standing possibility of such transformations does not show that the system now is what it would be if the transformation took place. No rules can be guaranteed against breach or repudiation; for it is never psychologically or physically impossible for human beings to break or repudiate them; and if enough do so for long enough, then the rules will cease to exist. But the existence of rules at any given time does not require that there should be these impossible guarantees against destruction. To say that at a given time there is a rule requiring judges to accept as law Acts of Parliament or Acts of Congress entails first, that there is general compliance with this requirement and that deviation or repudiation on the part of individual judges is rare; secondly, that when or if it occurs it is or would be treated by a preponderant majority as a subject of serious criticism and as wrong, even though the result of the consequent decision in a particular case cannot, because of the rule as to the finality of decisions, be counteracted except by legislation which concedes its validity though not its correctness. It is logically possible that human beings might break all their promises: at first, perhaps, with the sense that this was the wrong thing to do, and then with no such sense. Then the rule which makes it obligatory to keep promises would cease to exist; this would, however, be a poor support for the view that no such rule exists at present and that promises are not really binding. The parallel argument in the case of judges, based on the possibility of their engineering the destruction of the present system, is no stronger.

Before we leave the topic of rule-scepticism we must say a last word about its positive contention that rules are the predictions of courts' decisions. It is plain and has often been remarked that whatever truth there may be in this, it can at best apply to the statements of law ventured by private individuals or their advisers. It cannot apply to the courts' own statements of a legal rule. These must either be, as some extremer 'Realists' claimed, a verbal covering for the exercise of an unfettered discretion, or they must be the formulation of rules genuinely regarded by the courts from the internal point of view as a standard of correct decision. On the other hand, predictions of judicial decisions have undeniably an important place in the law. When the area of open texture is reached, very often all we can profitably offer in answer to the question: 'What is the law on this matter?' is a guarded prediction of what the courts will do. Moreover, even where what the rules require is clear to all, the statement of it may often be made in the form of a prediction of the courts' decision. But it is important to notice that predominantly in the latter case, and to a varying degree in the former, the basis for such prediction is the knowledge that the courts regard legal rules not as predictions, but as standards to be followed in decision, determinate enough, in spite of their open texture, to limit, though not to exclude, their discretion. Hence, in many cases, predictions of what a court will do are like the prediction we might make that chess-players will move the bishop diagonally: they rest ultimately on an appreciation of the non-predictive aspect of rules, and of the internal point of view of the rules as standards accepted by those to whom the predictions relate. This is only a further aspect of the fact already stressed in Chapter V that, though the existence of rules in any social group renders predictions possible and often reliable, it cannot be identified with them.

4. UNCERTAINTY IN THE RULE OF RECOGNITION

Formalism and rule-scepticism are the Scylla and Charybdis of juristic theory; they are great exaggerations, salutary where they correct each other, and the truth lies between them. Much indeed that cannot be attempted here needs to be done to characterize in informative detail this middle path, and to show the varied types of reasoning which courts characteristically use in exercising the creative function left to them by the open texture of law in statute or precedent. But we have said enough in this chapter to enable us to resume, with profit, the important topic deferred at the end of Chapter VI. This concerned the uncertainty, not of particular legal rules but of the rule of recognition and so of the ultimate criteria used by courts in identifying valid rules of law. The distinction between the uncertainty of a particular rule, and the uncertainty of the criterion used in identifying it as a rule of the system, is not itself, in all cases, a clear one. But it is clearest where the rules are statutory enactments with an authoritative text. The words of a statute and what it requires in a particular case may be perfectly plain; yet there may be doubts as to whether the legislature has power to legislate in this way. Sometimes the resolution of these doubts requires only the interpretation of another rule of law which conferred the legislative power, and the validity of this may not be in doubt. This will be the case, for example, where the validity of an enactment made by a subordinate authority is in question, because doubts arise as to the meaning of the parent Act of Parliament defining the subordinate authority's legislative powers. This is merely a case of the uncertainty or open texture of a particular statute and raises no fundamental question.

To be distinguished from such ordinary questions are those concerning the legal competence of the supreme legislature itself. These concern the ultimate criteria of legal validity; and they can arise even in a legal system like our own, in which there is no written constitution specifying the competence of the supreme legislature. In the overwhelming majority of cases the formula 'Whatever the Queen in Parliament enacts is law' is an adequate expression of the rule as to the legal competence of Parliament, and is accepted as an ultimate criterion for the identification of law, however open the rules thus identified may be at their periphery. But doubts can arise as to its meaning or scope; we can ask what is meant by 'enacted by Parliament' and when doubts arise they may be settled by the courts. What inference is to be drawn as to the place of courts within a legal system from the fact that the ultimate rule of a legal system may thus be in doubt and that courts may resolve the doubt? Does it require some qualification of the thesis that the foundation of a legal system is an accepted rule of recognition specifying the criteria of legal validity?

To answer these questions we shall consider here some aspects of the English doctrine of the sovereignty of Parliament, though, of course, similar doubts can arise in relation to ultimate criteria of legal validity in any system. Under the influence of the Austinian doctrine that law is essentially the product of a legally untrammelled will, older constitutional theorists wrote as if it was a logical necessity that there should be a legislature which was sovereign, in the sense that it is free, at every moment of its existence as a continuing body, not only from legal limitations imposed *ab extra*, but also from its own prior legislation. That Parliament is sovereign in this sense may now be regarded as established, and the principle that no earlier Parliament can preclude its 'successors' from repealing its legislation constitutes part of the ultimate rule of recognition used by the courts in identifying valid rules of law. It is, however, important to see that no necessity of logic, still less of nature, dictates that there should be such a Parliament; it is only one arrangement among others, equally conceivable, which has come to be accepted with us as the criterion of legal validity. Among these others is another principle which might equally well, perhaps better, deserve the name of 'sovereignty'. This is the principle that Parliament should *not* be incapable of limiting irrevocably the legislative competence of its successors but, on the contrary, should have this wider self-limiting power. Parliament would then at least once in its history be capable of exercising an even larger sphere of legislative competence than the accepted established doctrine allows to it. The requirement that at every moment of its existence Parliament should be free from legal limitations including even those imposed by itself is, after all, only one interpretation of the ambiguous idea of legal omnipotence. It in effect makes a choice between a *continuing* omnipotence in all matters not affecting the legislative competence of successive parliaments, and an unrestricted *self-embracing* omnipotence the exercise of which can only be enjoyed once. These two conceptions of omnipotence have their parallel in two conceptions of an omnipotent God: on the one hand, a God who at every moment of his existence enjoys the same powers and so is incapable of cutting down those powers, and, on the other, a God whose powers include the power to destroy for the future his omnipotence. Which form of omnipotence—continuing or self-embracing—our Parliament enjoys is an empirical question concerning the form of rule which is accepted as the ultimate criterion in identifying the law. Though it is a question about a rule lying at the base of a legal system, it is still a question of fact to which at any given moment of time, on some points at least, there may be a quite determinate answer. Thus it is clear that the presently accepted rule is one of continuing sovereignty, so that Parliament cannot protect its statutes from repeal.

Yet, as with every other rule, the fact that the rule of parliamentary sovereignty is determinate at this point does not mean that it is so at all points. Questions can be raised about it to which at present there is no answer which is clearly right or wrong. These can be settled only by a choice, made by someone to whose choices in this matter authority is eventually accorded. Such indeterminacies in the rule of parliamentary sovereignty present themselves in the following way. It is conceded under the present rule that Parliament cannot by statute irrevocably withdraw any topic from the scope of future legislation by Parliament; but a distinction may be drawn between an enactment simply purporting to do that and one which, while leaving it still open to Parliament to legislate on any topic, purports to alter the 'manner and form' of legislation. The latter may, for example, require that on certain issues no legislation shall be effective unless it is passed by a majority of the two Houses sitting together, or unless it is confirmed by a plebiscite. It may 'entrench' such a provision by the stipulation that the provision itself can be repealed only by the same special process. Such a partial alteration in the legislative process may well be consistent with the present rule that Parliament cannot irrevocably bind its successors; for what it does is not so much to *bind* successors, as to eliminate them *quoad* certain issues and transfer their legislative powers over these issues to the new special body. So it may be said that, in relation to these special issues, Parliament has not 'bound' or 'fettered' Parliament or diminished its continuing omnipotence, but has 'redefined' Parliament and what must be done to legislate.

Plainly, if this device were valid, Parliament could achieve by its use very much the same results as those which the accepted doctrine, that Parliament cannot bind its successors, seems to put beyond its power. For though, indeed, the difference between circumscribing the area over which Parliament can legislate, and merely changing the manner and form of legislation, is clear enough in some cases, in effect these categories shade into each other. A statute which, after fixing a minimum wage for engineers, provided that no bill concerning engineers' pay should have effect as law unless confirmed by resolution of the Engineers' Union and went on to entrench this provision, might indeed secure all that, in practice, could be done by a statue which fixed the wage 'for ever', and then crudely prohibited its repeal altogether. Yet an argument, which lawyers would recognize as having some force, can be made to show that although the latter would be ineffective under the present rule of continuing parliamentary sovereignty, the former would not. The steps of the argument consist of a succession of contentions as to what Parliament can do, each of which would command less assent than its predecessor though having some analogy with it. None of them can be ruled out as wrong or accepted with confidence as right; for we are in the area of open texture of the system's most fundamental rule. Here at any moment a question may arise to which there is no answer—only answers.

Thus it might be conceded that Parliament might irrevocably alter the present constitution of Parliament by abolishing the House of Lords altogether, and so going beyond the Parliament Acts of 1911 and 1949 which dispensed with its consent to certain legislation and which some authorities prefer to interpret as a mere revocable delegation of some of Parliament's powers to the Queen and Commons. It might also be conceded, as Dicey asserted,[1] that Parliament could destroy itself totally, by an Act declaring its powers at an end and repealing the legislation providing for the election of future Parliaments. If so, Parliament might validly accompany this legislative suicide by an Act transferring all its powers to some other body, say the Manchester Corporation. If it can do this, cannot it effectually do something less? Can it not put

---

[1] *The Law of the Constitution* (10th edn.), p. 68 n.

an end to its powers to legislate on certain matters and transfer these to a new composite entity which includes itself and some further body? On this footing may not section 4 of the Statute of Westminster, providing for the consent of a Dominion to any legislation affecting it, actually have done this in relation to Parliament's powers to legislate for a Dominion? The contention that this can effectively be repealed without the consent of the Dominion may not only, as Lord Sankey said, be 'theory' which 'has no relation to realities'. It may be bad theory—or at least no better than the opposite one. Finally, if Parliament can be reconstituted in these ways by its own action, why cannot it reconstitute itself by providing that the Engineers' Union shall be a necessary consenting element in certain types of legislation?

It is quite possible that some of the questionable propositions which constitute the doubtful, but not obviously mistaken, steps in this argument, will one day be endorsed or rejected by a court called on to decide the matter. Then we shall have an answer to the questions which they raise, and that answer, so long as the system exists, will have a unique authoritative status among the answers which might be given. The courts will have made determinate at this point the ultimate rule by which valid law is identified. Here 'the constitution is what the judges say it is' does *not* mean merely that particular decisions of supreme tribunals cannot be challenged. At first sight the spectacle seems paradoxical: here are courts exercising creative powers which settle the ultimate criteria by which the validity of the very laws, which confer upon them jurisdiction as judges, must itself be tested. How can a constitution confer authority to say what the constitution is? But the paradox vanishes if we remember that though every rule may be doubtful at some points, it is indeed a necessary condition of a legal system existing, that not every rule is open to doubt on all points. The possibility of courts having authority at any given time to decide these limiting questions concerning the ultimate criteria of validity, depends merely on the fact that, at that time, the application of those criteria to a vast area of law, including the rules which confer that authority, raises no doubts, though their precise scope and ambit do.

This answer, however, may to some seem too short a way with the question. It may appear to characterize very inadequately the activity of courts on the fringes of the fundamental rules which specify the criteria of legal validity; this may be because it assimilates the activity too closely to ordinary cases where courts exercise a creative choice in interpreting a particular statute which has proved indeterminate. It is clear that such ordinary cases must arise in any system, and so it seems obviously to be part, even if only an implied part, of the rules on which courts act that courts have jurisdiction to settle them by choosing between the alternatives which the statute leaves open, even if they prefer to disguise this choice as a discovery. But, at least in the absence of a written constitution, questions concerning the fundamental criteria of validity often seem *not* to have this previously envisageable quality, which makes it natural to say that, when they arise, the courts already have, under the existing rules, a clear authority to settle questions of this sort.

One form of 'formalist' error may perhaps just be that of thinking that every step taken by a court is covered by some general rule conferring in advance the authority to take it, so that its creative powers are *always* a form of delegated legislative power. The truth may be that, when courts settle previously unenvisaged questions concerning the most fundamental constitutional rules, they *get* their authority to decide them accepted after the questions have arisen and the decision has been given. Here all that succeeds is success. It is conceivable that the constitutional question at issue may divide society too fundamentally to permit of its disposition by a judicial decision. The issues in South Africa concerning the entrenched clauses of the South Africa Act, 1909, at one time threatened to be too divisive for legal settlement. But where less vital social issues are concerned, a very surprising piece of judicial law-making concerning the very sources of law may be calmly 'swallowed'. Where this is so, it will often in *retrospect* be said, and may genuinely appear, that there always was an 'inherent' power in the courts to do what they have done. Yet this may be a pious fiction, if the only evidence for it is the success of what has been done.

The manipulation by English courts of the rules concerning

the binding force of precedent is perhaps most honestly described in this last way as a successful bid to take powers and use them. Here power acquires authority *ex post facto* from success. Thus before the decision of the Court of Criminal Appeal in *Rex* v. *Taylor*[1] the question whether that court had authority to rule that it was not bound by its own precedents on matters concerning the liberty of the subject might have appeared entirely open. But the ruling was made and is now followed as law. The statement that the court always had an inherent power to rule in this way would surely only be a way of making the situation look more tidy than it really is. Here, at the fringe of these very fundamental things, we should welcome the rule-sceptic, as long as he does not forget that it is at the fringe that he is welcome; and does not blind us to the fact that what makes possible these striking developments by courts of the most fundamental rules is, in great measure, the prestige gathered by courts from their unquestionably rule-governed operations over the vast, central areas of the law.

[1] [1950] 2 KB 368.

JUSTICE AND MORALITY

We have found it necessary, in order to elucidate features distinctive of law as a means of social control, to introduce elements which cannot be constructed out of the ideas of an order, a threat, obedience, habits, and generality. Too much that is characteristic of law is distorted by the effort to explain it in these simple terms. Thus we found it necessary to distinguish from the idea of a general habit that of a social rule, and to emphasize the internal aspect of rules manifested in their use as guiding and critical standards of conduct. We then distinguished among rules between primary rules of obligation and secondary rules of recognition, change, and adjudication. The main theme of this book is that so many of the distinctive operations of the law, and so many of the ideas which constitute the framework of legal thought, require for their elucidation reference to one or both of these two types of rule, that their union may be justly regarded as the 'essence' of law, though they may not always be found together wherever the word 'law' is correctly used. Our justification for assigning to the union of primary and secondary rules this central place is not that they will there do the work of a dictionary, but that they have great explanatory power.

We must now turn our attention to the claim which, in the perennial discussion of the 'essence' or the 'nature' or 'the definition' of law, has been most frequently opposed to the simple imperative theory which we have found inadequate. This is the general contention that between law and morality there is a connection which is in some sense 'necessary', and that it is this which deserves to be taken as central, in any attempt to analyse or elucidate the notion of law. Advocates of this view might not be concerned to dispute our criticisms of the simple imperative theory. They might even concede that it was a useful advance; and that the union of primary and secondary rules was indeed more important than orders backed by threats as a starting-point for the understanding of law. Their argument would, however, be that this is not enough: that even these elements are of subordinate importance, and that until the 'necessary' relationship with morality is made explicit and its central importance seen, the mists which have so long clouded the understanding of law cannot be dissipated. From this point of view the questionable or challengeable cases of law would not merely be the law of primitive societies or international law, which have been considered doubtful because of their lack of a legislature, courts with compulsory jurisdiction, and centrally organized sanctions. Far more questionable from this point of view is the title to be treated as law of those municipal systems which exhibit the full complement of *juge, gendarme et legislateur* but fail to conform to certain fundamental requirements of justice or morality. In the words of St Augustine[1] 'What are states without justice but robber-bands enlarged?'

The claim that between law and morality there is a necessary connection has many important variants, not all of them conspicuous for their clarity. There are many possible interpretations of the key terms 'necessary' and 'morality' and these have not always been distinguished and separately considered by either advocates or critics. The clearest, perhaps, because it is the most extreme form of expression of this point of view, is that associated with the Thomist tradition of Natural Law. This comprises a twofold contention: first, that there are certain principles of true morality or justice, discoverable by human reason without the aid of revelation even though they have a divine origin; secondly, that man-made laws which conflict with these principles are not valid law, 'Lex iniusta non est lex.' Other variants of this general point of view take a different view of both the status of principles of morality and of the consequences of conflict between law and morality. Some conceive morality not as immutable principles of conduct or as discoverable by reason, but as expressions of human attitudes to conduct which may vary from society to society or from individual to individual. Theories of this form usually also hold that conflict between law and even the most fundamental requirements of morality is not sufficient to

---

[1] *De Civitate Dei*, IV, 4.

deprive a rule of its status as law; they interpret the 'necessary' connection between law and morality in a different way. They claim that for a legal system to exist there must be a widely diffused, though not necessarily universal, recognition of a moral obligation to obey the law, even though this may be overriden in particular cases by a stronger moral obligation not to obey particular morally iniquitous laws.

The full assessment of the different varieties of theory asserting a necessary connection between law and morals would take us far into moral philosophy. But something less than this may provide any thoughtful reader with enough to form a reasoned view of the truth and importance of such claims. For this purpose what is most needed is a separation and identification of some long-entangled issues, which we consider in this chapter and the next. The first of these issues concerns the distinction within the general sphere of morality of the specific idea of justice and the special features which account for its peculiarly intimate connection with law. The second concerns the characteristics which distinguish moral rules and principles not only from legal rules but from all other forms of social rule or standards of conduct. These two issues are the subject of this chapter; the third, which is the subject of the next, concerns the many different senses and ways in which legal rules and morals may be said to be related.

1. PRINCIPLES OF JUSTICE

The terms most frequently used by lawyers in the praise or condemnation of law or its administration are the words 'just' and 'unjust' and very often they write as if the ideas of justice and morality were coextensive. There are indeed very good reasons why justice should have a most prominent place in the criticism of legal arrangements; yet it is important to see that it is a distinct segment of morality, and that laws and the administration of laws may have or lack excellences of different kinds. Very little reflection on some common types of moral judgment is enough to show this special character of justice. A man guilty of gross cruelty to his child would often be judged to have done something morally *wrong*, *bad*, or even *wicked* or to have disregarded his moral *obligation* or duty to his child. But it would be strange to criticize his conduct as *unjust*. This is not because the word 'unjust' is too weak in condemnatory force, but because the point of moral criticism in terms of justice or injustice is usually different from, and more specific than, the other types of general moral criticism which are appropriate in this particular case and are expressed by words like 'wrong', 'bad', or 'wicked'. 'Unjust' would become appropriate if the man had arbitrarily selected one of his children for severer punishment than those given to others guilty of the same fault, or if he had punished the child for some offence without taking steps to see that he really was the wrongdoer. Similarly, when we turn from the criticism of individual conduct to the criticism of law, we might express our approval of a law requiring parents to send their children to school, by saying that it was a good law and our disapproval of a law forbidding the criticism of the Government, as by calling it a bad law. Such criticisms would not normally be couched in terms of 'justice' and 'injustice'. 'Just', on the other hand, would be the appropriate expression of approval of a law distributing the burden of taxation according to wealth; so 'unjust' would be appropriate for the expression of disapproval of a law which forbade coloured people to use the public means of transport or the parks. That just and unjust are more specific forms of moral criticism than good and bad or right and wrong, is plain from the fact that we might intelligibly claim that a law was good because it was just, or that it was bad because it was unjust, but not that it was just because good, or unjust because bad.

The distinctive features of justice and their special connection with law begin to emerge if it is observed that most of the criticisms made in terms of just and unjust could almost equally well be conveyed by the words 'fair' and 'unfair'. Fairness is plainly not coextensive with morality in general; references to it are mainly relevant in two situations in social life. One is when we are concerned not with a single individual's conduct but with the way in which *classes* of individuals are treated, when some burden or benefit falls to be distributed among them. Hence what is typically fair or unfair is a 'share'. The second situation is when some injury has been done and compensation or redress is claimed. These are not the only contexts where appraisals in terms of justice or fairness are made. We speak not only of distributions or compensations as just or fair but also of a judge as just or unjust; a trial as fair or unfair; and a person as justly or unjustly convicted. These are derivative applications of the notion of justice which are explicable once the primary application of justice to matters of distribution and compensation is understood.

The general principle latent in these diverse applications of the idea of justice is that individuals are entitled in respect of each other to a certain relative position of equality or inequality. This is something to be respected in the vicissitudes of social life when burdens or benefits fall to be distributed; it is also something to be restored when it is disturbed. Hence justice is traditionally thought of as maintaining or restoring a *balance* or *proportion*, and its leading precept is often formulated as 'Treat like cases alike'; though we need to add to the latter 'and treat different cases differently'. So when, in the name of justice, we protest against a law forbidding coloured people the use of the public parks, the point of such criticism is that such a law is bad, because in distributing the benefits of public amenities among the population it discriminates between persons who are, in all relevant respects, alike. Conversely, if a law is praised as just because it withdraws from some special section some privilege or immunity, e.g. in taxation, the guiding thought is that there is no such relevant difference between the privileged class and the rest of the community as to entitle them to the special treatment. These simple examples are, however, enough to show that, though 'Treat like cases alike and different cases differently' is a central element in the idea of justice, it is by itself incomplete and, until supplemented, cannot afford any determinate guide to conduct. This is so because any set of human beings will resemble each other in some respects and differ from each other in others and, until it is established what resemblance and differences are relevant, 'Treat like cases alike' must remain an empty form. To fill it we must know when, for the purposes in hand, cases are to be regarded as alike and what differences are relevant. Without this further supplement we cannot proceed to criticize laws or other social arrangements as unjust. It is not unjust for the law when it forbids homicide to treat the red-haired murderers in the same way as others; indeed it would be as unjust if it treated them differently, as it would be if it refused to treat differently the sane and the insane.

There is therefore a certain complexity in the structure of the idea of justice. We may say that it consists of two parts: a uniform or constant feature, summarized in the precept 'Treat like cases alike' and a shifting or varying criterion used in determining when, for any given purpose, cases are alike or different. In this respect justice is like the notions of what is genuine, or tall, or warm, which contain an implicit reference to a standard which varies with the classification of the thing to which they are applied. A tall child may be the same height as a short man, a warm winter the same temperature as a cold summer, and a fake diamond may be a genuine antique. But justice is far more complicated than these notions because the shifting standard of relevant resemblance between different cases incorporated in it not only varies with the type of subject to which it is applied, but may often be open to challenge even in relation to a single type of subject.

In certain cases, indeed, the resemblances and differences between human beings which are relevant for the criticism of legal arrangements as just or unjust are quite obvious. This is pre-eminently the case when we are concerned not with the justice or injustice of the *law* but of its *application* in particular cases. For here the relevant resemblances and differences between individuals, to which the person who administers the law must attend, are determined by the law itself. To say that the law against murder is justly applied is to say that it is impartially applied to all those and only those who are alike in having done what the law forbids; no prejudice or interest has deflected the administrator from treating them 'equally'. Consistently with this the procedural standards such as *'audi alteram partem'* 'let no one be a judge in his own cause' are thought of as requirements of justice, and in England and America are often referred to as principles of Natural Justice. This is so because they are guarantees of impartiality or objectivity, designed to secure that the law is applied to all those and only to those who are alike in the relevant respect marked out by the law itself.

The connection between this aspect of justice and the very notion of proceeding by rule is obviously very close. Indeed, it might be said that to apply a law justly to different cases is simply to take seriously the assertion that what is to be applied in different cases is the same general rule, without prejudice, interest, or caprice. This close connection between justice in the administration of the law and the very notion of a rule has tempted some famous thinkers to identify justice with conformity to law. Yet plainly this is an error unless 'law' is given some specially wide meaning; for such an account of justice leaves unexplained the fact that criticism in the name of justice is not confined to the administration of the law in particular cases, but the laws themselves are often criticized as just or unjust. Indeed there is no absurdity in conceding that an unjust law forbidding the access of coloured persons to the parks has been justly administered, in that only persons genuinely guilty of breaking the law were punished under it and then only after a fair trial.

When we turn from the justice or injustice of the administration of the law to the criticism of the law itself in these terms, it is plain that the law itself cannot now determine what resemblances and differences among individuals the law must recognize if its rules are to treat like cases alike and so be just. Here accordingly there is much room for doubt and dispute. Fundamental differences, in general moral and political outlook, may lead to irreconcilable differences and disagreement as to what characteristics of human beings are to be taken as relevant for the criticism of law as unjust. Thus, when in the previous example we stigmatized as unjust a law forbidding coloured people access to the parks, this was on the footing that, at least in the distribution of such amenities, differences of colour are irrelevant. Certainly in the modern world, the fact that human beings, of whatever colour, are capable of thought, feeling, and self-control, would be generally though not universally accepted as constituting crucial resemblances between them to which the law should attend. Hence, in most civilized countries there is a great measure of agreement that both the criminal law (conceived not only as restricting liberty but as providing protection from various sorts of harm) and the civil law (conceived as offering redress for harm), would be unjust if in the distribution of these burdens and benefits they discriminated between persons, by reference to such characteristics as colour or religious belief. And if, instead of these well-known *foci* of human prejudice, the law discriminated by reference to such obvious irrelevancies as height, weight, or beauty it would be both unjust and ludicrous. If murderers belonging to the established church were exempt from capital punishment, if only members of the peerage could sue for libel, if assaults on coloured persons were punished less severely than those on whites, the laws would in most modern communities be condemned as unjust on the footing that prima facie human beings should be treated alike and these privileges and immunities rested on no relevant ground.

Indeed so deeply embedded in modern man is the principle that prima facie human beings are entitled to be treated alike that almost universally where the laws do discriminate by reference to such matters as colour and race, lip-service at least is still widely paid to this principle. If such discriminations are attacked they are often defended by the assertion that the class discriminated against lack, or have not yet developed, certain essential human attributes; or it may be said that, regrettable though it is, the demands of justice requiring their equal treatment must be overridden in order to preserve something held to be of greater value, which would be jeopardized if such discriminations were not made. Yet though lip-service is now general, it is certainly possible to conceive of a morality which did not resort to these often disingenuous devices to justify discrimination and inequalities, but openly rejected the principle that prima facie human beings were to be treated alike. Instead, human beings might be thought of as falling naturally and unalterably into certain classes, so that some were naturally fitted to be free and others to be their slaves or, as Aristotle expressed it, the living instruments of others. Here the sense of prima-facie equality among men would be absent. Something of this view is to be found in Aristotle and Plato, though even there, there is more than a hint that any full defence of slavery would involve showing that those enslaved lacked the capacity for independent existence or differed from the free in their capacity to realize some ideal of the good life.

It is therefore clear that the criteria of relevant resemblances and differences may often vary with the fundamental moral outlook of a given person or society. Where this is so, assessments of the justice or injustice of the law may be met with counter-assertions inspired by a different morality. But sometimes a consideration of the object which the law in question is admittedly designed to realize may make clear the resemblances and differences which a just law should recognize and they may then be scarcely open to dispute. If a law provides for the relief of poverty then the requirement of the principle that 'Like cases be treated alike' would surely involve attention to the *need* of different claimants for relief. A similar criterion of need is implicitly recognized when the burden of taxation is adjusted by a graded income tax to the wealth of the individuals taxed. Sometimes what is relevant are the *capacities* of persons for a specific function with which the exercise of the law in question may be concerned. Laws which exclude from the franchise, or withhold the power to make wills or contracts from children, or the insane, are regarded as just because such persons lack the capacity, which sane adults are presumed to have, to make a rational use of these facilities. Such discriminations are made on grounds which are obviously relevant, whereas discriminations in these matters between the sexes or between persons of different colour are not; though of course it has been argued in defence of the subjection of women, or coloured people, that women or coloured people lack the white male's capacity for rational thought and decision. To argue thus is of course to admit that equal capacity for a particular function is the criterion of justice in the case of such law, though in the absence of any evidence that such capacity is lacking in women or coloured persons, again only lip-service is paid to this principle.

So far we have considered the justice or injustice of laws which may be viewed as *distributing* among individuals burdens and benefits. Some of the benefits are tangible, like poor relief, or food rations; others are intangible, like the protection from bodily harm given by the criminal law, or the facilities afforded by laws relating to testamentary or contractual capacity, or the right to vote. From distribution in this wide sense, we must distinguish *compensation* for injury done by one person to another. Here the connection between what is just and the central precept of justice 'Treat like cases alike and different cases differently' is certainly less direct. Yet it is not too indirect to be traced and may be seen in the following way. The laws which provide for the compensation by one person of another for torts or civil injuries might be considered unjust for two different reasons. They might, on the one hand, establish unfair privileges or immunities. This would be so if only peers could sue for libel, or if no white person were liable to a coloured person for trespass or assault. Such laws would violate, in a straightforward way, principles of fair distribution of the rights and duties of compensation. But such laws might also be unjust in a quite different way: for while making no unfair discriminations they might fail altogether to provide a remedy for certain types of injury inflicted by one person on another, even though morally compensation would be thought due. In this matter the law might be unjust while treating all alike.

The vice of such laws would then not be the maldistribution, but the refusal, to all alike, of compensation for injuries which it was morally wrong to inflict on others. The crudest case of such unjust refusal of redress would be a system in which no one could obtain damages for physical harm wantonly inflicted. It is worth observing that *this* injustice would still remain even if the criminal law prohibited such assaults under penalty. Few instances of anything so crude can be found, but the failure of English law to provide compensation for invasions of privacy, often found profitable by advertisers, has often been criticized in this way. Failure to provide compensation where morally it is held due is, however, also the gravamen of the charge of injustice against technicalities of the law of tort or contract which permit 'unjust enrichment' at the expense of another by some action considered morally wrong.

The connection between the justice and injustice of compensation for injury, and the principle 'Treat like cases alike and different cases differently', lies in the fact that outside the law there is a moral conviction that those with whom the law is concerned have a right to mutual forbearance from certain kinds of harmful conduct. Such a structure of reciprocal rights and obligations proscribing at least the grosser sorts of harm, constitutes the basis, though not the whole, of the morality of every social group. Its effect is to create among individuals a moral and, in a sense, an artificial equality to offset the inequalities of nature. For when the moral code forbids one man to rob or use violence on another even when superior strength or cunning would enable him to do so with impunity, the strong and cunning are put on a level with the weak and simple. Their cases are made morally alike. Hence the strong man who disregards morality and takes advantage of his strength to injure another is conceived as upsetting this equilibrium, or order of equality, established by morals; justice then requires that this moral status quo should as far as possible be restored by the wrongdoer. In simple cases of theft this would simply involve giving back the thing taken; and compensation for other injuries is an extension of this primitive notion. One who has physically injured another either intentionally or through negligence is thought of as having taken something from his victim; and though he has not literally done this, the figure is not too far-fetched: for he has profited at his victim's expense, even if it is only by indulging his wish to injure him or not sacrificing his ease to the duty of taking adequate precautions. Thus when laws provide compensation where justice demands it, they recognize indirectly the principle 'Treat like cases alike' by providing for the restoration, after disturbance, of the moral status quo in which victim and wrongdoer are on a footing of equality and so alike. Again, it is conceivable that there might be a moral outlook which did not put individuals on a footing of reciprocal equality in these matters. The moral code might forbid Barbarians to assault Greeks but allow Greeks to assault Barbarians. In such cases a Barbarian may be thought morally bound to compensate a Greek for injuries done though entitled to no such compensation himself. The moral order here would be one of inequality in which victim and wrongdoer were treated differently. For such an outlook, repellent though it may be to us, the law would be just only if it reflected this difference and treated different cases differently.

In this brief outline of justice we have considered only some of its simpler applications in order to show the specific form of excellence attributed to laws which are appraised as just.

Not only is this distinct from other values which laws may have or lack, but sometimes the demands of justice may conflict with other values. This may occur, when a court, in sentencing a particular offender for a crime which has become prevalent, passes a severer sentence than that passed in other similar cases, and avowedly does this 'as a warning'. There is here a sacrifice of the principle 'Treat like cases alike' to the general security or welfare of society. In civil cases, a similar conflict between justice and the general good is resolved in favour of the latter, when the law provides no remedy for some moral wrong because to enforce compensation in such cases might involve great difficulties of proof, or overburden the courts, or unduly hamper enterprise. There is a limit to the amount of law enforcement which any society can afford, even when moral wrong has been done. Conversely the law, in the name of the general welfare of society, may enforce compensation from one who has injured another, even where morally, as a matter of justice, it might not be thought due. This is often said to be the case when liability in tort is strict, i.e. independent of the intention to injure or failure to take care. This form of liability is sometimes defended on the ground that it is in the interest of 'society' that those accidentally injured should be compensated; and it is claimed that the easiest way of doing this is to place the burden on those whose activities, however carefully controlled, result in such accidents. They commonly have deep pockets and opportunities to insure. When this defence is made, there is in it an implicit appeal to the general welfare of society which, though it may be morally acceptable and sometimes even called '*social* justice', differs from the primary forms of justice which are concerned simply to redress, as far as possible, the status quo as between two individuals.

An important juncture point between ideas of justice and social good or welfare should be noticed. Very few social changes or laws are agreeable to or advance the welfare of all individuals alike. Only laws which provide for the most elementary needs, such as police protection or roads, come near to this. In most cases the law provides benefits for one class of the population only at the cost of depriving others of what they prefer. Provision for the poor can be made only out of the goods of others; compulsory school education for all may mean not only loss of liberty for those who wish to educate their children privately, but may be financed only at the cost of reducing or sacrificing capital investment in industry or old-age pensions or free medical services. When a choice has been made between such competing alternatives it may be defended as proper on the ground that it was for the 'public good' or the 'common good'. It is not clear what these phrases mean, since there seems to be no scale by which contributions of the various alternatives to the common good can be measured and the greater identified. It is, however, clear that a choice, made without prior consideration of the interests of all sections of the community would be open to criticism as merely partisan and unjust. It would, however, be rescued from *this* imputation if the claims of all had been impartially considered before legislation, even though in the result the claims of one section were subordinated to those of others.

Some might indeed argue that all that in fact could be meant by the claim that a choice between the competing claims of different classes or interests was made 'for the common good', was that the claims of all had been thus impartially surveyed before decision. Whether this is true or not, it seems clear that justice in this sense is at least a necessary condition to be satisfied by any legislative choice which purports to be for the common good. We have here a further aspect of distributive justice, differing from those simple forms which we have discussed. For here what is justly 'distributed' is not some specific benefit among a class of claimants to it, but impartial attention to and consideration of competing claims to different benefits.

2. MORAL AND LEGAL OBLIGATION

Justice constitutes one segment of morality primarily concerned not with individual conduct but with the ways in which *classes* of individuals are treated. It is this which gives justice its special relevance in the criticism of law and of other public or social institutions. It is the most public and the most legal of the virtues. But principles of justice do not exhaust the idea of morality; and not all criticism of law made on moral grounds is made in the name of justice. Laws may be condemned as morally bad simply because they require men to do particular actions which morality forbids individuals to do, or because they require men to abstain from doing those which are morally obligatory.

It is therefore necessary to characterize, in general terms, those principles, rules, and standards relating to the conduct of individuals which belong to morality and make conduct morally obligatory. Two related difficulties confront us here. The first is that the word 'morality' and all other associated or nearly synonymous terms like 'ethics', have their own considerable area of vagueness or 'open texture'. There are certain forms of principle or rule which some would rank as moral and which others would not. Secondly, even where there is agreement on this point and certain rules or principles are accepted as indisputably belonging to morality, there may still be great philosophical disagreement as to their *status* or relation to the rest of human knowledge and experience. Are they immutable principles which constitute part of the fabric of the Universe, not made by man, but awaiting discovery by the human intellect? Or are they expressions of changing human attitudes, choices, demands, or feelings? These are crude formulations of two extremes in moral philosophy. Between them lie many complicated and subtle variants, which philosophers have developed in the effort to elucidate the nature of morality.

In what follows we shall seek to evade these philosophical difficulties. We shall later[1] identify under the heads of 'Importance', 'Immunity from deliberate change', 'Voluntary character of moral offences', and 'The form of moral pressure' four cardinal features which are constantly found together in those principles, rules, and standards of conduct which are most commonly accounted 'moral'. These four features reflect different aspects of a characteristic and important function which such standards perform in social life or in the life of individuals. This alone would justify us in marking off whatever has these four features for separate consideration, and above all, for contrast and comparison with law.

[1] Below, p. 173 ff.

Moreover, the claim that morality has these four features is neutral between rival philosophical theories as to its *status* or 'fundamental' character. Certainly most, if not all, philosophers would agree that these four features were necessary in any moral rule or principle, though they would offer very different interpretations or explanations of the fact that morality possesses them. It may indeed be objected that these features though necessary are *only* necessary and not sufficient to distinguish morality from certain rules or principles of conduct which would be excluded from morality by a more stringent test. We shall refer to the facts on which such objections are based but we shall adhere to the wider sense of 'morality'. Our justification for this is both that this accords with much usage and that what the word in this wide sense designates, performs an important, distinguishable function in social and individual life.

We shall consider first the social phenomenon often referred to as '*the* morality' of a given society or the 'accepted' or 'conventional' morality of an actual social group. These phrases refer to standards of conduct which are widely shared in a particular society, and are to be contrasted with the moral principles or moral ideals which may govern an individual's life, but which he does not share with any considerable number of those with whom he lives. The basic element in the shared or accepted morality of a social group consists of rules of the kind which we have already described in Chapter V when we were concerned to elucidate the general idea of obligation, and which we there called primary rules of obligation. These rules are distinguished from others both by the serious social pressure by which they are supported, and by the considerable sacrifice of individual interest or inclination which compliance with them involves. In the same chapter we also drew a picture of a society at a stage in which such rules were the only means of social control. We noticed that at that stage there might be nothing corresponding to the clear distinction made, in more developed societies, between legal and moral rules. Possibly some embryonic form of this distinction might be present if there were some rules which were primarily maintained by threats of punishment for disobedience, and others maintained by appeals to presumed

respect for the rules or to feelings of guilt or remorse. When
this early stage is passed, and (the step from the pre-legal into
the legal world is taken, so that the means of social control
now includes a system of rules containing rules of recognition,
adjudication, and change, this contrast between legal and other
rules hardens into something definite) The primary rules of
obligation identified through the official system are now set
apart from other rules, which continue to exist side by side with
those officially recognized. In fact in our own, and indeed in
all communities which reach this stage, there are many types
of social rule and standard lying outside the legal system; only
some of these are usually thought and spoken of as moral,
though certain legal theorists have used the word 'moral' to
designate all non-legal rules.

Such non-legal rules may be distinguished and classified in
many different ways. Some are rules of very limited scope concerning only a particular sphere of conduct (e.g. dress) or activities
for which there are only intermittent opportunities, deliberately
created (ceremonies and games). Some rules are conceived as
applying to the social group in general; others to special sub-
groups within it, either marked off by certain characteristics as a
distinct social class, or by their own choice to meet or combine
for limited purposes. Some rules are considered to be binding by
virtue of agreement and may allow for voluntary withdrawal:
others are thought not to have their origin in agreement or any
other form of deliberate choice. Some rules when broken may
meet with no more than an assertion or reminder of the 'right'
thing to do (e.g. etiquette or rules of correct speech), others with
serious blame or contempt or more or less protracted exclusion
from the association concerned. Though no precise scale could be
constructed, a conception of the relative importance attributed to
these different types of rules is reflected both in the measure of
sacrifice of private interest which they demand, and the weight
of social pressure for conformity.

In all societies which have developed a legal system there
are, among its non-legal rules, some to which supreme importance is attached, and which in spite of crucial differences
have many similarities to its law. Very often the vocabulary
of 'rights', 'obligations', and 'duties' used to express the

requirements of legal rules is used with the addition of 'moral', to express the acts or forbearances required by these rules. In all communities there is a partial overlap in content between legal and moral obligation; though the requirements of legal rules are more specific and are hedged round with more detailed exceptions than their moral counterparts. Characteristically, moral obligation and duty, like many legal rules, concern what is to be done or not to be done in circumstances constantly recurring in the life of the group, rather than in rare or intermittent activities on deliberately selected occasions. What such rules require are either forbearances, or actions which are simple in the sense that no special skill or intellect is required for their performance. Moral obligations, like most legal obligations, are within the capacity of any normal adult. Compliance with these moral rules, as with legal rules, is taken as a matter of course, so that while breach attracts serious censure, conformity to moral obligation, again, like obedience to the law, is not a matter for praise except when marked by exceptional conscientiousness, endurance, or resistance to special temptation. Various classifications of moral obligations and duties may be made. Some belong to relatively distinct, enduring functions or roles, which not all members of society occupy. Such are the duties of a father or husband to care for his family. On the other hand, there are both general obligations which all normal adults are conceived as having throughout life (e.g. to abstain from violence) and special obligations which any such member may incur by entering into special relations with others (e.g. obligations to keep promises or return services rendered).

The obligations and duties recognized in moral rules of this most fundamental kind may vary from society to society or within a single society at different times. Some of them may reflect quite erroneous or even superstitious beliefs as to what is required for the health or safety of the group; in one society it may be a wife's duty to throw herself on her husband's funeral pyre, and in another, suicide may be an offence against common morality. There is a diversity among moral codes which may spring either from the peculiar but real needs of a given society, or from superstition or ignorance. Yet the social morality of societies which have reached the stage where this can be distinguished from its law, always includes certain obligations and duties, requiring the sacrifice of private inclination or interest which is essential to the survival of any society, so long as men and the world in which they live retain some of their most familiar and obvious characteristics. Among such rules obviously required for social life are those forbidding, or at least restricting, the free use of violence, rules requiring certain forms of honesty and truthfulness in dealings with others, and rules forbidding the destruction of tangible things or their seizure from others. If conformity with these most elementary rules were not thought a matter of course among any group of individuals, living in close proximity to each other, we should be doubtful of the description of the group as a society, and certain that it could not endure for long.

Moral and legal rules of obligation and duty have therefore certain striking similarities enough to show that their common vocabulary is no accident. These may be summarized as follows. They are alike in that they are conceived as binding independently of the consent of the individual bound and are supported by serious social pressure for conformity; compliance with both legal and moral obligations is regarded not as a matter for praise but as a minimum contribution to social life to be taken as a matter of course. Further both law and morals include rules governing the behaviour of individuals in situations constantly recurring throughout life rather than special activities or occasions, and though both may include much that is peculiar to the real or fancied needs of a particular society, both make demands which must obviously be satisfied by any group of human beings who are to succeed in living together. Hence some forms of prohibition of violence to person or property, and some requirements of honesty and truthfulness will be found in both alike. Yet, in spite of these similarities, it has seemed obvious to many that there are certain characteristics which law and morals cannot share, though in the history of jurisprudence these have proved most difficult to formulate.

The most famous attempt to convey in summary fashion their essential difference is the theory which asserts that, while legal rules only require 'external' behaviour and are indifferent to the motives, intentions, or other 'internal' accompaniments of conduct, morals on the other hand do not require any specific external actions but only a good will or proper intentions or motive. This really amounts to the surprising assertion that legal and moral rules properly understood could not ever have the same content; and though it does contain a hint of the truth it is, as it stands, profoundly misleading. It is in fact an inference, though a mistaken one, from certain important characteristics of morals, and particularly from certain differences between moral blame and legal punishment. If someone does something forbidden by moral rules or fails to do what they require, the fact that he did so unintentionally and in spite of every care is an excuse from *moral* blame; whereas a legal system or custom may have rules of 'strict liability' under which those who have broken the rules unintentionally and without 'fault' may be liable to punishment. So it is indeed true that while the notion of 'strict liability' in morals comes as near to being a contradiction in terms as anything in this sphere, it is something which may be merely open to criticism when found in a legal system. But this does not mean that morals require only good intention, will, or motives. Indeed to argue thus is, as we show later, to confuse the idea of an *excuse* with that of a *justification* for conduct.

None the less there is something of importance caricatured in this confused argument; the vague sense that the difference between law and morals is connected with a contrast between the 'internality' of the one and the 'externality' of the other is too recurrent a theme in speculation about law and morals to be altogether baseless. Rather than dismiss it, we shall treat it as a compendious statement of four cardinal related features which collectively serve to distinguish morality not only from legal rules but from other forms of social rule.

(i) *Importance.* To say that an essential feature of *any* moral rule or standard is that it is regarded as something of great importance to maintain may appear both truistic and vague. Yet this feature cannot be omitted in any faithful account of the morality of any social group or individual, nor can it be made more precise. It is manifested in many ways: first, in the simple fact that moral standards are maintained against the drive of strong passions which they restrict, and at the cost of sacrificing considerable personal interest; secondly, in the serious forms of social pressure exerted not only to obtain conformity in individual cases, but to secure that moral standards are taught or communicated as a matter of course to all in society; thirdly, in the general recognition that, if moral standards were not generally accepted, far-reaching and distasteful changes in the life of individuals would occur) In contrast with morals, the rules of deportment, manners, dress, and some, though not all, rules of law, occupy a relatively low place in the scale of serious importance. They may be tiresome to follow, but they do not demand great sacrifice: no great pressure is exerted to obtain conformity and no great alterations in other areas of social life would follow if they were not observed or changed. (Much of the importance thus ascribed to the maintenance of moral rules may be very simply explained on agreeably rationalistic lines; for even though they demand sacrifice of private interests on the part of the person bound, compliance with them secures vital interests which all share alike) It does so either by directly protecting persons from obvious harm or by maintaining the fabric of a tolerable, orderly society. But though the rationality of much social morality, as a protection from obvious harms, may be defended in this way, this simple utilitarian approach is not always possible; nor, where it is, should it be taken to represent the point of view of those who live by a morality. After all, a most prominent part of the morality of any society consists of rules concerning sexual behaviour, and it is far from clear that the importance attached to them is connected with the belief that the conduct they forbid is harmful to others; nor could such rules always be shown in fact to have this justification. (Even in a modern society which has ceased to look on its morality as divinely ordained, calculations of harmfulness to others do not account for the importance attached to moral regulation of sexual behaviour such as the common veto on homosexuality. Sexual functions and feelings are matter of such moment and emotional concern to all, that deviations from the accepted or normal forms of their expression easily become invested with an intrinsic 'pudor' or importance. They are abhorred, not out of conviction of their social harmfulness but simply as 'unnatural' or in themselves repugnant. Yet it would be absurd to deny the title of morality to emphatic social vetoes of this sort; indeed, sexual morality is perhaps the most prominent aspect of what plain men think morality to be. Of course the fact that society may view its own morality in this 'non-utilitarian' way does not mean that its rules are immune from criticism or condemnation, where their maintenance is judged useless or purchased at the cost of great suffering.

Legal rules, as we have seen, may correspond with moral rules in the sense of requiring or forbidding the same behaviour. Those that do so are no doubt felt to be as important as their moral counterparts. Yet importance is not essential to the status of all legal rules as it is to that of morals. A legal rule may be generally thought quite unimportant to maintain; indeed it may generally be agreed that it should be repealed: yet it remains a legal rule until it is repealed. It would, on the other hand, be absurd to think of a rule as part of the morality of a society even though no one thought it any longer important or worth maintaining. Old customs and traditions now maintained merely for old time's sake may, indeed, once have had the status of moral rules, but their status as part of morality has evaporated together with the importance attached to their observance and breach.

(ii) *Immunity from deliberate change.* It is characteristic of a legal system that new legal rules can be introduced and old ones changed or repealed by deliberate enactment, even though some laws may be protected from change by a written constitution limiting the competence of the supreme legislature. By contrast moral rules or principles *cannot* be brought into being or changed or eliminated in this way. To assert that this 'cannot' be is not, however, to deny that some conceivable state of affairs is actually the case, as the assertion that human beings 'cannot' alter the climate would be. Instead this assertion points to the following facts. It is perfectly good sense to say such things as 'As from 1 January 1960 it will be a criminal offence to do so-and-so' or 'As from 1 January 1960 it will be no longer illegal to do so-and-so' and to support such statements by reference to laws which have been enacted or repealed. By contrast such statements as 'As from tomorrow it will no longer be immoral to do so-and-so' or 'On 1 January last it became immoral to do so-and-so' and attempts to support these by reference to deliberate enactment would be astonishing paradoxes, if not senseless. For it is inconsistent with the part played by morality in the lives of individuals that moral rules, principles, or standards should be regarded, as laws are, as things capable of creation or change by deliberate act. Standards of conduct cannot be endowed with, or deprived of, moral status by human *fiat*, though the daily use of such concepts as enactment and repeal shows that the same is not true of law.

Much moral philosophy is devoted to the explanation of this feature of morality, and to the elucidation of the sense that morality is something 'there' to be recognized, not made by deliberate human choice. But the fact itself as distinct from its explanation is not a peculiarity of moral rules. This is why this feature of morality, though exceedingly important, cannot serve by itself to distinguish morality from all other forms of social norms. For in this respect, though not in others, any social tradition is like morals: tradition too is incapable of enactment or repeal by human *fiat*. The story, perhaps apocryphal, that the headmaster of a new English public school announced that, as from the beginning of the next term, it would be a tradition of the school that senior boys should wear a certain dress, depends for its comic effect wholly on the logical incompatibility of the notion of a tradition with that of deliberate enactment and choice. Rules acquire and lose the status of traditions by growing, being practised, ceasing to be practised, and decaying; and rules brought into being or eliminated otherwise than by these slow, involuntary processes could not thereby acquire or lose the status of tradition.

(The fact that morals and traditions cannot be directly changed, as laws may be, by legislative enactment must not be mistaken for immunity from other forms of change. Indeed though a moral rule or tradition cannot be repealed or changed by deliberate choice or enactment, the enactment or repeal of laws may well be among the causes of a change or decay of some moral standard or some tradition.) If a traditional practice such as the celebrations on Guy Fawkes night is forbidden by law and punished, the practice may cease and the tradition may disappear. Conversely, if the laws require military service from certain classes, this may ultimately develop a tradition among them which may well outlive the law.(So too legal enactments may set standards of honesty and humanity, which ultimately alter and raise the current morality; conversely, legal repression of practices thought morally obligatory may, in the end, cause the sense of their importance and so their status as morality to be lost; yet, very often, the law loses such battles with ingrained morality, and the moral rule continues in full vigour side by side with laws which forbid what it enjoins.)

These modes of change of tradition and morality in which the law may be a causal factor must be distinguished from legislative change or repeal. For though the acquisition or loss of *legal* status due to enactment may indeed be spoken of as the enacted statute's 'legal effect' this is not a contingent causal change, as the statute's eventual effect on morals and tradition is. This difference may be simply seen in the fact that while it is always possible to doubt whether a clear, valid, legal enactment will lead to a change in morals, no similar doubts could be entertained as to whether a clear, valid, legal enactment has changed the law.

The incompatibility of the idea of morality or tradition with that of change by deliberate enactment, must also be distinguished from the immunity conferred on certain laws in some systems by the restrictive clauses of a constitution. Such immunity is not a necessary element in the status of a law as a law, for this immunity may be removed by constitutional amendment. Unlike such legal immunity from legislative change, the incapacity of morals or tradition for similar modes of change is not something which varies from community to community or from time to time. It is incorporated in the meaning of these terms; the idea of a moral legislature with competence to make and change morals, as legal enactments make and change law, is repugnant to the whole notion of morality. When we come to consider international law we shall find it important to distinguish the mere *de facto* absence of a legislature, which may be regarded as a defect of the system, from the fundamental inconsistency which, as we have stressed here, is latent in the idea that moral rules or standards could be made or repealed by legislation.

(iii) *Voluntary character of moral offences.* The old conception that morals are exclusively concerned with what is 'internal' while law is concerned only with 'external' behaviour is in part a misstatement of the two features already discussed. But it is most often treated as a reference to certain prominent characteristics of moral responsibility and moral blame. If a person whose action, judged *ab extra*, has offended against moral rules or principles, succeeds in establishing that he did this unintentionally and in spite of every precaution that it was possible for him to take, he is excused from moral responsibility, and to blame him in these circumstances would itself be considered morally objectionable. Moral blame is excluded because he has done all that he could do. In any developed legal system the same is true up to a point; for the general requirement of *mens rea* is an element in criminal responsibility designed to secure that those who offend without carelessness, unwittingly, or in conditions in which they lacked the bodily or mental capacity to conform to the law, should be excused. A legal system would be open to serious moral condemnation if this were not so, at any rate in cases of serious crimes carrying severe punishments.

None the less admission of such excuses in all legal systems is qualified in many different ways. The real or alleged difficulties of proof of psychological facts may lead a legal system to refuse to investigate the actual mental states or capacities of particular individuals, and, instead, to use 'objective tests', whereby the individual charged with an offence is taken to have the capacities for control or ability to take precautions that a normal or 'reasonable' man would have. Some systems may refuse to consider 'volitional' as distinct from 'cognitive' disabilities; if so they confine the range of excuses to lack of intention or defects of knowledge. Again, the legal system may, for certain types of offence, impose 'strict liability' and make responsibility independent of *mens rea* altogether, except perhaps for the minimum requirement that the accused must possess normal muscular control.

It is therefore clear that legal responsibility is not necessarily excluded by the demonstration that an accused person could not have kept the law which he has broken; by contrast, in morals 'I could not help it' is always an excuse, and moral obligation would be altogether different from what it is if the moral 'ought' did not in this sense imply 'can'. Yet it is important to see that 'I could not help it' is only an excuse (though a good one), and to distinguish excuse from justification; for, as we have said, the claim that morals do not require external behaviour rests on a confusion of these two ideas. If good intentions were a justification for doing what moral rules forbid, there would be nothing to deplore in the action of a man who had accidentally and in spite of every care killed another. We should look upon it as we now look upon a man's killing another, when this is required as a necessary measure of self-defence. The latter is *justified* because killing, in such circumstances, is a kind of conduct which the system is not concerned to prevent and may even encourage, though it is of course an exception to a general prohibition of killing. Where someone is *excused* because he offended unintentionally, the underlying moral conception is not that this action is of a kind which it is the policy of the law to permit or even welcome; it is that when we investigate the mental condition of the particular offender, we find that he lacked the normal capacity to conform to the law's requirements. (Hence this aspect of the 'internality' of morals does not mean that morals is not a form of control of outward conduct; but only that it is a necessary condition for moral responsibility that the individual must have a certain type of control over his conduct. Even in morals there is a difference between 'He did not do the wrong thing' and 'He could not help doing what he did'.)

(iv) *The form of moral pressure.* A further distinguishing feature of morality is the characteristic form of moral pressure which is exerted in its support. This feature is closely related to the last and like it has powerfully contributed to the vague sense that moral is concerned with what is 'internal'. The facts which have led to this interpretation of morality are these. (If it were the case that whenever someone was about to break a rule of conduct, *only* threats of physical punishment or unpleasant consequences were used in argument to dissuade him, then it would be impossible to regard such a

rule as a part of the morality of the society, though this would not
be any objection to treating it as part of its law. Indeed the typical
form of legal pressure may well be said to consist in such threats.)
With morals on the other hand the typical form of pressure consists in appeals to the respect for the rules, as things important in
themselves, which is presumed to be shared by those addressed.
(So moral pressure is characteristically, though not exclusively,
exerted not by threats or by appeals to fear or interest, but by
reminders of the moral character of the action contemplated and
of the demands of morality.) 'That would be a lie', 'That would
be to break your promise'. (In the background there are indeed
the 'internal' moral analogues of fear of punishment; for it is
assumed that protests will awaken in those addressed a sense of
shame or guilt: they may be 'punished' by their own conscience.)
(Of course sometimes such distinctively moral appeals are accompanied by threats of physical punishment, or by appeals to ordinary personal interest; deviations from the moral code meet with
many different forms of hostile social reaction, ranging from
relatively informal expressions of contempt to severance of social
relations or ostracism.)But emphatic reminders of what the rules
demand, appeals to conscience, and reliance on the operation
of guilt and remorse, are the characteristic and most prominent
forms of pressure used for the support of social morality. That it
should be supported in just these ways is a simple consequence of
the acceptance of moral rules and standards, as things which it is
supremely and obviously important to maintain. Standards not
supported in these ways could not have the place in social and
personal life distinctive of moral obligation.)

3. MORAL IDEALS AND SOCIAL CRITICISM

Moral obligation and duty are the bedrock of social morality
but they are not the whole. Before we examine other forms
we shall, however, consider an objection to the way in which
we have characterized moral obligation. The fourfold criteria
which in the last section we used to distinguish it from other
forms of social standard or rule (importance, immunity from
deliberate change, the voluntary character of moral offences,
and the special form of moral pressure) are in a sense *formal*

criteria. They make no direct reference to any necessary content which rules or standards must have in order to be moral, nor even to any purpose which they must serve in social life. We have, indeed, insisted that in all moral codes there will be found some form of prohibition of the use of violence, to persons or things, and requirements of truthfulness, fair dealing, and respect for promises. These things, granted only certain very obvious truisms about human nature and the character of the physical world, can be seen in fact to be essential if human beings are to live continuously together in close proximity; and it therefore would be extraordinary if rules providing for them were not everywhere endowed with the moral importance and status which we have described. It seems clear that the sacrifice of personal interest which such rules *demand* is the price which must be paid in a world such as ours for living with others, and the protection they *afford* is the minimum which, for beings such as ourselves, makes living with others worth while. These simple facts constitute, as we argue in the next chapter, a core of indisputable truth in the doctrines of Natural Law.

Many moralists would wish to bring into the definition of morality as a further criterion beyond the four which we have offered, this connection, which seems so clear, between morality and human needs and interests. They would stipulate that nothing is to be recognized as part of morality unless it could survive rational criticism in terms of human interests, and so be shown to advance them (perhaps even in some fair or equal way), in the society whose rules they are. Some might even go further, and refuse to recognize as moral any principle or rule of conduct, unless the benefits of the for-bearances and actions it required were extended, beyond the boundaries of a particular society, to all who were themselves willing and able to respect such rules. We have, however, intentionally taken a broader view of morality, so as to include in it all social rules and standards which, in the actual practice of a society, exhibit the four features we have men-tioned. Some of these would survive criticism in the light of these further suggested tests; others would not but might be condemned as irrational or unenlightened or even barbarous. We have done this not merely because the weight of usage of the word 'moral' favours this broader meaning, but because to take the narrower restricted view, which would exclude these, would force us to divide in a very unrealistic manner elements in a social structure which function in an identical manner, in the lives of those who live by it. Moral prohibitions of conduct, which may not in fact harm others, are not only regarded with precisely the same instinctive respect as those that do; they enter together with the requirements of more rationally defensible rules into social estimates of character; and, with them, form part of the generally accepted picture of the life which individuals are expected and indeed are assumed to live.

It is, however, both true and important that morality includes much more than the *obligations* and *duties* which are recognized in the actual practice of social groups.(Obligation and duty are only the bedrock of morality, even of social morality, and there are forms of morality which extend beyond the accepted shared morality of particular societies.) Two further aspects of morality require attention here. First, even within the morality of a particular society, there exist side by side with the structure of mandatory moral obligations and duties and the relatively clear rules that define them, certain moral *ideals*. The realization of these is not taken, as duty is, as a matter of course, but as an achievement deserving praise.(The hero and the saint are extreme types of those who do *more* than their duty. What they do is not like obligation or duty, something which can be demanded of them, and failure to do it is not regarded as wrong or a matter for censure. On a humbler scale than the saint or hero, are those who are recognized in a society as deserving praise for the moral virtues which they manifest in daily life such as bravery, charity, benevolence, patience, or chastity. The connection between such socially recognized ideals and virtues and the primary mandatory forms of social obligation and duty is fairly clear. Many moral virtues are qualities consisting in the ability and disposition to carry forward beyond the limited extent which duty demands, the kind of concern for others' interests or sacrifice of personal interest which it does demand.) Benevolence and charity are examples of this.(Other moral virtues like temperance, patience, bravery, or conscientiousness are in a sense ancillary: they are qualities of character shown in exceptional devotion to duty or in the pursuit of substantive moral ideals in the face of special temptation or danger.)

The further reaches of morality take us in different ways beyond the confines of the obligations and ideals recognized in particular social groups to the principles and ideals used in the moral criticism of society itself; yet even here important connections remain with the primordial social form of morality. (It is always possible, when we come to examine the accepted morality either of our own or some other society, that we shall find much to criticize; it may, in the light of currently available knowledge, appear unnecessarily repressive, cruel, superstitious, or unenlightened. It may cramp human liberty, especially in the discussion and practice of religion or in experimentation with different forms of human life, even when only negligible benefits are thereby secured for others.) Above all, a given society's morality may extend its protections from harm to its own members only, or even only to certain classes, leaving a slave or helot class at the mercy of their masters' whims. Implicit in this type of criticism which (even though it might be rejected) would certainly be accorded recognition as 'moral' criticism, is the assumption that the arrangements of society, including its accepted morality, must satisfy two formal conditions, one of rationality and the other of generality. Thus it is implied in such criticism first that social arrangements should not rest on beliefs which can be shown to be mistaken, and secondly that the protections from harm, which morality characteristically affords through the actions and forbearances it demands, should be extended at least to all men who are able and willing themselves to observe such restrictions. Thus such moral criticism of society as that enshrined in watchwords like liberty, fraternity, equality, and the pursuit of happiness draws its moral character from the fact that it invites reform, either in the name of some value or combination of values already recognized (though perhaps to an inadequate extent) in all actual social moralities or in the name of a version of these, refined and extended so as to meet the two demands of rationality and generality.)

Of course it does not follow from the fact that criticism of the accepted morality or other social arrangements in the name of liberty or equality is itself recognized as *moral* criticism that the rejection of it in the names of other values may not also be moral. The denunciation of restriction on liberty might be met by the claim that the sacrifice of liberty to social or economic equality or security was itself justified. Such differences of weight or emphasis placed on different moral values may prove irreconcilable. They may amount to radically different ideal conceptions of society and form the moral basis of opposed political parties. One of the great justifications of democracy is that it permits experimentation and a revisable choice between such alternatives.

Finally, not all extensions of morality beyond the obligations and ideals generally recognized in a given society need take the form of social criticism. It is important to remember that morality has its private aspect, shown in the individual's recognition of ideals which he need not either share with others or regard as a source of criticism of others, still less of society as a whole. Lives may be ruled by dedication to the pursuit of heroic, romantic, aesthetic or scholarly ideals or, less agreeably, to mortification of the flesh. Here too, it could be argued that if we speak of morality, we do so because the values thus pursued by individuals are at least analogous to some of those recognized in the morality of their own society. But the analogy is surely not one of content, but one of form and function. For such ideals play, in the life of individuals, the same part as morality does in a society. They are ranked as supremely important, so that their pursuit is felt as duty to which other interests or desires are to be sacrificed; though conversions are possible the notion that such ideals could be adopted, changed, or eliminated by a deliberate choice is chimerical; and, finally, deviations from such ideals are 'punished' by the same conscience, guilt, and remorse as that to which social morality makes its primary appeal.

LAWS AND MORALS

1. NATURAL LAW AND LEGAL POSITIVISM

There are many different types of relation between law and morals and there is nothing which can be profitably singled out for study as *the* relation between them. Instead it is important to distinguish some of the many different things which may be meant by the assertion or denial that law and morals are related. Sometimes what is asserted is a kind of connection which few if any have ever denied; but its indisputable existence may be wrongly accepted as a sign of some more doubtful connection, or even mistaken for it. Thus, it cannot seriously be disputed that the development of law, at all times and places, has in fact been profoundly influenced both by the conventional morality and ideals of particular social groups, and also by forms of enlightened moral criticism urged by individuals, whose moral horizon has transcended the morality currently accepted. But it is possible to take this truth illicitly, as a warrant for a different proposition: namely that a legal system *must* exhibit some specific conformity with morality or justice, or *must* rest on a widely diffused conviction that there is a moral obligation to obey it. Again, though this proposition may, in some sense, be true, it does not follow from it that the criteria of legal validity of particular laws used in a legal system must include, tacitly if not explicitly, a reference to morality or justice.

Many other questions besides these may be said to concern the relations between law and morals. In this chapter we shall discuss only two of them, though both will involve some consideration of many others. The first is a question which may still be illuminatingly described as the issue between Natural Law and Legal Positivism, though each of these titles has come to be used for a range of different theses about law and morals. Here we shall take Legal Positivism to mean the simple contention that it is in no sense a necessary truth that laws reproduce or satisfy certain demands of morality, though in fact they have often done so. But just because those who have taken this view have either been silent or differed very much concerning the nature of morality, it is necessary to consider two very different forms in which Legal Positivism has been rejected. One of these is expressed most clearly in the classical theories of Natural Law: that there are certain principles of human conduct, awaiting discovery by human reason, with which man-made law must conform if it is to be valid. The other takes a different, less rationalist view of morality, and offers a different account of the ways in which legal validity is connected with moral value. We shall consider the first of these in this section and the next.

In the vast literature from Plato to the present day which is dedicated to the assertion, and also to the denial, of the proposition that the ways in which men ought to behave may be discovered by human reason, the disputants on one side seem to say to those on the other, 'You are blind if you cannot see this' only to receive in reply, 'You have been dreaming.' This is so, because the claim that there are true principles of right conduct, rationally discoverable, has not usually been advanced as a separate doctrine but was originally presented, and for long defended, as part of a general conception of nature, inanimate and living. This outlook is, in many ways, antithetic to the general conception of nature which constitutes the framework of modern secular thought. Hence it is that, to its critics, Natural Law theory has seemed to spring from deep and old confusions from which modern thought has triumphantly freed itself; while to its advocates, the critics appear merely to insist on surface trivialities, ignoring profounder truths.

Thus many modern critics have thought that the claim that laws of proper conduct may be discovered by human reason rested on a simple ambiguity of the word 'law', and that when this ambiguity was exposed Natural Law received its deathblow. It is in this way that John Stuart Mill dealt with Montesquieu, who in the first chapter of the *Esprit des Lois* naïvely inquires why it is that, while inanimate things such as the stars and also animals obey 'the law of their nature', man does not do so but falls into sin. This, Mill thought, revealed the perennial confusion between laws which formulate the course or regularities of nature, and laws which require men to behave in certain ways. The former, which can be discovered by observation and reasoning, may be called 'descriptive' and it is for the scientist thus to discover them; the latter cannot be so established, for they are not statements or descriptions of facts, but are 'prescriptions' or demands that men shall behave in certain ways. The answer therefore to Montesquieu's question is simple: prescriptive laws may be broken and yet remain laws, because that merely means that human beings do not do what they are told to do; but it is meaningless to say of the laws of nature, discovered by science, either that they can or cannot be broken. If the stars behave in ways contrary to the scientific laws which purport to describe their regular movements, these are not broken but they lose their title to be called 'laws' and must be reformulated. To these differences in the sense of 'law', there correspond systematic differences in the associated vocabulary of words like 'must', 'bound to', 'ought', and 'should'. So, on this view, belief in Natural Law is reducible to a very simple fallacy: a failure to perceive the very different senses which those law-impregnated words can bear. It is as if the believer had failed to perceive the very different meaning of such words in 'You are bound to report for military service' and 'It is bound to freeze if the wind goes round to the north'.

Critics like Bentham and Mill, who most fiercely attacked Natural Law, often attributed their opponents' confusion between these distinct senses of law, to the survival of the belief that the observed regularities of nature were prescribed or decreed by a Divine Governor of the Universe. On such a theocratic view, the only difference between the law of gravity and the Ten Commandments—God's law for Man—was, as Blackstone asserted, the relatively minor one that men, alone of created things, were endowed with reason and free will; and so unlike things, could discover and disobey the divine prescriptions. Natural Law has, however, not always been associated with belief in a Divine Governor or Lawgiver of the universe, and even where it has been, its characteristic tenets have not been logically dependent on that belief. Both the relevant sense of the word 'natural', which enters into

Natural Law, and its general outlook minimizing the difference, so obvious and so important to modern minds, between prescriptive and descriptive laws, have their roots in Greek thought which was, for this purpose, quite secular. Indeed, the continued reassertion of some form of Natural Law doctrine is due in part to the fact that its appeal is independent of both divine and human authority, and to the fact that despite a terminology, and much metaphysics, which few could now accept, it contains certain elementary truths of importance for the understanding of both morality and law. These we shall endeavour to disentangle from their metaphysical setting and restate here in simpler terms.

For modern secular thought the world of inanimate and living things, animals, and men is a scene of recurrent kinds of events and changes which exemplify certain regular connections. Some at least of these, human beings have discovered and formulated as laws of nature. To understand nature is, in this modern view, to bring to bear on some part of it, knowledge of these regularities. The structure of great scientific theories does not of course mirror in any simple way observable fact, events, or changes; often, indeed, a great part of such theories consists of abstract mathematical formulations with no direct counterpart in observable fact. Their connection with observable events and changes lies in the fact that, from these abstract formulations, generalizations may be deduced which do refer to, and may be confirmed or falsified by, observable events. A scientific theory's claim to forward our understanding of nature is therefore, in the last resort, dependent on its power to predict what will occur, which is based on generalizations of what regularly occurs. The law of gravity and the second law of thermodynamics are, for modern thought, laws of nature and more than mere mathematical constructions in virtue of the information they yield concerning the regularities of observable phenomena.

The doctrine of Natural Law is part of an older conception of nature in which the observable world is not merely a scene of such regularities, and knowledge of nature is not merely a knowledge of them. Instead, on this older outlook every nameable kind of existing thing, human, animate, and inanimate, is conceived not only as tending to maintain itself in existence but as proceeding towards a definite optimum state which is the specific good—or the *end* (τέλοζ, *finis*) appropriate for it.

This is the teleological conception of nature as containing in itself levels of excellence which things realize. The stages by which a thing of any given kind progresses to its specific or proper end are regular, and may be formulated in generalizations describing the thing's characteristic mode of change, or action, or development; to that extent the teleological view of nature overlaps with modern thought. The difference is that on the teleological view, the events regularly befalling things are not thought of *merely* as occurring regularly, and the questions whether they *do* occur regularly and whether they *should* occur or whether it is *good* that they occur are not regarded as separate questions. On the contrary (except for some rare monstrosities ascribed to 'chance'), what generally occurs can both be explained and evaluated as good or what ought to occur, by exhibiting it as a step towards the proper end or goal of the thing concerned. The laws of a thing's development therefore should show both how it should and how it does regularly behave or change.

This mode of thinking about nature seems strange when stated abstractly. It may appear less fantastic if we recall some of the ways in which even now we refer at least to living things, for a teleological view is still reflected in common ways of describing their development. Thus in the case of an acorn, growth into an oak is something which is not only regularly achieved by acorns, but is distinguished unlike its decay (which is also regular) as an optimum state of maturity in the light of which the intermediate stages are both explained and judged as good or bad, and the 'functions' of its various parts and structural changes identified. The normal growth of leaves is required if it is to obtain the moisture necessary for 'full' or 'proper' development, and it is the 'function' of leaves to supply this. Hence we think and speak of this growth as what 'ought naturally to occur'. In the case of the action or movements of inanimate things, such ways of talking seem much less plausible unless they are artefacts designed by human beings for a purpose. The notion that a stone on falling to the ground is realizing some appropriate 'end' or returning to its 'proper place', like a horse galloping home to a stable, is now somewhat comic.

Indeed, one of the difficulties in understanding a teleological view of nature is that just as it minimized the differences between statements of what regularly happens and statements of what ought to happen, so too it minimizes the difference, so important in modern thought, between human beings *with* a purpose of their own which they consciously strive to realize and other living or inanimate things. For in the teleological view of the world, man, like other things, is thought of as tending towards a specific optimum state or end which is set for him and the fact, that he, unlike other things, may do this consciously, is not conceived as a radical difference between him and the rest of nature. This specific human end or good is in part, like that of other living things, a condition of biological maturity and developed physical powers; but it also includes, as its distinctively human element, a development and excellence of mind and character manifested in thought and conduct. Unlike other things, man is able by reasoning and reflection to discover what the attainment of this excellence of mind and character involves and to desire it. Yet even so, on this teleological view, this optimum state is not man's good or end because he desires it; rather he desires it because it is already his natural end.

Again, much of this teleological point of view survives in some of the ways in which we think and speak of human beings. It is latent in our identification of certain things as human *needs* which it is *good* to satisfy and of certain things done to or suffered *by* human beings as *harm* or *injury*. Thus, though it is true that some men may refuse to eat or rest because they wish to die, we think of eating and resting as something more than things which men regularly do or just happen to desire. Food and rest are human needs, even if some refuse them when they are needed. Hence we say not only that it is natural for all men to eat and sleep, but that all men ought to eat and rest sometimes, or that it is naturally good to do these things. The force of the word 'naturally', in such judgments of human conduct, is to differentiate them both from judgments which reflect mere conventions or human prescriptions ('You ought to take off your hat'), the content of which cannot be discovered by thought or reflection, and also from judgments which merely indicate what is required for achieving some particular objective, which at a given time one man may happen to have and another may not. The same outlook is present in our conception of the *functions* of bodily organs and the line we draw between these and mere causal properties. We say it is the function of the heart to circulate the blood, but not that it is the function of a cancerous growth to cause death.

These crude examples designed to illustrate teleological elements still alive in ordinary thought about human action, are drawn from the lowly sphere of biological fact which man shares with other animals. It will be rightly observed that what makes sense of this mode of thought and expression is something entirely obvious: it is the tacit assumption that the proper end of human activity is survival, and this rests on the simple contingent fact that most men most of the time wish to continue in existence. The actions which we speak of as those which are naturally good to do, are those which are required for survival; the notions of a human need, of harm, and of the *function* of bodily organs or changes rest on the same simple fact. Certainly if we stop here, we shall have only a very attenuated version of Natural Law: for the classical exponents of this outlook conceived of survival (*perseverare in esse suo*) as merely the lowest stratum in a much more complex and far more debatable concept of the human end or good for man. Aristotle included in it the disinterested cultivation of the human intellect, and Aquinas the knowledge of God, and both these represent values which may be and have been challenged. Yet other thinkers, Hobbes and Hume among them, have been willing to lower their sights: they have seen in the modest aim of survival the central indisputable element which gives empirical good sense to the terminology of Natural Law. 'Human nature cannot by any means subsist without the association of individuals: and that association never could have place were no regard paid to the laws of equity and justice.'[1]

This simple thought has in fact very much to do with the

---

[1] Hume, *Treatise of Human Nature*, III. ii, 'Of Justice and Injustice'.

characteristics of both law and morals, and it can be disentangled
from more disputable parts of the general teleological outlook
in which the end or good for man appears as a specific way
of life about which, in fact, men may profoundly disagree.
Moreover, we can, in referring to survival, discard, as too
metaphysical for modern minds, the notion that this is something antecedently fixed which men necessarily desire because
it is their proper goal or end. Instead we may hold it to be a
mere contingent fact which could be otherwise, that in general
men do desire to live, and that we may mean nothing more by
calling survival a human goal or end than that men do desire it.
Yet even if we think of it in this common-sense way, survival
has still a special status in relation to human conduct and in our
thought about it, which parallels the prominence and the necessity ascribed to it in the orthodox formulations of Natural Law.
For it is not merely that an overwhelming majority of men do
wish to live, even at the cost of hideous misery, but that this is
reflected in whole structures of our thought and language, in
terms of which we describe the world and each other. We could
not subtract the general wish to live and leave intact concepts
like danger and safety, harm and benefit, need and function,
disease and cure; for these are ways of simultaneously describing and appraising things by reference to the contribution they
make to survival which is accepted as an aim.

There are, however, simpler, less philosophical, considerations
than these which show acceptance of survival as an aim to be
necessary, in a sense more directly relevant to the discussion of
human law and morals, We are committed to it as something
presupposed by the terms of the discussion; for our concern is
with social arrangements for continued existence, not with
those of a suicide club. We wish to know whether, among
these social arrangements, there are some which may illuminatingly be ranked as natural laws discoverable by reason, and
what their relation is to human law and morality. To raise
this or any other question concerning *how* men should live
together, we must assume that their aim, generally speaking, is to live. From this point the argument is a simple one.
Reflection on some very obvious generalizations—indeed
truisms—concerning human nature and the world in which

men live, show that as long as these hold good, there are certain rules of conduct which any social organization must contain if it is to be viable. Such rules do in fact constitute a common element in the law and conventional morality of all societies which have progressed to the point where these are distinguished as different forms of social control. With them are found, both in law and morals, much that is peculiar to a particular society and much that may seem arbitrary or a mere matter of choice. Such universally recognized principles of conduct which have a basis in elementary truths concerning human beings, their natural environment, and aims, may be considered the *minimum content* of Natural Law, in contrast with the more grandiose and more challengeable constructions which have often been proffered under that name. In the next section we shall consider, in the form of five truisms, the salient characteristics of human nature upon which this modest but important minimum rests.

2. THE MINIMUM CONTENT OF NATURAL LAW

In considering the simple truisms which we set forth here, and their connection with law and morals, it is important to observe that in each case the facts mentioned afford a *reason* why, given survival as an aim, law and morals should include a specific content. The general form of the argument is simply that without such a content laws and morals could not forward the minimum purpose of survival which men have in associating with each other. In the absence of this content men, as they are, would have no reason for obeying voluntarily any rules; and without a minimum of co-operation given voluntarily by those who find that it is in their interest to submit to and maintain the rules, coercion of others who would not voluntarily conform would be impossible. It is important to stress the distinctively rational connection between natural facts and the content of legal and moral rules in this approach, because it is both possible and important to inquire into quite different forms of connection between natural facts and legal or moral rules. Thus, the still young sciences of psychology and sociology may discover or may even have discovered that, unless certain physical, psychological, or economic conditions are satisfied, e.g. unless young children

are fed and nurtured in certain ways within the family, no system
of laws or code of morals can be established, or that only those
laws can function successfully which conform to a certain type.
Connections of this sort between natural conditions and systems
of rules are not mediated by *reasons*; for they do not relate the
existence of certain rules to the conscious aims or purpose of
those whose rules they are. Being fed in infancy in a certain
way may well be shown to be a necessary condition or even a
cause of a population developing or maintaining a moral or legal
code, but it is not a *reason* for their doing so. Such causal connections do not of course conflict with the connections which rest
on purposes or conscious aims; they may indeed be considered
more important or fundamental than the latter, since they may
actually explain why human beings have those conscious aims or
purposes which Natural Law takes as its starting-points. Causal
explanations of this type do not rest on truisms nor are they
mediated by conscious aims or purposes: they are for sociology
or psychology like other sciences to establish by the methods of
generalization and theory, resting on observation and, where
possible, on experiment. Such connections therefore are of a different kind from those which relate the content of certain legal
and moral rules to the facts stated in the following truisms.

(i) *Human vulnerability.* The common requirements of law and
morality consist for the most part not of active services to be
rendered but of forbearances, which are usually formulated in
negative form as prohibitions. Of these the most important for
social life are those that restrict the use of violence in killing or
inflicting bodily harm. The basic character of such rules may
be brought out in a question: If there were not these rules what
point could there be for beings such as ourselves in having rules
of *any* other kind? The force of this rhetorical question rests on
the fact that men are both occasionally prone to, and normally
vulnerable to, bodily attack. Yet though this is a truism it is not
a necessary truth; for things might have been, and might one
day be, otherwise. There are species of animals whose physical
structure (including exoskeletons or a carapace) renders them
virtually immune from attack by other members of their species
and animals who have no organs enabling them to attack. If men

were to lose their vulnerability to each other there would vanish one obvious reason for the most characteristic provision of law and morals: *Thou shalt not kill.*

(ii) *Approximate equality.* Men differ from each other in physical strength, agility, and even more in intellectual capacity. None the less it is a fact of quite major importance for the understanding of different forms of law and morality, that no individual is so much more powerful than others, that he is able, without co-operation, to dominate or subdue them for more than a short period. Even the strongest must sleep at times and, when asleep, loses temporarily his superiority. This fact of approximate equality, more than any other, makes obvious the necessity for a system of mutual forbearance and compromise which is the base of both legal and moral obligation. Social life with its rules requiring such forbearances is irksome at times; but it is at any rate less nasty, less brutish, and less short than unrestrained aggression for beings thus approximately equal. It is, of course, entirely consistent with this and an equal truism that when such a system of forbearance is established there will always be some who will wish to exploit it, by simultaneously living within its shelter and breaking its restrictions. This, indeed is, as we later show, one of the natural facts which makes the step from merely moral to organized, legal forms of control a necessary one. Again, things might have been otherwise. Instead of being approximately equal there might have been some men immensely stronger than others and better able to dispense with rest, either because some were in these ways far above the present average, or because most were far below it. Such exceptional men might have much to gain by aggression and little to gain from mutual forbearance or compromise with others. But we need not have recourse to the fantasy of giants among pygmies to see the cardinal importance of the fact of approximate equality: for it is illustrated better by the facts of international life, where there are (or were) vast disparities in strength and vulnerability between the states. This inequality, as we shall later see, between the units of international law is one of the things that has imparted to it a character so different from municipal law and limited the extent to which it is capable of operating as an organized coercive system.

(iii) *Limited altruism*. Men are not devils dominated by a wish to exterminate each other, and the demonstration that, given only the modest aim of survival, the basic rules of law and morals are necessities, must not be identified with the false view that men are predominantly selfish and have no disinterested interest in the survival and welfare of their fellows. But if men are not devils, neither are they angels; and the fact that they are a mean between these two extremes is something which makes a system of mutual forbearances both necessary and possible. With angels, never tempted to harm others, rules requiring forbearances would not be necessary. With devils prepared to destroy, reckless of the cost to themselves, they would be impossible. As things are, human altruism is limited in range and intermittent, and the tendencies to aggression are frequent enough to be fatal to social life if not controlled.

(iv) *Limited resources*. It is a merely contingent fact that human beings need food, clothes, and shelter; that these do not exist at hand in limitless abundance; but are scarce, have to be grown or won from nature, or have to be constructed by human toil. These facts alone make indispensable some minimal form of the institution of property (though not necessarily individual property), and the distinctive kind of rule which requires respect for it. The simplest forms of property are to be seen in rules excluding persons generally other than the 'owner' from entry on, or the use of land, or from taking or using material things. If crops are to grow, land must be secure from indiscriminate entry, and food must, in the intervals between its growth or capture and consumption, be secure from being taken by others. At all times and places life itself depends on these minimal forbearances. Again, in this respect, things might have been otherwise than they are. The human organism might have been constructed like plants, capable of extracting food from air, or what it needs might have grown without cultivation in limitless abundance.

The rules which we have so far discussed are *static* rules, in the sense that the obligations they impose and the incidence of these obligations are not variable by individuals. But the division of labour, which all but the smallest groups must develop to obtain adequate supplies, brings with it the need for rules which are *dynamic* in the sense that they enable individuals to create obligations and to vary their incidence. Among these are rules enabling men to transfer, exchange, or sell their products; for these transactions involve the capacity to alter the incidence of those initial rights and obligations which define the simplest form of property. The same inescapable division of labour, and perennial need for co-operation, are also factors which make other forms of dynamic or obligation-creating rule necessary in social life. These secure the recognition of promises as a source of obligation. By this device individuals are enabled by words, spoken or written, to make themselves liable to blame or punishment for failure to act in certain stipulated ways. Where altruism is not unlimited, a standing procedure providing for such self-binding operations is required in order to create a minimum form of confidence in the future behaviour of others, and to ensure the predictability necessary for co-operation. This is most obviously needed where what is to be exchanged or jointly planned are mutual services, or wherever goods which are to be exchanged or sold are not simultaneously or immediately available.

(v) *Limited understanding and strength of will.* The facts that make rules respecting persons, property, and promises necessary in social life are simple and their mutual benefits are obvious. Most men are capable of seeing them and of sacrificing the immediate short-term interests which conformity to such rules demands. They may indeed obey, from a variety of motives: some from prudential calculation that the sacrifices are worth the gains, some from a disinterested interest in the welfare of others, and some because they look upon the rules as worthy of respect in themselves and find their ideals in devotion to them. On the other hand, neither understanding of long-term interest, nor the strength or goodness of will, upon which the efficacy of these different motives towards obedience depends, are shared by all men alike. All are tempted at times to prefer their own immediate interests and, in the absence of a special organization for their detection and punishment, many would succumb to the temptation. No doubt the advantages of mutual forbearance are so palpable that the number and strength of those who would co-operate voluntarily in a coercive system will normally be greater than any likely combination of malefactors. Yet, except in very small closely-knit societies, submission to the system of restraints would be folly if there were no organization for the coercion of those who would then try to obtain the advantages of the system without submitting to its obligations. 'Sanctions' are therefore required not as the normal motive for obedience, but as a *guarantee* that those who would voluntarily obey shall not be sacrificed to those who would not. To obey, without this, would be to risk going to the wall. Given this standing danger, what reason demands is *voluntary* co-operation in a *coercive* system.

It is to be observed that the same natural fact of approximate equality between men is of crucial importance in the efficacy of organized sanctions. If some men were vastly more powerful than others, and so not dependent on their forbearance, the strength of the malefactors might exceed that of the supporters of law and order. Given such inequalities, the use of sanctions could not be successful and would involve dangers at least as great as those which they were designed to suppress. In these circumstances instead of social life being based on a system of mutual forbearances, with force used only intermittently against a minority of malefactors, the only viable system would be one in which the weak submitted to the strong on the best terms they could make and lived under their 'protection'. This, because of the scarcity of resources, would lead to a number of conflicting power centres, each grouped round its 'strong man': these might intermittently war with each other, though the natural sanction, never negligible, of the risk of defeat might ensure an uneasy peace. Rules of a sort might then be accepted for the regulation of issues over which the 'powers' were unwilling to fight. Again we need not think in fanciful terms of pygmies and giants in order to understand the simple logistics of approximate equality and its importance for law. The international scene, where the units concerned have differed vastly in strength, affords illustration enough. For centuries the disparities between states have resulted in a system where organized sanctions have been impossible, and law has been confined to matters which did not affect 'vital' issues. How far atomic weapons, when available to all, will redress the balance of unequal power, and bring forms of control more closely resembling municipal criminal law, remains to be seen.

The simple truisms we have discussed not only disclose the core of good sense in the doctrine of Natural Law. They are of vital importance for the understanding of law and morals, and they explain why the definition of the basic forms of these in purely formal terms, without reference to any specific content or social needs, has proved so inadequate. Perhaps the major benefit to jurisprudence from this outlook is the escape it affords from certain misleading dichotomies which often obscure the discussion of the characteristics of law. Thus, for example, the traditional question whether every legal system *must* provide for sanctions can be presented in a fresh and clearer light, when we command the view of things presented by this simple version of Natural Law. We shall no longer have to choose between two unsuitable alternatives which are often taken as exhaustive: on the one hand, that of saying that this is required by 'the' meaning of the words 'law' or 'legal system', and on the other, that of saying that it is 'just a fact' that most legal systems do provide for sanctions. Neither of these alternatives is satisfactory. There are no settled principles forbidding the use of the word 'law' of systems where there are no centrally organized sanctions, and there is good reason (though no compulsion) for using the expression 'international law' of a system, which has none. On the other hand, we do need to distinguish the place that sanctions must have within a municipal system, if it is to serve the minimum purposes of beings constituted as men are. We can say, given the setting of natural facts and aims, which make sanctions both possible and necessary in a municipal system, that this is a *natural necessity*; and some such phrase is needed also to convey the status of the minimum forms of protection for persons, property, and promises which are similarly indispensable features of municipal law. It is in this form that we should reply to the positivist thesis that 'law may have any content'. For it is a truth of some importance that for the adequate description not only of law but of many other social institutions, a place must be reserved, besides definitions and ordinary statements of fact, for a third category of statements:

those the truth of which is contingent on human beings and
the world they live in retaining the salient characteristics which
they have.

3. LEGAL VALIDITY AND MORAL VALUE

The protections and benefits provided by the system of mutual
forbearances which underlies both law and morals may, in different societies, be extended to very different ranges of persons. It is
true that the denial of these elementary protections to any class of
human beings, willing to accept the corresponding restrictions,
would offend the principles of morality and justice to which all
modern states pay, at any rate, lip-service. Their professed moral
outlook is, in general, permeated by the conception that in these
fundamentals at least, human beings are entitled to be treated
alike and that differences of treatment require more to justify
them than just an appeal to the interests of others.

Yet it is plain that neither the law nor the accepted morality of
societies need extend their minimal protections and benefits to
all within their scope, and often they have not done so. In slave-
owning societies the sense that the slaves are human beings, not
mere objects to be used, may be lost by the dominant group, who
may yet remain morally most sensitive to each other's claims
and interests. Huckleberry Finn, when asked if the explosion
of a steamboat boiler had hurt anyone, replied, 'No'm: killed a
nigger.' Aunt Sally's comment 'Well it's lucky because sometimes
people do get hurt' sums up a whole morality which has often
prevailed among men. Where it does prevail, as Huck found
to his cost, to extend to slaves the concern for others which is
natural between members of the dominant group may well
be looked on as a grave moral offence, bringing with it all the
sequelae of moral guilt. Nazi Germany and South Africa offer
parallels unpleasantly near to us in time.

Though the law of some societies has occasionally been
in advance of the accepted morality, normally law follows
morality and even the homicide of a slave may be regarded
only as a waste of public resources or as an offence against the
master whose property he is. Even where slavery is not officially recognized, discriminations on grounds of race, colour,

or creed may produce a legal system and a social morality which does not recognize that all men are entitled to a minimum of protection from others.

These painful facts of human history are enough to show that, though a society to be viable must offer *some* of its members a system of mutual forbearances, it need not, unfortunately, offer them to all. It is true, as we have already emphasized in discussing the need for and the possibility of sanctions, that if a system of rules is to be imposed by force on any, there must be a sufficient number who accept it voluntarily. Without their voluntary co-operation, thus creating *authority*, the coercive power of law and government cannot be established. But coercive power, thus established on its basis of authority, may be used in two principal ways. It may be exerted only against malefactors who, though they are afforded the protection of the rules, yet selfishly break them. On the other hand, it may be used to subdue and maintain, in a position of permanent inferiority, a subject group whose size, relatively to the master group, may be large or small, depending on the means of coercion, solidarity, and discipline available to the latter, and the helplessness or inability to organize of the former. For those thus oppressed there may be nothing in the system to command their loyalty but only things to fear. They are its victims, not its beneficiaries.

In the earlier chapters of this book we stressed the fact that the existence of a legal system is a social phenomenon which always presents two aspects, to both of which we must attend if our view of it is to be realistic. It involves the attitudes and behaviour involved in the voluntary acceptance of rules and also the simpler attitudes and behaviour involved in mere obedience or acquiescence.

Hence a society with law contains those who look upon its rules from the internal point of view as accepted standards of behaviour, and not merely as reliable predictions of what will befall them, at the hands of officials, if they disobey. But it also comprises those upon whom, either because they are malefactors or mere helpless victims of the system, these legal standards have to be imposed by force or threat of force; they are concerned with the rules merely as a source of possible punishment. The balance between these two components will be determined by many different factors. If the system is fair and caters genuinely for the vital interests of all those from whom it demands obedience, it may gain and retain the allegiance of most for most of the time, and will accordingly be stable. On the other hand, it may be a narrow and exclusive system run in the interests of the dominant group, and it may be made continually more repressive and unstable with the latent threat of upheaval. Between these two extremes various combinations of these attitudes to law are to be found, often in the same individual.

Reflection on this aspect of things reveals a sobering truth: the step from the simple form of society, where primary rules of obligation are the only means of social control, into the legal world with its centrally organized legislature, courts, officials, and sanctions brings its solid gains at a certain cost. The gains are those of adaptability to change, certainty, and efficiency, and these are immense; the cost is the risk that the centrally organized power may well be used for the oppression of numbers with whose support it can dispense, in a way that the simpler regime of primary rules could not. Because this risk has materialized and may do so again, the claim that there is some further way in which law *must* conform to morals beyond that which we have exhibited as the minimum content of Natural Law, needs very careful scrutiny. Many such assertions either fail to make clear the sense in which the connection between law and morals is alleged to be necessary; or upon examination they turn out to mean something which is both true and important, but which it is most confusing to present as a necessary connection between law and morals. We shall end this chapter by examining six forms of this claim.

(i) *Power and authority.* It is often said that a legal system must rest on a sense of moral obligation or on the conviction of the moral value of the system, since it does not and cannot rest on mere power of man over man. We have ourselves stressed, in the earlier chapters of this book, the inadequacy of orders backed by threats and habits of obedience for the understanding of the foundations of a legal system and the idea of legal validity. Not only do these require for their elucidation the notion of an accepted rule of recognition, as we have argued at length in Chapter VI, but, as we have seen in this chapter, a necessary condition of the existence of coercive power is that some at least must voluntarily co-operate in the system and accept its rules. In this sense it is true that the coercive power of law presupposes its accepted authority. But the dichotomy of 'law based merely on power' and 'law which is accepted as morally binding' is not exhaustive. Not only may vast numbers be coerced by laws which they do not regard as morally binding, but it is not even true that those who do accept the system voluntarily, must conceive of themselves as morally bound to do so, though the system will be most stable when they do so. In fact, their allegiance to the system may be based on many different considerations: calculations of long-term interest; disinterested interest in others; an unreflecting inherited or traditional attitude; or the mere wish to do as others do. There is indeed no reason why those who accept the authority of the system should not examine their conscience and decide that, morally, they ought not to accept it, yet for a variety of reasons continue to do so.

These commonplaces may have become obscured by the general use of the same vocabulary to express both the legal and the moral obligations which men acknowledge. Those who accept the authority of a legal system look upon it from the internal point of view, and express their sense of its requirements in internal statements couched in the normative language which is common to both law and morals: 'I (You) ought', 'I (he) must', 'I (they) have an obligation'. Yet they are not thereby committed to a *moral* judgment that it is morally right to do what the law requires. No doubt if nothing else is said, there is a presumption that any one who speaks in these ways of his or others' legal obligations, does not think that there is any moral or other reason against fulfilling them. This, however, does not show that nothing can be acknowledged as legally obligatory unless it is accepted as morally obligatory. The presumption which we have mentioned rests on the fact that it will often be pointless to acknowledge or point out a legal obligation, if the speaker has conclusive reasons, moral or otherwise, to urge against fulfilling it.

(ii) *The influence of morality on law.* The law of every modern state shows at a thousand points the influence of both the accepted social morality and wider moral ideals. These influences enter into law either abruptly and avowedly through legislation, or silently and piecemeal through the judicial process. In some systems, as in the United States, the ultimate criteria of legal validity explicitly incorporate principles of justice or substantive moral values; in other systems, as in England, where there are no formal restrictions on the competence of the supreme legislature, its legislation may yet no less scrupulously conform to justice or morality. The further ways in which law mirrors morality are myriad, and still insufficiently studied: statutes may be a mere legal shell and demand by their express terms to be filled out with the aid of moral principles; the range of enforceable contracts may be limited by reference to conceptions of morality and fairness; liability for both civil and criminal wrongs may be adjusted to prevailing views of moral responsibility. No 'positivist' could deny that these are facts, or that the stability of legal systems depends in part upon such types of correspondence with morals. If this is what is meant by the necessary connection of law and morals, its existence should be conceded.

(iii) *Interpretation*. Laws require interpretation if they are to be applied to concrete cases, and once the myths which obscure the nature of the judicial processes are dispelled by realistic study, it is patent, as we have shown in Chapter VII, that the open texture of law leaves a vast field for a creative activity which some call legislative. Neither in interpreting statutes nor precedents are judges confined to the alternatives of blind, arbitrary choice, or 'mechanical' deduction from rules with predetermined meaning. Very often their choice is guided by an assumption that the purpose of the rules which they are interpreting is a reasonable one, so that the rules are not intended to work injustice or offend settled moral principles. Judicial decision, especially on matters of high constitutional import, often involves a choice between moral values, and not merely the application of some single outstanding moral principle; for it is folly to believe that where the meaning of the law is in doubt, morality always has a clear answer to offer. At this point judges may again make a choice which is neither arbitrary nor mechanical; and here often display characteristic judicial virtues, the special appropriateness of which to legal decision explains why some feel reluctant to call such judicial activity 'legislative'. These virtues are: impartiality and neutrality in surveying the alternatives; consideration for the interest of all who will be affected; and a concern to deploy some acceptable general principle as a reasoned basis for decision. No doubt because a plurality of such principles is always possible it cannot be *demonstrated* that a decision is uniquely correct: but it may be made acceptable as the reasoned product of informed impartial choice. In all this we have the 'weighing' and 'balancing' characteristic of the effort to do justice between competing interests.

Few would deny the importance of these elements, which may well be called 'moral', in rendering decisions acceptable; and the loose and changing tradition or canons of interpretation, which in most systems govern interpretation, often vaguely incorporate them. Yet if these facts are tendered as evidence of the *necessary* connection of law and morals, we need to remember that the same principles have been honoured nearly as much in the breach as in the observance. For, from Austin to the present day, reminders that such elements *should* guide decision have come, in the main, from critics who have found that judicial law-making has often been blind to social values, 'automatic', or inadequately reasoned.

(iv) *The criticism of law.* Sometimes the claim that there is a necessary connection between law and morality comes to no more than the assertion that a *good* legal system must conform at certain points, such as those already mentioned in the last paragraph, to the requirements of justice and morality. Some may regard this as an obvious truism; but it is not a tautology, and in fact, in the criticism of law, there may be disagreement both as to the appropriate moral standards and as to the required points of conformity. Does the morality, with which law must conform if it is to be good, mean the accepted morality of the group whose law it is, even though this may rest on superstition or may withhold its benefits and protection from slaves or subject classes? Or does morality mean standards which are enlightened in the sense that they rest on rational beliefs as to matters of fact, and accept all human beings as entitled to equal consideration and respect?

No doubt the contention that a legal system must treat all human beings within its scope as entitled to certain basic protections and freedoms, is now generally accepted as a statement of an ideal of obvious relevance in the criticism of law. Even where practice departs from it, lip service to this ideal is usually forthcoming. It may even be the case that a morality which does not take this view of the right of all men to equal consideration, can be shown by philosophy to be involved in some inner contradiction, dogmatism, or irrationality. If so, the enlightened morality which recognizes these rights has special credentials as the true morality, and is not just one among many possible moralities. These are claims which cannot be investigated here, but even if they are conceded, they cannot alter, and should not obscure, the fact that municipal legal systems, with their characteristic structure of primary and secondary rules, have long endured though they have flouted these principles of justice. What, if anything, is to be gained from denying that iniquitous rules are law, we consider below.

(v) *Principles of legality and justice.* It may be said that the distinction between a good legal system which conforms at certain points to morality and justice, and a legal system which does not, is a fallacious one, because a minimum of justice is necessarily realized whenever human behaviour is controlled by general rules publicly announced and judicially applied. Indeed we have already pointed out,[1] in analysing the idea of justice, that its simplest form (justice in the application of the law) consists in no more than taking seriously the notion that what is to be applied to a multiplicity of different persons is the same general rule, undeflected by prejudice, interest, or caprice. This impartiality is what the procedural standards known to English and American lawyers as principles of 'Natural Justice' are designed to secure. Hence, though the most odious laws may be justly applied, we have, in the bare notion of applying a general rule of law, the germ at least of justice.

Further aspects of this minimum form of justice which might well be called 'natural' emerge if we study what is in fact

---

[1] p. 160 above.

involved in any method of social control—rules of games as well as law—which consists primarily of general standards of conduct communicated to classes of persons, who are then expected to understand and conform to the rules without further official direction. If social control of this sort is to function, the rules must satisfy certain conditions: they must be intelligible and within the capacity of most to obey, and in general they must not be retrospective, though exceptionally they may be. This means that, for the most part, those who are eventually punished for breach of the rules will have had the ability and opportunity to obey. Plainly these features of control by rule are closely related to the requirements of justice which lawyers term principles of legality. Indeed one critic of positivism has seen in these aspects of control by rules, something amounting to a necessary connection between law and morality, and suggested that they be called 'the inner morality of law'. Again, if this is what the necessary connection of law and morality means, we may accept it. It is unfortunately compatible with very great iniquity.

(vi) *Legal validity and resistance to law.* However incautiously they may have formulated their general outlook, few legal theorists classed as positivists would have been concerned to deny the forms of connection between law and morals discussed under the last five headings. What then was the concern of the great battle-cries of legal positivism: 'The existence of law is one thing; its merit or demerit another';[1] 'The law of a State is not an ideal but something which actually exists … it is not that which ought to be, but that which is';[2] 'Legal norms may have any kind of content'?[3]

What these thinkers were, in the main, concerned to promote was clarity and honesty in the formulation of the theoretical and moral issues raised by the existence of particular laws which were morally iniquitous but were enacted in proper form, clear in meaning, and satisfied all the acknowledged criteria of validity of a system. Their view was that, in thinking about such laws, both the theorist and the unfortunate official or private citizen who was called on to

---

[1] Austin, *The Province of Jurisprudence Defined*, Lecture V, pp. 184–5.
[2] Gray, *The Nature and Sources of the Law*, s. 213.
[3] Kelsen, *General Theory of Law and State*, p. 113.

apply or obey them, could only be confused by an invitation to refuse the title of 'law' or 'valid' to them. They thought that, to confront these problems, simpler, more candid resources were available, which would bring into focus far better, every relevant intellectual and moral consideration: we should say, 'This is law; but it is too iniquitous to be applied or obeyed.'

The opposed point of view is one which appears attractive when, after revolution or major upheavals, the Courts of a system have to consider their attitude to the moral iniquities committed in legal form by private citizens or officials under an earlier regime. Their punishment may be felt socially desirable, and yet, to procure it by frankly retrospective legislation, making criminal what was permitted or even required by the law of the earlier regime, may be difficult, itself morally odious, or perhaps not possible. In these circumstances it may seem natural to exploit the moral implications latent in the vocabulary of the law and especially in words like *ius, recht, diritto, droit* which are laden with the theory of Natural Law. It may then appear tempting to say that enactments which enjoined or permitted iniquity should not be recognized as valid, or have the quality of law, even if the system in which they were enacted acknowledged no restriction upon the legislative competence of its legislature. It is in this form that Natural Law arguments were revived in Germany after the last war in response to the acute social problems left by the iniquities of Nazi rule and its defeat. Should informers who, for selfish ends, procured the imprisonment of others for offences against monstrous statutes passed during the Nazi regime, be punished? Was it possible to convict them in the courts of post-war Germany on the footing that such statutes violated the Natural Law and were therefore void so that the victims' imprisonment for breach of such statutes was in fact unlawful, and procuring it was itself an offence?[1] Simple as the issue looks between those who would accept and those

---

[1] See the judgment of 27 July 1949, Oberlandesgericht Bamberg, 5 *Süddeutsche Juristen-Zeitung*, 207: discussed at length in H. L. A. Hart, 'Legal Positivism and the Separation of Law and Morals', in 71. *Harvard L. Rev.* (1958), 598, and in L. Fuller, 'Positivism and Fidelity to Law', ibid., p. 630. But note corrected account of this judgment below, pp. 303–4.

who would repudiate the view that morally iniquitous rules cannot be law, the disputants seem often very unclear as to its general character. It is true that we are here concerned with alternative ways of formulating a moral decision not to apply, obey, or allow others to plead in their defence morally iniquitous rules: yet the issue is ill presented as a verbal one. Neither side to the dispute would be content if they were told, 'Yes: you are right, the correct way in English (or in German) of putting that sort of point is to say what you have said.' So, though the positivist might point to a weight of English usage, showing that there is no contradiction in asserting that a rule of law is too iniquitous to be obeyed, and that it does not follow from the proposition that a rule is too iniquitous to obey that it is not a valid rule of law, their opponents would hardly regard this as disposing of the case.

Plainly we cannot grapple adequately with this issue if we see it as one concerning the proprieties of linguistic usage. For what really is at stake is the comparative merit of a wider and a narrower concept or way of classifying rules, which belong to a system of rules generally effective in social life. If we are to make a reasoned choice between these concepts, it must be because one is superior to the other in the way in which it will assist our theoretical inquiries, or advance and clarify our moral deliberations, or both.

The wider of these two rival concepts of law includes the narrower. If we adopt the wider concept, this will lead us in theoretical inquiries to group and consider together as 'law' all rules which are valid by the formal tests of a system of primary and secondary rules, even though some of them offend against a society's own morality or against what we may hold to be an enlightened or true morality. If we adopt the narrower concept we shall exclude from 'law' such morally offensive rules. It seems clear that nothing is to be gained in the theoretical or scientific study of law as a social phenomenon by adopting the narrower concept: it would lead us to exclude certain rules even though they exhibit all the other complex characteristics of law. Nothing, surely, but confusion could follow from a proposal to leave the study of such rules to another discipline, and certainly no history or other form of legal study has found it profitable to do this. If we adopt the wider concept of law, we can accommodate within it the study of whatever special features morally iniquitous laws have, and the reaction of society to them. Hence the use of the narrower concept here must inevitably split, in a confusing way, our effort to understand both the development and potentialities of the specific method of social control to be seen in a system of primary and secondary rules. Study of its use involves study of its abuse.

What then of the practical merits of the narrower concept of law in moral deliberation? In what way is it better, when faced with morally iniquitous demands, to think 'This is in no sense law' rather than 'This is law but too iniquitous to obey or apply'? Would this make men more clear-headed or readier to disobey when morality demands it? Would it lead to better ways of disposing of the problems such as the Nazi regime left behind? No doubt ideas have their influence; but it scarcely seems that an effort to train and educate men in the use of a narrower concept of legal validity, in which there is no place for valid but morally iniquitous laws, is likely to lead to a stiffening of resistance to evil, in the face of threats of organized power, or a clearer realization of what is morally at stake when obedience is demanded. So long as human beings can gain sufficient co-operation from some to enable them to dominate others, they will use the forms of law as one of their instruments. Wicked men will enact wicked rules which others will enforce. What surely is most needed in order to make men clear-sighted in confronting the official abuse of power, is that they should preserve the sense that the certification of something as legally valid is not conclusive of the question of obedience, and that, however great the aura of majesty or authority which the official system may have, its demands must in the end be submitted to a moral scrutiny. This sense, that there is something outside the official system, by reference to which in the last resort the individual must solve his problems of obedience, is surely more likely to be kept alive among those who are accustomed to think that rules of law may be iniquitous, than among those who think that nothing iniquitous can anywhere have the status of law.

But perhaps a stronger reason for preferring the wider concept of law, which will enable us to think and say, 'This is law but iniquitous', is that to withhold legal recognition from iniquitous rules may grossly oversimplify the variety of moral issues to which they give rise. Older writers who, like Bentham and Austin, insisted on the distinction between what law is and what it ought to be, did so partly because they thought that unless men kept these separate they might, without counting the cost to society, make hasty judgments that laws were invalid and ought not to be obeyed. But besides this danger of anarchy, which they may well have overrated, there is another form of oversimplification. If we narrow our point of view and think only of the person who is called upon to *obey* evil rules, we may regard it as a matter of indifference whether or not he thinks that he is faced with a valid rule of 'law' so long as he sees its moral iniquity and does what morality requires. But besides the moral question of obedience (Am I to do this evil thing?) there is Socrates' question of submission: Am I to submit to punishment for disobedience or make my escape? There is also the question which confronted the post-war German courts, 'Are we to punish those who did evil things when they were permitted by evil rules then in force?' These questions raise very different problems of morality and justice, which we need to consider independently of each other: they cannot be solved by a refusal, made once and for all, to recognize evil laws as valid for any purpose. This is too crude a way with delicate and complex moral issues.

A concept of law which allows the invalidity of law to be distinguished from its immorality, enables us to see the complexity and variety of these separate issues; whereas a narrow concept of law which denies legal validity to iniquitous rules may blind us to them. It may be conceded that the German informers, who for selfish ends procured the punishment of others under monstrous laws, did what morality forbad; yet morality may also demand that the state should punish only those who, in doing evil, did what the state at the time forbad. This is the principle *of nulla poena sine lege*. If inroads have to be made on this principle in order to avert something held to be a greater evil than its sacrifice, it is vital that the issues at stake be clearly identified. A case of retroactive punishment should not be made to look like an ordinary case of punishment for an act illegal at the time. At least it can be claimed for the simple positivist doctrine that morally iniquitous rules may still be law, that this offers no disguise for the choice between evils which, in extreme circumstances, may have to be made.

X

INTERNATIONAL LAW

I. SOURCES OF DOUBT

The idea of a union of primary and secondary rules to which so important a place has been assigned in this book may be regarded as a mean between juristic extremes. For legal theory has sought the key to the understanding of law sometimes in the simple idea of an order backed by threats and sometimes in the complex idea of morality. With both of these law has certainly many affinities and connections; yet, as we have seen, there is a perennial danger of exaggerating these and of obscuring the special features which distinguish law from other means of social control. It is a virtue of the idea which we have taken as central that it permits us to see the multiple relationships between law, coercion, and morality for what they are, and to consider afresh in what, if any, sense these are necessary.

Though the idea of the union of primary and secondary rules has these virtues, and though it would accord with usage to treat the existence of this characteristic union of rules as a sufficient condition for the application of the expression 'legal system', we have not claimed that the word 'law' must be defined in its terms. It is because we make no such claim to identify or regulate in this way the use of words like 'law' or 'legal', that this book is offered as an elucidation of the *concept* of law, rather than a definition of 'law' which might naturally be expected to provide a rule or rules for the use of these expressions. Consistently with this aim, we investigated, in the last chapter, the claim made in the German cases, that the title of valid law should be withheld from certain rules on account of their moral iniquity, even though they belonged to an existing system of primary and secondary rules. In the end we rejected this claim; but we did so, not because it conflicted with the view that rules belonging to such a system must be called 'law', nor because it conflicted with the weight of usage.

Instead we criticized the attempt to narrow the class of valid laws by the extrusion of what was morally iniquitous, on the ground that to do this did not advance or clarify either theoretical inquiries or moral deliberation. For these purposes, the broader concept which is consistent with so much usage and which would permit us to regard rules however morally iniquitous as law, proved on examination to be adequate.

International law presents us with the converse case. For, though it is consistent with the usage of the last 150 years to use the expression 'law' here, the absence of an international legislature, courts with compulsory jurisdiction, and centrally organized sanctions have inspired misgivings, at any rate in the breasts of legal theorists. The absence of these institutions means that the rules for states resemble that simple form of social structure, consisting only of primary rules of obligation, which, when we find it among societies of individuals, we are accustomed to contrast with a developed legal system. It is indeed arguable, as we shall show, that international law not only lacks the secondary rules of change and adjudication which provide for legislature and courts, but also a unifying rule of recognition specifying 'sources' of law and providing general criteria for the identification of its rules. These differences are indeed striking and the question 'Is international law really law?' can hardly be put aside. But in this case also, we shall neither dismiss the doubts, which many feel, with a simple reminder of the existing usage; nor shall we simply confirm them on the footing that the existence of a union of primary and secondary rules is a necessary as well as a sufficient condition for the proper use of the expression 'legal system'. Instead we shall inquire into the detailed character of the doubts which have been felt, and, as in the German case, we shall ask whether the common wider usage that speaks of 'international law' is likely to obstruct any practical or theoretical aim.

Though we shall devote to it only a single chapter some writers have proposed an even shorter treatment for this question concerning the character of international law. To them it has seemed that the question 'Is international law really law?' has only arisen or survived, because a trivial question about the meaning of words has been mistaken for a serious question about the nature of things: since the facts which differentiate international law from municipal law are clear and well known, the only question to be settled is whether we should observe the existing convention or depart from it; and this is a matter for each person to settle for himself. But this short way with the question is surely too short. It is true that among the reasons which have led theorists to hesitate over the extension of the word 'law' to international law, a too simple, and indeed absurd view, of what justifies the application of the same word to many different things has played some part. The variety of types of principle which commonly guide the extension of general classifying terms has too often been ignored in jurisprudence. None the less, the sources of doubt about international law are deeper, and more interesting than these mistaken views about the use of words. Moreover, the two alternatives offered by this short way with the question ('Shall we observe the existing convention or shall we depart from it?') are not exhaustive; for, besides them, there is the alternative of making explicit and examining the principles that have in fact guided the existing usage.

The short way suggested would indeed be appropriate if we were dealing with a proper name. If someone were to ask whether the place called 'London' is *really* London, all we could do would be to remind him of the convention and leave him to abide by it or choose another name to suit his taste. It would be absurd, in such a case, to ask on what principle London was so called and whether this principle was acceptable. This would be absurd because, whereas the allotment of proper names rests *only* on an *ad hoc* convention, the extension of the general terms of any serious discipline is never without its principle or rationale, though it may not be obvious what that is. When as, in the present case, the extension is queried by those who in effect say, 'We know that it is called law, but is it really law?', what is demanded—no doubt obscurely—is that the principle be made explicit and its credentials inspected.

We shall consider two principal sources of doubt concerning the legal character of international law and, with them, the steps which theorists have taken to meet these doubts.

Both forms of doubt arise from an adverse comparison of international law with municipal law, which is taken as the clear, standard example of what law is. The first has its roots deep in the conception of law as fundamentally a matter of orders backed by threats and contrasts the character of the *rules* of international law with those of municipal law. The second form of doubt springs from the obscure belief that states are fundamentally incapable of being the subjects of legal obligation, and contrasts the character of the *subjects* of international law with those of municipal law.

2. OBLIGATIONS AND SANCTIONS

The doubts which we shall consider are often expressed in the opening chapters of books on international law in the form of the question 'How can international law be binding?' Yet there is something very confusing in this favourite form of question; and before we can deal with it we must face a prior question to which the answer is by no means clear. This prior question is: what is meant by saying of a whole system of law that it is 'binding'? The statement that a particular rule of a system is binding on a particular person is one familiar to lawyers and tolerably clear in meaning. We may paraphrase it by the assertion that the rule in question is a valid rule, and under it the person in question has some obligation or duty. Besides this, there are some situations in which more general statements of this form are made. We may be doubtful in certain circumstances whether one legal system or another applies to a particular person. Such doubts may arise in the conflict of laws or in public international law. We may ask, in the former case, whether French or English Law is binding on a particular person as regards a particular transaction, and in the latter case we may ask whether the inhabitants of, for example, enemy-occupied Belgium, were bound by what the exiled government claimed was Belgian law or by the ordinances of the occupying power. But in both these cases, the questions are questions of law which arise *within* some system of law (municipal or international) and are settled by reference to the rules or principles of that system. They do not call in question the general character of the rules, but only their scope or applicability in given circumstances to particular persons or transactions. Plainly the question, 'Is international law binding?' and its congeners 'How can international law be binding?' or 'What makes international law binding?' are questions of a different order. They express a doubt not about the applicability, but about the general legal status of international law: this doubt would be more candidly expressed in the form 'Can such rules as these be meaningfully and truthfully said ever to give rise to obligations?' As the discussions in the books show, one source of doubt on this point is simply the absence from the system of centrally organized sanctions. This is one point of adverse comparison with municipal law, the rules of which are taken to be unquestionably 'binding' and to be paradigms of legal obligation. From this stage the further argument is simple: if for this reason the rules of international law are not 'binding', it is surely indefensible to take seriously their classification as law; for however tolerant the modes of common speech may be, this is too great a difference to be overlooked. All speculation about the nature of law begins from the assumption that its existence at least makes certain conduct obligatory.

In considering this argument we shall give it the benefit of every doubt concerning the facts of the international system. We shall take it that neither Article 16 of the Covenant of the League of Nations nor Chapter VII of the United Nations Charter introduced into international law anything which can be equated with the sanctions of municipal law. In spite of the Korean war and of whatever moral may be drawn from the Suez incident, we shall suppose that, whenever their use is of importance, the law enforcement provisions of the Charter are likely to be paralysed by the veto and must be said to exist only on paper.

To argue that international law is not binding because of its lack of organized sanctions is tacitly to accept the analysis of obligation contained in the theory that law is essentially a matter of orders backed by threats. This theory, as we have seen, identifies 'having an obligation' or 'being bound' with 'likely to suffer the sanction or punishment threatened for disobedience'. Yet, as we have argued, this identification distorts the role played in all legal thought and discourse of the ideas of obligation and duty. Even in municipal law, where there are effective organized sanctions, we must distinguish, for the variety of reasons given in Chapter III, the meaning of the external predictive statement 'I (you) are likely to suffer for disobedience', from the internal normative statement 'I (you) have an obligation to act thus' which assesses a particular person's situation from the point of view of rules accepted as guiding standards of behaviour. It is true that not all rules give rise to obligations or duties; and it is also true that the rules which do so generally call for some sacrifice of private interests, and are generally supported by serious demands for conformity and insistent criticism of deviations. Yet once we free ourselves from the predictive analysis and its parent conception of law as essentially an order backed by threats, there seems no good reason for limiting the normative idea of obligation to rules supported by organized sanctions.

We must, however, consider another form of the argument, more plausible because it is not committed to definition of obligation in terms of the likelihood of threatened sanctions. The sceptic may point out that there are in a municipal system, as we have ourselves stressed, certain provisions which are justifiably called necessary; among these are primary rules of obligation, prohibiting the free use of violence, and rules providing for the official use of force as a sanction for these and other rules. If such rules and organized sanctions supporting them are in this sense necessary for municipal law, are they not equally so for international law? That they are may be maintained without insisting that this follows from the very meaning of words like 'binding' or 'obligation'.

The answer to the argument in this form is to be found in those elementary truths about human beings and their environment which constitute the enduring psychological and physical setting of municipal law. In societies of individuals, approximately equal in physical strength and vulnerability, physical sanctions are both necessary and possible. They are required in order that those who would voluntarily submit to the restraints of law shall not be mere victims of malefactors who would, in the absence of such sanctions, reap the advantages of respect for law on the part of others, without respecting it themselves. Among individuals living in close proximity to each other, opportunities for injuring others, by guile, if not by open attack, are so great, and the chances of escape so considerable, that no mere natural deterrents could in any but the simplest forms of society be adequate to restrain those too wicked, too stupid, or too weak to obey the law. Yet, because of the same fact of approximate equality and the patent advantages of submission to a system of restraints, no combination of malefactors is likely to exceed in strength those who would voluntarily co-operate in its maintenance. In these circumstances, which constitute the background of municipal law, sanctions may successfully be used against malefactors with relatively small risks, and the threat of them will add much to whatever natural deterrents there may be. But, just because the simple truisms which hold good for individuals do not hold good for states, and the factual background to international law is so different from that of municipal law, there is neither a similar necessity for sanctions (desirable though it may be that international law should be supported by them) nor a similar prospect of their safe and efficacious use.

This is so because aggression between states is very unlike that between individuals. The use of violence between states must be public, and though there is no international police force, there can be very little certainty that it will remain a matter between aggressor and victim, as a murder or theft, in the absence of a police force, might. To initiate a war is, even for the strongest power, to risk much for an outcome which is rarely predictable with reasonable confidence. On the other hand, because of the inequality of states, there can be no standing assurance that the combined strength of those on the side of international order is likely to preponderate over the powers tempted to aggression. Hence the organization and use of sanctions may involve fearful risks and the threat of them add little to the natural deterrents. Against this very different background of fact, international law has developed in a form different from that of municipal law. In a population of a modern state, if there were no organized repression and punishment of crime, violence and theft would be hourly expected; but for states, long years of peace have intervened between disastrous wars. These years of peace are only rationally to be expected, given the risks and stakes of war and the mutual needs of states; but they are worth regulating by rules which differ from those of municipal law in (among other things) not providing for their enforcement by any central organ. Yet what these rules require is thought and spoken of as obligatory; there is general pressure for conformity to the rules; claims and admissions are based on them and their breach is held to justify not only insistent demands for compensation, but reprisals and counter-measures. When the rules are disregarded, it is not on the footing that they are not binding; instead efforts are made to conceal the facts. It may of course be said that such rules are efficacious only so far as they concern issues over which states are unwilling to fight. This may be so, and may reflect adversely on the importance of the system and its value to humanity. Yet that even so much may be secured shows that no simple deduction can be made from the necessity of organized sanctions to municipal law, in its setting of physical and psychological facts, to the conclusion that without them international law, in its very different setting, imposes no obligations, is not 'binding', and so not worth the title of 'law'.

3. OBLIGATION AND THE SOVEREIGNTY OF STATES

Great Britain, Belgium, Greece, Soviet Russia have rights and obligations under international law and so are among its subjects. They are random examples of states which the layman would think of as independent and the lawyer would recognize as 'sovereign'. One of the most persistent sources of perplexity about the obligatory character of international law has been the difficulty felt in accepting or explaining the fact that a state which is sovereign may also be 'bound' by, or have an obligation under, international law. This form of scepticism is, in a sense, more extreme than the objection that international law is not binding because it lacks sanctions. For whereas that would be met if one day international law were reinforced by a system of sanctions, the present objection is based on a radical inconsistency, said or felt to exist, in the conception of a state which is at once sovereign and subject to law.

Examination of this objection involves a scrutiny of the

notion of sovereignty, applied not to a legislature or to some other element or person *within* a state, but to a state itself. Whenever the word 'sovereign' appears in jurisprudence, there is a tendency to associate with it the idea of a person above the law whose word is law for his inferiors or subjects. We have seen in the early chapters of this book how bad a guide this seductive notion is to the structure of a municipal legal system; but it has been an even more potent source of confusion in the theory of international law. It is, of course, *possible* to think of a state along such lines, as if it were a species of Superman—a Being inherently lawless but the source of law for its subjects. From the sixteenth century onwards, the symbolical identification of state and monarch ('L'état c'est moi') may have encouraged this idea which has been the dubious inspiration of much political as well as legal theory. But it is important for the understanding of international law to shake off these associations. The expression 'a state' is not the name of some person or thing inherently or 'by nature' outside the law; it is a way of referring to two facts: first, that a population inhabiting a territory lives under that form of ordered government provided by a legal system with its characteristic structure of legislature, courts, and primary rules; and, secondly, that the government enjoys a vaguely defined degree of independence.

The word 'state' has certainly its own large area of vagueness but what has been said will suffice to display its central meaning. States such as Great Britain or Brazil, the United States or Italy, again to take random examples, possess a very large measure of independence from both legal and factual control by any authorities or persons outside their borders, and would rank as 'sovereign states' in international law. On the other hand, individual states which are members of a federal union, such as the United States, are subject in many different ways to the authority and control of the federal government and constitution. Yet the independence which even these federated states retain is large if we compare it with the position, say, of an English county, of which the word 'state' would not be used at all. A county may have a local council discharging, for its area, some of the functions of a legislature, but its meagre powers are subordinate to those of Parliament and, except in certain minor respects, the area of the county is subject to the same laws and government as the rest of the country.

Between these extremes there are many different types and degrees of dependence (and so of independence) between territorial units which possess an ordered government. Colonies, protectorates, suzerainties, trust territories, confederations, present fascinating problems of classification from this point of view. In most cases the dependence of one unit on another is expressed in legal forms, so that what is law in the territory of the dependent unit will, at least on certain issues, ultimately depend on lawmaking operations in the other.

In some cases, however, the legal system of the dependent territory may not reflect its dependence. This may be so either because it is merely formally independent and the territory is in fact governed, through puppets, from outside; or it may be so because the dependent territory has a real autonomy over its internal but not its external affairs, and its dependence on another country in external affairs does not require expression as part of its domestic law. Dependence of one territorial unit on another in these various ways is not, however, the only form in which its independence may be limited. The limiting factor may be not the power or authority of another such unit, but an international authority affecting units which are alike independent of each other. It is possible to imagine many different forms of international authority and correspondingly many different limitations on the independence of states. The possibilities include, among many others, a world legislature on the model of the British Parliament, possessing legally unlimited powers to regulate the internal and external affairs of all; a federal legislature on the model of Congress, with legal competence only over specified matters or one limited by guarantees of specific rights of the constituent units; a regime in which the only form of legal control consists of rules generally accepted as applicable to all; and finally a regime in which the only form of obligation recognized is contractual or self-imposed, so that a state's independence is legally limited only by its own act.

It is salutary to consider this range of possibilities because merely to realize that there are many possible forms and

degrees of dependence and independence, is a step toward
answering the claim that because states are sovereign they
'*cannot*' be subject to or bound by international law or '*can*' only
be bound by some specific form of international law. For the
word 'sovereign' means here no more than 'independent'; and,
like the latter, is negative in force: a sovereign state is one *not*
subject to certain types of control, and its sovereignty is that
area of conduct in which it is autonomous. Some measure of
autonomy is imported, as we have seen, by the very meaning of
the word state but the contention that this '*must*' be unlimited
or '*can*' only be limited by certain types of obligation is at best
the assertion of a claim that states ought to be free of all other
restraints, and at worst is an unreasoned dogma. For if in fact we
find that there exists among states a given form of international
authority, the sovereignty of states is to that extent limited, and
it has just that extent which the rules allow. Hence we can only
know which states are sovereign, and what the extent of their
sovereignty is, when we know what the rules are; just as we
can only know whether an Englishman or an American is free
and the extent of his freedom when we know what English or
American law is. The rules of international law are indeed vague
and conflicting on many points, so that doubt about the area of
independence left to states is far greater than that concerning
the extent of a citizen's freedom under municipal law. None the
less, these difficulties do not validate the *a priori* argument which
attempts to deduce the general character of international law
from an absolute sovereignty, which is assumed, without reference to international law, to belong to states.

It is worth observing that an uncritical use of the idea of
sovereignty has spread similar confusion in the theory both
of municipal and international law, and demands in both a
similar corrective. Under its influence, we are led to believe
that there *must* in every municipal legal system be a sovereign
legislator subject to no legal limitations; just as we are led to
believe that international law *must* be of a certain character
because states are sovereign and incapable of legal limitation save by themselves. In both cases, belief in the necessary
existence of the legally unlimited sovereign prejudges a question which we can only answer when we examine the actual

280

...ion for municipal law is: what is the extent of
...gislative authority recognized in this system? For
...1 law it is: what is the maximum area of autonomy
...rules allow to states?

...the simplest answer to the present objection is that it
inve...s the order in which questions must be considered. There is
no way of knowing what sovereignty states have, till we know
what the forms of international law are and whether or not they
are mere empty forms. Much juristic debate has been confused
because this principle has been ignored, and it is profitable to
consider in its light those theories of international law which
are known as 'voluntarist' or theories of 'auto-limitation'. These
attempted to reconcile the (absolute) sovereignty of states with
the existence of binding rules of international law, by treating
all international obligations as self-imposed like the obligation which arises from a promise. Such theories are in fact the
counterpart in international law of the social contract theories
of political science. The latter sought to explain the facts that
individuals, 'naturally' free and independent, were yet bound by
municipal law, by treating the obligation to obey the law as one
arising from a contract which those bound had made with each
other, and in some cases with their rulers. We shall not consider
here the well-known objections to this theory when taken literally, nor its value when taken merely as an illuminating analogy.
Instead we shall draw from its history a threefold argument
against the voluntarist theories of international law.

First, these theories fail completely to explain how it is known
that states '*can*' only be bound by self-imposed obligations, or
why this view of their sovereignty should be accepted, in advance
of any examination of the actual character of international law.
Is there anything more to support it besides the fact that it has
often been repeated? Secondly, there is something incoherent
in the argument designed to show that states, because of their
sovereignty, *can* only be subject to or bound by rules which they
have imposed upon themselves. In some very extreme forms of
'auto-limitation' theory, a state's agreement or treaty engagements
are treated as mere declarations of its proposed future conduct, and
failure to perform is not considered to be a breach of any obligation.

This, though very much at variance with the facts, has at least the merit of consistency: it is the simple theory that the absolute sovereignty of states is inconsistent with obligation of any kind, so that, like Parliament, a state cannot bind itself. The less extreme view that a state may impose obligations on itself by promise, agreement, or treaty is not, however, consistent with the theory that states are subject only to rules which they have thus imposed on themselves. For, in order that words, spoken or written, should in certain circumstances function as a promise, agreement, or treaty, and so give rise to obligations and confer rights which others may claim, *rules* must already exist providing that a state is bound to do whatever it undertakes by appropriate words to do. Such rules presupposed in the very notion of a self-imposed obligation obviously cannot derive *their* obligatory status from a self-imposed obligation to obey them.

It is true that every specific *action* which a given state was bound to do might in theory derive its obligatory character from a promise; none the less this could only be the case if the *rule* that promises, &c., create obligations is applicable to the state independently of any promise. In any society, whether composed of individuals or states, what is necessary and sufficient, in order that the words of a promise, agreement, or treaty should give rise to obligations, is that rules providing for this and specifying a procedure for these self-binding operations should be generally, though they need not be universally, acknowledged. Where they are acknowledged the individual or state who wittingly uses these procedures is bound thereby, whether he or it chooses to be bound or not. Hence, even this most voluntary form of social obligation involves some rules which are binding independently of the choice of the party bound by them, and this, in the case of states, is inconsistent with the supposition that their sovereignty demands freedom from all such rules.

Thirdly there are the facts. We must distinguish the *a priori* claim just criticized, that states *can* only be bound by self-imposed obligations, from the claim that though they could be bound in other ways under a different system, in fact no other form of obligation for states exists under the present rules of international law. It is, of course, possible that the system might be one of this wholly consensual form, and both assertions and repudiations of this view of its character are to be found in the writings of jurists, in the opinions of judges, even of international courts, and in the declarations of states. Only a dispassionate survey of the actual practice of states can show whether this view is correct or not. It is true that modern international law is very largely treaty law, and elaborate attempts have been made to show that rules which appear to be binding on states without their prior consent do in fact rest on consent, though this may have been given only 'tacitly' or has to be 'inferred'. Though not all are fictions, some at least of these attempts to reduce to one the forms of international obligation excite the same suspicion as the notion of a 'tacit command' which, as we have seen, was designed to perform a similar, though more obviously spurious, simplification of municipal law.

A detailed scrutiny of the claim that all international obligation arises from the consent of the party bound, cannot be undertaken here, but two clear and important exceptions to this doctrine must be noticed. The first is the case of a new state. It has never been doubted that when a new, independent state emerges into existence, as did Iraq in 1932, and Israel in 1948, it is bound by the general obligations of international law including, among others, the rules that give binding force to treaties. Here the attempt to rest the new state's international obligations on a 'tacit' or 'inferred' consent seems wholly threadbare. The second case is that of a state acquiring territory or undergoing some other change, which brings with it, for the first time, the incidence of obligations under rules which previously it had no opportunity either to observe or break, and to which it had no occasion to give or withhold consent. If a state, previously without access to the sea, acquires maritime territory, it is clear that this is enough to make it subject to all the rules of international law relating to the territorial waters and the high seas. Besides these, there are more debatable cases, mainly relating to the effect on non-parties of general or multilateral treaties; but these two important exceptions are enough to justify the suspicion that the general theory that all international obligation is self-imposed has been inspired by too much abstract dogma and too little respect for the facts.

4. INTERNATIONAL LAW AND MORALITY

In Chapter V we considered the simple form of social structure which consists of primary rules of obligation alone, and we saw that, for all but the smallest most tightly knit and isolated societies, it suffered from grave defects. Such a regime must be static, its rules altering only by the slow processes of growth and decay; the identification of the rules must be uncertain; and the ascertainment of the fact of their violation in particular cases, and the application of social pressure to offenders must be haphazard, time-wasting, and weak. We found it illuminating to conceive the secondary rules of recognition, change, and adjudication characteristic of municipal law as different though related remedies for these different defects.

In form, international law resembles such a regime of primary rules, even though the content of its often elaborate rules are very unlike those of a primitive society, and many of its concepts, methods, and techniques are the same as those of modern municipal law. Very often jurists have thought that these formal differences between international and municipal law can best be expressed by classifying the former as 'morality'. Yet it seems clear that to mark the difference in this way is to invite confusion.

Sometimes insistence that the rules governing the relations between states are only moral rules, is inspired by the old dogmatism, that any form of social structure that is not reducible to orders backed by threats can only be a form of 'morality'. It is, of course, possible to use the word 'morality' in this very comprehensive way; so used, it provides a conceptual wastepaper basket into which will go the rules of games, clubs, etiquette, the fundamental provisions of constitutional law and international law, together with rules and principles which we ordinarily think of as moral ones, such as the common prohibitions of cruelty, dishonesty, or lying. The objection to this procedure is that between what is thus classed together as 'morality' there are such important differences of both form and social function, that no conceivable purpose, practical or theoretical, could be served by so crude a classification. Within the category of morality thus artificially widened, we should have to mark out afresh the old distinctions which it blurs.

In the particular case of international law there are a number of different reasons for resisting the classification of its rules as 'morality'. The first is that states often reproach each other for immoral conduct or praise themselves or others for living up to the standard of international morality. No doubt *one* of the virtues which states may show or fail to show is that of abiding by international law, but that does not mean that that law is morality. In fact the appraisal of states' conduct in terms of morality is recognizably different from the formulation of claims, demands, and the acknowledgements of rights and obligations under the rules of international law. In Chapter IX we listed certain features which might be taken as defining characteristics of social morality: among them was the distinctive form of moral pressure by which moral rules are primarily supported. This consists not of appeals to fear or threats of retaliation or demands for compensation, but of appeals to conscience, made in the expectation that once the person addressed is reminded of the moral principle at stake, he may be led by guilt or shame to respect it and make amends.

Claims under international law are not couched in such terms though of course, as in municipal law, they may be joined with a moral appeal. What predominate in the arguments, often technical, which states address to each other over disputed matters of international law, are references to precedents, treaties, and juristic writings; often no mention is made of moral right or wrong, good or bad. Hence the claim that the Peking Government has or has not a right under international law to expel the Nationalist forces from Formosa is very different from the question whether this is fair, just, or a morally good or bad thing to do, and is backed by characteristically different arguments. No doubt in the relations between states there are half-way houses between what is clearly law and what is clearly morality, analogous to the standards of politeness and courtesy recognized in private life. Such is the sphere of international 'comity' exemplified in the privilege extended to diplomatic envoys of receiving goods intended for personal use free of duty.

A more important ground of distinction is the following. The rules of international law, like those of municipal law, are often morally quite indifferent. A rule may exist because it is convenient or necessary to have some clear fixed rule about the subjects with which it is concerned, but not because any moral importance is attached to the particular rule. It may well be but one of a large number of possible rules, any one of which would have done equally well. Hence legal rules, municipal and international, commonly contain much specific detail, and draw arbitrary distinctions, which would be unintelligible as elements in moral rules or principles. It is true that we must not be dogmatic about the possible content of social morality: as we saw in Chapter IX the morality of a social group may contain much by way of injunction which may appear absurd or superstitious when viewed in the light of modern knowledge. So it is possible, though difficult, to imagine that men with general beliefs very different from ours, might come to attach *moral* importance to driving on the left instead of the right of the road or could come to feel moral guilt if they broke a promise witnessed by two witnesses, but no such guilt if it was witnessed by one. Though such strange moralities are possible, it yet remains true that a morality cannot (logically) contain rules which are generally held by those who subscribe to them to be in no way preferable to alternatives and of no intrinsic importance. Law, however, though it also contains much that is of moral importance, can and does contain just such rules, and the arbitrary distinctions, formalities, and highly specific detail which would be most difficult to understand as part of morality, are consequently natural and easily comprehensible features of law. For one of the typical functions of law, unlike morality, is to introduce just these elements in order to maximize certainty and predictability and to facilitate the proof or assessments of claims. Regard for forms and detail carried to excess, has earned for law the reproaches of 'formalism' and 'legalism'; yet it is important to remember that these vices are exaggerations of some of the law's distinctive qualities.

It is for this reason that just as we expect a municipal legal system, but not morality, to tell us how many witnesses a validly executed will must have, so we expect international law, but not morality, to tell us such things as the number of days a belligerent vessel may stay for refueling or repairs in a neutral port; the width of territorial waters; the methods to be used in their measurement. All these things are necessary and desirable provisions for *legal rules* to make, but so long as the sense is retained that such rules may equally well take any of several forms, or are important only as one among many possible means to specific ends, they remain distinct from rules which have the status in individual or social life characteristic of morality. Of course not all the rules of international law are of this formal, or arbitrary, or morally neutral kind. The point is only that legal rules *can* and moral rules *cannot* be of this kind.

The difference in character between international law and anything which we naturally think of as morality has another aspect. Though the effect of a law requiring or proscribing certain practices might ultimately be to bring about changes in the morality of a group, the notion of a legislature making or repealing moral rules is, as we saw in Chapter VII, an absurd one. A legislature cannot introduce a new rule and give it the status of a moral rule by its *fiat*, just as it cannot, by the same means, give a rule the status of a tradition, though the reasons why this is so may not be the same in the two cases. Accordingly morality does not merely lack or happen not to have a legislature; the very idea of change by human legislative *fiat* is repugnant to the idea of morality. This is so because we conceive of morality as the ultimate standard by which human actions (legislative or otherwise) are evaluated. The contrast with international law is clear. There is nothing in the nature or function of international law which is similarly inconsistent with the idea that the rules might be subject to legislative change; the lack of a legislature is just a lack which many think of as a defect one day to be repaired.

Finally we must notice a parallel in the theory of international law between the argument, criticized in Chapter IX, that even if particular rules of municipal law may conflict with morality, none the less the system as a whole must rest on a generally diffused conviction that there is a moral obligation to obey its rules, though this may be overridden in special exceptional cases. It has often been said in the discussion of the 'foundations' of international law, that in the last resort, the rules of international law *must* rest on the conviction of states that there is a moral obligation to obey them; yet, if this means more than that the obligations which they recognize are not enforceable by officially organized sanctions, there seems no reason to accept it. Of course it is possible to think of circumstances which would certainly justify our saying that a state considered some course of conduct required by international law morally obligatory, and acted for that reason. It might, for example, continue to perform the obligations of an onerous treaty because of the manifest harm to humanity that would follow if confidence in treaties was severely shaken, or because of the sense that it was only fair to shoulder the irksome burdens of a code from which it, in its turn, had profited in the past when the burden fell on others. Precisely whose motives, thoughts and feelings on such matters of moral conviction are to be attributed to the state is a question which need not detain us here.

But though there *may* be such a sense of moral obligation it is difficult to see why or in what sense it *must* exist as a condition of the existence of international law. It is clear that in the practice of states certain rules are regularly respected even at the cost of certain sacrifices; claims are formulated by reference to them; breaches of the rules expose the offender to serious criticism and are held to justify claims for compensation or retaliation. These, surely, are all the elements required to support the statement that there exist among states rules imposing obligations upon them. The proof that 'binding' rules in any society exist, is simply that they are thought of, spoken of, and function as such. What more is required by way of 'foundations' and why, if more is required, must it be a foundation of moral obligation? It is, of course, true that rules could not exist or function in the relations between states unless a preponderant majority accepted the rules and voluntarily co-operated in maintaining them. It is true also that the pressure exercised on those who break or threaten to break the rules is often relatively weak, and has usually been decentralized or unorganized. But as in the case of individuals, who voluntarily accept the far more strongly coercive system of municipal law, the motives for voluntarily supporting such a system may be extremely diverse. It may well be that any form of legal order is at its healthiest when there is a generally diffused sense that it is morally obligatory to conform to it. None the less, adherence to law may not be motivated by it, but by calculations of long-term interest, or by the wish to continue a tradition or by disinterested concern for others. There seems no good reason for identifying any of these as a necessary condition of the existence of law either among individuals or states.

5. ANALOGIES OF FORM AND CONTENT

To the innocent eye, the formal structure of international law lacking a legislature, courts with compulsory jurisdiction and officially organized sanctions, appears very different from that of municipal law. It resembles, as we have said, in form though not at all in content, a simple regime of primary or customary law. Yet some theorists, in their anxiety to defend against the sceptic the title of international law to be called 'law', have succumbed to the temptation to minimize these formal differences, and to exaggerate the analogies which can be found in international law to legislation or other desirable formal features of municipal law. Thus, it has been claimed that war, ending with a treaty whereby the defeated power cedes territory, or assumes obligations, or accepts some diminished form of independence, is essentially a legislative act; for, like legislation, it is an imposed legal change. Few would now be impressed by this analogy, or think that it helped to show that international law had an equal title with municipal law to be called 'law'; for one of the salient differences between municipal and international law is that the former usually does not, and the latter does, recognize the validity of agreements extorted by violence.

A variety of other, more respectable analogies have been stressed by those who consider the title of 'law' to depend on them. The fact that in almost all cases the judgment of the International Court and its predecessor, the Permanent Court of International Justice, have been duly carried out by the parties, has often been emphasized as if this somehow offset the fact that, in contrast with municipal courts, no state can be brought before these international tribunals without its prior consent. Analogies have also been found between the use of force, legally regulated and officially administered, as a sanction in municipal law and 'decentralized sanctions', i.e. the resort to war or forceful retaliation by a state which claims that its rights under international law have been violated by another. That there is some analogy is plain; but its significance must be assessed in the light of the equally plain fact that, whereas a municipal court has a compulsory jurisdiction to investigate the rights and wrongs of 'self help', and to punish a wrongful resort to it, no international court has a similar jurisdiction.

Some of these dubious analogies may be considered to have been much strengthened by the obligations which states have assumed under the United Nations Charter. But, again, any assessment of their strength is worth little if it ignores the extent to which the law enforcement provisions of the Charter, admirable on paper, have been paralysed by the veto and the ideological divisions and alliances of the great powers. The reply, sometimes made, that the law-enforcement provisions of municipal law *might* also be paralysed by a general strike is scarcely convincing; for in our comparison between municipal law and international law we are concerned with what exists in fact, and here the facts are undeniably different.

There is, however, one suggested formal analogy between international and municipal law which deserves some scrutiny here. Kelsen and many modern theorists insist that, like municipal law, international law possesses and indeed must possess a 'basic norm', or what we have termed a rule of recognition, by reference to which the validity of the other rules of the system is assessed, and in virtue of which the rules constitute a single system. The opposed view is that this analogy of structure is false: international law simply consists of a *set* of separate primary rules of obligation which are not united in this manner. It is, in the usual terminology of international lawyers, a set of customary rules of which the rule giving binding force to treaties is one. It is notorious that those who have embarked on the task have found very great difficulties in formulating the 'basic norm' of international law. Candidates for this position include the principle *pacta sunt servanda*. This has, however, been abandoned by most theorists, since it seems incompatible with the fact that not all obligations under international law arise from '*pacta*', however widely that term is construed. So it has been replaced by something less familiar: the so-called rule that 'States should behave as they customarily behave'.

We shall not discuss the merits of these and other rival formulations of the basic norm of international law; instead we shall question the assumption that it must contain such an element. Here the first and perhaps the last question to ask is: why should we make this *a priori* assumption (for that is what it is) and so prejudge the actual character of the rules of international law? For it is surely conceivable (and perhaps has often been the case) that a society may live by rules imposing obligations on its members as 'binding', even though they are regarded simply as a set of separate rules, not unified by or deriving their validity from any more basic rule. It is plain that the mere existence of rules does not involve the existence of such a basic rule. In most modern societies there are rules of etiquette, and, though we do not think of them as imposing obligations, we may well talk of such rules as existing; yet we would not look for, nor could we find, a basic rule of etiquette from which the validity of the separate rules was derivable. Such rules do not form a system but a mere set, and, of course, the inconveniences of this form of social control, where matters more important than those of etiquette are at stake, are considerable. They have already been described in Chapter V. Yet if rules are in fact accepted as standards of conduct, and supported with appropriate forms of social pressure distinctive of obligatory rules, nothing more is required to show that they are binding rules, even though, in this simple form of social structure, we have not something which we do have in municipal law: namely a way of demonstrating the validity of individual rules by reference to some ultimate rule of the system.

There are of course a number of questions which we can ask about rules which constitute not a system but a simple set. We can, for example, ask questions about their historical origin, or questions concerning the causal influences that have fostered the growth of the rules. We can also ask questions about the value of the rules to those who live by them, and whether they regard themselves as morally bound to obey them or obey from some other motive. But we cannot ask in the simpler case one kind of question which we can ask concerning the rules of a system enriched, as municipal law is, by a basic norm or secondary rule of recognition. In the simpler case we cannot ask: 'From what ultimate provision of the system do the separate rules derive their validity or "binding force"?' For there is no such provision and need be none. It is, therefore, a mistake to suppose that a basic rule or rule of recognition is a generally necessary condition of the existence of rules of obligation or 'binding' rules. This is not a necessity, but a luxury, found in advanced social systems whose members not merely come to accept separate rules piecemeal, but are committed to the acceptance in advance of general classes of rule, marked out by general criteria of validity. In the simpler form of society we must wait and see whether a rule gets accepted as a rule or not; in a system with a basic rule of recognition we can say before a rule is actually made, that it *will* be valid *if* it conforms to the requirements of the rule of recognition.

The same point may be presented in a different form. When such a rule of recognition is added to the simple set of separate rules, it not only brings with it the advantages of system and ease of identification, but it makes possible for the first time a new form of statement. These are internal statements about the validity of the rules; for we can now ask in a new sense, 'What provision of the system makes this rule binding?' or, in Kelsen's language, 'What, within the system, is the reason of its validity?' The answers to these new questions are provided by the basic rule of recognition. But though, in the simpler structure, the validity of the rules cannot thus be demonstrated by reference to any more basic rule, this does not mean that there is some question about the rules or their binding force or validity which is left unexplained. It is not the case that there is some mystery as to why the rules in such a simple social structure are binding, which a basic rule, if only we could find it, would resolve. The rules of the simple structure are, like the basic rule of the more advanced systems, binding if they are accepted and function as such. These simple truths about different forms of social structure can, however, easily be obscured by the obstinate search for unity and system where these desirable elements are not in fact to be found.

There is indeed something comic in the efforts made to fashion a basic rule for the most simple forms of social structure which exist without one. It is as if we were to insist that a naked savage *must* really be dressed in some invisible variety of modern dress. Unfortunately, there is also here a standing possibility of confusion. We may be persuaded to treat as a basic rule, something which is an empty repetition of the mere fact that the society concerned (whether of individuals or states) observes certain standards of conduct as obligatory rules. This is surely the status of the strange basic norm which has been suggested for international law: 'States should behave as they have customarily behaved'. For it says nothing more than that those who accept certain rules must also observe a rule that the rules ought to be observed. This is a mere useless reduplication of the fact that a set of rules are accepted by states as binding rules.

Again once we emancipate ourselves from the assumption that international law *must* contain a basic rule, the question to be faced is one of fact. What is the actual character of the rules as they function in the relations between states? Different interpretations of the phenomena to be observed are of course possible; but it is submitted that there is no basic rule providing general criteria of validity for the rules of international law, and that the rules which are in fact operative constitute not a system but a set of rules, among which are the rules providing for the binding force of treaties. It is true that, on many important matters, the relations between states are regulated by multilateral treaties, and it is sometimes argued that these may bind states that are not parties. If this were generally recognized, such treaties would in fact be legislative enactments and international law would have distinct criteria of validity for its rules. A basic rule of recognition could then be formulated which would represent an actual feature of the system and would be more than an empty restatement of the fact that a set of rules are in fact observed by states. Perhaps international law is at present in a stage of transition towards acceptance of this and other forms which would bring it nearer in structure to a municipal system. If, and when, this transition is completed the formal analogies, which at present seem thin and even delusive, would acquire substance, and the sceptic's last doubts about the legal 'quality' of international law may then be laid to rest. Till this stage is reached the analogies are surely those of function and content, not of form. Those of function emerge most clearly when we reflect on the ways in which international law differs from morality, some of which we examined in the last section. The analogies of content consist in the range of principles, concepts, and methods which are common to both municipal and international law, and make the lawyers' technique freely transferable from the one to the other. Bentham, the inventor of the expression 'international law', defended it simply by saying that it was 'sufficiently analogous'[1] to municipal law. To this, two comments are perhaps worth adding. First, that the analogy is one of content not of form: secondly, that, in this analogy of content, no other social rules are so close to municipal law as those of international law.

[1] *Principles of Morals and Legislation*, XVII. 25, n. 1.

POSTSCRIPT

INTRODUCTORY

This book was first published thirty-two years ago. Since then jurisprudence and philosophy have come much closer together and the subject of legal theory has been greatly developed both in this country and in the United States. I would like to think that this book helped to stimulate this development even if among academic lawyers and philosophers, critics of its main doctrines have been at least as numerous as converts to them. However that may be, it is the case that though I originally wrote the book with English undergraduate readers in mind, it has achieved a much wider circulation and has generated a vast subsidiary literature of critical comment in the English-speaking world and in several countries where translations of the book have appeared. Much of this critical literature consists of articles in legal and philosophical journals, but in addition a number of important books have been published in which various doctrines of this book have been taken as targets for criticism and a starting-point for the exposition of the critics' own legal theories.

Though I have fired a few shots across the bows of some of my critics, notably the late Professor Lon Fuller[1] and Professor R. M. Dworkin,[2] I have hitherto made no general comprehensive reply to any of them; I have preferred to watch and learn from a most instructive running debate in which some of the critics have differed from others as much as they

---

[1] See my review of his *The Morality of Law* (1964), 78 *Harvard Law Review* 1281 (1965), reprinted in my *Essays in Jurisprudence and Philosophy* (1983), p. 343. [Note: Footnotes to the Postscript that are enclosed in square brackets were added by the editors.]

[2] See my 'Law in the Perspective of Philosophy: 1776–1976', 51 *New York University Law Review* 538 (1976); 'American Jurisprudence through English Eyes: The Nightmare and the Noble Dream', 11 *Georgia Law Review* 969 (1977); 'Between Utility and Rights', 79 *Columbia Law Review* 828 (1979). All the foregoing are reprinted in *Essays in Jurisprudence and Philosophy*. See also 'Legal Duty and Obligation', chap. VI in my *Essays on Bentham* (1982), and 'Comment' in R. Gavison (ed.), *Issues in Contemporary Legal Philosophy* (1987), p. 35.

have differed from me. But in this Postscript I attempt to reply to some of the wide-ranging criticisms urged by Dworkin in many of the seminal articles collected in his *Taking Rights Seriously* (1977) and *A Matter of Principle* (1985) and in his book *Law's Empire* (1986).[3] I focus in this Postscript mainly on Dworkin's criticisms because he has not only argued that nearly all the distinctive theses of this book are radically mistaken, but he has called in question the whole conception of legal theory and of what it should do which is implicit in the book. Dworkin's arguments against the main themes of the book have been broadly consistent over the years, but there have been some important changes both in the substance of some arguments and in the terminology in which they are expressed. Some of his criticisms which were prominent in his earlier essays do not appear in his later work, though they have not been explicitly withdrawn. Such earlier criticisms have, however, gained a wide currency and are very influential, and I have therefore thought fit to reply to them as well as to his later criticisms.

The first and longer section of this Postscript is concerned with Dworkin's arguments. But I consider in a second section the claims of a number of other critics that in my exposition of some of my theses there are not only obscurities and inaccuracies but at certain points actual incoherence and contradiction.[4] Here I have to admit that in more instances than I care to contemplate my critics have been right and I take the opportunity of this Postscript to clarify what is obscure, and to revise what I originally wrote where it is incoherent or contradictory.

I. THE NATURE OF LEGAL THEORY

My aim in this book was to provide a theory of what law is which is both general and descriptive. It is *general* in the sense that it is not tied to any particular legal system or legal culture, but seeks to give an explanatory and clarifying account of law as a complex social and political institution with a rule-governed (and in that sense 'normative') aspect. This

---

[3] Cited hereinafter as *TRS*, *AMP*, and *LE* respectively.

[4] [Hart did not complete the second of the two sections mentioned here. See Editors' Note.]

institution, in spite of many variations in different cultures and in different times, has taken the same general form and structure, though many misunderstandings and obscuring myths, calling for clarification, have clustered round it. The starting-point for this clarificatory task is the widespread common knowledge of the salient features of a modern municipal legal system which on page 3 of this book I attribute to any educated man. My account is *descriptive* in that it is morally neutral and has no justificatory aims: it does not seek to justify or commend on moral or other grounds the forms and structures which appear in my general account of law, though a clear understanding of these is, I think, an important preliminary to any useful moral criticism of law.

As a means of carrying out this descriptive enterprise my book makes repeated use of a number of concepts such as *duty-imposing rules, power-conferring rules, rules of recognition, rules of change, acceptance of rules, internal and external points of view, internal and external statements*, and *legal validity*. These concepts focus attention on elements in terms of which a variety of legal institutions and legal practices may be illuminatingly analysed and answers may be given to questions, concerning the general nature of law, which reflection on these institutions and practices has prompted. These include such questions as: What are rules? How do rules differ from mere habits or regularities of behaviour? Are there radically different types of legal rules? How may rules be related? What is it for rules to form a system? How are legal rules, and the authority they have, related on the one hand to threats, and on the other to moral requirements?[5]

Legal theory conceived in this manner as both descriptive and general is a radically different enterprise from Dworkin's conception of legal theory (or 'jurisprudence' as he often terms it) as in part evaluative and justificatory and as 'addressed to a particular legal culture',[6] which is usually the theorist's own and in Dworkin's case is that of Anglo-American law. The central task of legal theory so conceived is termed by Dworkin 'interpretive'[7] and is partly evaluative, since it consists in the

---

[5] See H. L. A. Hart, 'Comment', in Gavison, above, n. 2, p. 35.
[6] *LE* 102.   [7] *LE* chap. 3.

identification of the principles which both best 'fit' or cohere with the settled law and legal practices of a legal system and also provide the best moral justification for them, thus showing the law 'in its best light'.[8] For Dworkin the principles thus identified are not only parts of a theory of the law but are also implicit parts of the law itself. So for him 'Jurisprudence is the general part of adjudication, silent prologue to any decision at law'.[9] In his earlier work such principles were designated simply as 'the soundest theory of law',[10] but in his latest work, *Law's Empire*, he characterizes these principles and the particular propositions of law which follow from them as law in an 'interpretive sense'. The settled legal practices or paradigms of law which such interpretive theory is to interpret are termed by Dworkin 'preinterpretive',[11] and a theorist is taken to have no difficulty and no theoretical task to perform in identifying such preinterpretive data since they are settled as a matter of the general consensus of the lawyers of particular legal systems.[12]

It is not obvious why there should be or indeed could be any significant conflict between enterprises so different as my own and Dworkin's conceptions of legal theory. Thus much of Dworkin's work, including *Law's Empire*, is devoted to the elaboration of the comparative merits of three different accounts of the way in which law ('past political decisions')[13] justifies coercion, and so yields three forms of legal theory which he calls 'conventionalism', 'legal pragmatism', and 'law as integrity'.[14] All that he writes about these three types of theory is of great interest and importance as contributions to an evaluative justificatory jurisprudence and I am not concerned to dispute his elaboration of these interpretive ideas[15] except in so far as he claims that positivist legal theory such as that presented in this book can be illuminatingly re-stated as such an interpretive theory. This latter claim is

---

[8] *LE* 90.   [9] *LE* 90.   [10] *TRS* 66.   [11] *LE* 65–66.

[12] But Dworkin warns that the identification of such preinterpretive law may itself involve interpretation. See *LE* 66.

[13] *LE* 93.   [14] *LE* 94.

[15] But note that some critics, e.g. Michael Moore in his 'The Interpretive Turn in Modern Theory: A Turn for the Worse?', 41 *Stanford Law Review* 871 (1989), at 947–8, while accepting that legal practice is interpretive in Dworkin's sense, deny that legal theory can be interpretive.

in my view mistaken and I give below my reasons for objecting to any such interpretive version of my theory.

But in his books Dworkin appears to rule out general and descriptive legal theory as misguided or at best simply useless. 'Useful theories of law', he says, are 'interpretive of a particular stage of a historically developing practice'[16] and he had earlier written that 'the flat distinction between description and evaluation' has 'enfeebled legal theory'.[17]

I find it hard to follow Dworkin's precise reasons for rejecting descriptive legal theory or 'jurisprudence' as he often calls it. His central objection seems to be that legal theory must take account of an internal perspective on the law which is the viewpoint of an insider or participant in a legal system, and no adequate account of this internal perspective can be provided by a descriptive theory whose viewpoint is not that of a participant but that of an external observer.[18] But there is in fact nothing in the project of a descriptive jurisprudence as exemplified in my book to preclude a non-participant external observer from describing the ways in which participants view the law from such an internal point of view. So I explained in this book at some length that participants manifest their internal point of view in accepting the law as providing guides to their conduct and standards of criticism. Of course a descriptive legal theorist does not as such himself share the participants' acceptance of the law in these ways, but he can and should describe such acceptance, as indeed I have attempted to do in this book. It is true that for this purpose the descriptive legal theorist must *understand* what it is to adopt the internal point of view and in that limited sense he must be able to put himself in the place of an insider; but this is not to accept the law or share or endorse the insider's internal point of view or in any other way to surrender his descriptive stance.

Dworkin in his criticism of descriptive jurisprudence seems

---

[16] *LE* 102; cf. 'General theories of law, for us, are general interpretations of our own judicial practice.' *LE* 410.

[17] *AMP* 148; cf. 'theories of law cannot sensibly be understood as...neutral accounts of social practice', in 'A Reply by Ronald Dworkin', Marshall Cohen (ed.), *Ronald Dworkin and Contemporary Jurisprudence* (1983) [cited hereinafter as *RDCJ*], p. 247 at 254.   [18] [See LE 13–14.]

to rule out this obvious possibility of an external observer taking account in this descriptive way of a participant's internal viewpoint since, as I have said, he identifies jurisprudence as 'the general part of adjudication', and this is to treat jurisprudence or legal theory as itself a part of a system's law seen from the internal viewpoint of its judicial participants. But the descriptive legal theorist may understand and describe the insider's internal perspective on the law without adopting or sharing it. Even if (as Neil MacCormick[19] and many other critics have argued) the participant's internal perspective manifested in the acceptance of the law as providing guides to conduct and standards of criticism necessarily also included a belief that there are *moral* reasons for conforming to the law's requirements and *moral* justification of its use of coercion, this would also be something for a morally neutral descriptive jurisprudence to record but not to endorse or share.

However, in response to my claim that the partly evaluative issues which Dworkin calls 'interpretive' are not the only proper issues for jurisprudence and legal theory, and that there is an important place for general and descriptive jurisprudence, he has conceded that this is so, and he has explained that his observations such as 'jurisprudence is the general part of adjudication' need qualification, since this, as he now says, is only 'true of jurisprudence about the question of sense'.[20] This is an important and welcome correction of what appeared to be the extravagant and indeed, as Dworkin himself has termed it, 'imperialist', claim that the only proper form of legal theory is interpretive and evaluative.

But I find still very perplexing the implications of the following cautionary words which Dworkin has now coupled with his withdrawal of his seemingly imperialist claim: 'But it is worth stressing how pervasive that question [of sense] is in the issues that general theories, like Hart's, have mainly discussed.'[21] The relevance of this caution is not clear. The issues which I have discussed (see the list on p. 240 above)

---

[19] [See *Legal Reasoning and Legal Theory* (1978), 63–4, 139–40.]

[20] R. M. Dworkin, 'Legal Theory and the Problem of Sense', in R. Gavison (ed.), *Issues in Contemporary Legal Philosophy: The Influence of H. L. A. Hart* (1987), at 19.

[21] Ibid.

include questions such as the relation of law to coercive threats on the one hand and to moral requirements on the other, and the point of Dworkin's caution seems to be that in discussing such issues even the descriptive legal theorist will have to face questions concerning the sense or meaning of propositions of law which can only be satisfactorily answered by an interpretive and partly evaluative legal theory. If this were really the case, in order to determine the sense of any given proposition of law even the descriptive legal theorist must ask and answer the interpretive and evaluative question, 'What meaning must be assigned to this proposition if it is to follow from principles which best fit the settled law and best justify it?' But even if it were true that the general and descriptive legal theorist seeking an answer to the kind of questions that I have mentioned must determine the meaning of propositions of law in many different legal systems, there seems no reason to accept the view that this *must* be determined by his asking Dworkin's interpretive and evaluative question. Moreover, even if the judges and lawyers of all the legal systems of which the general and descriptive legal theorist had to take account themselves did in fact settle questions of meaning in this interpretive and partly evaluative way, this would be something for the general descriptive theorist to record as a fact on which to base his general descriptive conclusions as to the meaning of such propositions of law. It would of course be a serious error to suppose that because these conclusions were so based they must themselves be interpretive and evaluative and that in offering them the theorist had shifted from the task of description to that of interpretation and evaluation. Description may still be description, even when what is described is an evaluation.

2. THE NATURE OF LEGAL POSITIVISM

(i) *Positivism as a Semantic Theory*

My book is taken by Dworkin as a representative work of modern legal positivism distinguished from earlier versions, such as those of Bentham and Austin, mainly by its rejection of their imperative theories of law and their conception that all law emanates from a legally unlimited sovereign legislative person or body. Dworkin finds in my version of legal positivism a large number of different though related errors. The most fundamental of these errors is the view that the truth of propositions of law such as those that describe legal rights and legal duties depends only on questions of plain historical fact including facts about individual beliefs and social attitudes.[22] The facts on which the truth of propositions of law depends constitute what Dworkin calls 'the grounds of law',[23] and the positivist according to him wrongly takes these to be fixed by linguistic rules, shared by judges and lawyers, which govern the use and so the meaning of the word 'law' both when this appears in statements of what 'the law' of a particular system is on a particular point and in statements about what 'law' (i.e. law in general) is.[24] From this positivist view of law it would follow that the only disagreements that there can be about questions of law are those which concern the existence or non-existence of such historical facts; there can be no theoretical disagreements or controversy as to what constitutes the 'grounds' of law.

Dworkin devotes many illuminating pages of his criticism of legal positivism to showing that theoretical disagreement as to what constitutes the grounds of law is, contrary to the positivist's view, a prominent feature of Anglo-American legal practices. Against the view that these are uncontroversially fixed by linguistic rules shared by lawyers and judges, Dworkin urges that they are essentially controversial, since amongst them are not only historical facts but very frequently controversial moral judgments and value judgments.

Dworkin offers two very different accounts of how it is that positivists such as myself have come to adopt this their radically mistaken view. According to the first of these accounts, positivists believe that if what the grounds of law are was not uncontroversially fixed by rules, but was a controversial matter allowing theoretical disagreements, then the word 'law' would *mean* different things to different people and in using it they would be simply talking past each other, not communicating about the same thing. This belief thus imputed to the positivist is in Dworkin's view wholly mistaken, and he calls the

---

[22] *LE* 6 ff.   [23] *LE* 4.   [24] *LE* 31 ff.

argument against controversial grounds of law which the positivist is supposed to base on it the 'semantic sting'[25] because it rests on a theory about the meaning of the word 'law'. So in *Law's Empire* he set out to draw this 'semantic sting'.

Though in the first chapter of *Law's Empire* I am classed with Austin as a semantic theorist and so as deriving a plain-fact positivist theory of law from the meaning of the word 'law', and suffering from the semantic sting, in fact nothing in my book or in anything else I have written supports such an account of my theory. Thus, my doctrine that developed municipal legal systems contain a rule of recognition specifying the criteria for the identification of the laws which courts have to apply may be mistaken, but I nowhere base this doctrine on the mistaken idea that it is part of the meaning of the word 'law' that there should be such a rule of recognition in all legal systems, or on the even more mistaken idea that if the criteria for the identification of the grounds of law were not uncontroversially fixed, 'law' would *mean* different things to different people.

Indeed this last argument ascribed to me confuses the *meaning* of a concept with the criteria for its *application*, and so far from accepting this I expressly drew attention (on page 160 of this book), in explaining the concept of justice, to the fact that the criteria for the application of a concept with a constant meaning may both vary and be controversial. To make this clear I drew in effect the same distinction between a concept and different conceptions of a concept which figures so prominently in Dworkin's later work.[26]

Lastly, Dworkin also insists that the positivist's claim that his theory of law is not a semantic theory, but a descriptive account of the distinctive features of law in general as a complex social phenomenon, presents a contrast with semantic theory which is empty and misleading. His argument[27] is that since one of the distinctive features of law as a social phenomenon is that lawyers debate the truth of propositions of law

---

[25] LE 45.

[26] On this distinction see John Rawls, *A Theory of Justice* (1971), pp. 5–6, 10. [In distinguishing the concept of justice from conceptions of justice, Rawls states, 'Here I follow H. L. A. Hart, *The Concept of Law* ... pp. 155–159.' (First edition.) See *A Theory of Justice*, p. 5 n. 1.]   [27] *LE* 418–19, n. 29.

and 'explain' this by reference to the meaning of such propositions, such a descriptive theory of law must after all be semantic.[28]
This argument seems to me to confuse the meaning of 'law' with
the meaning of propositions of law. A semantic theory of law
is said by Dworkin to be a theory that the very meaning of the
word 'law' makes law depend on certain specific criteria. But
propositions of law are typically statements not of what 'law' is
but of what *the law* is, i.e. what the law of some system permits
or requires or empowers people to do. So even if the meaning
of such propositions of law was determined by definitions or by
their truth-conditions this does not lead to the conclusion that
the very meaning of the word 'law' makes law depend on certain
specific criteria. This would only be the case if the criteria provided by a system's rule of recognition and the need for such a
rule were derived from the meaning of the word 'law'. But there
is no trace of such a doctrine in my work.[29]

There is one further respect in which Dworkin misrepresents my form of legal positivism. He treats my doctrine of
the rule of recognition as requiring that the criteria which
it provides for the identification of law must consist only of
historical facts and so as an example of 'plain-fact positivism'.[30]
But though my main examples of the criteria provided by the
rule of recognition are matters of what Dworkin has called
'pedigree',[31] concerned only with the manner in which laws
are adopted or created by legal institutions and not with their
content, I expressly state both in this book (p. 72) and in my
earlier article on 'Positivism and the Separation of Law and
Morals'[32] that in some systems of law, as in the United States,
the ultimate criteria of legal validity might explicitly incorporate besides pedigree, principles of justice or substantive
moral values, and these may form the content·of legal constitutional restraints. In ascribing 'plain-fact' positivism to me
in *Law's Empire* Dworkin ignores this aspect of my theory. So

---

[28] See *LE* 31–3.

[29] See p. 209 of this book, where I repudiate any such doctrine.

[30] [This phrase is Hart's, and does not appear in *LE*.]

[31] *TRS* 17.

[32] 71 *Harvard Law Review* 598 (1958), reprinted in my *Essays on Jurisprudence and Philosophy* (see esp. pp. 54–5).

the 'semantic' version of plain-fact positivism which he attributes to me is plainly not mine, nor is mine any form of plain-fact positivism.

(ii) *Positivism as an Interpretive Theory*

Dworkin's second account of plain-fact positivism does not treat it as a semantic theory or as based on linguistic considerations but attempts to reconstruct it as a form of Dworkinian interpretive theory called by him 'conventionalism'. According to this theory (which Dworkin ultimately rejects as defective) the positivist, in the guise of an interpretive theorist committed to showing the law in the best light, presents the criteria of law as consisting of plain facts, uncontroversially fixed not, as in the semantic version, by the vocabulary of law but by a conviction which is shared by judges and lawyers. This casts a favourable light on law because it shows it as securing something of great value to the subjects of the law: namely that the occasions for legal coercion are made to depend on plain facts available to all, so that all will have fair warning before coercion is used. This Dworkin calls 'the ideal of protected expectations',[33] but its merits for him do not in the end outweigh its various defects.

But this interpretivist account of positivism as conventionalism cannot be represented as a plausible version or reconstruction of my theory of law. This is so for two reasons. First, as I have already stated, my theory is not a plain-fact theory of positivism since amongst the criteria of law it admits values, not only 'plain' facts. But secondly and more importantly, whereas Dworkin's interpretive legal theory in all its forms rests on the presupposition that the point or purpose of law and legal practice is to justify coercion,[34] it certainly is not and never has been my view that law has this as its point or purpose. Like other forms of positivism my theory makes no claim to identify the point or purpose of law and legal practices as such; so there is nothing in my theory to support Dworkin's view, which I certainly do not share, that the purpose of law is to justify the use of coercion. In fact

---

[33] *LE* 117.   [34] [*LE* 93.]

I think it quite vain to seek any more specific purpose which law as such serves beyond providing guides to human conduct and standards of criticism of such conduct. This will not of course serve to distinguish laws from other rules or principles with the same general aims; the distinctive features of law are the provision it makes by secondary rules for the identification, change, and enforcement of its standards and the general claim it makes to priority over other standards. However, even if my theory were wholly committed to plain-fact positivism in the form of conventionalism which protects expectations by guaranteeing that prior notice of the occasions for legal coercion will be generally available, this would only show that I view this as a particular moral merit which law has, not that the whole purpose of law as such is to provide this. Since the occasions for legal coercion are mainly cases where the primary function of the law in guiding the conduct of its subjects has broken down, legal coercion, though of course an important matter, is a secondary function. Its justification cannot be sensibly taken to be the point or purpose of the law as such.

Dworkin's reasons for reconstructing my legal theory as a conventionalist interpretive theory which makes the claim that legal coercion is only justified 'when it conforms to conventional understandings'[35] rest on my account of the Elements of Law in Chapter V Section 3 of this book. There I exhibit the secondary rules of recognition, change, and adjudication, as remedies for the defects of an imagined simple regime consisting only of primary rules of obligation. These defects are the *uncertainty* as to the identity of the rules, their *static* quality, and the time-wasting *inefficiency* of the diffuse social pressure by which alone the rules are enforced. But in presenting these secondary rules as remedies for such defects I nowhere make any claim that legal coercion is only *justified* when it conforms to these rules, still less that the provision of such justification is the point or purpose of the law in general. Indeed the only reference which I make to coercion in my discussion of secondary rules is to the time-wasting *inefficiency* of leaving the enforcement of the rules to diffuse social pressure instead of

---

[35] *LE* 429 n. 3.

to organized sanctions administered by courts. But plainly a remedy for inefficiency is not a justification.

It is of course true that the addition to the regime of primary rules of obligation of a secondary rule of recognition will, by frequently enabling individuals to identify in advance the occasions for coercion, help to justify its use in the sense that it will exclude one moral objection to its use. But the certainty and knowledge in advance of the requirements of the law which the rule of recognition will bring is not only of importance where coercion is in issue: it is equally crucial for the intelligent exercise of legal powers (e.g. to make wills or contracts) and generally for the intelligent planning of private and public life. The justification of coercion to which the rule of recognition contributes therefore cannot be represented as its general point or purpose, still less can it be represented as the general point or purpose of the law as a whole. Nothing in my theory suggests that it can.

(iii) *Soft Positivism*

Dworkin in attributing to me a doctrine of 'plain-fact positivism' has mistakenly treated my theory as not only requiring (as it does) that the existence and authority of the rule of recognition should depend on the fact of its acceptance by the courts, but also as requiring (as it does not) that the criteria of legal validity which the rule provides should consist exclusively of the specific kind of plain fact which he calls 'pedigree' matters and which concern the manner and form of law-creation or adoption. This is doubly mistaken. First, it ignores my explicit acknowledgement that the rule of recognition may incorporate as criteria of legal validity conformity with moral principles or substantive values; so my doctrine is what has been called 'soft positivism' and not as in Dworkin's version of it 'plain-fact' positivism. Secondly, there is nothing in my book to suggest that the plain-fact criteria provided by the rule of recognition must be solely matters of pedigree; they may instead be substantive constraints on the content of legislation such as the Sixteenth or Nineteenth Amendments to the United States Constitution respecting the establishment of religion or abridgements of the right to vote.

But this reply does not meet Dworkin's most basic criticisms, for in replying to other theorists who have also adopted some form of soft positivism,[36] he has made important criticisms of it which if valid would apply to my theory and so call for an answer here.

Dworkin's most fundamental criticism is that there is a deep inconsistency between soft positivism, which permits the identification of the law to depend on controversial matters of conformity with moral or other value judgments, and the general positivist 'picture' of law as essentially concerned to provide reliable public standards of conduct which can be identified with certainty as matters of plain fact without dependence on controversial moral arguments.[37] To establish such inconsistency between soft positivism and the rest of my theory Dworkin would cite my account of the rule of recognition as curing, among other defects, the uncertainty of the imagined pre-legal regime of custom-type primary rules of obligation.

This criticism of soft positivism seems to me to exaggerate both the degree of certainty which a consistent positivist must attribute to a body of legal standards and the uncertainty which will result if the criteria of legal validity include conformity with specific moral principles or values. It is of course true that an important function of the rule of recognition is to promote the certainty with which the law may be ascertained. This it would fail to do if the tests which it introduced for law not only raise controversial issues in some cases but raise them in all or most cases. But the exclusion of all uncertainty at whatever costs in other values is not a goal which I have ever envisaged for the rule of recognition. This is made plain, or so I had hoped, both by my explicit statement in this book that the rule of recognition itself as well as particular rules of law identified by reference to it may have a debatable 'penumbra' of uncertainty.[38] There is also my general argument that, even if laws could be framed that could settle in advance all possible questions that could arise about their meaning, to adopt such laws would often war with other aims which law should cherish.[39] A margin of uncertainty should

---

[36] See his replies to E. P. Soper and J. L. Coleman in *RDCJ* 247 ff. and 252 ff.

[37] *RDCJ* 248. [38] [See this book, pp. 123, 147–54.]

[39] [See this book, p. 128.]

be tolerated, and indeed welcomed in the case of many legal rules, so that an informed judicial decision can be made when the composition of an unforeseen case is known and the issues at stake in its decision can be identified and so rationally settled. Only if the certainty-providing function of the rule of recognition is treated as paramount and overriding could the form of soft positivism that includes among the criteria of law conformity with moral principles or values which may be controversial be regarded as inconsistent. The underlying question here concerns the degree or extent of uncertainty which a legal system can tolerate if it is to make any significant advance from a decentralized regime of custom-type rules in providing generally reliable and determinate guides to conduct identifiable in advance.

Dworkin's second criticism of the consistency of my version of soft positivism raises different and more complex issues concerning the determinacy and completeness of law. My view advanced in this book is that legal rules and principles identified in general terms by the criteria provided by the rule of recognition often have what I call frequently 'open texture', so that when the question is whether a given rule applies to a particular case the law fails to determine an answer either way and so proves partially indeterminate. Such cases are not merely 'hard cases', controversial in the sense that reasonable and informed lawyers may disagree about which answer is legally correct, but the law in such cases is fundamentally *incomplete*: it provides *no* answer to the questions at issue in such cases. They are legally unregulated and in order to reach a decision in such cases the courts must exercise the restricted law-making function which I call 'discretion'. Dworkin rejects the idea that the law may be incomplete in this way and leave gaps to be filled by the exercise of such a law-creating discretion. This view he thinks is a mistaken inference from the fact that a proposition of law asserting the existence of a legal right or a legal duty may be controversial and so a matter about which reasonable and informed men may disagree, and when they do disagree there is often no way of demonstrating conclusively whether it is true or false. Such an inference is mistaken because when a proposition of law is thus controversial there may none the less still be 'facts of the matter' in virtue of which it is true or false, and though its truth or falsity cannot be demonstrated, arguments that it is true may still be assessed as better than arguments that it is false and vice versa. This distinction between law that is controversial and law that is incomplete or indeterminate is a matter of considerable importance for Dworkin's interpretive theory, since according to that theory a proposition of law is true only if in conjunction with other premises it follows from principles which both best fit the legal system's institutional history and also provide the best moral justification for it. Hence for Dworkin the truth of any proposition of law ultimately depends on the truth of a moral judgment as to what best justifies and since for him moral judgments are essentially controversial, so are all propositions of law.

For Dworkin the idea of a criterion of legal validity the application of which involves a controversial moral judgment presents no theoretical difficulty; it can still be in his view a genuine test for pre-existing law because its controversial character is perfectly compatible with there being facts (in many cases moral facts) in virtue of which it is true.

But soft positivism, which allows that a criterion of legal validity may be in part a moral test is, so Dworkin claims, involved in a second inconsistency, in addition to that already discussed on pp. 251–2 above. For it is not only inconsistent with the positivist 'picture' of law as identifiable with certainty, but inconsistent also with the wish which he attributes to positivists to make 'the objective standing of propositions of law'[40] independent of any commitment to any controversial philosophical theory of the status of moral judgments. For a moral test can be a test for pre-existing law only if there are objective moral facts in virtue of which moral judgments are true. But that there are such objective moral facts is a controversial philosophical theory; if there are no such facts, a judge, told to apply a moral test, can only treat this as a call for the exercise by him of a law-making discretion in accordance with his best understanding of morality and its requirements and subject to whatever constraints on this are imposed by the legal system.

I still think legal theory should avoid commitment to

[40] RDCJ 250.

controversial philosophical theories of the general status of moral
judgments and should leave open, as I do in this book (p. 168),
the general question of whether they have what Dworkin calls
'objective standing'. For whatever the answer is to this philosophical question, the judge's duty will be the same: namely, to
make the best moral judgment he can on any moral issues he
may have to decide. It will not matter for any practical purpose
whether in so deciding cases the judge is *making* law in accordance with morality (subject to whatever constraints are imposed
by law) or alternatively is guided by his moral judgment as to
what already *existing* law is revealed by a moral test for law. Of
course, if the question of the objective standing of moral judgments is left open by legal theory, as I claim it should be, then
soft positivism cannot be simply characterized as the theory that
moral principles or values may be among the criteria of legal
validity, since if it is an open question whether moral principles
and values have objective standing, it must also be an open question whether 'soft positivist' provisions purporting to include
conformity with them among the tests for existing law can have
that effect or instead, can only constitute directions to courts to
make law in accordance with morality.

It is to be observed that some theorists, notably Raz, hold that
whatever the status of moral judgments may be, whenever the law
requires courts to apply moral standards to determining the law
it thereby grants the courts discretion and directs them to use it
according to their best moral judgment in making what is a new
law; it does not thereby convert morality into pre-existing law.[41]

3. THE NATURE OF RULES

(i) *The Practice Theory of Rules*

At various points in this book I draw attention to the distinction
between internal and external statements of law and between
internal and external aspects of law.

To explain these distinctions and their importance I started
(pp. 56–7) by examining not the highly complex case of a

---

[41] See J. Raz, 'Dworkin: A New Link in the Chain', 74 *California Law Review*
1103 (1986), at 1110, 1115–16.

legal system which comprises both enacted and custom-type rules, but the simpler case (to which the same distinctions between internal and external apply) of the custom-type rules of any social group large or small, and these I call 'social rules'. The account I have given of these has become known as 'the practice theory' of rules because it treats the social rules of a group as constituted by a form of social practice comprising both patterns of conduct regularly followed by most members of the group and a distinctive normative attitude to such patterns of conduct which I have called 'acceptance'. This consists in the standing disposition of individuals to take such patterns of conduct both as guides to their own future conduct and as standards of criticism which may legitimate demands and various forms of pressure for conformity. The external point of view of social rules is that of an observer of their practice, and the internal point of view is that of a participant in such practice who accepts the rules as guides to conduct and as standards of criticism.

My practice theory of social rules has been extensively criticized by Dworkin, who, as I have already mentioned, makes a similar but in fact in many ways a very different distinction between a sociologist's external description of a community's social rules and the internal point of view of a participant who appeals to the rules for the purpose of evaluation and criticism of his own and others' conduct.[42] Some of Dworkin's criticism of my original account of social rules is certainly sound and important for the understanding of law, and in what follows here I indicate the considerable modifications in my original account which I now think necessary.

(i) My account is, as Dworkin has claimed, defective in ignoring the important difference between a consensus of *convention* manifested in a group's conventional rules and a consensus of independent *conviction* manifested in the concurrent practices of a group. Rules are conventional social practices if the general conformity of a group to them is part of the reasons which its individual members have for acceptance; by contrast merely concurrent practices such as the

---

[42] [See *LE* 13–14.]

shared morality of a group are constituted not by convention but by the fact that members of the group have and generally act on the same but independent reasons for behaving in certain specific ways.

(ii) My account of social rules is, as Dworkin has also rightly claimed, applicable only to rules which are conventional in the sense I have now explained. This considerably narrows the scope of my practice theory and I do not now regard it as a sound explanation of morality, either individual or social. But the theory remains as a faithful account of conventional social rules which include, besides ordinary social customs (which may or may not be recognized as having legal force), certain important legal rules including the rule of recognition, which is in effect a form of judicial customary rule existing only if it is accepted and practised in the law-identifying and law-applying operations of the courts. Enacted legal rules by contrast, though they are identifiable as valid legal rules by the criteria provided by the rule of recognition, may exist as legal rules from the moment of their enactment before any occasion for their practice has arisen and the practice theory is not applicable to them.

Dworkin's central criticism of the practice theory of rules is that it mistakenly takes a social rule to be constituted by its social practice and so treats the statement that such a rule exists merely as a statement of the external sociological fact that the practice-conditions for the existence of the rule are satisfied.[43] That account cannot, so Dworkin argues, explain the *normative* character possessed by even the simplest conventional rule. For these rules establish *duties* and *reasons for action* to which appeal is made when such rules are cited, as they commonly are, in criticism of conduct and in support of demands for action. This reason-giving and duty-establishing feature of rules constitutes their distinctive normative character and shows that their existence cannot consist in a merely factual state of affairs as do the practices and attitudes which according to the practice theory constitute the existence of a social rule. According to Dworkin, a normative rule with these distinctive features can only exist if there is 'a certain normative

---

[43] [See *TRS* 48–58.]

state of affairs'.[44] I find these quoted words tantalizingly obscure: from the discussion of the example of the Churchgoers' Rule (males must bare their heads in church)[45] Dworkin, it appears, means by a normative state of affairs the existence of good moral grounds or justification for doing what the rule requires, so he argues that while the mere regular practice of churchgoers removing hats in church cannot constitute the rule it may help to justify it by creating ways of giving offence and by giving rise to expectations which are good grounds for a rule requiring the removal of hats in church. If this is what Dworkin means by a normative state of affairs required to warrant the assertion of a normative rule his account of the existence conditions of a social rule seems to me far too strong. For it seems to require not only that the participants who appeal to rules as establishing duties or providing reasons for action must believe that there are good moral grounds or justification for conforming to the rules, but that there must actually be such good grounds. Plainly a society may have rules accepted by its members which are morally iniquitous, such as rules prohibiting persons of certain colour from using public facilities such as parks or bathing beaches. Indeed, even the weaker condition that for the existence of a social rule it must only be the case that participants must *believe* that there are good moral grounds for conforming to it is far too strong as a general condition for the existence of social rules. For some rules may be accepted simply out of deference to tradition or the wish to identify with others or in the belief that society knows best what is to the advantage of individuals. These attitudes may coexist with a more or less vivid realization that the rules are morally objectionable. Of course a conventional rule may both be and be believed to be morally sound and justified. But when the question arises as to why those who have accepted conventional rules as a guide to their behaviour or as standards of criticism have done so I see no reason for selecting from the many answers to be given (see pp. 203, 232 of this book) a belief in the moral justification of rules as the sole possible or adequate answer.

Finally, Dworkin argues that the practice theory of rules

---

[44] *TRS* 51. [45] [*TRS* 50-8; see this book, pp. 124-5.]

even if restricted to conventional rules must be abandoned
because it cannot accommodate the idea that the scope of a
conventional rule may be controversial and so the subject of
disagreement.[46] He does not deny that there are some uncontroversial rules constituted by regular practice and acceptance,
but he claims that rules so constituted include only relatively
unimportant cases such as the rules of some games; but in this
book a rule as important and as little controversial as a legal
system's basic rule of recognition is treated as a rule constituted
by the uniform practice of the courts in accepting it as a guide
to their law-applying and law-enforcing operations. Against
this Dworkin contends that in hard cases there are frequent
theoretical disagreements between judges as to what the law
on some subject is and that these show that the appearance of
uncontroversiality and general acceptance is an illusion. Of
course the frequency and importance of such disagreements
cannot be denied but appeals to their existence used as an argument against the applicability of the practice theory to the rule
of recognition rest on a misunderstanding of the function of the
rule. It assumes that the rule is meant to determine completely
the legal result in particular cases, so that any legal issue arising
in any case could simply be solved by mere appeal to the criteria
or tests provided by the rule. But this is a misconception: the
function of the rule is to determine only the general conditions
which correct legal decisions must satisfy in modern systems
of law. The rule does this most often by supplying criteria of
validity which Dworkin calls matters of pedigree and which
refer not to the content of the law but to the manner and form
in which the laws are created or adopted; but as I have said
(p. 250) in addition to such pedigree matters the rule of recognition may supply tests relating not to the factual content of
laws but to their conformity with substantive moral values or
principles. Of course in particular cases judges may disagree as
to whether such tests are satisfied or not and a moral test in the
rule of recognition will not resolve such disagreement. Judges
may be agreed on the relevance of such tests as something settled
by established judicial practice even though they disagree as

---

[46] [TRS 58.]

to what the tests require in particular cases. To the rule of recognition viewed in this way the practice theory of rules is fully applicable.

(ii) *Rules and Principles*

For long the best known of Dworkin's criticisms of this book was that it mistakenly represents law as consisting solely of 'all-or-nothing' rules, and ignores a different kind of legal standard, namely legal principles, which play an important and distinctive part in legal reasoning and adjudication. Some critics who have found this defect in my work have conceived of it as a more or less isolated fault which I could repair simply by including legal principles along with legal rules as components of a legal system, and they have thought that I could do this without abandoning or seriously modifying any of the main themes of the book. But Dworkin, who was the first to press this line of criticism, has insisted that legal principles could only be included in my theory of law at the cost of surrender of its central doctrines. If I were to admit that law consists in part of principles I could not, according to him, consistently maintain, as I have done, that the law of a system is identified by criteria provided by a rule of recognition accepted in the practice of the courts, or that the courts exercise a genuine though interstitial law-making power or discretion in those cases where the existing explicit law fails to dictate a decision, or that there is no important necessary or conceptual connection between law and morality. These doctrines are not only central to my theory of law but are often taken to constitute the core of modern legal positivism; so their abandonment would be a matter of some moment.

In this section of my reply I consider various aspects of the criticism that I have ignored legal principles and I attempt to show that whatever is valid in this criticism can be accommodated without any serious consequences for my theory as a whole. But I certainly wish to confess now that I said far too little in my book about the topic of adjudication and legal reasoning and, in particular, about arguments from what my critics call legal principles. I now agree that it is a defect of this book that principles are touched upon only in passing.

But what precisely is it that I am charged with ignoring?

What are legal principles, and how do they differ from legal rules? As used by legal writers 'principles' often include a vast array of theoretical and practical considerations only some of which are relevant to the issues which Dworkin meant to raise. Even if the expression 'principle' is taken to be limited to standards of conduct including the conduct of courts in deciding cases, there are different ways of drawing a contrast between rules and such principles. However, I think all my critics who have accused me of ignoring principles would agree that there are at least two features which distinguish them from rules. The first is a matter of degree: principles are, relatively to rules, broad, general, or unspecific, in the sense that often what would be regarded as a number of distinct rules can be exhibited as the exemplifications or instantiations of a single principle. The second feature is that principles, because they refer more or less explicitly to some purpose, goal, entitlement, or value, are regarded from some point of view as desirable to maintain, or to adhere to, and so not only as providing an explanation or rationale of the rules which exemplify them, but as at least contributing to their justification.

Besides these two relatively uncontroversial features of breadth and desirability from some point of view which account for the explanatory and justificatory role of principles in relation to rules, there is a third distinguishing feature which I myself think is a matter of degree whereas Dworkin who regards it as crucial does not. Rules, according to him, function in the reasoning of those who apply them in an 'all-or-nothing manner' in the sense that if a rule is valid and applicable at all to a given case then it 'necessitates' i.e. conclusively determines the legal result or outcome.[47] Among the examples which he gave of legal rules are those prescribing a maximum speed of 60 m.p.h. on the turnpike road or statutes regulating the making, proof, and efficacy of wills such as the statutory rule that a will is invalid unless signed by two witnesses. Legal principles, according to Dworkin, differ from such all-or-nothing rules because when they are applicable they do not 'necessitate' a decision but point towards or count

[47] [*TRS* 24.]

in favour of a decision, or state a reason which may be over-ridden but which the courts take into account as inclining in one direction or another. I shall, for short, call this feature of principles their 'non-conclusive' character. Some examples given by Dworkin of such non-conclusive principles are relatively specific, such as 'the courts must examine purchase agreements [for automobiles] closely to see if consumer and public interests are treated fairly';[48] others have much wider scope, such as 'no man may profit from his own wrong';[49] and in fact many of the most important constitutional restrictions on the powers of the United States Congress and on state legislation such as the provisions of the First, Fifth, and Fourteenth Amendments to the United States Constitution function as non-conclusive principles.[50] Legal principles, according to Dworkin, differ from rules because they have a dimension of *weight*[51] but not of validity, and hence it is that in conflict with another principle of greater weight, one principle may be overridden and fail to determine a decision, but none the less will survive intact to be used in other cases where it may win in competition with some other principle of lesser weight. Rules, on the other hand, are either valid or invalid but do not have this dimension of weight, so if as initially formulated they conflict, only one of them according to Dworkin can be valid, and a rule which loses in competition with another must be reformulated so as to make it consistent with its competitor and hence inapplicable to the given case.[52]

I see no reason to accept either this sharp contrast between legal principles and legal rules, or the view that if a valid rule is applicable to a given case it must, unlike a principle, always determine the outcome of the case. There is no reason why a legal system should not recognize that a valid rule determines a result in cases to which it is applicable, except where another rule, judged to be more important, is also applicable to the same case. So a rule which is defeated in

---

[48] *TRS* 24, quoting from *Henningsen v. Bloomfield Motors, Inc.*, 32 NJ 358, 161 A.2d 69 (1960) at 387, 161 A.2d at 85.   [49] *TRS* 25–6.

[50] [Dworkin discusses whether the First Amendment is a rule or a principle at *TRS* 27.]   [51] [*TRS* 26.]

[52] *TRS* 24–7.

competition with a more important rule in a given case may, like a principle, survive to determine the outcome in other cases where it is judged to be more important than another competing rule.[53]

So law for Dworkin comprises both all-or-nothing rules and non-conclusive principles, and he does not think that this difference between them is a matter of degree. But I do not think that Dworkin's position can be coherent. His earliest examples imply that rules may come into conflict with principles and that a principle will sometimes win in competition with a rule and sometimes lose. The cases he cites include *Riggs* v. *Palmer*,[54] in which the principle that a man may not be permitted to profit from his own wrongdoing was held notwithstanding the clear language of the statutory rules governing the effect of a will to preclude a murderer inheriting under his victim's will. This is an example of a principle winning in competition with a rule, but the existence of such competition surely shows that rules do not have an all-or-nothing character, since they are liable to be brought into such conflict with principles which may outweigh them. Even if we describe such cases (as Dworkin at times suggests) not as conflicts between rules and principles, but as a conflict between the principle explaining and justifying the rule under consideration and some other principle, the sharp contrast between all-or-nothing rules and non-conclusive principles disappears; for on this view a rule will fail to determine a result in a case to which it is applicable according to its terms if its justifying principle is outweighed by another. The same is true if (as Dworkin also suggests) we think of a principle as providing a reason for a new interpretation of some clearly formulated legal rule.[55]

This incoherence in the claim that a legal system consists both of all-or-nothing rules and non-conclusive principles may be cured if we admit that the distinction is a matter of degree.

---

[53] Raz and Waluchow have emphasized this important point to which I had failed to draw attention. See J. Raz, 'Legal Principles and the Limits of the Law', 81 *Yale LJ* 823 (1972) at 832–4 and W. J. Waluchow, 'Herculean Positivism', 5 *Oxford Journal of Legal Studies* 187 (1985) at 189–92.

[54] 115 N.Y. 506, 22 N.E. 188 (1889); *TRS* 23; see also *LE* 15 ff.

[55] [For Dworkin's discussion see *TRS* 22–8 and *LE* 15–20.]

Certainly a reasonable contrast can be made between near-conclusive rules, the satisfaction of whose conditions of application suffices to determine the legal result except in a few instances (where its provisions may conflict with another rule judged of greater importance) and generally non-conclusive principles which merely point towards a decision but may very frequently fail to determine it.

I certainly think that arguments from such non-conclusive principles are an important feature of adjudication and legal reasoning, and that it should be marked by an appropriate terminology. Much credit is due to Dworkin for having shown and illustrated their importance and their role in legal reasoning, and certainly it was a serious mistake on my part not to have stressed their non-conclusive force. But I certainly did not intend in my use of the word 'rule' to claim that legal systems comprise only 'all-or-nothing' or near-conclusive rules. I not only drew attention (see pp. 130–3 of this book) to what I termed (perhaps infelicitously) 'variable legal standards' which specify factors to be taken into account and weighed against others, but I attempted (see pp. 133–4) to explain why some areas of conduct were suitable for regulation not by such variable standards as 'due care' but rather by near-conclusive rules prohibiting or requiring the same specific actions in all but rare cases. So it is that we have rules against murder and theft and not merely principles requiring due respect for human life and property.

4. PRINCIPLES AND THE RULE OF RECOGNITION

Pedigree and Interpretation

Dworkin has claimed that legal principles cannot be identified by criteria provided by a rule of recognition manifested in the practice of the courts and that, since principles are essential elements of law, the doctrine of a rule of recognition must be abandoned. According to him, legal principles can only be identified by constructive interpretation as members of the unique set of principles which both best fits and best justifies the whole institutional history of the settled law of a legal system. Of course no court, English or American, has ever explicitly adopted such a system-wide holistic criterion for identifying the law, and Dworkin concedes that no actual human judge as distinct from his mythical ideal judge 'Hercules' could accomplish the feat of constructing an interpretation of all his country's law at once. None the less the courts in his view are most illuminatingly understood as trying to 'imitate Hercules' in a limited way and viewing their judgments in this way serves, he thinks, to bring to light 'the hidden structure'.[56]

The most famous example, familiar to English lawyers, of the identification of principles by a limited form of constructive interpretation is Lord Atkin's formulation in the case of *Donoghue* v. *Stevenson*[57] of the previously unformulated 'neighbour principle' as underlying the various separate rules establishing a duty of care in different situations.

I do not find plausible the view that in such limited exercises of constructive interpretation judges are best understood as trying to imitate Hercules' holistic system-wide approach. But my present criticism is that preoccupation with constructive interpretation has led Dworkin to ignore the fact that many legal principles owe their status not to their content serving as interpretation of settled law, but to what he calls their 'pedigree'; that is the manner of their creation or adoption by a recognized authoritative source. This preoccupation has, I think, in fact led him into a double error: first, to the belief that legal principles cannot be identified by their pedigree, and secondly to the belief that a rule of recognition can only provide pedigree criteria. Both these beliefs are mistaken; the first is so because there is nothing in the non-conclusive character of principles nor in their other features to preclude their identification by pedigree criteria. For plainly a provision in a written constitution or a constitutional amendment or a statute may be taken as intended to operate in the non-conclusive way characteristic of principles, as providing reasons for decision which may be outweighed in cases where some other rule or principle presents stronger reasons for an alternative decision. Dworkin himself envisaged that the First Amendment of the United States Constitution, providing that Congress shall not abridge freedom of speech, is to be

[56] *LE* 265.   [57] [1932] A.C. 562.

interpreted in just that way.[58] Also some legal principles, including some basic principles of the Common Law, such as that no
man may profit from his own wrongdoing, are identified as law
by the 'pedigree' test in that they have been consistently invoked
by courts in ranges of different cases as providing reasons for
decision, which must be taken into account, though liable to be
overridden in some cases by reasons pointing the other way. In
face of such examples of legal principles identified by pedigree
criteria, no general argument that the inclusion of principles
as part of the law entails the abandonment of the doctrine of a
rule of recognition could succeed. In fact, as I show below, their
inclusion is not only consistent with, but actually requires acceptance of that doctrine.

If it is conceded, as surely it must be, that there are at least
some legal principles which may be 'captured' or identified as
law by pedigree criteria provided by a rule of recognition, then
Dworkin's criticism must be reduced to the more modest claim
that there are many legal principles that cannot be so captured
because they are too numerous, too fleeting, or too liable to
change or modification, or have no feature which would permit
their identification as principles of law by reference to any other
test than that of belonging to that coherent scheme of principles
which both best fits the institutional history and practices of the
system and best justifies them. At first sight this interpretivist
test seems not to be an alternative to a criterion provided by
a rule of recognition, but, as some critics have urged,[59] only a
complex 'soft-positivist' form of such a criterion identifying
principles by their content not by their pedigree. It is true that
a rule of recognition containing such an interpretive criterion
could not, for the reasons discussed on pp. 251 ff. above, secure
the degree of certainty in identifying the law which according
to Dworkin a positivist would wish. None the less, to show that
the interpretive test criterion was part of a conventional pattern
of law-recognition would still be a good theoretical explanation

---

[58] [See TRS 27.]

[59] See, e.g., E. P. Soper, 'Legal Theory and the Obligation of a Judge', *RDCJ*
p. 3 at 16; J. Coleman, 'Negative and Positive Positivism', *RDCJ* p. 28; D. Lyons,
'Principles, Positivism and Legal Theory', 87 *Yale Law Journal* 415 (1977).

of its legal status. So there is certainly no incompatibility such as Dworkin claims between the admission of principles as part of the law and the doctrine of a rule of recognition.

The argument of the last two paragraphs is enough to show that contrary to Dworkin's contention the acceptance of principles as part of the law is consistent with the doctrine of a rule of recognition, even if Dworkin's interpretive test were as he claims the sole appropriate criterion for identifying them. But in fact a stronger conclusion is warranted: namely that a rule of recognition is necessary if legal principles are to be identified by such a criterion. This is so because the starting-point for the identification of any legal principle to be brought to light by Dworkin's interpretive test is some specific area of the settled law which the principle fits and helps to justify. The use of that criterion therefore presupposes the identification of the settled law, and for that to be possible a rule of recognition specifying the sources of law and the relationships of superiority and subordination holding between them is necessary. In the terminology of *Law's Empire*, the legal rules and practices which constitute the starting-points for the interpretive task of identifying underlying or implicit legal principles constitute 'preinterpretive law', and much that Dworkin says about it appears to endorse the view that for its identification something very like a rule of recognition identifying the authoritative sources of law as described in this book is necessary. The main difference between my view and Dworkin's here is that whereas I ascribe the general agreement found among judges as to the criteria for the identification of the sources of law to their shared acceptance of *rules* providing such criteria, Dworkin prefers to speak not of rules but of 'consensus'[60] and 'paradigms'[61] and 'assumptions'[62] which members of the same interpretive community share. Of course, as Dworkin has made clear, there is an important distinction between a consensus of independent convictions where the concurrence of others is not part of the reason which each party to the consensus has for concurring, and a consensus of convention where it is such a part. Certainly the rule of recognition is treated in my book as resting on a

---

[60] [*LE* 65–6, 91–2.]   [61] [*LE* 72–3.]   [62] [*LE* 47, 67.]

conventional form of judicial consensus. That it does so rest
seems quite clear at least in English and American law for surely
an English judge's reason for treating Parliament's legislation (or
an American judge's reason for treating the Constitution) as a
source of law having supremacy over other sources includes the
fact that his judicial colleagues concur in this as their predecessors have done. Indeed Dworkin himself speaks of the doctrine
of legislative supremacy as a brute fact of legal history which
limits the role which a judge's conviction can play[63] and he states
that 'the interpretive attitude cannot survive unless members of
the same interpretive community share at least roughly the same
assumptions' about 'what counts as part of the practice'.[64] I conclude therefore that whatever differences may remain between
rules and the 'assumptions' and 'consensus' and 'paradigms' of
which Dworkin speaks, his explanation of the judicial identification of the sources of law is substantially the same as mine.

However, large theoretical differences remain between
mine and Dworkin's view. For Dworkin would certainly
reject my treatment of his interpretive test for legal principles
as merely the specific form taken in some legal systems by a
conventional rule of recognition whose existence and authority depend on its acceptance by the courts. This would in
his view utterly misrepresent and demean the project of a
'constructive' interpretation designed to show the law in the
best moral light, which in Dworkin's view is involved in the
identification of the law. For this style of interpretation is not
conceived by him as a method of law recognition required by
a mere conventional rule accepted by the judges and lawyers
of particular legal systems. Instead he presents it as a central
feature of much social thought and social practice besides
law and as showing 'a deep connection among all forms of
interpretation', including interpretation as it is understood in
literary criticism and even in the natural sciences.[65] However,
even if this interpretive criterion is not merely a pattern of law
recognition required by a conventional rule and has affinities
and connections with interpretation as it is understood in
other disciplines, the fact remains that if there are any legal

---

[63] [*LE* 401.]   [64] *LE* 67.   [65] *LE* 53.

systems in which Dworkin's holistic interpretive criterion is actually used to identify legal principles it could perfectly well be that
in such systems that criterion is provided by a conventional rule of
recognition. But since there are no actual legal systems where this
full holistic criterion is used, but only systems like English law
and American law where more modest exercises of constructive
interpretation are undertaken in cases like *Donoghue* v. *Stevenson* to
identify latent legal principles, the only question to be considered
is whether such exercises are to be understood as the application
of a criterion provided by a conventional rule of recognition or in
some other way, and if so what their legal status is.

5. LAW AND MORALITY

(i) *Rights and Duties*

I argue in this book that though there are many different
contingent connections between law and morality there are no
necessary conceptual connections between the content of law
and morality; and hence morally iniquitous provisions may be
valid as legal rules or principles. One aspect of this form of the
separation of law from morality is that there can be legal rights
and duties which have no moral justification or force whatever.
Dworkin has rejected this idea in favour of the view (ultimately
derived from his own interpretive theory of law) that there
must be at least prima-facie moral grounds for assertions of the
existence of legal rights and duties. So he regards the idea that
'legal rights must be understood as [a] species of moral rights' as
a 'crucial'[66] element in his legal theory and says that the opposed
positivist doctrine belongs to 'the peculiar world of legal essen-
tialism'[67] in which it is just given to us to know pre-analytically
that there can be legal rights and duties without any moral
ground or force. It is I think important for understanding the
kind of contribution which a general descriptive jurisprudence
can make to the understanding of law to see that whatever the
merits of his general interpretive theory may be, Dworkin's criticism of the doctrine that legal rights and duties may be devoid of
moral force or justification is mistaken. It is so for the following

[66] *RDCJ* 260.   [67] *RDCJ* 259.

reasons: legal rights and duties are the point at which the law with its coercive resources respectively protects individual freedom and restricts it or confers on individuals or denies to them the power to avail themselves of the law's coercive machinery. So whether the laws are morally good or bad, just or unjust, rights and duties demand attention as focal points in the operations of the law which are of supreme importance to human beings and independently of moral merits of the laws. It is therefore untrue that statements of legal rights and duties can only make sense in the real world if there is some moral ground for asserting their existence.

(ii) *The Identification of the Law*

The most fundamental difference relating to connections between law and morality between the legal theory developed in this book and Dworkin's theory concerns the identification of the law. According to my theory, the existence and content of the law can be identified by reference to the social sources of the law (e.g. legislation, judicial decisions, social customs) without reference to morality except where the law thus identified has itself incorporated moral criteria for the identification of the law. In Dworkin's interpretive theory, on the other hand, every proposition of law stating what the law on some subject is necessarily involves a moral judgment, since according to his holistic interpretive theory propositions of law are true only if with other premises they follow from that set of principles which both best fit all the settled law identified by reference to the social sources of the law and provide the best moral justification for it. This overall holistic interpretive theory has therefore a double function: it serves both to identify the law and to provide moral justification for it.

Such was Dworkin's theory, briefly summarized, prior to his introduction in *Law's Empire* of the distinction between 'interpretive' and 'preinterpretive' law. Considered as an alternative to the positivist's theory that the existence and content of the law may be identified without reference to morality, Dworkin's theory as it originally stood was vulnerable to the following criticism. Where the law identified by reference to its social sources is morally iniquitous, principles providing

the best 'justification' for it could only be the least iniquitous of principles fitting that law. But such least iniquitous
principles can have no justifying force and cannot constitute
any moral limit or constraint on what can count as law and
since they cannot fail to fit any legal system, however evil,
the theory purporting to identify law by reference to them is
indistinguishable from the positivist theory that the law may
be identified without any reference to morality. Principles
which are morally sound by the standards of what Dworkin
has called 'background morality'[68] and not merely the morally
soundest of those principles which fit the law may indeed
provide moral limits or constraints upon what can count as
law. I do not dissent in any way from that proposition but it is
fully compatible with my claim that the law may be identified
without reference to morality.

In introducing his later distinction between interpretive and
preinterpretive law Dworkin concedes that there may be legal
systems so evil that no interpretation of their laws which we
could find morally acceptable is possible. When this is so we
may, as he explains, resort to what he calls 'internal scepticism'[69]
and deny that such systems are law. But since our resources for
describing such situations are highly flexible we are not bound
to come to that conclusion when we can instead say that legal
systems however evil are law in a preinterpretive sense.[70] So we
are not forced to say of even the worst of the Nazi laws that
they are not law since they may differ only in their iniquitous
moral content from the laws of morally acceptable regimes while
sharing with them many distinctive features of law (e.g. forms
of law creation, forms of adjudication and enforcement). There
may be reasons enough in many contexts and for many purposes
to disregard the moral difference and say with the positivist that
such evil systems are law. To this Dworkin would only add as it
were a rider manifesting his general adherence to his interpretive
point of view that such evil systems are law only in a preinterpretive sense.

I find that this appeal to the flexibility of our language and

---

[68] [*TRS* 112, 128, and see *TRS* 93.]
[69] *LE* 78–9.   [70] [*LE* 103.]

the introduction at this point of the distinction between interpretive and preinterpretive law concedes rather than weakens the
positivist's case. For it does little more than convey the message
that while he insists that in a descriptive jurisprudence the law
may be identified without reference to morality, things are
otherwise for a justificatory interpretive jurisprudence according
to which the identification of the law always involves a moral
judgment as to what best justifies the settled law. This message of
course gives no reason for the positivist to abandon his descriptive
enterprise, nor is it intended to do so but even this message has to
be qualified, for the law may be so evil that 'internal scepticism'
is in order, in which case the interpretation of the law involves
no moral judgment and interpretation as Dworkin understands it
must be given up.[71]

One further modification by Dworkin of his interpretive
theory has an important bearing on his account of legal rights.
In his holistic theory as originally expounded the identification
of law and its justification are both treated as following from
that unique set of principles which both best fit all of the settled
law of a system and best justify it. Such principles therefore have,
as I have said, a double function. But since the settled law of a
system may be so evil that no overall justifying interpretation
of its law is possible, Dworkin has observed that these two
functions may become separated, leaving only principles of
law identified without reference to any morality. But such law
cannot establish any rights having the prima-facie moral force
which Dworkin claims all legal rights have. Yet as Dworkin
later recognized, even where the system is so wicked that no
moral or justifying interpretation of law as a whole is possible
there may still be situations where individuals may properly be
said to have rights with at least prima-facie moral force.[72] That
would be so where the system contains laws (e.g. those relating
to the formation and enforcement of contracts) which may not be
affected by the general wickedness of the system and individuals
may have relied on such laws in planning their lives or making
dispositions of property. To cater for such situations Dworkin
qualifies his original idea that legal rights and duties with

[71] [*LE* 105.]   [72] [*LE* 105–6.]

prima-facie moral force must flow from a general interpretive theory of the law, and he recognizes such situations as constituting independently of his general theory 'special reasons' for ascribing legal rights with some moral force to individuals.

6. JUDICIAL DISCRETION[73]

The sharpest direct conflict between the legal theory of this book and Dworkin's theory arises from my contention that in any legal system there will always be certain legally unregulated cases in which on some point no decision either way is dictated by the law and the law is accordingly partly indeterminate or incomplete. If in such cases the judge is to reach a decision and is not, as Bentham once advocated, to disclaim jurisdiction or to refer the points not regulated by the existing law to the legislature to decide, he must exercise his *discretion* and *make* law for the case instead of merely applying already pre-existing settled law. So in such legally unprovided-for or unregulated cases the judge both makes new law and applies the established law which both confers and constrains his law-making powers.

This picture of the law as in part indeterminate or incomplete and of the judge as filling the gaps by exercising a limited law-creating discretion is rejected by Dworkin as a misleading account both of the law and of judicial reasoning. He claims in effect that what is incomplete is not the law but the positivist's picture of it, and that this is so will emerge from his own 'interpretive' account of the law as including besides the *explicit* settled law identified by reference to its social sources, *implicit* legal principles which are those principles which both best fit or cohere with the explicit law and also provide the best moral justification for it. On this interpretive view, the law is never incomplete or indeterminate, so the judge never has occasion to step outside the law and exercise a law-creating power in order to reach a decision. It is therefore to such implicit principles, with their moral dimensions, that courts should turn in those 'hard cases' where

---

[73] [An alternative version of the opening paragraph of this section appears in an endnote.]

the social sources of the law fail to determine a decision on some point of law.

It is important that the law-creating powers which I ascribe to the judges to regulate cases left partly unregulated by the law are different from those of a legislature: not only are the judge's powers subject to many constraints *narrowing his choice* from which a legislature may be quite free, but since the judge's powers are exercised only to dispose of particular instant cases he cannot use these to introduce large-scale reforms or new codes. So his powers are *interstitial* as well as subject to many substantive constraints. None the less there will be points where the existing law fails to dictate any decision as the correct one, and to decide cases where this is so the judge must exercise his law-making powers. But he must not do this arbitrarily: that is he must always have some general reasons justifying his decision and he must act as a conscientious legislator would by deciding according to his own beliefs and values. But if he satisfies these conditions he is entitled to follow standards or reasons for decision which are not dictated by the law and may differ from those followed by other judges faced with similar hard cases.

Against my account of the courts as exercising such a limited discretionary power to settle cases left incompletely regulated by the law, Dworkin directs three main criticisms. The first is that this account is a false description of the judicial process and of what courts do in 'hard cases'.[74] To show this Dworkin appeals to the language used by judges and lawyers in describing the judge's task, and to the phenomenology of judicial decision-making. Judges, it is said, in deciding cases and lawyers pressing them to decide in their favour, do not speak of the judge as 'making' the law even in novel cases. Even in the hardest of such cases the judge often betrays no awareness that there are, as the positivist suggests, two completely different stages in the process of decision: one in which the judge first finds that the existing law fails to dictate a decision either way; and the other in which he then turns away from the existing law to make law for the parties *de novo* and *ex post facto* according to his idea of what is best. Instead,

---

[74] [*TRS* 81; cf. *LE* 37–9.]

lawyers address the judge as if he was always concerned to discover and enforce existing law and the judge speaks as if the law were a gapless system of entitlements in which a solution for every case awaits his discovery, not his invention.

There is no doubt that the familiar rhetoric of the judicial process encourages the idea that there are in a developed legal system no legally unregulated cases. But how seriously is this to be taken? There is of course a long European tradition and a doctrine of the division of powers which dramatizes the distinction between Legislator and Judge and insists that the Judge always is, what he is when the existing law is clear, the mere 'mouthpiece' of a law which he does not make or mould. But it is important to distinguish the ritual language used by judges and lawyers in deciding cases in their courts from their more reflective general statements about the judicial process. Judges of the stature of Oliver Wendell Holmes and Cardozo in the United States, or Lord Macmillan or Lord Radcliffe or Lord Reid in England, and a host of other lawyers, both academic and practising, have insisted that there are cases left incompletely regulated by the law where the judge has an inescapable though 'interstitial' law-making task, and that so far as the law is concerned many cases could be decided either way.

One principal consideration helps to explain resistance to the claim that judges sometimes both make and apply law and also elucidates the main features which distinguish judicial from a legislature's law-making. This is the importance characteristically attached by courts when deciding unregulated cases to proceeding by analogy so as to ensure that the new law they make, though it *is* new law, is in accordance with principles or underpinning reasons recognized as already having a footing in the existing law. It is true that when particular statutes or precedents prove indeterminate, or when the explicit law is silent, judges do not just push away their law books and start to legislate without further guidance from the law. Very often, in deciding such cases, they cite some general principle or some general aim or purpose which some considerable relevant area of the existing law can be understood as exemplifying or advancing and which points towards a determinate answer for the instant hard case. This indeed

the very nucleus of the 'constructive interpretation' which
so prominent a feature of Dworkin's theory of adjudication.
But though this procedure certainly defers, it does not eliminate
the moment for judicial law-making, since in any hard case different principles supporting competing analogies may present
themselves and a judge will often have to choose between them,
relying, like a conscientious legislator, on his sense of what is best
and not on any already established order of priorities prescribed
for him by law. Only if for all such cases there was always to
be found in the existing law some unique set of higher-order
principles assigning relative weights or priorities to such competing lower-order principles, would the moment for judicial
law-making be not merely deferred but eliminated.

Dworkin's other criticisms of my account of judicial discretion condemn it not as descriptively false but for endorsing a
form of law-making which is undemocratic and unjust.[75] Judges
are not usually elected and in a democracy, so it is claimed, only
the elected representatives of the people should have law-making
powers. There are many answers to this criticism. That judges
should be entrusted with law-making powers to deal with disputes which the law fails to regulate may be regarded as a necessary price to pay for avoiding the inconvenience of alternative
methods of regulating them such as reference to the legislature;
and the price may seem small if judges are constrained in the
exercise of these powers and cannot fashion codes or wide
reforms but only rules to deal with the specific issues thrown up
by particular cases. Secondly, the delegation of limited legislative
powers to the executive is a familiar feature of modern democ-
racies and such delegation to the judiciary seems a no greater
menace to democracy. In both forms of delegation an elected
legislature will normally have residual control and may repeal
or amend any subordinate laws which it finds unacceptable. It
is true that when, as in the USA, the legislature's powers are
limited by a written constitution and the courts have extensive
powers of review a *democratically elected* legislature may find itself
unable to reverse a piece of judicial legislation. Then ultimate

democratic control can be secured only through the cumbrous machinery of constitutional amendment. That is the price which must be paid for legal constraints on government.

Dworkin makes the further accusation that judicial lawmaking is unjust and condemns it as a form of retrospective or *ex post facto* law-making which is, of course, commonly regarded as unjust. But the reason for regarding retrospective law-making as unjust is that it disappoints the justified expectations of those who, in acting, have relied on the assumption that the legal consequences of their acts will be determined by the known state of the law established at the time of their acts. This objection, however, even if it has force against a court's retrospective change or over-ruling of clearly established law, seems quite irrelevant in hard cases since these are cases which the law has left incompletely regulated and where there is no known state of clear established law to justify expectations.

NOTES

The text of this book is self-contained, and the reader may find it best to read each chapter through before turning to these notes. The footnotes in the text give only the sources of quotations, and references to cases or statutes cited. The following notes are designed to bring to the reader's attention matters of three different kinds, viz.: (i) further illustrations or examples of general statements made in the text; (ii) writings in which the views adopted or referred to in the text are further expounded or criticized; (iii) suggestions for the further investigation of questions raised in the text. All references to this book are indicated simply by chapter and section numbers, e.g. Chapter 1, s. 1. The following abbreviations are used:

Austin, *The Province*	Austin, *The Province of Jurisprudence Determined* (ed. Hart, London, 1954)
Austin, *The Lectures*	Austin, *Lectures on the Philosophy of Positive Law.*
Kelsen, *General Theory*	Kelsen, *General Theory of Law and State.*
BYBIL	*British Year Book of International Law.*
HLR	*Harvard Law Review.*
LQR	*Law Quarterly Review.*
MLR	*Modern Law Review.*
PAS	*Proceedings of the Aristotelian Society.*

CHAPTER I

Pages 1–2. Each of the quotations on these pages from Llewellyn, Holmes, Gray, Austin, and Kelsen, are paradoxical or exaggerated ways of emphasizing some aspect of law which, in the author's view, is either obscured by ordinary legal terminology, or has been unduly neglected by previous theorists. In the case of any important jurist, it is frequently profitable to defer consideration of the question whether his statements about law are literally true or false, and to examine first, the detailed reasons given by him in support of his statements and secondly, the conception or theory of law which his statement is designed to displace.

A similar use of paradoxical or exaggerated assertions, as a method of emphasizing neglected truths is familiar in philosophy. See J. Wisdom, 'Metaphysics and Verification' in *Philosophy and Psychoanalysis* (1953); Frank, *Law and the Modern Mind* (London, 1949), Appendix VII ('Notes on Fictions').

The doctrines asserted or implied in each of the five quotations on these pages are examined in Chapter VII, ss. 2 and 3 (Holmes,

Gray, and Llewellyn); Chapter IV, ss. 3 and 4 (Austin); and Chapter III, s. 1, pp. 35–42 (Kelsen).

Page 4. Standard cases and borderline cases. The feature of language referred to here is generally discussed under the heading of 'The Open Texture of Law' in Chapter VII, s. 1. It is something to be kept in mind not only when a definition is expressly sought for general terms like 'law', 'state', 'crime', &c., but also when attempts are made to characterize the reasoning involved in the application of rules, framed in general terms, to particular cases. Among legal writers who have stressed the importance of this feature of language are: Austin, *The Province*, Lecture VI, pp. 202–7, and *Lectures in Jurisprudence* (5th edn., 1885), p. 997 ('Note on Interpretation'); Glanville Williams, 'International Law and the Controversy Concerning the Word "Law"', *22 BYBIL* (1945), and 'Language in the Law' (five articles), *61* and *62 LQR* (1945–6). On the latter, however, see comments by J. Wisdom in 'Gods' and in 'Philosophy, Metaphysics and Psycho-Analysis', both in *Philosophy and Psycho-Analysis* (1953).

Page 6. Austin on obligation. See *The Province,* Lecture I, pp. 14–18; *The Lectures,* Lectures 22 and 23. The idea of obligation and the differences between 'having an obligation' and 'being obliged' by coercion are examined in detail in Chapter V, s. 2. On Austin's analysis see notes to Chapter II, below, p. 282.

Page 8. Legal and moral obligation. The claim that law is best understood through its connection with morality is examined in Chapters VIII and IX. It has taken very many different forms. Sometimes, as in the classical and scholastic theories of Natural Law, this claim is associated with the assertion that fundamental moral distinctions are 'objective truths' discoverable by human reason; but many other jurists, equally concerned to stress the interdependence of law and morals, are not committed to this view of the nature of morality. See notes to Chapter IX, below, p. 302.

Page 10. Scandinavian legal theory and the idea of a binding rule. The most important works of this school, for English readers, are Hägerström (1868–1939), *Inquiries into the Nature of Law and Morals* (trans. Broad, 1953), and Olivecrona, *Law as Fact* (1939). The clearest statement of their views on the character of legal rules is to be found in Olivecrona, op. cit. His criticism of the predictive analysis of legal rules favoured by many American jurists (see op. cit., pp. 85–8, 213–15) should be compared with the similar criticisms in Kelsen, *General Theory* (pp. 165 ff., 'The Prediction of the Legal Function'). It is worth inquiring why such different conclusions as to the character of legal rules are drawn by these two jurists in spite of their agreement on many points. For criticisms of the Scandinavian School, see Hart, review of Hägerström, op. cit. in 30 *Philosophy* (1955); 'Scandinavian Realism', *Cambridge Law Journal* (1959); Marshall, 'Law in a Cold Climate', *Juridical Review* (1956).

Page 12. *Rule-scepticism in American legal theory.* See Chapter VII, ss. 1 and 2 on 'Formalism and Rule-scepticism', where some of the principal doctrines which have come to be known as 'Legal Realism' are examined.

Pages 12–13. *Doubt as to meaning of common words.* For cases on the meaning of 'sign' or 'signature' see 34 Halsbury, *Laws of England* (2nd edn.), paras. 165–9 and In the Estate of Cook (1960), 1 AER 689 and cases there cited.

Page 13. *Definition.* For a general modern view of the forms and functions of definition see Robinson, *Definition* (Oxford, 1952). The inadequacy of the traditional definition *per genus et differentiam* as a method of elucidating legal terms is discussed by Bentham, *Fragment on Government* (notes to Chapter V, s. 6), and Ogden, *Bentham's Theory of Fictions* (pp. 75–104). See also Hart, 'Definition and Theory in Jurisprudence', *70 LQR* (1954), and Cohen and Hart, 'Theory and Definition in Jurisprudence,' *PAS* Suppl. vol. xxix (1955).

For the definition of the term 'law' see Glanville Williams, op. cit.; R. Wollheim, 'The Nature of Law' in *2 Political Studies* (1954); and Kantorowicz, *The Definition of Law* (1958), esp. Chapter 1. On the general need for, and clarificatory function of, a definition of terms, though no doubts are felt about their day-to-day use in particular cases, see Ryle, *Philosophical Arguments* (1945); Austin, 'A Plea for Excuses', *57 PAS* (1956–7), pp. 15 ff.

Page 15. *General terms and common qualities.* The uncritical belief that if a general term (e.g. 'law', 'state', 'nation', 'crime', 'good', 'just') is correctly used, then the range of instances to which it is applied must all share 'common qualities' has been the source of much confusion. Much time and ingenuity has been wasted in jurisprudence in the vain attempt to discover, for the purposes of definition, the common qualities which are, on this view, held to be the *only* respectable reason for using the same word of many different things (see Glanville Williams, op. cit. It is however important to notice that this mistaken view of the character of general words does not always involve the further confusion of 'verbal questions' with questions of fact which this author suggests).

Understanding of the different ways in which the several instances of a general term may be related is of particular importance in the case of legal, moral, and political terms. For analogy: see Aristotle, *Nicomachean Ethics*, i, ch. 6 (where it is suggested that the different instances of 'good' may be so related), Austin, *The Province*, Lecture V, pp. 119–24. For different relationships to a central case, e.g. healthy: see Aristotle, *Categories*, chap. 1 and examples in *Topics*, 1, chap. 15, ii, chap. 9, of 'paronyms'. For the notion of 'family resemblance': see Wittgenstein, *Philosophical Investigations*, i, paras. 66–76. Cf. Chapter VIII, s. 1 on the structure of the term 'just'. Wittgenstein's advice (op. cit., para. 66) is peculiarly relevant to the analysis of legal and political terms. Considering the definition of 'game' he said, 'Don't say there *must* be something common or they would not be called 'games', but *look* and *see* whether there is anything common to all. For if you look at them you will not see anything common to *all* but similarities, relationships, and a whole series at that.'

CHAPTER II

Page 18. *The varieties of imperatives.* The classification of imperatives as 'orders', 'pleas', 'comments', &c., which depends upon many circumstances such as the social situation and relationships of the parties and their intentions as to the use of force, is as yet a virtually untapped subject of inquiry. Most philosophical discussion of imperatives is concerned either with (1) the relationships between imperative and indicative or descriptive language and the possibilities of reducing the former to the latter (see Bohnert, 'The Semiotic Status of Commands', *12 Philosophy of Science* (1945)), or (2) the question whether any, and if so what, deductive relationships exist between imperatives (see Hare, 'Imperative Sentences', 58 *Mind* (1949), also *The Language of Morals* (1952); Hofstadter and McKinsey, 'The Logic of Imperatives', *6 Philosophy of Science* (1939); Hall, *What is Value* (1952), chap. 6; and Ross, 'Imperatives and Logic', *11 Philosophy of Science* (1944)). Study of these logical questions is important; but there is also great need for a discrimination of the varieties of imperatives by reference to contextual social situations. To ask in what standard sorts of situation would the use of sentences in the grammatical imperative mood be normally classed as 'orders', 'pleas', 'requests', 'commands', 'directions', 'instructions', &c., is a method of discovering not merely facts about language, but the similarities and differences, recognized in language, between various social situations and relationships. The appreciation of these is of great importance for the study of law, morals, and sociology.

Page 18. *Imperatives as the expressions of the wish that others should act or abstain from action.* In characterizing in this way the standard use of the imperative mood in language, care must be taken to distinguish the case where the speaker simply reveals that he wishes another to act in a certain way, as a piece of information about himself, from the case where he speaks with the intention that the other shall be moved thereby to act as the speaker wishes. The indicative not the imperative mood would normally be appropriate in the former case (see on this distinction Hägerström, *Inquiries into the Nature of Law and Morals*, chap. 3, s. 4, pp. 116–26). But though it is necessary, it is not sufficient to characterize the standard use of the imperative mood that the speaker's purpose in speaking is that the other should act in the way he wishes; for it is also necessary that the speaker should intend the person addressed to recognize that this is his purpose in speaking and to be influenced thereby to act as the speaker desires. For this complication (which is neglected in the text) see Grice, 'Meaning', *66 Philosophical Review* (1957) and Hart, 'Signs and Words', *2 The Philosophical Quarterly* (1952).

Page 19. *The gunman situation, orders and obedience.* One of the difficulties to be faced in the analysis of the general notion of an 'imperative' is that no word exists for what is common to orders, commands, requests, and many other varieties, i.e. the expression of intention that another should or should not do some action; similarly no single word exists for the performance of, or abstention from, such action. All the natural expressions (such as 'orders', 'demands', 'obedience', 'compliance') are coloured by the special features of the different situations in which they are normally used. Even the most colourless of these, viz. 'telling to' suggests some ascendancy of one party over the other. For the purpose of describing the gunman situation we have chosen the expressions 'orders' and 'obedience' since it would be perfectly natural to say of the gunman that he *ordered* the clerk to hand over the money, and that the clerk *obeyed.* It is true that the abstract *nouns* 'orders' and 'obedience' would not naturally be used to describe this situation, since some suggestion of authority attaches to the former and the latter is often considered a virtue. But in expounding and criticizing the theory of law as coercive orders we have used the nouns 'orders' and 'obedience' as well as the verbs 'order' and 'obey' without these implications of authority or propriety. This is a matter of convenience and does not prejudge any issue. Both Bentham (in *Fragment of Government,* chap. i, note to para. 12) and Austin (*The Province,* p. 14) use the word 'obedience' in this way. Bentham was aware of all the difficulties mentioned here (see *Of Laws in General,* 298 n.a.).

Page 20. *Law as coercive orders: relation to Austin's doctrine.* The simple model of law as coercive orders constructed in Section 2 of this chapter differs from Austin's doctrine in *The Province* in the following respects.

(*a*) *Terminology.* The phrases 'order backed by threats' and 'coercive orders' are used instead of 'command' for the reasons given in the text.

(*b*) *Generality of laws.* Austin (op. cit., p. 19) distinguishes between 'laws' and 'particular commands' and asserts that a command is a law or rule if it 'obliges generally to acts or forbearances of a class'. On this view a command would be a law even if it were 'addressed' by the sovereign to a single individual so long as it required him to do or abstain from a class or kind of action and not merely a single act or a set of different actions specified individually. In the model of a legal system constructed in the text the orders are general, both in the sense that they apply to classes of individuals and refer to classes of acts.

(*c*) *Fear and obligation.* Austin occasionally suggests that a person is bound or obliged only if he *actually* fears the sanction (op. cit., pp. 15 and 24, and *The Lectures*, Lecture 22 (5th edn.), p. 444, 'The party is *bound* or *obliged* to do or forbear because he is obnoxious to the evil and because he fears the evil'). His main doctrine, however, seems to be that it is enough that there is the '*smallest* chance of incurring the slightest evil' whether the person bound fears it or not (*The Province*, p. 16). In the model of law as coercive orders we have stipulated only that there should be a *general belief* that disobedience is likely to be followed by the threatened evil.

(*d*) *Power and legal obligation.* Similarly, in his analysis of command and obligation, Austin at first suggests that the author of the command must actually possess the power (be 'able and willing') to inflict the eventual evil; but he later weakens this requirement to the smallest chance of the smallest evil (op. cit., pp. 14, 16). See on these ambiguities in Austin's definitions of command and obligation Hart, 'Legal and Moral Obligation', in Melden, *Essays in Moral Philosophy* (1958), and Chapter V, s. 2.

(*e*) *Exceptions.* Austin treats declaratory laws, permissive laws (e.g. repealing enactments), and imperfect laws as exceptions to his general definition of law in terms of command (op. cit., pp. 25–9). This has been disregarded in the text of this chapter.

(*f*) *The legislature as sovereign.* Austin held that in a democracy the electorate, and not their representatives in the legislature, constitute or form part of the sovereign body, though in the United Kingdom the only use made by the electorate of its sovereignty is to appoint its representatives, and to delegate to them the rest of their sovereign powers. Though he claimed that 'accurately speaking' this is the true position, he permitted himself to speak (as all constitutional writers do) of Parliament as possessing the sovereignty (op. cit., Lecture VI, pp. 228–35). In the text of this chapter a legislature such as Parliament is identified with the sovereign; but see Chapter IV, s. 4, for a detailed scrutiny of this aspect of Austin's doctrine.

(g) *Refinements and qualifications of Austin's doctrine.* In later chapters of this book certain ideas which have been used in defending Austin's theory against criticisms are considered in detail, though they are not reproduced in the model constructed in this chapter. These ideas were introduced by Austin himself though, in some cases, only in a sketchy or inchoate form, anticipating doctrines of later writers such as Kelsen. They include the notion of a 'tacit' command (see Chapter III, s. 3, above, p. 45, and Chapter IV, s. 2, above, p. 64); nullity as a sanction (Chapter III, s. 1); the doctrine that the 'real' law is a rule addressed to officials requiring them to apply sanctions (Chapter III, s. 1); the electorate as an extraordinary sovereign legislature (Chapter IV, s. 4); the unity and continuity of the sovereign body (Chapter IV, s. 4, p. 76). In any assessment of Austin attention should be paid to W. L. Morison, 'Some Myth about Positivism', *68 Yale Law Journal*, 1958, which corrects serious misunderstandings of earlier writers on Austin. See also A. Agnelli, *John Austin alle origini del positi o giuridico* (1959), chap. 5.

CHAPTER III

Page 26. The varieties of law. The pursuit of a general definition of law has obscured differences in form and function between different types of legal rules. The argument of this book is that the differences between rules which impose obligations, or duties, and rules which confer powers, is of crucial importance in jurisprudence. Law can be best understood as a union of these two diverse types of rule. This is, accordingly, the main distinction between types of legal rule stressed in this chapter but many other distinctions could and, for some purposes, should be drawn (see Daube, *Forms of Roman Legislation* (1956), for further illuminating classifications of laws, reflecting their diverse social functions which is often evidenced by their linguistic form).

Page 27. Duties in criminal and civil law. In order to focus attention on the distinction between rules imposing duties and rules conferring powers, we have neglected many distinctions between the duties of the criminal law and those in tort and contract. Some theorists, impressed by these differences, have argued that, in contract and tort, the 'primary' or 'antecedent' duties to do or abstain from certain acts (e.g. to perform some act stipulated by contract or to abstain from libel) are illusory and the only 'genuine' duties are remedial or sanctioning duties to pay compensation in certain eventualities, including failure to perform the so-called primary duty (see Holmes, *The Common Law*, chap. 8, criticized by Buckland in *Some Reflections on Jurisprudence*, p. 96, and in 'The Nature of Contractual Obligation', *8 Cambridge Law Journal* (1944); cf. Jenks, *The New Jurisprudence*, p. 179).

Page 27. Obligation and duty. In Anglo-American Law these terms are now roughly synonymous though, except in abstract discussions of the law's requirements (e.g. the analysis of legal obligation as opposed to moral obligation), it is unusual to refer to the criminal law as imposing obligations. The word 'obligation' is, perhaps, still most commonly used by lawyers to refer to contract or other cases, such as the obligation to pay compensation after the commission of a tort, where a determinate individual has a right against another determinate individual (right *in personam*). In other cases 'duty' is more commonly used. This is all that now survives in modern English legal usage of the original meaning of the Roman *obligatio* as a *vinculum juris* binding together determinate individuals (see Salmond, *Jurisprudence*, 11th edn., chap. 10, p. 260 and chap. 21; cf. also Chapter V, s. 2).

Page 28. Power-conferring rules. In continental jurisprudence rules which confer legal powers are sometimes referred to as 'norms of competence' (see Kelsen, *General Theory*, p. 90 and A. Ross, *On Law and Justice* (1958), pp. 34, 50–9, 203–25). Ross distinguishes between private and social competence (and so between private dispositions such as a contract and public legal acts). He also observes that norms of competence do not prescribe duties. 'The norm of competence is not immediately in itself a directive; it does not prescribe a procedure as a duty.... The norm of competence itself does not say that the competent person is obligated to exercise his competence' (op, cit., p. 207). It is, however, to be noted that in spite of making these distinctions, Ross adopts the view criticized in this chapter (above, pp. 35–42) that norms of competence are reducible to 'norms of conduct' since both types of norm must 'be interpreted as directives to the Courts' (op. cit., p. 33).

In considering the criticism in the text of the various attempts to eliminate the distinction between these two types of rule or to show that it is merely superficial, forms of social life other than law, where this distinction appears important, should be remembered. In morals, the vague rules which determine whether a person has

made a binding promise confer limited powers of moral legislation on individuals and so need to be distinguished from rules
which impose duties *in invitum* (see Melden, 'On Promising', *65*
Mind (1956); Austin, 'Other Minds', *PAS* Suppl. vol. xx (1946),
reprinted in *Logic and Language*, 2nd series; Hart, 'Legal and Moral
Obligation', in Melden, *Essays on Moral Philosophy*). The rules of any
complex game may also be profitably studied from this point of
view. Some rules (analogous to the criminal law) prohibit, under
penalty, certain types of behaviour, e.g. fouling or disrespect to the
referee. Other rules define the jurisdiction of officials of the game
(referee, scorer, or umpire); others again define what must be done
to score (e.g. goals or runs). Fulfilling the conditions for making
a run or a goal marks a crucial phase towards winning; failure
to fulfil them is a failure to score and from that point of view a
'nullity'. Here, prima facie, are different types of rule with diverse
functions in the game. Yet a theorist might claim that they could
and should be reduced to one type either because failure to score
('nullity') might be regarded as a 'sanction' or penalty for prohibited
behaviour, or because all rules might be interpreted as directions to
the officials to take certain steps (e.g. record a score or send players
off the field) under certain circumstances. To reduce the two types
of rule in this way to a single type would, however, obscure their
character and subordinate what is of central importance in the
game to what is merely ancillary. It is worth considering how far
the reductionist legal theories, criticized in this chapter, similarly
obscure the diverse functions which different types of legal rules
have in the system of social activity of which they form part.

Page 29. *Rules conferring judicial powers and additional rules imposing*
duties on the judge. The distinction between these two types of
rule remains although the same conduct may be treated *both* as
an excess of jurisdiction, rendering a judicial decision liable to be
quashed as a nullity, *and* as a breach of duty under a special rule
requiring a judge not to exceed his jurisdiction. This would be the
case if an injunction could be obtained to prevent a judge trying
a case outside his jurisdiction (or behaving in other ways which
would invalidate his decision) or if penalties were prescribed for
such behaviour. Similarly if a legally disqualified person partici-
pates in official proceedings this may expose him to a penalty as
well as rendering the proceedings invalid. (See for such a penalty
Local Government Act 1933, s. 76; *Rands* v. *Oldroyd* (1958), 3 AER
344. This Act, however, provides that the proceedings of a local
authority shall not be invalidated by a defect in qualifications of
its members (ib. Schedule III, Part 5 (5)).

Page 33. *Nullity as a sanction.* Austin adopts but does not develop this conception in *The Lectures*, Lecture 23, but see the criticisms of Buckland, op. cit., chap. 10.

Page 35. *Power-conferring rules as fragments of rules imposing duties.* The extreme version of this theory is elaborated by Kelsen in conjunction with the theory that the primary rules of law are the rules requiring courts or officials to apply sanctions under certain conditions (see *General Theory*, pp. 58–63 and (with reference to constitutional law) ib., pp. 143–4). 'The norms of the constitution are thus not independent complete norms; they are intrinsic parts of all the legal norms which the Courts and other organs have to apply'). This doctrine is qualified by its restriction to a 'static' as distinct from a 'dynamic' presentation of the law (ib., p. 144). Kelsen's exposition is also complicated by his claim that in the case of rules conferring private powers, e.g. to make a contract, the 'secondary norm' or duties created by the contract is 'not a mere auxiliary construction of juristic theory' (op. cit., pp. 90 and 137). But in essentials Kelsen's theory is that criticized in this chapter. See, for a simpler version, Ross's doctrine that 'Norms of competence are norms of conduct in indirect formulation' (Ross, op. cit., p. 50). For the more moderate theory reducing all rules to rules creating duties see Bentham, *Of Laws in General*, chap. 16 and Appendices A–B.

Page 39. *Legal duties as predictions and sanctions as taxes on conduct.* For both these theories see Holmes, 'The Path of the Law (1897), in *Collected Legal Papers*. Holmes thought it was necessary to wash the idea of duty in 'cynical acid', because it had become confused with moral duty. 'We fill the word with all the content which we draw from morals' (op. cit. 173). But the conception of legal rules as standards of conduct does not necessitate their identification with moral standards (see Chapter V, s. 2). For criticisms of Holmes's identification of duty with the 'prophecy that if he [the Bad Man] does certain things he will be subjected to disagreeable consequences' (loc. cit.) see A. H. Campbell, review of Frank's 'Courts on Trial', *13 MLR* (1950); and also Chapter V, s. 2, Chapter VII, ss. 2 and 3.

The American courts have found difficulty in distinguishing a penalty from a tax, for the purposes of Article 1, s. 8 of the US Constitution which confers power to tax on Congress. See *Charles C. Steward Machine Co.* v. *Davis*, 301 US 548 (1937).

Page 41. *The individual as duty-bearer and as private legislator.* Cf. Kelsen's account of legal capacity and private autonomy (*General Theory*, pp. 90 and 136).

Page 42. *Legislation binding the legislator.* For criticisms of imperative theories of law on the ground that orders and commands apply only to others, see Baier, *The Moral Point of View* (1958), pp. 136–9. Some philosophers, however, accept the idea of a self-addressed command, and even use it in their analysis of first person moral judgments (see Hare, *The Language of Morals*, chaps. 11 and 12 on 'Ought'). For the analogy suggested in the text between legislation and the making of a promise see Kelsen, *General Theory*, p. 36.

Page 45. Custom and tacit commands. The doctrine criticized in the text is Austin's (see *The Province*, Lecture I, pp. 30–3 and *The Lectures*, Lecture 30). For the notion of tacit command and its use in explaining, consistently with imperative theory, the recognition of various forms of law, see Bentham's doctrines of 'adoption' and 'susception' in *Of Laws in General*, p. 21; Morison, 'Some Myth about Positivism', *68 Yale Law Journal* (1958); and also Chapter IV, s. 2. For criticism of the notion of a tacit command see Gray, *The Nature and Sources of the Law*, ss. 193–9.

Page 49. Imperative theories and statutory interpretation. The doctrine that laws are essentially orders and so expressions of the will or intention of a legislator is open to many criticisms besides those urged in this chapter. By some critics it has been held responsible for a misleading conception of the task of statutory interpretation as a search for 'the intention' of the legislator, without regard to the fact that where the legislature is a complex artificial body there may not only be difficulties in finding or producing evidence of its intention but no clear meaning is given to the phrase 'the legislature's intention' (see Hägerström, *Inquiries into the Nature of Law and Morals*, chap. iii, pp. 74–97, and for the fiction involved in the idea of legislative intention see Payne, 'The Intention of the Legislature in the Interpretation of Statute', *Current Legal Problems* (1956); cf. Kelsen, *General Theory*, p. 33, on the 'will' of the legislator).

CHAPTER IV

Page 50. Austin on sovereignty. The theory of sovereignty examined in this chapter is that expounded by Austin in *The Province*, Lectures V and VI. We have interpreted him as not merely offering certain formal definitions or an abstract scheme for the logical arrangement of a legal system, but as making the factual claim that in all societies, such as England or the United States, where there is law a sovereign with the attributes defined by Austin is somewhere to be found, though this may be obscured by different constitutional and legal forms. Some theorists have interpreted Austin differently as making no such factual claims (see Stone, *The Province and Function of Law*, chaps. 2 and 6, and especially pp. 60, 61, 138, 155 in which Austin's efforts to identify the sovereign in various communities are treated as irrelevant diversions from his main purpose). For criticisms of this view of Austin's doctrine see Morison, 'Some Myth about Positivism', loc. cit., pp. 217–22. Cf. Sidgwick, *The Elements of Politics,* Appendix (A) 'On Austin's Theory of Sovereignty'.

Page 54. *The continuity of legislative authority in Austin.* The brief references in *The Province* to persons who 'take the sovereignty in the way of succession' (Lecture V, pp. 152–4) are suggestive but obscure. Austin seems to admit that to account for the continuity of sovereignty through a succession of changing persons who acquire it, something more is required in addition to his key notions of 'habitual obedience' and 'commands', but he never clearly identifies the further element. He speaks in this connection of a *'title'*, and of *'claims'* to succeed and also of a *'legitimate'* title, though all these expressions, as normally used, imply the existence of a *rule* regulating the succession and not merely *habits* of obedience to successive sovereigns. Austin's explanation of these terms and of the expressions 'generic title' and 'the generic mode' of acquiring sovereignty which he uses has to be spelt out of his doctrine concerning the 'determinate' character of the sovereign (op. cit., Lecture V, pp. 145–55). Here he distinguishes the case where the person or persons who are sovereign are identified individually, e.g. by name, from the case where they are identified 'as answering to some generic description'. Thus (to take the simplest example) in an hereditary monarchy the generic description might be 'the eldest living male descendant' of some given ancestor; in a parliamentary democracy it would be a highly complex description reproducing the qualifications for membership of the legislature.

Austin's view seems to be that when a person satisfies such a 'generic' description he has a 'title' or 'right' to succeed. This explanation in terms of the generic *description* of the sovereign is, as it stands, inadequate, unless Austin means by a 'description' in this context an accepted *rule* regulating the succession. For there is plainly a distinction between the case in which the members of a society each *as a matter of fact* habitually obey whoever for the time being answers to a certain description, and one in which a rule is accepted that whoever answers this description has a *right* or *title* to be obeyed. This is parallel to the difference between the case of persons who move a chess piece habitually in a certain way and those who, as well as doing this, accept the rule that this is the *right* way to move it. If there is to be a 'right' or 'title' to succeed, there must be a rule providing for the succession. Austin's doctrine of generic descriptions cannot take the place of such a rule though it plainly reveals its necessity. For somewhat similar criticism of Austin's failure to admit the notion of a rule qualifying persons as legislators, see Gray, *The Nature and Sources of the Law*, chap, iii, esp. ss. 151–7. Austin's account in Lecture V of the unity and the corporate or 'collegiate' capacity of the sovereign body suffers from the same defect (see s. 4 of this chapter).

Page 55. *Rules and habits.* The internal aspect of rules which is stressed here is discussed further in Chapters V, s. 2, p. 88 and s. 3, p. 98, VI, s. 1, and VII, s. 3. See also Hart, 'Theory and Definition in Jurisprudence', *29 PAS* Suppl. vol. (1955), pp. 247–50. For a similar view see Winch on 'Rules and Habits' in *The Idea of a Social Science* (1958), chap. ii, pp. 57–65, chap. iii, pp. 84–94; Piddington, 'Malinowski's Theory of Needs' in *Man and Culture* (ed. Firth).

Page 60. *General acceptance of fundamental constitutional rules.* The complex of different attitudes to rules of law on the part of officials and private citizens which is involved in the acceptance of a constitution and so in the existence of a legal system is examined further in Chapter V, s. 2, pp. 88–91, and Chapter VI, s. 2, pp. 114–17. See also Jennings, *The Law of the Constitution* (3rd edn.), Appendix 3: 'A Note on the Theory of Law'.

Page 63. *Hobbes and the theory of tacit commands.* See *ante*, Chapter III, s. 3, and notes thereto; also Sidgwick, *Elements of Politics*, Appendix A. For the partly similar 'realist' theory that even statutes of a contemporary legislature are not law until they are enforced, see Gray, *The Nature and Sources of the Law*, chap. 4; J. Frank, *Law and the Modern Mind*, chap. 13.

Page 66. *Legal limitations on legislative power.* Unlike Austin, Bentham held that the supreme power might be limited by 'express convention' and that laws made in breach of the convention would be void. See *A Fragment on Government*, chap. 4, paras. 26 and 34–8. Austin's argument against the possibility of a legal limitation on the power of the sovereign rests on the assumption that to be subject to such a limitation is to be subject to a *duty*. See *The Province*, Lecture VI, pp. 254–68. In fact, limitations on legislative authority consist of *disabilities* not duties (see Hohfeld, *Fundamental Legal Conceptions* (1923), chap. i).

Page 68. *Provisions as to manner and form of legislation.* The difficulty of distinguishing these from substantive limitations on legislative power is considered further in Chapter VII, s. 4, pp. 149–52. See Marshall, *Parliamentary Sovereignty and the Commonwealth* (1957), chaps. 1–6, for an exhaustive discussion of the distinction between 'defining' and 'fettering' the capacities of a sovereign body.

Page 72. *Constitutional safeguards and judicial review.* For constitutions where no judicial review is permitted see Wheare, *Modern Constitutions*, chap. 7. They include Switzerland (except cantonal legislation), the Third French Republic, Holland, Sweden. For the refusal of the US Supreme Court to adjudicate claims of unconstitutionality which raise 'political questions' see *Luther* v. *Borden*, 7 Howard 1 12 L. Ed. 581 (1849); Frankfurter, 'The Supreme Court', in *14 Encyclopaedia of the Social Sciences*, pp. 474–6.

Page 74. The electorate as an 'extraordinary legislature'. For Austin's use of this notion in the effort to escape the objection that in many systems the ordinary legislature is subject to legal limitations, see *The Province*, Lecture VI, pp. 222–33 and 245–51.

Page 76. Legislators in their private and in their official capacity. Austin frequently distinguishes between members of the sovereign body 'considered severally' and 'considered as members or in their collegiate and sovereign capacity' *(The Province*, Lecture VI, pp. 261–6). But this distinction involves the idea of a rule regulating the legislative activity of the sovereign body. Austin only hints at an analysis of the notion of official or collegiate capacity in the unsatisfactory terms of a 'generic description' (see above note on p. 54).

Page 78. Limited scope of amending powers. See proviso to Article V of the United States Constitution. Articles 1 and 20 of the Basic Law of the German Federal Republic (1949) are placed altogether outside the scope of the amending power conferred by Article 79 (3). See also Article 1 and Article 102 of the Constitution of Turkey (1945).

CHAPTER V

Page 83. Obligation as the likelihood of threatened harm. For 'predictive' analyses of obligation see Austin, *The Province*, Lecture 1, pp. 15–24, and *The Lectures*, Lecture 22; Bentham, *A Fragment on Government*, chap. 5, esp. para. 6 and note thereto; Holmes, *The Path of the Law*. Austin's analysis is criticized in Hart, 'Legal and Moral Obligation' in Melden, *Essays in Moral Philosophy*. For the general notion of obligation, cf. Nowell-Smith, *Ethics* (1954), chap. 14.

Page 87. Obligation and the figure of a bond ('vinculum juris'). See A. H. Campbell, *The Structure of Stairs Institute* (Glasgow, 1954), p. 31. Duty is derived through the French *devoir* from the Latin *debitum*. Hence the latent idea of a debt.

Page 88. Obligation and feelings of compulsion. Ross analyses the concept of validity in terms of two elements, viz. the effectiveness of the rule and 'the way it is felt to be motivating, that is, socially binding'. This involves an analysis of obligation in terms of a mental experience accompanying experienced patterns of behaviour. See Ross, *On Law and Justice*, chaps. i and ii, and *Kritik der sogenannten praktischen Erkenntniss* (1933), p. 280. For an elaborate discussion of the idea of duty in its relation to feeling see Hägerström, *Inquiries into the Nature of Law and Morals*, pp. 127–200, on which see Broad, 'Hägerström's Account of Sense of Duty and Certain Allied Experiences', *26 Philosophy* (1951); Hart, 'Scandinavian Realism' in *Cambridge Law Journal* (1959), pp. 236–40.

Page 86. The internal aspect of rules. The contrast between the external predictive point of view of the observer and the internal point of view of those who accept and use the rules as guides is made, though not in these terms, by Dickinson, 'Legal Rules. Their Function in the Process of Decision', *79 University of Pennsylvania Law Review*, p. 833 (1931). Cf. L. J. Cohen, *The Principles of World Citizenship* (1954), chap. 3. It is to be noted that from the external point of view, i.e. that of an observer who does not accept the rules of the society which he is observing, many different types of statements may be made, viz. (i) he may merely record the regularities of behaviour on the part of those who comply with the rules as if they were mere habits, without referring to the fact that these patterns are regarded by members of the society as standards of correct behaviour; (ii) he may, in addition, record the regular hostile reaction to deviations from the usual pattern of behaviour as something habitual, again without referring to the fact that such deviations are regarded by members of the society as reasons and justifications for such reactions; (iii) he may record not only such observable regularities of behaviour and reactions but also *the fact that* members of the society accept certain rules as standards of behaviour, and that the observable behaviour and reactions are regarded by *them* as required or justified by the rules. It is important to distinguish the external statement of fact asserting that members of society accept a given rule from the internal statement of the rule made by one who himself accepts it. See Wedberg, 'Some Problems on the Logical Analysis of Legal Science', *17 Theoria* (1951); Hart, 'Theory and Definition in Jurisprudence', *29 PAS* Suppl. vol. (1955), pp. 247–50. See also Chapter VI, s. 1, pp. 102–5 and 109–10.

Page 91. Customary rules in primitive communities. Few societies have existed in which legislative and adjudicative organs and centrally organized sanctions were all entirely lacking. For studies of the nearest approximations to this state see Malinowski, *Crime and Custom in Savage Society*; A. S. Diamond, *Primitive Law* (1935), chap. 18; Llewellyn and Hoebel, *The Cheyenne Way* (1941).

Page 94. Adjudication without organized sanctions. For primitive societies in which provision is made for the settlement of disputes by rudimentary forms of adjudication though no system of centrally organized sanctions for enforcing decisions exists, see Evans-Pritchard on 'ordered anarchy' in *The Nuer* (1940), pp. 117 ff., quoted in Gluckman, *The Judicial Process among the Barotse* (1955), p. 262. In Roman law an elaborate system of litigation long preceded the provision of State machinery for enforcing judgments in civil cases. Until the later empire the successful plaintiff, if the defendant failed to pay, was left to seize him or his property. See Schulz, *Classical Roman Law*, p. 26.

Page 94. The step from the pre-legal into the legal world. See Baier on 'Law and Custom' in *The Moral Point of View*, pp. 127–33.

Page 94. Rule of recognition. For further discussion of this element in a legal system and its relation to Kelsen's Basic Norm (*Grundnorm*) see Chapter VI, s. 1 and Chapter X, s. 5 and notes thereto.

Page 95. Authoritative texts of rules. In Rome, according to tradition, the XII Tables were set up on bronze tablets in the market-place in response to the demands of the Plebeians for publication of an authoritative text of the law. From the meagre evidence available it seems unlikely that the XII Tables departed much from the traditional customary rules.

Page 96. Contracts, wills, &c., as the exercise of legislative powers. See, for this comparison, Kelsen, *General Theory*, p. 136, on the legal transaction as a 'law creating act'.

CHAPTER VI

Page 100. Rule of recognition and Kelsen's 'basic norm'. One of the central theses of this book is that the foundations of a legal system consist not in a general habit of obedience to a legally unlimited sovereign, but in an ultimate rule of recognition providing authoritative criteria for the identification of valid rules of the system. This thesis resembles in some ways Kelsen's conception of a basic norm, and, more closely, Salmond's insufficiently elaborated conception of 'ultimate legal principles' (see Kelsen, *General Theory*, pp. 110–24, 131–4, 369–73, 395–6, and Salmond, *Jurisprudence*, 11th edn., p. 137 and Appendix I). A different terminology from Kelsen's has, however, been adopted in this book because the view taken here differs from Kelsen's in the following major respects.

    1. The question whether a rule of recognition exists and what its content is, i.e. what the criteria of validity in any given legal system are, is regarded throughout this book as an empirical, though complex, question of fact. This is true even though it is also true that normally, when a lawyer operating within the system asserts that some particular rule is valid he does not *explicitly state* but *tacitly*

presupposes the fact that the rule of recognition (by reference to which he has tested the validity of the particular rule) exists as the accepted rule of recognition of the system. If challenged, what is thus presupposed but left unstated could be established by appeal to the facts, i.e. to the actual practice of the courts and officials of the system when identifying the law which they are to apply. Kelsen's terminology classifying the basic norm as a 'juristic hypothesis' (ib. xv), 'hypothetical' (ib. 396), a 'postulated ultimate rule' (ib. 113), a 'rule existing in the juristic consciousness' (ib. 116), 'an assumption' (ib. 396), obscures, if it is not actually inconsistent with, the point stressed in this book, viz. that the question what the criteria of legal validity in any legal system are is a question of fact. It is a factual question though it is one *about* the existence and content of a rule. Cf. Ago, 'Positive Law and International Law' in *51 American Journal of International Law* (1957), pp. 703–7.

2. Kelsen speaks of 'presupposing the *validity*' of the basic norm. For the reasons given in the text (pp. 108–110) no question concerning the validity or invalidity of the generally accepted rule of recognition as distinct from the factual question of its existence can arise.

3. Kelsen's basic norm has in a sense always the same content; for it is, in all legal systems, simply the rule that the constitution or those 'who laid down the first constitution' ought to be obeyed (*General Theory*, pp. 115–16). This appearance of uniformity and simplicity may be misleading. If a constitution specifying the various sources of law is a living reality in the sense that the courts and officials of the system actually identify the law in accordance with the criteria it provides, then the constitution is accepted and actually exists. It seems a needless reduplication to suggest that there is a further rule to the effect that the constitution (or those who 'laid it down') are to be obeyed. This is particularly clear where, as in the United Kingdom, there is no written constitution: here there seems no place for the rule 'that the constitution is to be obeyed' in addition to the rule that certain criteria of validity (e.g. enactment by the Queen in Parliament) are to be used in identifying the law. This is the accepted rule and it is mystifying to speak of a rule that this rule be obeyed.

4. Kelsen's view (*General Theory*, pp. 373–5, 408–10) is that it is logically impossible to regard a particular rule of law as valid and at the same time to accept, as morally binding, a moral rule forbidding the behaviour required by the legal rule. No such consequences follow from the account of legal validity given in this book. One reason for using the expression 'rule of recognition' instead of a '*basic*' norm' is to avoid any commitment to Kelsen's view of the conflict between law and morals.

Page 101. *Sources of law.* Some writers distinguish 'formal' or 'legal' from 'historical' or 'material' sources of laws (Salmond, *Jurisprudence*, 11th edn., chap. v). This is criticized by Allen, *Law in the Making,* 6th edn., p. 260, but this distinction, interpreted as a differentiation of two senses of the word 'source', is important (see Kelsen, *General Theory*, pp. 131–2, 152–3). In one sense (i.e. 'material', 'historical') a source is simply the causal or historical influences which account for the existence of a given rule of law at a given time and place: in this sense the source of certain contemporary English rules of law may be rules of Roman law or Canon law or even rules of popular morality. But when it is said that 'statute' is a source of law, the word 'source' refers not to mere historical or causal influences but to one of the criteria of legal validity accepted in the legal system in question. Enactment as a statute by a competent legislature is the *reason* why a given statutory rule is valid law and not merely the *cause* of its existence. This distinction between the historical cause and the reason for the validity of a given rule of law can be drawn only where the system contains a rule of recognition, under which certain things (enactment by a legislature, customary practice, or precedent) are accepted as identifying marks of valid law.

But this clear distinction between historical or causal sources and legal or formal ones may be blurred in actual practice and it is this which has led writers such as Allen (op. cit.) to criticize the distinction. In systems where a statute is a formal or legal source of law, a court in deciding a case is bound to attend to a relevant statute though no doubt it is left considerable freedom in interpreting the meaning of the statutory language (see Chapter VII, s. 1). But sometimes much more than freedom of interpretation is left to the judge. Where he considers that no statute or other formal source of law determines the case before him, he may base his decision on e.g. a text of the Digest, or the writings of a French jurist (see, for example, Allen, op. cit., 260 f.). The legal system does not *require* him to use these sources, but it is accepted as perfectly proper that he should do so. They are therefore more than merely historical or causal influences since such writings are recognized as 'good reasons' for decisions. Perhaps we might speak of such sources as 'permissive' legal sources to distinguish them both from 'mandatory' legal or formal sources such as statute and from historical or material sources.

Page 103. *Legal validity and efficacy.* Kelsen distinguishes between the efficacy of a legal order which is, on the whole, efficacious and the efficacy of a particular norm (*General Theory*, pp. 41–2, 118–22). For him a norm is valid if, and only if, it belongs to a system which is *on the whole* efficacious. This view he also expresses, perhaps more obscurely, by saying that the efficacy of the system as a whole is a *conditio sine qua non* (a necessary condition) though not a *conditio per quam* (a sufficient condition: *sed quaere*) of the validity of its rules. The point of this distinction, expressed in the terminology of this book, is as follows. The general efficacy of the system is not a criterion of validity provided by the rule of recognition of a legal system, but is presupposed though not explicitly stated whenever a rule of the system is identified as a valid rule of the system by reference to its criteria of validity, and unless the system is in general efficacious, no meaningful statement of validity can be made. The view adopted in the text differs from Kelsen on this point since it is here argued that though the efficacy of the system is the *normal context* for making statements of validity, none the less, in special circumstances, such statements may be meaningful even if the system is no longer efficacious (see *ante*, p. 104).

Kelsen also discusses under the head of *desuetudo* the possibility of a legal system making the validity of a rule depend on its continued efficacy. In such a case efficacy (of a particular rule) would be part of the system's criteria of validity and not a mere 'presupposition' (op. cit., pp. 119–22).

Page 104. *Validity and prediction.* For the view that a statement that a law is valid is a prediction of future judicial behaviour and its special motivating feeling, see Ross, *On Law and Justice*, chaps. 1 and 2, criticized in Hart, 'Scandinavian Realism' in *Cambridge Law Journal* (1959).

Page 106. *Constitutions with limited amending powers.* See the cases of Western Germany and Turkey in notes to Chapter IV, *ante*, p. 290.

Page 111. *Conventional categories and constitutional structures.* For the allegedly exhaustive division into 'law' and 'convention' see Dicey, *Law of the Constitution*, 10th edn., pp. 23 ff.; Wheare, *Modern Constitutions*, chap. i.

Page 111. *The rule of recognition: law or fact?* See the arguments for and against its classification as political fact in Wade, 'The Basis of Legal Sovereignty', *Cambridge Law Journal* (1955), especially p. 189, and Marshall, *Parliamentary Sovereignty and the Commonwealth*, pp. 43–6.

Page 112. *The existence of a legal system, habitual obedience, and the acceptance of the rule of recognition.* For the dangers of oversimplifying the complex social phenomenon which involves both the ordinary citizen's obedience and acceptance on the part of officials of constitutional rules, see Chapter IV, s. 1, pp. 60–1, and Hughes, 'The

Existence of a Legal System', 35 *New York University LR* (1960), p. 1010, criticizing justly, on this point, the terminology used in Hart, 'Legal and Moral Obligation' in *Essays in Moral Philosophy* (Melden edn., 1958).

Page 118. *Partial breakdown of legal order.* Only a few of the many possible half-way states between full normal existence and non-existence of a legal system are noticed in the text. Revolution is discussed from the legal point of view in Kelsen, *General Theory*, pp. 117 ff., 219 ff., and at length by Cattaneo in *II Concetto di Revoluzione nella Scienza del Diritto* (1960). The interruption of a legal system by enemy occupation may take many different forms, some of which have been categorized in international law: see McNair, 'Municipal Effects of Belligerent Occupation', *57 LQR* (1941), and the theoretical discussion by Goodhart in 'An Apology for Jurisprudence' in *Interpretations of Modern Legal Philosophies*, pp. 288 ff.

Page 120. *The embryology of a legal system.* The development from colony to dominion traced in Wheare, *The Statute of Westminster and Dominion Status,* 5th edn., is a rewarding field of study for legal theory. See also Latham, *The Law and the Commonwealth* (1949). Latham was the first to interpret the constitutional development of the Commonwealth in terms of the growth of a new basic norm with a 'local root'. See also Marshall, op. cit., esp. chap. vii on Canada, and Wheare, *The Constitutional Structure of the Commonwealth* (1960), chap. 4 on 'Autochthony'.

Page 121. *Renunciation of legislative power.* See the discussion of the legal effect of s. 4 of the Statute of Westminster in Wheare, *The Statute of Westminster and Dominion Status,* 5th edn., pp. 297–8; *British Coal Corporation* v. *The King* (1935), AC 500; Dixon, 'The Law and the Constitution', *51 LQR* (1935); Marshall, op. cit., pp. 146 ff.; also Chapter VII, s. 4.

Page 121. *Independence not recognized by the parent system.* See the discussion of the Irish Free State in Wheare, op. cit.; *Moore* v. *AG for the Irish Free State* (1935), AC 484; *Ryan* v. *Lennon* (1935), IRR 170.

Page 121. *Factual assertions and statements of law concerning the existence of a legal system.* Kelsen's account (op. cit., pp. 373–83) of the possible relationships between municipal law and international law ('primacy of national law or primacy of international law') assumes that the statement that a legal system exists *must* be a statement of law, made from the point of view of one legal system about another, accepting the other system as 'valid' and as forming a single system with itself. The common-sense view that municipal law and international law constitute separate legal systems, involves treating the statement that a legal system (national or international) exists, as a statement of fact. This for Kelsen is unacceptable 'pluralism' (Kelsen, loc. cit.; Jones, 'The "Pure" Theory of International Law', *16 BYBIL* 1935), see Hart 'Kelsen's Doctrine of the Unity of Law' in *Ethics and Social Justice*, vol. 4 of *Contemporary Philosophical Thought* (New York, 1970).

Page 122. *South Africa.* For a full examination of the important juristic lesson to be learnt from the South African constitutional troubles, see Marshall, op. cit., chap. 11.

CHAPTER VII

Page 125. *Communication of rules by examples.* For a characterization of the use of precedent in these terms see Levi, 'An Introduction to Legal Reasoning', s. 1 in 15 *University of Chicago Law Review* (1948). Wittgenstein in *Philosophical Investigations* (esp. i, ss. 208–38) makes many important observations concerning the notions of teaching and following rules. See the discussion of Wittgenstein in Winch, *The Idea of a Social Science*, pp. 24–33, 91-3.

Page 128. *Open texture of verbally formulated rules.* For the idea of open texture see Waismann on 'Verifiability' in *Essays on Logic and Language*, i (Flew edn.), pp. 117–30. For its relevance to legal reasoning see Dewey, 'Logical Method and Law', *10 Cornell Law Quarterly* (1924); Stone, *The Province and Function of Law*, chap. vi; Hart, 'Theory and Definition in Jurisprudence,' *29 PAS* Suppl. vol., 1955, pp. 258–64, and 'Positivism and the Separation of Law and Morals', *71 HLR* (1958), pp. 606–12.

Page 129. *Formalism and conceptualism.* Near synonyms for these expressions, used in legal writings, are 'mechanical' or 'automatic' jurisprudence, 'the jurisprudence of conceptions', 'the excessive use of logic'. See Pound, 'Mechanical Jurisprudence', *8 Columbia Law Review* (1908) and *Interpretations of Legal History*, chap. 6. It is not always clear precisely what vice is referred to in these terms. See Jensen, *The Nature of Legal Argument*, chap. i and review by Honoré, *74 LQR* (1958), p. 296; Hart, op. cit., *71 HLR*, pp. 608–12.

Page 131. *Legal standards and specific rules.* The most illuminating general discussion of the character and relationships between these forms of legal control is in Dickinson, *Administrative Justice and the Supremacy of Law*, pp. 128–40.

Page 131. *Legal standards implemented by administrative rule-making.* In the United States the federal regulatory agencies such as the Interstate Commerce Commission and the Federal Trade Commission make rules implementing broad standards of 'fair competition', 'just and reasonable rates', &c. (See Schwartz, *An Introduction to American Administrative Law*, pp. 6–18, 33–7.) In England a similar rule-making function is carried out by the executive though usually without the formal quasi-judicial hearing of interested parties, familiar in the United States. Cf. the Welfare Regulations made under s. 46 of the Factories Act 1957 and the Building Regulations made under s. 60 of the same Act. The powers of the Transport Tribunal under the Transport Act 1947 to settle a 'charges scheme' after hearing objectors approximates more closely to the American model.

Page 132. Standards of care. For an illuminating analysis of the constituents of a duty of care see the opinion of Learned Hand J. in *US* v. *Carroll Towing Co.* (1947), 159 F 2nd 169, 173. For the desirability of replacing general standards by specific rules see Holmes, *The Common Law*, Lecture, 3, pp. 111–19, criticized in Dickinson, op. cit., p. 146–50.

Page 133. Control by specific rules. For the conditions making hard and fast rules rather than flexible standards the appropriate form of control, see Dickinson, op. cit., pp. 128–32, 145–50.

Page 134. Precedent and the legislative activity of Courts. For a modern general account of the English use of precedent see R. Cross, *Precedent in English Law* (1961). A well-known illustration of the narrowing process referred to in the text is *L. & S. W. Railway Co.* v. *Gomm* (1880), 20 Ch.D. 562, narrowing the rule in *Tulk* v. *Moxhay* (1848), 2 Ph. 774.

Page 136. Varieties of rule-scepticism. American writing on this subject can be illuminatingly read as a debate. Thus the arguments of Frank in *Law and the Modern Mind* (esp. chap. i and Appendix 2, 'Notes on Rule Fetishism and Realism'), and Llewellyn, *The Bramble Bush*, should be considered in the light of Dickinson, 'Legal Rules: Their Function in the Process of Decision', *79 University of Pennsylvania Law Review* (1931); 'The Law behind the Law', *29 Columbia Law Review* (1929); 'The Problem of the Unprovided Case' in *Recueil d'Etudes sur les sources de droit en l'honneur de F. Geny*, 11 chap. 5; and Kantorowicz, 'Some Rationalism about Realism' in *43 Yale Law Review* (1934).

Page 139. The sceptic as a disappointed absolutist. See Miller, 'Rules and Exceptions', *66 International Journal of Ethics* (1956).

Page 140. Intuitive application of rules. See Hutcheson, 'The Judgement Intuitive'; 'The Function of the "Hunch" in Judicial Decision', *14 Cornell Law Quarterly* (1928).

Page 141. 'The constitution is what the judges say it is.' This is attributed to Chief Justice Hughes of the United States in Hendel, *Charles Evan*

Hughes and the Supreme Court (1951), pp. 11–12. But see C. E. Hughes, *The Defence Court of the United States* (1966 edn.), pp. 37, 41 on the duty of Judges to interpret the Constitution apart from personal political views.

Page 149. *Alternative analyses of the sovereignty of Parliament.* See H. W. R. Wade, 'The Basis of Legal Sovereignty', *Cambridge Law Journal* (1955), criticized in Marshall, *Parliamentary Sovereignty and the Commonwealth*, chaps. 4 and 5.

Page 149. *Parliamentary sovereignty and divine omnipotence.* See Mackie, 'Evil and Omnipotence', *Mind*, 1955, p. 211.

Page 150. *Binding or redefining Parliament.* On this distinction see Friedmann, 'Trethowan's Case, Parliamentary Sovereignty and the Limits of Legal Change', *24 Australian Law Journal* (1950); Cowen, 'Legislature and Judiciary', 15 *MLR* (1952), and *16 MLR* (1953); Dixon, 'The Law and the Constitution', *51 LQR* (1935); Marshall, op. cit., chap. 4.

Page 151. *Parliament Acts 1911 and 1949.* For the interpretation of these as authorizing a form of delegated legislation see H. W. R. Wade, op. cit., and Marshall, op. cit., pp. 44–6.

Page 152. *Statute of Westminster, s. 4.* The weight of authority supports the view that the enactment of this section could not constitute an irrevocable termination of the power to enact legislation for a dominion without its consent. See *British Coal Corporation* v. *The King* (1935), AC 500; Wheare, *The Statute of Westminster and Dominion Status*, 5th edn., pp. 297–8; Marshall, op. cit., pp. 146–7. The contrary view that 'Freedom once conferred cannot be revoked' was expressed by the South African Courts in *Ndlwana* v. *Hofmeyr* (1937), AD 229 at 237.

CHAPTER VIII

Page 157. *Justice as a distinct segment of morality.* Aristotle in *Nicomachean Ethics*, Book 5, chaps, 1–3, exhibits justice as specifically concerned with the maintenance or restoration of a balance or proportion (ἀναλογία) between persons. The best modern elucidations of the idea of justice are Sidgwick, *The Method of Ethics*, chap. 6, and Perelman, *De la Justice* (1945), followed in Ross, *On Law and Justice*, chap. 12. There is historical matter of great interest in Del Vecchio's *Justice*, reviewed by Hart in *28 Philosophy* (1953).

Page 161. *Justice in the application of the law.* The temptation to treat this aspect of justice as exhaustive of the idea of justice perhaps accounts for Hobbes's statement that 'no law can be unjust' (*Leviathan*, chap. 30). Austin in *The Province*, Lecture VI, p. 260 n., expresses the view that 'just is a term of relative import' and 'is uttered with relation to a determinate law which a speaker assumes as a standard of comparison'. Thus for him a law may be morally unjust if 'tried by' positive morality or the law of God. Austin thought that Hobbes merely meant that a law cannot be *legally* unjust.

Page 162. Justice and equality. For instructive discussions of the status of the principle that prima facie human beings should be treated alike, and its connections with the idea of justice, see Benn and Peters, *Social Principles and the Democratic State*, chap. 5, 'Justice and Equality'; J. Rawls, 'Justice as Fairness', *Philosophical Review* (1958); Raphael, 'Equality and Equity', *21 Philosophy* (1946), and 'Justice and Liberty', *51 PAS* (1951–2).

Page 162. Aristotle on slavery. See *Politics*, i, chap. ii, 3–22. He held that some who were slaves were not so 'by nature' and for them slavery was not just or expedient.

Page 163. Justice and compensation. This is clearly distinguished by Aristotle from justice in distribution, op. cit., Book V, chap. 4, though the unifying principle that there is, in all applications of the idea of justice, a 'just' or proper proportion (ἀναλογία) to be maintained or restored is stressed. See H. Jackson, *Book 5 of the Nicomachean Ethics* (Commentary: 1879).

Page 164. Legal compensation for invasions of privacy. For the argument that the law should recognize the right to privacy and that the principles of the common law require its recognition, see Warren and Brandeis, 'The Right to Privacy', *4 HLR* (1890) and the dissenting judgment of Gray J., in *Roberson* v. *Rochester Folding Box Co.* (1902), 171 NY 538. The English law of torts does not protect privacy as such, though it is now extensively protected in the United States. See for English law *Tolley* v. *J. S. Fry and Sons Ltd.* (1931), AC 333.

Page 166. Conflict of justice between individuals and wider social interests. See the discussion of strict liability and of vicarious liability in tort, in Prosser on *Torts*, chaps. 10 and 11, and Friedmann, *Law in a Changing Society*, chap. 5. On the justification of strict liability in crime see Glanville Williams, *The Criminal Law*, chap. 7; Friedmann, op. cit., chap. 6.

Page 166. Justice and the 'common good'. See Benn and Peters, *Social Principles and the Democratic State*, chap. 13, where seeking the common good is identified with acting justly or attending to the interests of all members of a society in a spirit of impartiality. This identification of the 'common good' with justice is not universally accepted. See Sidgwick, *The Method of Ethics*, chap. 3.

Page 167. *Moral obligation.* For the need to distinguish the obligation and duties of social morality both from moral ideals and personal morality, see Urmson, 'Saints and Heroes' in *Essays on Moral Philosophy* (Melden ed.); Whiteley, 'On Defining "Morality"', in *20 Analysis* (1960); Strawson, 'Social Morality and Individual Ideal' in *Philosophy* (1961); Bradley, *Ethical Studies*, chaps. 5 and 6.

Page 169. *The morality of a social group.* Austin in *The Province* uses the expression 'positive morality' to distinguish the actual morality observed within a society from the 'law of God', which constitutes for him the ultimate standards by which both positive morality and positive law are to be tested. This marks the very important distinction between a social morality and those moral principles which transcend it and are used in criticism of it. Austin's 'positive morality', however, includes all social rules other than positive law; it embraces rules of etiquette, games, clubs, and international law, as well as what is ordinarily thought and spoken of as morality. This wide use of the term morality obscures too many important distinctions of form and social function. See Chapter X, s. 4.

Page 172. *Essential rules.* See Chapter IX, s. 2, for the development of the idea that rules restricting the use of violence and requiring respect for property and promises constitute a 'minimum content' of Natural Law underlying both positive law and social morality.

Pages 172–3. *Law and external behaviour.* The view criticized in the text that whereas the law requires external behaviour, morality does not, has been inherited by jurists from Kant's distinction between juridical and ethical laws. See the General Introduction to the Metaphysic of Morals in Hastie, *Kant's Philosophy of Law* (1887), pp. 14 and 20–4. A modern restatement of this doctrine is in Kantorowicz, *The Definition of Law*, pp. 43–51, criticized by Hughes in 'The Existence of a Legal System', 35 *New York University LR* (1960).

Page 178. *Mens rea and objective standards.* See Holmes, *The Common Law*, Lecture 11; Hall, *Principles of Criminal Law*, chaps. 5 and 6; Hart, 'Legal Responsibility and Excuses', in *Determinism and Freedom* (ed. Hook).

Page 179. *Justification and excuse.* On this distinction in the law of homicide see Kenny, *Outlines of Criminal Law* (24th edn.), pp. 109–16. For its general moral importance see Austin, 'A Plea for Excuses', 57 *PAS* (1956–7); Hart, 'Prolegomenon to the Principles of Punishment', 60 *PAS* (1959–60), p. 12. For a similar distinction see Bentham, *Of Laws in General*, pp. 121–2 on 'exemption' and 'exculpation'.

Page 181. *Morality, human needs, and interests.* For the view that the criterion for calling a rule a moral rule is that it is the product of reasoned and impartial consideration of the interests of those affected, see Benn and Peters, *Social Principles of the Democratic State*, chap. 2. Contrast Devlin, *The Enforcement of Morals* (1959).

CHAPTER IX

Page 185. *Natural Law.* The existence of a vast literature of comment on classical, scholastic, and modern conceptions of Natural Law and the ambiguities of the expression 'positivism' (see below) often make it difficult to see precisely what issue is at stake when Natural Law is opposed to Legal Positivism. An effort is made in the text to identify one such issue. But very little can be gained from a discussion of this subject if only secondary sources are read. Some first-hand acquaintance with the vocabulary and philosophical pre-suppositions of the primary sources is indispensable. The following represent an easily accessible minimum. Aristotle, *Physics*, ii, chap. 8 (trans. Ross, Oxford); Aquinas, *Summa Theologica*, I-II, Quaestiones 90–7 (available with translation in D'Entrèves, *Aquinas: Selected Political Writings*, Oxford, 1948); Grotius, *On the Law of War and Peace; Prolegomena* (trans. in The Classics of International Law, vol. 3, Oxford, 1925); Blackstone, *Commentaries*, Introduction, s. 2. *Page* 185. *Legal Positivism.* The expression 'positivism' is used in contemporary Anglo-American literature to designate one or more of the following contentions: (1) that laws are commands of human beings; (2) that there is no necessary connection between law and morals, or law as it is and law as it ought to be; (3) that the analysis or study of meanings of legal concepts is an important study to be distinguished from (though in no way hostile to) historical inquiries, sociological inquiries, and the critical appraisal of law in terms of morals, social aims, functions, &c.; (4) that a legal system is a 'closed logical system' in which correct decisions can be deduced from predetermined legal rules by logical means alone; (5) that moral judgments cannot be established, as statements of fact can, by rational argument, evidence or proof ('non cognitivism in ethics'). Bentham and Austin held the views expressed in (1), (2), and (3) but not those in (4) and (5); Kelsen holds those expressed in (2), (3), and (5) but not those in (1) or (4). Contention (4)is often ascribed to 'analytical jurists' but apparently without good reason. In continental literature the expression 'positivism' is often used for the general repudiation of the claim that some principles or rules of human conduct are discoverable by reason alone. See the valuable discussion of the ambiguities of 'positivism' by Ago, op. cit., in *51 American Journal of International Law* (1957).

Page 186. *Mill on Natural Law.* See his Essay on Nature in *Nature, the Utility of Religion and Theism.*

Page 187. *Blackstone and Bentham on Natural Law.* Blackstone, loc. cit., and Bentham, *Comment on the Commentaries*, ss. 1–6.

Page 193. *The minimum content of natural law.* This empirical version of natural law is based on Hobbes, *Leviathan*, chaps. 14 and 15, and Hume, *Treatise of Human Nature*, Book III, part 2; esp. ss. 2 and 4–7.

Page 200. *Huckleberry Finn.* Mark Twain's novel is a profound study of the moral dilemma created by the existence of a social morality which runs counter to the sympathies of an individual and to humanitarianism. It is a valuable corrective of the identification of all morality with the latter.

Page 200. *Slavery.* For Aristotle a slave was 'a living instrument'. (*Politics*, I, chaps. 2–4).

Page 203. *The influence of morality on law.* Valuable studies of the ways in which the *development* of law has been influenced by morality are Ames, 'Law and Morals', *22 HLR* (1908); Pound, *Law and Morals* (1926); Goodhart, *English Law and the Moral Law* (1953). Austin fully recognized this factual or causal connection. See *The Province*, Lecture V, p. 162.

Page 204. *Interpretation.* On the place of moral considerations in the interpretation of law see Lamont, *The Value Judgment*, pp. 296–31; Wechsler, 'Towards Neutral Principles of Constitutional Law', *73 HLR* i, p. 960; Hart, op. cit., in *71 HLR*, pp. 606–15, and Fuller's criticism, ib. 661 *ad fin.* For Austin's recognition of the area left open for judicial choice between 'competing analogies' and his criticism of the judges' failure to adapt their decisions to the standard of utility, see *The Lectures*, Lectures 37 and 38.

Page 205. *Criticism of law and the right of all men to equal consideration.* See Benn and Peters, *Social Principles and the Democratic State*, chaps. 2 and 5, and Baier, *The Moral Point of View*, chap. 8, for the view that the recognition of such a right is not merely one among many possible moralities but a defining feature of true morality.

Page 206. *Principles of legality and justice.* See Hall, *Principles of Criminal Law,* chap. i and, for the 'internal morality of law', see Fuller, op. cit., *71 HLR* (1958), pp. 644–8.

Page 208. *Revival of Natural Law doctrines in post-war Germany.* See for a discussion of the later views of G. Radbruch, Hart, and reply by Fuller in op. cit. in *71 HLR* (1958). The discussion there of the decision of the Oberlandsgericht Bamberg of July 1949, in which a

wife who had denounced her husband for an offence against a
Nazi statute of 1934 was convicted of unlawfully depriving him
of his freedom, proceeded on the footing that the account of the
case in *64 HLR* (1951), p. 1005, was correct and that the German
court held the statute of 1934 to be invalid. The accuracy of this
account has recently been challenged by Pappe, 'On the Validity
of Judicial Decisions in the Nazi Era', *23 MLR* (1960). Dr Pappe's
criticism is well founded and the case as discussed by Hart should
strictly be regarded as hypothetical. As Dr Pappe shows (op. cit.,
p. 263), in the actual case the court (Provincial Court of Appeal),
after accepting the theoretical possibility that statutes might be
unlawful if they violated Natural Law, held that the Nazi statute
in question did not violate it; the accused was held guilty of an
unlawful deprivation of liberty since she had no duty to inform,
but did so for purely personal reasons and must have realized that
to do so was in the circumstances 'contrary to the sound conscience
and sense of justice of all decent human beings'. Dr Pappe's careful
analysis of a decision of the German Supreme Court in a similar
case should be studied (ib., p. 268 *ad fin.*).

CHAPTER X

Page 214. *'Is international law really law?'* For the view that this is a
merely verbal question mistaken for a question of fact see Glanville
Williams, op. cit., in *22 BYBIL* (1945).

Page 215. *Sources of doubt.* For a constructive general survey see A.
H. Campbell, 'International Law and the Student of Jurisprudence'
in 35 *Grotius Society Proceedings* (1950); Gihl, 'The Legal Character
and Sources of International Law' in *Scandinavian Studies in Law*
(1957).

Page 216. *'How can international law be binding?'* This question
(sometimes referred to as 'the problem of the binding force' of
international law) is raised by Fischer Williams, *Chapters on Current
International Law*, pp. 11–27; Brierly, *The Law of Nations*, 5th edn.
(1955), chap. 2; *The Basis of Obligation in International Law* (1958),
chap. 1. See also Fitzmaurice, 'The Foundations of the Authority
of International Law and the Problem of Enforcement' in *19 MLR*
(1956). These authors do not explicitly discuss the meaning of the
assertion that a system of rules is (or is not) binding.

Page 217. *Sanctions in International Law.* For the position under Art. 16
of the Covenant of the League of Nations see Fischer Williams,
'Sanctions under the Covenant' in *17 BYBIL* (1936). For sanctions
under chapter vii of the UN Charter see Kelsen, 'Sanctions in

International Law under the Charter of U.N.', *31 Iowa LR* (1946), and Tucker, 'The Interpretation of War under present International Law', *4 The International Law Quarterly* (1951). On the Korean War, see Stone, *Legal Controls of International Conflict* (1954), chap. ix, Discourse 14. It is of course arguable that the Uniting for Peace Resolution showed that the United Nations was not 'paralyzed'.

Page 220. International Law thought and spoken of as obligatory. See Jessup, *A Modern Law of Nations*, chap. 1, and 'The Reality of International Law', *118 Foreign Affairs* (1940).

Page 220. The Sovereignty of States. For a clear exposition of the view that 'sovereignty is only a name given to so much of the international field as is left by law to the individual action of states' see Fischer Williams, op. cit., pp. 10–11, 285–99, and *Aspects of Modern International Law*, pp. 24–6, and Van Kleffens, 'Sovereignty and International Law', *Recueil des Cours* (1953), i, pp. 82–3.

Page 221. The State. For the notion of a 'state' and types of dependent states see Brierly, *The Law of Nations*, chap. 4.

Page 224. Voluntarist and 'Auto-limitation' theories. The principal authors are Jellinek, *Die Rechtliche Natur der Staatsverträge*; Triepel, 'Les Rapports entre le droit interne et la droit internationale', *Recueil des Cours* (1923). The extreme view is that of Zorn, *Grundzüge des Völkerrechts*. See the critical discussion of this form of 'positivism' in Gihl, op. cit., in *Scandinavian Studies in Law* (1957); Starke, *An Introduction to International Law*, chap. 1; Fischer Williams, *Chapters on Current International Law*, pp. 11–16.

Page 224. Obligation and consent. The view that no rule of international law is binding on a state without its prior consent, express or tacit, has been expressed by English courts (see *R. v. Keyn* 1876, 2 Ex. Div. 63, 'The Franconia') and also by the Permanent Court of International Justice. See *The Lotus*, PCIJ Series A, No. 10.

Page 226. New States and States acquiring maritime territory. See Kelsen, *Principles of International Law*, pp. 312–13.

Page 226. Effect on non-parties of general international treaties. See Kelsen, op. cit., 345 ff.; Starke, op. cit., chap. 1; Brierly, op. cit., chap. vii, pp. 251–2.

Page 227. Comprehensive use of term 'morality'. See Austin on 'positive morality' in *The Province*, Lecture V, pp. 125–9, 141–2.

Page 230. Moral obligation to obey international law. For the view that this is 'the foundation' of international law see Lauterpacht, Introduction to Brierly's *The Base of Obligation in International Law*, xviii, and Brierly, ib., chap. 1.

Page 232. Treaty imposed by force as legislation. See Scott, 'The Legal Nature of International Law' in *American Journal of International Law* (1907) at pp. 837, 862–4. For criticism of the common description of general treaties as 'international legislation' see Jennings, 'The Progressive Development of International Law and its Codification', *24 BYBIL* (1947) at p. 303.

Page 233. Decentralized sanctions. See Kelsen, op. cit., p. 20, and Tucker in op. cit., *4 International Law Quarterly* (1951).

Page 233. The basic norm of international law. For its formulation as *pacta sunt servanda* see Anzilotti, *Corso di diritto internazionale* (1923), p. 40. For the substitution of 'States ought to behave as they have customarily behaved' see Kelsen, *General Theory*, p. 369, and *Principles of International Law*, p. 418. See the important critical discussion by Gihl, *International Legislation* (1937) and op. cit. in *Scandinavian Studies in Law* (1957), pp. 62 ff. For the fuller development of the interpretation of international law as containing no basic norm see Ago, 'Positive Law and International Law' in *51 American Journal of International Law* (1957) and *Scienza giuridica e diritto internazionale* (1958). Gihl draws the conclusion that in spite of Article 38 of the Statute of the International Court international law has no formal sources of law. See for an attempt to formulate for international law an 'initial hypothesis' which seems open to similar criticisms to those urged in the text, Lauterpacht, *The Future of Law in the International Community*, pp. 420–3.

Page 237. Analogy of content between international law and municipal law. See Campbell, op. cit. in *35 Grotius Society Proceedings* (1950), p. 121 *ad fin.,* and the discussion of treaties and the rules governing acquisition of territory, prescriptions, leases, mandates, servitudes, &c., in Lauterpacht, *Private Law Sources and Analogies of International Law* (1927).

Page 272. [An alternative beginning to this section is included here, as it was not discarded.]

> Throughout the long sequence of his writings on adjudication Dworkin has unswervingly maintained his denial that the courts have discretion in the sense of a law-creating power to decide cases left incompletely regulated by the existing law. Indeed he has argued that apart from some trivial exceptions there are no such cases, since as he has famously said, there is always a single 'right answer' to any meaningful question as to what the law is on any point of law arising in any case.[1]

---

[1] [See his 'No Right Answer?' in P. M. S. Hacker and J. Raz (eds.), *Law, Morality and Society* (1977), pp. 58–84; reprinted with revisions as 'Is There Really No Right Answer in Hard Cases?' *AMP*, chap. 5.]

But notwithstanding this appearance of an unchanging doctrine, Dworkin's later introduction of interpretive ideas into his legal theory and his claim that all propositions of law are 'interpretive' in the special sense which he has given to this expression, has (as Raz was the first to make clear)[2] brought the substance of this position very close to my own in recognizing that the courts in fact have and frequently exercise a law-creating discretion. Arguably before the introduction of interpretive ideas into his theory there seemed to be a great difference between our respective accounts of adjudication, because Dworkin's earlier denial of judicial discretion in the strong sense and his insistence that there is always a right answer were associated with the idea that the judge's role in deciding cases was to *discern* and *enforce existing law*. But this earlier conception which of course conflicted very sharply with my claim that the courts in deciding cases often exercise a law-creating discretion does not figure at all in

[The text of the alternative beginning to Section 6 ends at this point.]

[2] [See J. Raz. 'Dworkin: A New Link in the Chain', 74 *California Law Review*, 1103 (1986) at 1110, 1115–16.]

NOTES TO THE THIRD EDITION

Leslie Green

Hart's own notes have been left unaltered in this edition. They remain useful for understanding nuances in his argument, thoughts not elaborated in the main text, and some comparisons between his own views and those of others. As a scholarly resource, however, they are often superseded. What follows are pointers to more recent work in English that elaborates or criticizes his arguments. No attempt is made to be comprehensive—the literature is enormous—but only to suggest some items that will be of particular use to students. Where possible I have chosen works by Hart's most persistent interlocutors and by others who directly engage or develop his writings.

There are many general works on Hart's legal philosophy. Two good book-length treatments are Neil MacCormick, *H. L. A. Hart* (2nd edn., Stanford University Press, 2008; all page references in these notes are to 1st edn., 1981) and Michael D. Bayles, *Hart's Legal Philosophy: An Examination* (Kluwer Academic, 1992). A brief overview is Joseph Raz's obituary 'H. L. A. Hart (1907–1992)' (1993) 5 *Utilitas* 145. For Hart's life and influences, see Nicola Lacey, *A Life of H. L. A. Hart: The Nightmare and the Noble Dream* (Oxford University Press, 2004).

CHAPTER I

Pages 3–4. Common knowledge about the law. For discussion of the importance of ordinary understandings, and self-understanding, to legal theory see Joseph Raz, *Between Authority and Interpretation* (Oxford University Press, 2009), chap. 2.

Page 4. Borderline cases of legal systems. Hart's point is that philosophic controversy about law does not usually result from the existence of borderline cases. Ronald Dworkin agrees: see *Law's Empire* (Harvard University Press, 1986) 40–3. For doubts about whether domestic legal systems *are* the central case of law see John Griffiths, 'What is Legal Pluralism?' (1986) 24 *Journal of Legal Pluralism & Unofficial Law* 1; William Twining, *General Jurisprudence: Understanding Law from a Global Perspective* (Cambridge University Press, 2009), chap. 4; and Keith Culver and Michael Giudice, *Legality's Borders* (Oxford University Press, 2010).

Pages 6–13. Recurrent issues. Hart later thought of the agenda for legal philosophy somewhat differently. In 1967 he added to the issues treated in this book problems of legal reasoning and problems in the criticism of law, including the appropriate standards to judge law by, and the basis for law's moral authority. See 'Problems of the Philosophy of Law', chap. 3 of his *Essays in Jurisprudence and Philosophy* (Oxford University Press, 1983).

For contrasting views of the agenda for legal theory see Ronald Dworkin, *Taking Rights Seriously* (rev. edn., Harvard University Press, 1978) 14–16; Ronald Dworkin, *Law's Empire* 1–6; John Finnis, *Natural Law and Natural Rights* (2nd edn., Oxford University Press, 2011), chap. 1; and Hugh Collins, *Marxism and Law* (Oxford University Press, 1984) chap. 1. For an assessment of progress on Hart's agenda see Leslie Green, 'General Jurisprudence: A 25th Anniversary Essay' (2005) 25 *Oxford Journal of Legal Studies* 565.

Page 14. The relationship between word and object. See P. M. S. Hacker, 'Hart's Philosophy of Law' in P. M. S. Hacker and J. Raz eds., *Law, Morality, and Society: Essays in Honour of H. L. A. Hart* (Oxford University Press, 1977) esp. 2–12; and Neil MacCormick, *H. L. A. Hart* 12–19. Dworkin interprets Hart as holding 'that lawyers all follow certain linguistic criteria for judging propositions of law'—this is the basis of the 'semantic sting' argument, *Law's Empire* 45–6. Criticism of this aspect of Hart's methodology can also be found in Nicos Stavropoulos, 'Hart's Semantics' in Jules Coleman ed., *Hart's Postscript* (Oxford University Press, 2001) and, on different grounds, in Brian Leiter, 'Beyond the Hart/Dworkin Debate: The Methodology Problem in Jurisprudence'; (2003) 48 *American Journal of Jurisprudence* 17, esp. 43–51.

On the semantics of 'law' see Jules Coleman and Ori Simchen, 'Law' (2003) 9 *Legal Theory* 1. For doubts about whether jurisprudence has any stake in semantics see Joseph Raz, *Ethics in the Public Domain* (rev. edn., Oxford University Press, 1995, chap. 9, esp. 195–8) and Joseph Raz, *Between Authority and Interpretation*, 49–59. For general doubts about the linguistic approach to political theory see David Miller, 'Linguistic Philosophy and Political Theory', in David Miller and Larry Siedentop eds., *The Nature of Political Theory* (Oxford University Press, 1983).

Pages 15–16. Definition per genus et differentiam. For a critique of Hart's position see P. M. S. Hacker, 'Definition in Jurisprudence' (1969) 19 *Philosophical Quarterly* 343.

Page 16. A central set of elements which form a common part of the answer. They are presented at 91–9. Whether or not these amount to a 'conceptual analysis' of 'law' or 'legal system' depends on what one takes such an analysis to require. Compare Frank Jackson, *From Metaphysics to Ethics: A Defense of Conceptual Analysis* (Oxford University Press, 1998) and Colin McGinn, *Truth by Analysis: Games, Names, and Philosophy* (Oxford University Press, 2012), esp. chap. 2.

On the relationship between a theory of Hart's sort and sociological theory see H. L. A. Hart, 'Analytical Jurisprudence in Mid-Twentieth Century: A Reply to Professor Bodenheimer' (1956) 105 *University of Pennsylvania Law Review* 953; M. Krygier, '"The Concept of Law" and Social Theory' (1982) 2 *Oxford Journal of Legal Studies* 155; B. Z. Tamanaha, 'Socio-Legal Positivism and a General Jurisprudence' (2001) 21 *Oxford Journal of Legal Studies* 1; and Denis Galligan, 'Legal Theory and Empirical Research' in Peter Cane and Herbert Kritzer eds., *Oxford Handbook of Empirical Legal Research* (Oxford University Press, 2010).

CHAPTER II

Page 18. *Austin's theory.* Hart makes it clear that he is discussing a simplified reconstruction of Austin's theory (itself a simplified version of Bentham's theory). For Austin's own views see W. L. Morison, *John Austin* (Stanford University Press, 1982); and W. E. Rumble, *The Thought of John Austin: Jurisprudence, Colonial Reform, and the British Constitution* (Athlone Press, 1985). For a treatment of English legal thought in the period see Michael Lobban, *The Common Law and English Jurisprudence 1760–1850* (Oxford University Press, 1991).

Pages 18–20. *Law as imperatives.* See also Neil MacCormick, 'Legal Obligation and the Imperative Fallacy', in A. W. B. Simpson ed., *Oxford Essays in Jurisprudence*, 2nd series (Oxford University Press, 1973). For the suggestion that something of an imperatival theory survives even in Hart, see G. J. Postema, 'Law as Command: The Model of Command in Modern Jurisprudence' (2001) 11 *Philosophical Issues* 470. For attempts to save aspects of an imperatival theory see Matthew H. Kramer, *In Defense of Legal Positivism: Law Without Trimmings* (Oxford University Press, 1999) 83–7; and Robert Ladenson, 'In Defense of a Hobbesian Conception of Law' (1980) 9 *Philosophy and Public Affairs* 134.

Pages 20–2. *The generality of law.* For thicker and thinner interpretations of generality compare Friedrich Hayek, *Law, Legislation, and Liberty*, Vol. I (University of Chicago Press, 1973), chap. 2;

Lon L. Fuller, *The Morality of Law* (rev. edn., Yale University Press, 1969), 46 ff.; and Timothy Endicott, 'The Generality of Law' in Luís Duarte d'Almeida, Andrea Dolcetti, and James Edwards eds., *Reading The Concept of Law* (Hart Publishing, 2013).

Pages 24–5. Supremacy and Independence. See also Joseph Raz, *The Concept of a Legal System* (2nd edn., Oxford University Press, 1980) chap. 1.

CHAPTER III

Pages 27–32. Power conferring rules. Hart revises his view in 'Legal Powers', chap. 8 of his *Essays on Bentham: Jurisprudence and Political Theory* (Oxford University Press, 1982). On power conferring rules more generally see Joseph Raz, *Practical Reason and Norms* (2nd edn., Oxford University Press, 1990) 97–106, and the symposium with Joseph Raz and D. N. MacCormick on 'Voluntary Obligation and Normative Powers' (1972) *Proceedings of the Aristotelian Society*, supp. vol. xlvi, 59. On public powers see G. H. Von Wright, *Norm and Action* (The Humanities Press, 1963) chap. 10; and Eugenio Bulygin, 'On Norms of Competence' (1992) 11 *Law and Philosophy* 201.

Page 32. Taxonomy of laws. For a more fine-grained classification see A. M. Honoré, 'Real Laws' in P. M. S. Hacker and J. Raz eds., *Law, Morality and Society.*

Pages 38–9. Sanctions and the social functions of law. See Hans Oberdiek, 'The Role of Sanctions and Coercion in Understanding Law and Legal Systems' (1976) 71 *American Journal of Jurisprudence* 21; Joseph Raz, *Practical Reason and Norms* 157–62; John Finnis, *Natural Law and Natural Rights* 266–70; Grant Lamond, 'Coercion and the Nature of Law' (2001) 7 *Legal Theory* 35; and Frederick Schauer, 'Was Austin Right After All? On the Role of Sanctions in a Theory of Law' (2010) 23 *Ratio Juris* 1. For the idea that law serves to 'license' coercion, see Ronald Dworkin, *Law's Empire*, chap. 3, esp. 92–4.

Pages 38–42. The 'bad man's' point of view. See William Twining, 'The Bad Man Revisited' (1972) 58 *Cornell Law Review* 275. Stephen Perry argues that Hart's theory lacks the resources to sideline the bad man's point of view: see 'Holmes versus Hart: The Bad Man in Legal Theory' in Steven J. Burton ed., *The Path of the Law and Its Influence: The Legacy of Oliver Wendell Holmes Jr.*

(Cambridge University Press, 2000). Attempts to understand law wholly as an incentivizing device persist, especially among economists. See Richard Posner, *Economic Analysis of Law* (8th edn., Aspen Publishers, 2010), and his *The Problems of Jurisprudence* (Harvard University Press, 1990); the most sophisticated treatment is Lewis A. Kornhauser, 'The Normativity of Law' (1999) 1 *American Law and Economics Review* 3.

Pages 44–9. Custom as a source of law. See John Gardner, 'Some Types of Law', chap. 3 of his *Law as a Leap of Faith* (Oxford University Press, 2012); and the essays in Amanda Perreau-Saussine and James B. Murphy eds., *The Nature of Customary Law: Legal, Historical and Philosophical Perspectives* (Cambridge University Press, 2007). Dworkin argues that Hart cannot explain custom consistently with his doctrine of the rule of recognition: *Taking Rights Seriously* 41–4.

CHAPTER IV

Pages 55–7. On the nature of social rules. For criticism of Hart's 'practice theory' of rules see G. J. Warnock, *The Object of Morality* (Methuen, 1971), chap. 4; Ronald Dworkin, *Taking Rights Seriously* 48–58; and Joseph Raz, *Practical Reason and Norms* 49–58.

In later work Hart makes another suggestion about rules, by developing a thought about commands. He says commands are 'peremptory', i.e. 'intended to preclude or cut off any independent deliberation by the hearer of the merits pro and con of doing the act' and that they are 'content-independent': 'intended to function as a reason independently of the nature or character of the actions to be done'. He then claims that 'the general recognition in a society of the commander's words as peremptory reasons for action is equivalent to the existence of a social rule' (258): H. L. A. Hart, 'Commands and Authoritative Legal Reasons', chap. 10 of his *Essays on Bentham*. Hart introduced the idea of 'content-independent' reasons in 'Legal and Moral Obligation' in A. I. Melden ed., *Essays in Moral Philosophy* (University of Washington Press, 1958) 82–107. The idea is developed in Joseph Raz, *The Morality of Freedom* (Oxford University Press, 1986) chap. 2; and in Leslie Green, *The Authority of the State* (Oxford University Press, 1990) 36–42. It is criticized by P. Markwick, 'Law and Content-Independent Reasons' (2000) 20 *Oxford Journal of Legal Studies* 579.

Pages 56–8. *The 'internal aspect' of law.* Note that Hart often uses 'internal point of view' and 'internal aspect' interchangeably (e.g. at 88–9). On the general idea see Neil MacCormick, *H. L. A. Hart* 29–40. For discussion of ambiguities in it see Stephen Perry, 'Hart on Social Rules and the Foundations of Law: Liberating the Internal Point of View' (2006) 75 *Fordham Law Review* 1171; and Scott J. Shapiro, 'What is the Internal Point of View?' (2006) 75 *Fordham Law Review* 1157. For its methodological importance in legal theory see Joseph Raz, *Between Authority and Interpretation*, chap. 2. For criticism of the methodological point see Stephen Perry, 'Interpretation and Methodology in Legal Theory' in Andrei Marmor ed., *Law and Interpretation* (Oxford University Press, 1997) and John Finnis, *Natural Law and Natural Rights*, chap. 1. Finnis's objections are in turn subjected to scrutiny by Julie Dickson, *Evaluation and Legal Theory* (Hart Publishing, 2001), chaps. 2–4.

Pages 66–71. *Legal limitations on legislative power.* Hart examines Bentham's attempts to understand legally limited government in 'Sovereignty and Legally Limited Government', chap. 9 of his *Essays on Bentham*. For Raz's criticisms of Austin on illimitability see *The Concept of a Legal System*, chap. 2. Geoffrey Marshall discusses implications Austin's analysis might have for constitutional law in his *Constitutional Theory* (Oxford University Press, 1980), chap. 1, 3.

CHAPTER V

Pages 80–1. *Primary and secondary rules.* Hart uses this distinction inconsistently to mark a difference of (a) normative type (81: primary rules as duty-imposing, secondary rules as power-conferring); (b) object (94, 97: primary rules govern conduct, secondary rules govern rules); (c) social function (40–1: primary rules direct behaviour, secondary rules provide facilities); (d) importance (91, 235: primary rules are essential to human society, secondary rules are valuable but optional); and (e) genesis (91, 95: primary rules emerge first, secondary rules later). Some of these variations are noticed in Colin Tapper, 'Powers and Secondary Rules of Change' in A. W. B. Simpson ed., *Oxford Essays in Jurisprudence* 248–68; Neil MacCormick, *H. L. A. Hart* 103–6; Joseph Raz, *The Authority of Law* (Oxford University Press, 1979) 177–9; and P. M. S. Hacker, 'Hart's Philosophy of Law' in P. M. S. Hacker and Joseph Raz eds., *Law, Morality, and Society* 19–21.

Pages 82–7. The nature of obligations. The point of usage that Hart invokes (82) is open to doubt: Edgar Page, 'On Being Obliged' (1973) 82 *Mind* 283. And note that the analysis (86–7) is an account of the circumstances in which rules 'are *thought of* as giving rise to obligations' (87, emphasis added); it is not a justificatory account. Note also that the distinction between obligation-imposing rules and others is for Hart a matter of degree: it depends on how serious the pressure to conformity is, and on how important the rules are thought to be.

Hart revisits the issue in 'Legal Duty and Obligation', chap. 6 of his *Essays on Bentham*, where he tackles Bentham's view and responds to some criticisms by Dworkin and Raz. Here he suggests that statements of legal duties 'refer to actions which are due from or owed by the subjects having the duty, in the sense that they may be properly demanded or extracted from them' (160). It is unclear how this relates to his earlier account.

Pages 88–91. Predictive theories and the 'external' point of view. Statements of legal obligations are typically intended to be practical, i.e. action-guiding, and not theoretical, e.g. action-predicting. Hart thinks that to capture this we need to understand law from the 'internal' point of view of one who 'accepts' the obligation-imposing rules (see notes to pages 56–8, above). Kelsen proposes that we understand the connection between obligation and action using the sui-generis principle of 'imputation': *Pure Theory of Law* (tr. Max Knight, University of California Press, 1967) 75–81. Raz proposes understanding it from a 'detached' legal point of view: *Practical Reason and Norms* 170–7. For helpful discussion see Kevin Toh, 'Raz on Detachment, Acceptance and Describability' (2007) 27 *Oxford Journal of Legal Studies* 403.

Pages 91–8. The emergence of law. For the methodological presuppositions of Hart's claims concerning the transition from pre-legal to legal society see Neil MacCormick, *H. L. A. Hart*, chap. 9 esp. 106–8. Contrast John Finnis, *Natural Law and Natural Rights*, chap. 1 esp. 6–18. On the idea of 'defects' in simple social orders see Leslie Green, 'Introduction' to this volume (above, xlix–l).

For criticism of Hart's conception of the rule of recognition see Joseph Raz, *The Concept of a Legal System*, chap. 8, esp. 197–200; Joseph Raz, *The Authority of Law*, chap. 5 esp. 90–7; Ronald Dworkin, *Taking Rights Seriously* 39–45, 62–8. For his interpretation of the rule of recognition as involving a semantic doctrine, see Ronald Dworkin, *Law's Empire* 31–5.

CHAPTER VI

Pages 100–1. *Sources of law.* On the theoretical importance of the idea that law has sources see Joseph Raz, *The Authority of Law*, chap. 3. On common law and custom as sources see Gerald J. Postema, *Bentham and the Common Law Tradition* (Oxford University Press, 1986); and John Gardner, 'Some Types of Law', chap. 3 of his *Law as a Leap of Faith*.

Pages 101–3. *The rule of recognition and the practice of the courts.* For Hart, ultimate rules of recognition inhere in customary practices of officials. If an official is someone identified as such by law, it may seem that circularity looms: something is law only if it is identified by the rule of recognition; something is a rule of recognition only if it is practised by officials; someone is an official only if so empowered by law. For resolutions see Neil MacCormick, *H. L. A. Hart* 108–20; and Michael Bayles, *Hart's Legal Philosophy* 81–3.

Pages 103–4. *Legal validity.* Hart mostly treats 'validity' as a matter of system membership. Contrast Kelsen, *Pure Theory of Law* 10–15, 193–5: ' "valid" means that it is binding—that an individual ought to behave in the manner determined by the norm' (193). For various senses of 'validity' in legal contexts see J. W. Harris, *Law and Legal Science: An Inquiry into the Concepts Legal Rule and Legal System* (Oxford University Press, 1979), chap. 4. Joseph Raz assesses Hart's account of validity in *The Authority of Law*, chap. 8. On the possibility of degrees of validity, see John Finnis, *Natural Law and Natural Rights* 276–81.

Pages 103–5. *The efficacy of law.* Hart's definition of efficacy applies only to mandatory rules ('the fact that a rule of law which requires certain behaviour is obeyed more often than not': 103). What of the efficacy of permissive or power conferring rules? See Joseph Raz, *The Concept of a Legal System*, chap. 9; *The Authority of Law*, chap. 5 esp. 85–90. See also Gerald Postema, 'Conformity, Custom, and Congruence: Rethinking the Efficacy of Law' in Matthew H. Kramer *et al.* eds., *The Legacy of H. L. A. Hart: Legal, Political, and Moral Philosophy* (Oxford University Press, 2008).

Pages 105–10. *The rule of recognition as ultimate and supreme.* Hart uses the term 'rule of recognition' to refer to a customary social rule that provides criteria for assessing the validity of all othe rules in that legal system, but which is not itself validated by any other rule. To note:

(1) The rule of recognition is a customary rule of judges and other officials, but it is not legislated and is not positive law. In particular, it is not the formal constitution or any part of it. (Such a constitution must *itself* be validated by the rule of recognition.) Confusion abounds on this point. For discussion see: Kent Greenawalt, 'The Rule of Recognition and the Constitution' (1987) 85 *Michigan Law Review* 621; and essays in Matthew Adler and Kenneth Himma eds., *The Rule of Recognition and the U.S. Constitution* (Oxford University Press, 2009); John Gardner, 'Can there be a Written Constitution' in Leslie Green and Brian Leiter eds., *Oxford Studies in Philosophy of Law,* vol. I (Oxford University Press, 2011), and chap. 4 of his *Law as a Leap of Faith* (Oxford University Press, 2012).

(2) Although Hart says the rule of recognition specifies features which provide 'conclusive affirmative indication that it is a rule of the group' (94) and that it is 'a rule for conclusive identification of the primary rules' (95) this cannot be understood to mean that its criteria are complete and determinate: he expressly denies that (147–54, 257–9).

(3) Hart assumes without argument that each legal system has exactly one rule of recognition. This is open to doubt: Joseph Raz, *The Authority of Law* 95–6.

Pages 114–16. *Officials and secondary rules.* Two different questions are commonly fused: (a) Whose conduct *constitutes* the rule of recognition? (b) Whose conduct is *regulated by* the rule of recognition? In answering (a) Hart sometimes refers to 'officials' (115, 116) and sometimes to 'judges' (108, 116, cf. 256). Joseph Raz argues for the special importance of law-applying officials, such as judges: *The Authority of Law*, chap. 6. With respect to (b) there is no room for doubt: the rule of recognition binds all officials. Note that the primacy of officials, and law-applying officials, is not a doctrine of political morality. It is consistent with everything Hart argues that it is regrettable that courts have the impact they do. On that political question see, e.g. Mark Tushnet, *Taking the Constitution Away from the Courts* (Princeton University Press, 1999).

Pages 116–17. *Obedience and the ordinary citizen.* These are key passages for understanding Hart's assessment of law as a social institution. He argues not only that law brings moral risks, but that those risks are intimately connected to its nature. See Jeremy Waldron, 'All We Like Sheep' (1999) 12 *Canadian Journal of Law and Jurisprudence* 169 and Leslie Green, 'Positivism and the Inseparability of Law and Morals' (2008) 83 *New York University Law Review* 1035 esp. 1052–4.

Pages 117–23. Pathology of a legal system. See also John Finnis, 'Revolutions and Continuity of Law', chap. 21 of his *Philosophy of Law: Collected Essays Volume IV* (Oxford University Press, 2011). Possibilities for interaction between legal systems are explored in Neil MacCormick, *Questioning Sovereignty: Law, State and Nation in the European Commonwealth* (Oxford University Press, 1999) chap. 7.

CHAPTER VII

Pages 124–8. Open texture of law. For a general discussion, see Avishai Margalit, 'Open Texture' (1979) 3 *Meaning and Use* 141. On Hart's use of 'open texture' see Brian Bix, *Law, Language, and Legal Determinacy* (Oxford University Press, 1993), chap. 1. For other sources of indeterminacy in law see Kelsen, *Pure Theory of Law* 348–56. For Dworkin's criticisms of indeterminacy and resultant discretion see *Taking Rights Seriously* 31–9, chap. 4, 13 and *A Matter of Principle* (Harvard University Press, 1986), chap. 5. Dworkin's critique finds favour in David Brink, 'Legal Theory, Legal Interpretation and Judicial Review'(1988) 17 *Philosophy & Public Affairs* 105 and in Nicos Stavropoulos, 'Hart's Semantics' in Jules Coleman ed., *Hart's Postscript* esp. 88–98; but not in Andrei Marmor, *Interpretation and Legal Theory* 2nd edn. (Hart Publishing, 2005), chap. 7.

Pages 128–34. General rules and particular cases. On the nature of rule-based decision-making see David Lyons, *Forms and Limits of Utilitarianism* (Oxford University Press, 1965); and Frederick Schauer, *Playing By the Rules: A Philosophical Examination of Rule-Based Decision-Making in Law and in Life* (Oxford University Press, 1991), esp. chap. 5; and Larry Alexander and Emily Sherwin, *The Rule of Rules: Morality, Rules, and Dilemmas of Law* (Duke University Press, 2001), chaps. 1, 2.

Pages 128–9. Paradigm cases. Timothy Endicott defends Hart's understanding of the role of paradigm cases in *Vagueness in Law* (Oxford University Press, 2000) chap. 7. Ronald Dworkin rejects it in *Law's Empire*, chap. 3 esp. 90–4. See in response

Endicott, 'Herbert Hart and the Semantic Sting' in Jules Coleman ed., *Hart's Postscript* (Oxford University Press, 2001).

Pages 129–30. '*Formalism*'. The term is also used in other ways: see Martin Stone, 'Formalism' in Jules Coleman and Scott Shapiro eds., *The Oxford Handbook of Jurisprudence and Philosophy of Law* (Oxford University Press, 2002).

Pages 130–2. *Indeterminacy and discretion*. Law is indeterminate when it fails to justify a *unique* answer to an intelligible legal question, i.e. when the law is incomplete. This is not the same as a legal case being 'hard': that may be true when there is a unique answer that is either not obvious or is subject to disagreement. It is also not the same as the suggestion that law in fact (causally) determines judicial decisions: the law can be fully determinate and yet judges may not know it, or may know it and decide not to apply it. Legal determinacy does not entail decisional predictability. (Cf. Brian Leiter, 'Legal Indeterminacy' (1995) 1 *Legal Theory* 481.) What Hart defends is law's justificatory indeterminacy. For a rejection of Hart's thesis see Ronald Dworkin, 'No Right Answer?' in P. M. S. Hacker and Joseph Raz eds., *Law, Morality and Society*; and also Ronald Dworkin, 'On Gaps in the Law' in Paul Amselek and Neil MacCormick eds., *Controversies About Law's Ontology* (Edinburgh University Press, 1991). For a defence see Joseph Raz, *The Authority of Law*, chap. 4.

Pages 131–3. *Rules and variable standards*. Here Hart is not discussing *whether* one should have rules, but what *kind* of rules would be appropriate to various circumstances. American lawyers, influenced by Henry Hart (no relation) and Albert Sacks, sometimes distinguish 'rules' and 'standards'; for H. L. A. Hart, standards are one kind of rule. For the distinction see Henry M. Hart and Albert Sacks, *The Legal Process: Basic Problems in the Making and Application of Law* (W. N. Eskridge, Jr. and P. P. Frickey eds., Foundation Press, 1994) 139–41; and Pierre J. Schlag, 'Rules and Standards' (1985) 33 *UCLA Law Review* 379. Similarly, what are often called 'principles' are included in Hart's idea of rules, and he rejects any categorical distinction between them such as is drawn by Dworkin in *Taking Rights Seriously* 22–8. See Hart's comments in the Postscript (261–3); as well as Joseph Raz, 'Legal Principles and the Limits of Law' (1972) 81 *Yale Law Journal* 823; and Larry Alexander and Ken Kress, 'Against Legal Principles' (1997) 82 *Iowa Law Review* 739.

Pages 134–5. *Precedent*. The literature is very rich. See A. W. B. Simpson, 'The Common Law and Legal Theory' in

A. W. B. Simpson ed., *Oxford Essays in Jurisprudence*; Ronald Dworkin, *Taking Rights Seriously* 110–23; Neil MacCormick, *Legal Reasoning and Legal Theory* (rev, edn., Oxford University Press, 1994); Laurence Goldstein ed., *Precedent in Law* (Oxford University Press, 1987); Stephen Perry, 'Judicial Obligation, Precedent and the Common Law' (1987) 7 *Oxford Journal of Legal Studies* 215; Frederick Schauer, 'Precedent' (1987) 39 *Stanford Law Review* 571; Susan Hurley, 'Coherence, Hypothetical Cases, and Precedent' (1990) 10 *Oxford Journal of Legal Studies* 221; Larry Alexander, 'Precedent' in Dennis Patterson ed., *A Companion to the Philosophy of Law and Legal Theory* (Blackwell, 1996); Neil Duxbury, *The Nature and Authority of Precedent* (Cambridge University Press, 2008).

Pages 136–41. *Varieties of rule scepticism*. See also Hart's essay 'American Jurisprudence through English Eyes: The Nightmare and the Noble Dream', chap. 4 of his *Essays in Jurisprudence and Philosophy*. The most prominent rule-sceptics since Hart's book was written were lawyers of the American 'Critical Legal Studies' movement. Influential, if philosophically uninformed discussions include Roberto Unger, *The Critical Legal Studies Movement* (Harvard University Press, 1986) esp. 1–14, and Duncan Kennedy, *A Critique of Adjudication [fin de siècle]* (Harvard University Press, 1997). For a critical discussion of earlier 'CLS' literature see Ken Kress, 'Legal Indeterminacy' (1989) 77 *California Law Review* 283. See also John Finnis, 'On the Critical Legal Studies Movement', chap. 13 of his *Philosophy of Law*, and Andrew Altman, *Critical Legal Studies: A Liberal Critique* (Princeton University Press, 1990). Brian Leiter discusses Hart's varieties of rule scepticism in 'Legal Realism and Legal Positivism Reconsidered', chap. 2 of his *Naturalizing Jurisprudence* (Oxford University Press, 2007).

CHAPTER VIII

Pages 157–60. *Principles of Justice*. John Rawls, who was importantly influenced by Hart, treats the subject matter of justice in John Rawls, *A Theory of Justice* rev. edn. (Harvard University Press, 1999) chap. 1, esp. 6–10. For a useful review emphasizing the distributive character of principles of justice see David Miller, *Social Justice* (Oxford University Press, 1976) chap. 1.

Pages 159–60. '*Treat like cases alike*'. Hart's suggestion that this is a kind of justice has been debated: David Lyons, 'On Formal Justice'

(1972) 58 *Cornell Law Review* 833; Matthew Kramer, 'Justice as Constancy' (1997) 16 *Law and Philosophy* 561; John Gardner, 'The Virtue of Justice and the Character of Law', chap. 10 of his *Law as a Leap of Faith*. Dworkin associates treating like cases alike not with bare consistency, but with his ideal of 'integrity': 'Integrity demands that the public standards of the community be both made and seen, so far as this is possible, to express a single, coherent scheme of justice and fairness in the right relation' (*Law's Empire* 219). For doubts see Denise Réaume, 'Is Integrity a Virtue? Dworkin's Theory of Legal Obligation' (1989) 39 *University of Toronto Law Journal* 380; and Joseph Raz, *Ethics in the Public Domain* 319–25.

Pages 161–4. *Distributive and compensatory justice.* The traditional classification of 'forms' of justice and the relations between them is unclear. On distributive and corrective justice in particular see Jules Coleman, *Risks and Wrongs* (rev. edn., Oxford University Press, 1992); Stephen Perry, 'On the Relationship between Corrective and Distributive Justice' in Jeremy Horder ed., *Oxford Essays in Jurisprudence*, 4th series (Oxford University Press, 2000); John Finnis, *Natural Law and Natural Rights* 173–84; and John Gardner, 'What is Tort Law For? Part 1: The Place of Corrective Justice' (2011) 30 *Law and Philosophy* 1.

Pages 166–7. *Justice and other values.* John Rawls claims that justice is the first virtue of social institutions in *A Theory of Justice*, rev. edn. 3–4. The view is considered in John Gardner, 'The Virtue of Justice and the Character of Law', chap. 10 of his *Law as a Leap of Faith*; and in Jeremy Waldron, 'The Primacy of Justice' (2003) 9 *Legal Theory* 269.

Pages 169–70. *Conventional morality.* Hart distinguishes 'positive' and 'critical' morality. Positive, or customary, or conventional morality is the morality actually accepted by a given social group; critical morality is sound, or correct morality, the morality the group *ought* to accept: H. L. A. Hart, *Law, Liberty, and Morality* (Stanford University Press, 1963) 17–24. Dworkin argues that not every set of socially accepted attitudes towards conduct can count as a morality: some are merely hatreds, phobias, etc. *Taking Rights Seriously* 248–55. W. J. Waluchow argues that there is a positive 'community constitutional morality' that is not simply a matter of convention but presupposed by a community's institutions: *A Common Law Theory of Judicial Review: The Living Tree* (Cambridge University Press, 2007).

Pages 183–4. *Moral criticism of society.* See Patrick Devlin, *The Enforcement of Morals* (Oxford University Press, 1965);

H. L. A. Hart, *Law, Liberty and Morality*; Ronald Dworkin, *Taking Rights Seriously*, chap. 10; and Robert P. George, *Making Men Moral: Civil Liberties and Public Morality* (Oxford University Press, 1993); chap. 2.

CHAPTER IX

Pages 185–6. Positivism and the 'separability thesis'. Hart says 'it is in no sense a necessary truth that laws reproduce or satisfy certain demands of morality'. (In his Holmes Lecture he says 'there is no necessary connection between law and morals': H. L. A. Hart, 'Positivism and the Separation of Law and Morals' (1957) 71 *Harvard Law Review* 593, at 601 n. 25.) This separability thesis is puzzling, not least because Hart himself appears to defend two necessary connections between law and morality, in the connection between rules and justice (see Notes to 159–60) and in the 'minimum content' thesis (see Note to 193). For various attempts to sort out the puzzle see John Gardner, 'Legal Positivism: 5½ Myths', chap. 2 of his *Law as a Leap of Faith*, Matthew H. Kramer, 'On The Separability of Law and Morality' (2004) 17 *Canadian Journal of Law and Jurisprudence* 315; James Morauta, 'Three Separation Theses' (2004) 23 *Law and Philosophy* 111; and Leslie Green, 'Positivism and the Inseparability of Law and Morals' (2008) 83 *New York University Law Review* 1035.

Pages 185–93. Classical theories of natural law. For a descendant of the view Hart describes, but with neo-Thomist inflections, see John Finnis, *Natural Law and Natural Rights*; also Mark C. Murphy, *Natural Law in Jurisprudence and Politics* (Cambridge University Press, 2006). Compare Nigel Simmonds, *Law as a Moral Idea* (Oxford University Press, 2007). On the relationships between natural law and positivism see John Finnis, 'The Truth in Legal Positivism', chap. 7 of his *Philosophy of Law*. On the (lack of) relationship between natural law moral theories, theories of legal interpretation, and natural law jurisprudential theories see Philip Soper 'Some Confusions about Natural Law' (1992) 90 *Michigan Law Review* 2393.

Pages 193–200. The 'minimum content' thesis. No system of rules is a legal system unless it addresses itself to a 'minimum content' of things that are universally valuable, given human nature and the world we live in. For amendments to Hart's list see Neil MacCormick, *H. L. A. Hart* 92–9; and John Finnis, *Natural Law and Natural Rights*, chap. IV. For a different approach to the necessary content of law see Joseph Raz, *Practical Reason and Norms* 162–70.

Page 203. The shared vocabulary of law and morality. For a different explanation of why law and morality share terms like 'obligation', 'right', 'liberty', etc. see Joseph Raz, *The Authority of Law*, chap. 8. Hart responds in his *Essays on Bentham* 153–61.

Pages 203–4. The incorporation of morality in law. Here, and more insistently in the Postscript, Hart says that 'In some systems...the ultimate criteria of legal validity explicitly incorporate principles of justice or substantive moral values...'. Hart calls this 'soft' positivism; it is now usually called the 'incorporation thesis' or 'inclusive legal positivism'. The literature can be technical. For a good overview see K. E. Himma, 'Inclusive Legal Positivism' in Jules Coleman and Scott Shapiro eds., *The Oxford Handbook of Jurisprudence and Philosophy of Law*. For criticism of Hart's position see Joseph Raz, *The Authority of Law*, chap. 3, and Raz, *Between Authority and Interpretation*, chap. 7. Developing the inclusive positivist position are Jules Coleman, 'Negative and Positive Positivism' (1982) 11 *Journal of Legal Studies* 139; Jules Coleman, *The Practice of Principle: In Defence of a Pragmatist Approach to Legal Theory* (Oxford University Press, 2001), chap. 8; and W. J. Waluchow, *Inclusive Legal Positivism* (Oxford University Press, 1994). Dworkin criticizes Hart's approach (as adopted by Philip Soper and David Lyons) in *Taking Rights Seriously* 345–50; he criticizes Coleman's approach in 'Thirty Years On' (2002) 115 *Harvard Law Review* 1655.

Pages 206–7. Principles of legality and justice. Lon L. Fuller's account is influential: *The Morality of Law* (rev. edn., Yale University Press, 1969) 46–91; and see Hart's review 'Lon L. Fuller, "The Morality of Law"', chap. 16 of his *Essays in Jurisprudence and Philosophy*. On the significance of the disputes between Hart and Fuller see the papers in Peter Cane ed., *The Hart–Fuller Debate: 50 Years On* (Hart Publishing, 2010). Raz discusses the relationship between the rule of law and the nature of law in *The Authority of Law*, chap. 11. Dworkin re-articulates his theory around the value of the rule of law ('legality') in 'Hart's Postscript and the Character of Political Philosophy' (2004) 24 *Oxford Journal of Legal Studies* 1, 3–37.

Pages 207–12. Legal validity and resistance to law. For a contemporary version of Radbruch's thesis that laws that do not at least attempt to secure justice are invalid, see Robert Alexy, *The Argument from Injustice: A Reply to Legal Positivism* (Bonnie L. Paulson and

Stanley L. Paulson trs., Oxford University Press, 2002). On the moral claims of law to our obedience, see Joseph Raz, *The Authority of Law*, chaps. 12–15; A. J. Simmons, *Moral Principles and Political Obligations* (Princeton University Press, 1979); Leslie Green, *The Authority of the State*; W. A. Edmundson, *Three Anarchical Fallacies: An Essay on Political Authority* (Cambridge University Press, 1998).

Pages 208–12. *Defending a 'broad' concept of law.* Several writers develop Hart's claim that a positivistic concept of law could 'advance and clarify our moral deliberations' (209). Hart never says this claim is needed to make his case for the soundness of his analysis: he regards it either as a supplementary consideration, or as a reply to those who charge that the broad concept of law is politically dangerous. In the literature there is also an ambiguity between the claim that *the concept of law* ought to be adjusted to bring morally good outcomes and the claim that *the content of the law* ought to be adjusted to bring morally good outcomes (for example, by attempting to narrow judicial duty to the application of source-based materials). Compare: Neil MacCormick, 'A Moralistic Case for A-Moralistic Law' (1985) 20 *Valparaiso Law Review* 1; Thomas Campbell, *The Legal Theory of Ethical Positivism* (Dartmouth, 1996); Jeremy Waldron, 'Normative (or Ethical) Positivism' in Jules Coleman ed., *Hart's Postscript*; and Liam Murphy, 'The Political Question about the Concept of Law' in ibid.

CHAPTER X

Pages 220–6. *Sovereign states and international law.* On the compatibility of sovereignty and the constraints of international law see Timothy Endicott, 'The Logic of Freedom and Power' in Samantha Besson and John Tasioulas eds., *The Philosophy of International Law* (Oxford University Press, 2010). For the relationship between state sovereignty and the rule of law see Jeremy Waldron, 'The Rule of International Law' (2006) 30 *Harvard Journal of Law and Public Policy* 15. There have been attempts to reconstrue sovereignty in light of various emerging forms of transnational authority: see Neil MacCormick, *Questioning Sovereignty*. For doubts about the de facto power of 'sovereign' states in the contemporary world see Saskia Sassen, *Losing Control? Sovereignty in an Age of Globalization* (Columbia University Press, 1996).

Pages 227–32. *International law and morality.* A highly influential discussion of the application of principles of justice in the international domain is John Rawls, *The Law of Peoples* (Harvard University Press, 1999). See also Allen Buchanan, *Justice, Legitimacy, and Self-Determination: Moral Foundations for International Law* (Oxford University Press, 2003). For a 'realist' view according to which states do, and ought to, comply with international law only to advance their national self-interest see Jack L. Goldsmith and Eric A. Posner, *The Limits of International Law* (Oxford University Press, 2005).

Pages 232–7. Analogies of form and content. For the suggestion that international law is now more systematized than it was when Hart wrote, see Samantha Besson and John Tasioulas' 'Introduction' to their edited collection *The Philosophy of International Law*, and sources cited therein. See also Allen Buchanan and David Golove, 'Philosophy of International Law' in Jules L. Coleman and Scott Shapiro eds., *The Oxford Handbook of Jurisprudence and Philosophy of Law*.

POSTSCRIPT

This is perhaps the only postscript about which a whole book has been produced:

Jules Coleman ed., *Hart's Postscript*. The essays are all valuable in understanding not only the Postscript, but also Hart's theory. See also Ronald Dworkin, 'Hart's Postscript and the Character of Political Philosophy' (2004) 24 *Oxford Journal of Legal Studies* 1.

INDEX

(N.B. References to pages after p. 276 are to the Notes)

Adjudication, rules of, 96–99; theory of 259, 275; *and see* Courts, Judges.

Agnelli, A., 283.

Ago, 293, 302, 306.

Allen, C. K., 294.

Ames, J. B., 303.

Analogy, 16, 81, 274, 280, 306.

Anzilotti, D., 306.

Aquinas, 8n., 191, 302.

Aristotle, 162, 191, 280, 300, 302, 303.

Atkin, Lord, 264.

Augustine, St., 8n., 14, 156.

Austin, John, 1, 6, 7, 8, 16, 17, 18, 19, 20, 21n., 23, 25, 60, 63, 73, 74, 81, 149, 207, 211, 244, 246, 277, 278, 280, 281, 282, 283, 285, 286, 287, 288, 289, 290, 299, 300, 301, 302, 303, 305.

Austin, J. L., 14, 279, 301.

Authority, 19–20, 98; legislative, 58–64, 70. distinguished from power, 63, 201, 202–3.

Baier, K., 287, 292, 303.

Basic Norm, *see* Kelsen, H., and Recognition, Rule of.

Benn, S. I., and Peters, R. S., 300, 302, 303.

Bentham, Jeremy, 17, 63, 187, 211, 237, 244, 272, 279, 28l, 286, 287, 289, 290, 301, 302, 303.

Blackstone, 187, 302, 303.

Bohnert, H. G., 280.

Bradley, F. H., 301.

Brierly, J. L., 304, 305.

Broad, C. D., 291.

Buckland, W. W., 284, 286.

Campbell, A. H., 286, 290, 304, 306.

Cardozo, B., 274.

Cattaneo, M., 296.

Certainty of Law, *see* Uncertainty.

Change, rule of, 95–9; *and see* Legislation.

Cicero, xvii.

Cohen, L. J., 279, 291.

Cohen, M., 242.

Coleman, J., 251, 265.

Commands, 16, 19–20; *and see* Imperatives; Orders; Tacit commands.

Commonwealth, emergence of independent legal systems in, 120–2, 296; *and see* Constitutional Law; Westminster, Statute of.

Conceptualism, 123, 129–30, 297; *and see* Formalism.

Constitutional Law: as 'positive morality', 1. restricting legislature, 68–70, 71–8, 289–90. amendment of, 72–3, 77–8, 290. *And see* Legislature; Limitations, Legal Parliament; Recognition, Rule of; South Africa; United States.

Contracts, 9, 28, 38, 41, 96; *and see* Promises.

Conventions of British Constitution, 111, 295.

Conventions, rules as, xxii–xxiv.

Courts, 2, 5, 29–30, 40, 97, 136, 137.
  and rule of recognition, 65–6, 113–17, 148–9, 152–4.
  creative function of, 132–6, 141–7, 272, 273–6.
  finality and infallibility of, 141–7.
  And see Adjudication; Judges; Precedent; Realism.

Cowen, D. V., 299.

Criminal Law, 6–7, 9, 24, 27, 28, 32, 33, 37, 40–1, 79,87.

Cross, R., 298.

Custom, legal status of, 44–8, 64, 68, 91, 287, 291, 292; *and see* Rules, Primary; Tacit Command.

Daube, D., 283.

Definition, 13–17: of law, 6, 208–12, 213–15, 239–40, 279.

Del Vecchio, G., 299.

Democracy:
  judges in a, 275.
  legislators in a, 60.
  sovereign in a, 50, 73–6.

Devlin, L.J., 302.

Dewey, J., 297.

Diamond, A. S., 291.

Dicey, A. V., in, 151, 295.

Dickinson, J., 291, 297, 298.

Discretion:
  of rule-making bodies, 132.
  of Courts, 141—7, 252, 254, 259, 272–3, 275–6.
  of scorer in a game, 142–6.

Division of Labour, law as involving, xxvii–xxx.

Dixon, Sir O., 296, 299.

Duties, 7, 27–8, 41–2, 170–1, 268–9, 271.
  distinguished from disability, 69–70.
  character of rules imposing, 87, 256.
  and obligation, 284.
  and predictions, 286.
  And see Obligation; Rules.

Dworkin, R. M., xviii, xxviii, liv, 238–76, 306–7.

Efficacy of Law, 103–4, 294–5.

Electorate as sovereign, 48, 71–8, 290.

Evans-Pritchard, E. E., 292.

Existence:
  of a legal system, 60–1, 112–17, 295–6.
  of a rule, 109–10.

Fiction involved in rules, 12.

Fitzmaurice, G. G., 304.

Formalism, 124–54, 297; *and see* Conceptualism.

Foucault, M., xx.

Frank, Jerome, 277, 286, 289, 291.

Frankfurter, F., 290.

Friedmann, W., 299, 300.

Fuller, L. L., 2o8n., 238, 303.

Games:
  variety of rules in, 9, 31.
  scoring rule in, 34, 59, 102.
  theory that all rules are addressed to officials applied to, 40, 285.
  internal aspect of rules in, 56–7.
  persistence of law illustrated by umpire's decision in, 63.

move in chess and compliance with rules in, 140–1.

scorer's discretion in and theory that law is what Courts do, 142–5.

definition of, 280.

Gavison, R., 238, 240.

Germany:
Nazi, 200, 208.

revival of natural law arguments in post-war, 208–12, 303–4.

Gihl, T., 304, 305, 306.

Gluckman, M., 292.

Goodhart, A. L., 296, 303.

Gray, J. C., 1, 141, 207, 278, 287, 289.

Grice, P., 281.

Grotius, 302.

Habits and rules, 9–12, 55–60, 289; *and see* Obedience; Rules.

Hagerstrom, A., 279, 281, 287, 291.

Hall, J., 303.

Hand, Learned, 298.

Hare, R. M., 280, 287.

Hart, H. L. A., 208n.1, 279, 281, 282, 285, 289, 290, 291, 295, 296, 297, 299, 301, 303, 304. [*See also* 238 ff.]

Hoadly, Bishop, 141, 145.

Hobbes, T., 63, 191, 289, 299–300, 303.

Hofstadter, A., and McKinvey, J. C. C., 280.

Hohfeld, W. N., 289.

Holmes, O. W., J., 1, 8, 274, 278, 286, 290, 298, 301.

Huckleberry Finn, 200, 303.

Hughes, C. E., C. J., 298–9.

Hughes, G., 295, 301.

Honore, A. M., 297.

Hume, D., xlviii, lv, 191, 303.

Hutcheson, J. C., 298.

Imperatives, varieties of, 18–20, 280–1; *and see* Commands; Orders; Tacit Command.

Independence:
of a legal system, 24, 25, 119–22, 296.

of a state, 221–6.

Internal and External Points of View, 89–91, 242–3, 254; *and see* Rules, internal aspect of.

International Law, li–lii, 3, 4, 68, 79, 119, 122, 156, 177, 195, 198, 213–37, 304–6.

Interpretation, 204–5, 263–8.

Iraq, 226.

Israel, 226.

Jackson, H., 300.

Jellinek., G., 305.

Jenks, E., 284.

Jennings, R., 306.

Jennings, W. Ivor, 289.

Jensen, O. C., 297.

Jessup, P. C., 305.

Jones, J. W., 297.

Judges:
powers of, 29, 41, 96–7.

duties of, 29.

phenomenology of decision making by, 273–4.

And see Courts.

Jurisdiction, 29–30, 36, 97–8; *and see* Courts.

Justice, 7–8, 155–67, 246, 99–300.

'germ of justice' thesis, xxxvi–xxxviii, 160, 206–7.

in distribution, 158–64, 167.

in compensation, 163–6.

natural, 160, 206.

Kant, I., 301.
Kantorowicz, H., 279, 298, 301.
Kelsen, H., xix, xxxi, xxxv, xliii, xlvi, 2, 18, 35–6, 207, 233, 278, 283, 284, 286, 287, 292–3, 294–5, 296–7, 302, 304, 305, 306; *and see* Recognition, Rule of.

Lamont, W. D., 303.
Latham, R. T., 296.
Lauterpacht, H., 305, 306.
League of Nations, 217.
Legal System:
   existence of, 61, 112–17, 295.
   distinguished from a set of separate rules, 92–3, 34–7, 249.
   interruption of, 118–19.
   emergence of new, 120–1.
   partial breakdown of, 122–3.
   And see Revolution.
Legal Theory, v–vi, 1–2, 6–17.
   as descriptive, v, 240, 242–4.
   as general, 239—40, 242, 44.
   as evaluative and interpretive, 40–4, 248–9, 269, 271.
   as semantic, 244–8.
   imperative, vi, 244, *and see* Orders.
   And see Natural Law; Positivism, Legal, Realism, Legal.
Legislation, 22, 30–31, 98, 2–3, 286–7.
   self-binding, 42–4, 286–7.
   authority of, 54–5, 58–63, 88–9.
   legal limits on, 66–71.
   manner and form of, 68, 71, 50–2, 289.

   dependence on language of, 24–8.
   and morality, 176–8, 29–30.
   and international law, 229–31, 232–3, 305.
Legislature, 5, 48, 275, 282–3; *and see* Legislation; Sovereign.
Limitations, legal on legislature, 66–71, 73, 74, 77, 106.
Linguistic analysis in Hart's theory, xlvii–xlviii.
Lyons, D., 265.

Macmillan, Lord, 274.
Marshall, G., 279, 289, 295, 96, 297, 299.
Melden, A., 282, 285, 290, 01.
Mill, J. S., 186, 187, 303.
Miller, 298.
Montesquieu, 186, 187.
Moore, M., 241.
Morality:
   and law, xxxiii–xliv, 7–8, 17, 86, 85–212, 268–72.
   characterization of, 155–84, 27–30, 301.
   obligations of, 169–82.
   'internality' of, 172–3, 79–80.
   importance of, 173–5.
   immunity of from deliberate change, 175–8.
   and voluntary action, 178–9.
   social pressure supporting, 79–80.
   ideals of, 182–3.
   personal forms of, 184.
   and human interests, 180–2.
   and criticism of law, 155–67, 83–4, 205–6.
   and legal validity, xxxviii–xliv, 200–12, 253–4.

and development of law,
203–4, 303.
and international law,
27–32.
And see Natural Law.
Morison, W. L., 283, 287, 88.

Natural Justice, 160, 206.
Natural Law, 8, 156, 181,
185–200, 302, 303.
concept of nature in,
88–91.
empirical version of, 191–3.
minimum content of,
xxxiv–xxxvi, 93–200.
revival of in post-war
Germany, 208–12, 303–4.
Negligence, 132–3.
Normative language, 57, 86,
117; *and see* Obligation;
Rules.
Nowell-Smith, P., 290.
Nuer, The, 292.
Nullity, 28, 30–1, 33–5, 49,
285, 286.

Obedience, 19, 30, 31–2.
habit of, 24, 50–66, 75, 76–7.
and continuity of legislative
authority, 51–61.
and persistence of laws,
1–6.
and existence of a legal system,
112–17. *And see* Habits and
rules.
Obligation, xxiii–xxiv, 6–7, 27,
43–4, 2–91, 284.
analysis of in terms of rules,
2–91, 290.
and feelings of compulsion, 8,
138, 290.
and prediction of sanction,
10–11, 83–5, 88–91, 37–9.

having an, distinguished
from being obliged, 82–3,
90, 282.
moral and legal, 167–70.
in international law,
216–26.
and duty, 284.
Officials, 20–1, 38–9, 60–1,
90–8, 113–17.
Olivecrona, K., 278.
Open texture of law, 123,
28–36, 145, 147, 204, 52,
272–3, 278, 297.
Orders:
backed by threats or coercive,
6, 16, 19, 20–5.
and rules conferring powers,
28–32.
and legislation, 42.
inadequacy of for analysis of
law, 48–9, 79–80.
And see Imperatives;
Commands; Tacit
Command; Rules.

Pappe, H., 304.
Parliament, 25, 107.
sovereignty of, 67, 74–8, 107,
111, 149–52, 282–3, 299.
and Commonwealth, 120–1,
296.
Parliament Acts 1911 and 1949,
151–2.
Payne, D. J., 287.
Perelman, Ch., 299.
Piddington, R., 289.
Plato, 162, 186.
Pluralism, of values, lii.
Positivism, legal, xix,
xxxviii–xliv, 8, 185–6,
207, 212, 241, 244–54,
259, 265, 268, 269–70, 71,
272, 302.

Pound, R., 297, 303.
Powers, *see* Rules, conferring powers.
Precedent, 124–6, 27, 134–5, 154, 297, 298.
Primitive law, xlix–li, 3, 4, 84, 91–2, 156, 291.
Promises, 34, 43–4, 197, 225–6.
Prosser, W. L., 300.
Punishment, 7, 10–11, 27, 34, 6–7, 39. 89, 173, 179–80; *and see* Sanction; Criminal Law.

Radbruch, G., 303.
Radcliffe, Lord, 277.
Raphael, D., 300.
Rawls, J., 246, 300.
Raz, J., xliii–xliv, 254, 262.
Realism, legal, 65, 136–47, 289, 298; *and see* Courts, Rules.
Recognition, Rule of, xx–xxii, 94–5, 96–9, 100–10, 246, 247, 250, 251–2, 256, 258, 259, 263–6, 268, 292–3, 294, 295.
   uncertainty of, 122, 123, 47–54, 251.
   and Courts, 115–17, 267.
   in international law, 233–6, 306.
   And see Kelsen; Validity.
Reid, Lord, 274.
Revolution, 118–20, 296.
Rights, 7, 54–5, 58–9, 88, 268–9, 271–2.
Robinson, R., 279.
Ross, A., 280, 284, 286, 290, 295, 299.
Rules:
   varieties of, 8–10, 27–33, 170–2.
   conferring powers distinguished from rules

imposing obligations or duties, xxxii–xxxiii, 26–49, 80–1, 283–6.
contrasted with habits, 9–11, 55–60, 289.
indeterminacy of, xlii–xliii
internal aspect of, 56–7, 88–90, 99, 102–3, 104, 108, 115–16, 117, 201, 242, 255, 289, 291.
place in jurisprudence, xxiv–xxvii.
'practice theory of', xxi–xxiii, 254–9. scepticism as to existence of, 2–13, 124–54.
and obligations, 85–91.
and predictions, 137–47.
different social functions of, 38–42, 284–5.
acceptance of, 55–61, 113–117, 255, 257.
primary, regime of, 91–4.
law as combination of primary and secondary, 79–99, 117, 213, 249–50.
distinguished from variable standards, 131–4, 263, 297–8.
connexion with justice, 160–1, 206–7.
and difference between 'convention' and 'conviction', 255–6, 266
normative character of, 256–7.
and principles, 259–68.
And see Recognition, Rule of; Normative language.
Ryle, G., 279.

Salmond, J., 284, 292, 294.
Sanction, xxx–xxxiii, 27, 33–5, 36–8, 48, 98, 198–200, 216–20, 291–2, 304–5, 306; *and see* Nullity; Orders.
Sankey, Lord, 152.

Scandinavian legal theory, 10, 278; *and see* Hägerström, Olivecrona; Ross.

Schulz, F., 292.

Scott, J. B., 306.

Sidgwick, H., 288, 289, 299.

Social construction in jurisprudence, xvii–xviii

Sociology, and jurisprudence, xlv–xlvii.

Soper, E., 251, 265.

Sources of Law, 95, 97, 101, 106, 264–7, 269, 294; *and see* Recognition, Rule of; Statutes as merely sources of law; Validity.

South Africa, constitutional problems in, 71–3, 122–3, 153, 200, 297, 299.

Sovereign, 25, 50–78, 148–52, 223–6, 287–9.

Sovereignty of States, 220–6, 305.

State, 50, 53, 98, 195, 220–6, 305, 306.

Statutes as merely sources of law, 2, 64–6, 137.

Statute of Westminster, 152, 299.

Starke, J. G., 305.

Stone, J., 287, 297, 305.

Strawson, P. F., 301.

Strict liability, 166, 173, 178–9.

Switzerland, constitution of, 72, 290.

Tacit command or order, 44–5, 63–5, 77–8, 80, 226, 287, 289.

Taxes contrasted with punishment, 39.

Tort, laws of, 27, 300.

Triepel, H., 305.

Tucker, R. W., 305, 306.

Twain, Mark, 303.

Uncertainty: of legal rules, 12, 124–33, 147–54, 251–2, 272–3.
of precedent, 125, 134–5.
And see Open texture.

United Nations Charter, 217, 233, 304–5.

United States of America, constitution of, 13, 36, 72, 73, 74, 78, 106, 145, 250, 261, 264, 290.

Urmson, J. O., 301.

Validity, Legal, 69, 98–9, 100–10, 200, 247, 250, 251, 253, 254, 294–5.
of morally iniquitous rules, 207–12, 268.
And see Recognition, Rule of.

Van Kief fens, E. N., 305.

Wade, H. W. R., 295, 299.

Waismann, F., 297.

Waluchow, W. J., 262.

Warren, S. D., and Brandeis, L. D., 300.

Wechsler, H, 303.

Wedberg, A., 291.

Wheare, K. C., 289, 295, 296, 299.

Wills, 9, 12, 28, 30, 34, 36–8, 41, 96.

Williams, Glanville L., 278, 279, 300, 304.

Williams, J. F., 304, 305.

Winch, P., 289, 297.

Wisdom, J., 277, 278.

Wittgenstein, L., 280, 297.

Wollheim, R., 279.

Zorn, P., 305.